LONGSTREET HIGHROAD GUIDE
TO THE

CALIFORNIA
SIERRA NEVADA

BY MARK GROSSI

FOREWORD BY THE WILDERNESS SOCIETY

LONGSTREET
ATLANTA, GEORGIA

Published by
LONGSTREET PRESS, INC.
2140 Newmarket Parkway
Suite 122
Marietta, Georgia 30067

Great efforts have been made to make the information in this book as accurate as possible. However, over time, trails are rerouted and signs and landmarks may change. If you find a change has occurred to a trail in the book, please let us know so we can correct future editions. *A word of caution:* Outdoor recreation by its nature is potentially hazardous. All participants in such activities must assume all responsibility for their own actions and safety. The scope of this book does not cover all potential hazards and risks involved in outdoor recreation activities.

Printed by RR Donnelley & Sons, Harrisonburg, VA

1st printing 2000

Library of Congress Catalog Number 00-104190

ISBN: 1-56352-592-5

Book editing, design, and cartography by Lenz Design & Communications, Inc., Decatur, Georgia. www.lenzdesign.org. Online version: www.sherpaguides.com

Cover illustration by Thomas Moran, *Picturesque America*, 1872

Cover design by Richard J. Lenz, Decatur, Georgia

Illustrations by Danny Woodard, Loganville, Georgia

Photographs: National Park Service: Pages 1, 17, 20, 172, 251, and 317. Kathleen Watson: Pages 7, 75, 125, 152, and 165. Mark Grossi: Pages 184, 201, 230, and 307.

Then it seemed to me the Sierra should be called not the Nevada or Snowy Range, but the Range of Light. And after 10 years spent in the heart of it, rejoicing and wondering, bathing in the glorious floods of light, seeing sunbursts of morning among the icy peaks, the noonday radiance on the trees and rocks and snow, the flush of the aspenglow, and a thousand dashing waterfalls with their marvelous abundance of irised spray, it seems to me above all others the Range of Light, the most divinely beautiful of all the mountain chains I have ever seen.

—John Muir, *The Mountains of California, 1894.*

Bernadette—

Let's go
hiking!

Mark Grossi

Contents

California

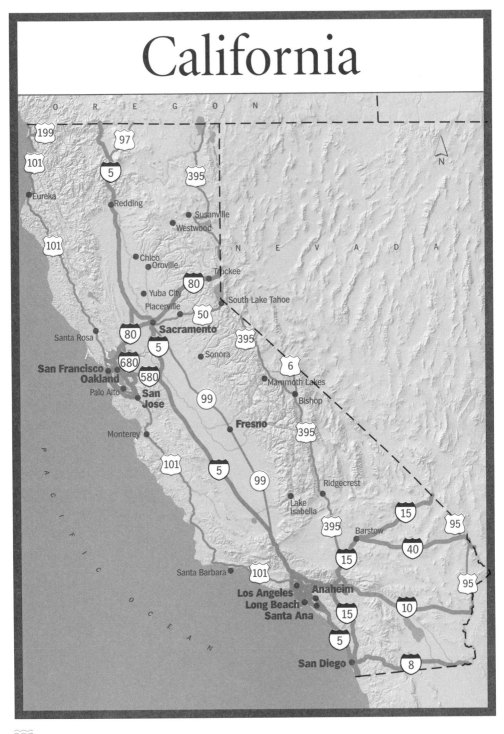

How Your Highroad Guide is Organized

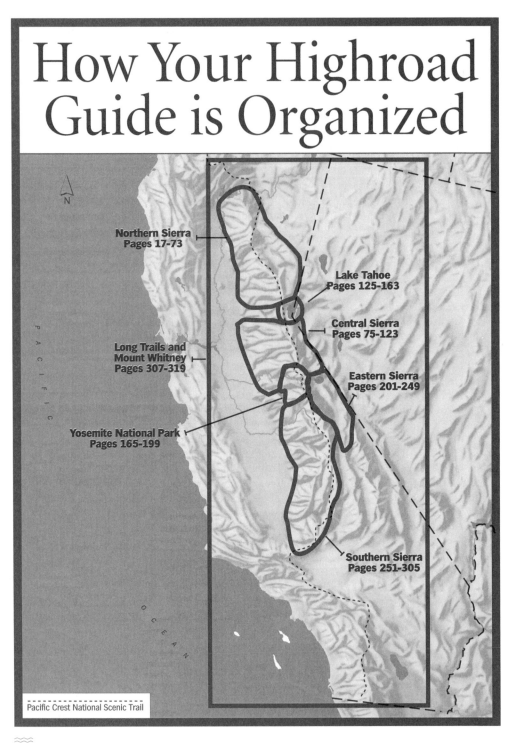

Northern Sierra
Pages 17-73

Lake Tahoe
Pages 125-163

Central Sierra
Pages 75-123

Long Trails and
Mount Whitney
Pages 307-319

Eastern Sierra
Pages 201-249

Yosemite National Park
Pages 165-199

Southern Sierra
Pages 251-305

Pacific Crest National Scenic Trail

How To Use Your Longstreet Highroad Guide

The *Longstreet Highroad Guide to the California Sierra Nevada* includes a wealth of detailed information on the best of what the Sierra Nevada has to offer, including hiking, camping, fishing, scenic driving, biking, and canoeing. The Longstreet Highroad Guide also presents information on the natural history of the mountains, plus interesting facts about Sierra Nevada flora and fauna, giving the reader a starting point to learn more about what makes these mountains special.

The mountain range is divided into six major sections, and each section is covered in its own chapter. There is also a chapter called Long Trails and Mount Whitney, as well as an introduction to the natural history of the Sierra Nevada.

The maps in the book are keyed by figure numbers and referenced in the text. These maps are intended to help orient both casual and expert mountain enthusiasts. Below is a legend to explain symbols used on the maps. Remember that hiking trails frequently change as they fall into disuse or new trails are created. Serious hikers may want to purchase additional maps from the U.S. Geological Service before they set out on a long hike. Sources are listed on the maps.

A word of caution: The mountains can be dangerous. Weather can change suddenly, rocks can be slippery, and wild animals can act in unexpected ways. Use common sense when in the mountains so all your memories will be happy ones.

Legend

Symbol	Description	Symbol	Description	Symbol	Description
	Amphitheater		Wheelchair Accessible		Special Areas
P	Parking		First Aid Station		Town or City
	Telephone		Picnic Shelter		Physiographic Region/ Misc. Boundary
?	Information		Horse Trail		Appalachian Trail
	Picnicking		Horse Stable		Regular Trail
	Dumping Station		Shower		State Boundary
	Swimming		Biking	70	Interstate
	Fishing		Comfort/Rest Station	522	U.S. Route
	Interpretive Trail		Cross-Country Ski Trail	643	State Highway
A	Camping		Snowmobile Trail	SR2010	State Route
	Bathroom		Park Boundary	T470	Township Road

Foreword

For many people, the Sierra Nevada—California's Range of Light—is the most conspicuous, if not revered geographic feature in the Golden State. In Spanish, *sierra* means "jagged range" and *nevada* means "snowed upon." Stretching roughly from Lassen Volcanic National Park in the north to the Inyo and Sequoia national forests in the south and from the oak woodlands of its western foothills to its eastern juncture with the Great Basin, the Sierra Nevada is one of the largest mountain ranges in the world.

Ever since the Spanish Franciscan missionary Pedro Font looked east from San Francisco and saw a great white range, the Sierra Nevada has been looked to for inspiration. For some, the range is best known for places like the incomparable Yosemite Valley, Mount Whitney, and the cobalt blue Lake Tahoe. For others, the Sierra Nevada evokes thoughts of a storied history, marked by events such as the Gold Rush and people like members of the Donner Party and Ishi—the last California Indian living in the wild.

Much of the Sierra Nevada—almost 13 million acres—is public land owned by the American people and is found within 10 national forests and Yosemite, Sequoia-Kings Canyon, and Lassen Volcanic national parks.

The Sierra Nevada range is also home to a rapidly growing population. As a result, the economy of the Sierra is rapidly becoming robust, diverse, and far more resilient than in the past. Friendly communities, high quality of life, open space, and outdoor recreation are drawing new residents, new businesses, and new wealth to the Sierra.

These changes will bring new challenges. What will the future hold for the Sierra Nevada? As Kevin Starr, the respected California state librarian has said, "Once again, as in the past, the Sierra Nevada challenges us to ask basic questions. Are we worthy of these great mountains, rivers, and lakes? Or is ours a long nightmare of wasteful consumption and improper stewardship? One hundred and fifty years ago the Sierra Nevada awed mankind into humility and silence. Today, it is time for men and women to begin a new dialogue with the Range of Light: a dialogue based upon the knowledge that the mountains that have inspired so much appreciation can also be lost."

To know the Sierra is to love the Sierra. And it is through knowing an area that a sense of place is attained. And it is a sense of place that leads to wise management and good stewardship. *The Longstreet Highroad Guide to the Sierra Nevada* by Mark Grossi will help bring about a new understanding of the Sierra Nevada, a new sense of place so important to its future.

—Jay Thomas Watson, California/Nevada Regional Director, The Wilderness Society

Preface

What will it be—the mountains or the beach? That's usually the question if you're heading outdoors in California. The beach has always been the big lure in California, especially if you come from an inland place. But as millions would now attest, the Sierra Nevada holds a charm and splendor quite apart from the coast. Maybe it's because the crowds were getting so big at the beach, but visitors these days are placing Yosemite National Park and Lake Tahoe on their itinerary right next to Malibu or Big Sur. When they get to these Sierra playgrounds, people discover natural history, cultural depth, and days filled with hiking, biking, kayaking, horseback riding, picnicking, rock climbing, fishing, backpacking, and sight-seeing.

But besides Tahoe and Yosemite, is there anywhere else to go in the Sierra? My mission in this book was to answer that question. Yes, I wanted to tell the story of Tahoe and Yosemite too, but there is so much more that often goes unexplored. There are plenty of guidebooks on the Sierra, but this represents one of the few that tackles the entire 400-mile range. It is also one of the few that combines the science of the Sierra with the nuts and bolts of where to go and what to do.

With 10 national forest, 3 national parks, and numerous state parks, it is a lot to digest and consider for anyone planning a trip to the Sierra. The glacial wonders of Yosemite and the awe-inspiring size of Tahoe are just the beginning. The Sierra also includes the tallest mountain in the lower 48 states, Mount Whitney, and the deepest river canyon in the country, Kings Canyon. The primitive backcountry throughout the range makes it a hiking and backpacking attraction for people from around the world.

But the Sierra has its own set of problems. Thirty-two million people—California's population—living anywhere close to a mountain range will have an impact. Air pollution from the state's growing population is beginning to affect trees in the Southern Sierra. Streams are becoming polluted, and amphibians are disappearing here as fast as they are anywhere in the world.

More houses and cabins are sprouting every year in the foothills and front country of the Sierra. Tahoe's clear mountain water is in jeopardy as watersheds become contaminated. The forests continue to grow thicker with vegetation because too many fires have been

WESTERN
REDCEDAR
(Thuja plicata)

ELK
(Cervus elaphus)
Also called "wapiti" — the Indian word for "white" — referring to the light color of the animal's rump, elk herds are distributed through mountain forests and valleys in the West.

extinguished in the past century. The threat of catastrophic fire confronts forest managers throughout the range.

I felt I understood many of these issues because I grew up in the San Joaquin Valley next to the Southern Sierra and have written about the Central and Eastern Sierra over the past decade. But I learned a lot about my own back yard. The number of things I did not know about my own home state still amazes me. But considering that it is a full day of nonstop driving from the Southern Sierra to reach the northern edge of range, it's no wonder that there are few people who have an understanding of the entire range.

With a fuller knowledge and deeper appreciation of the Sierra, I feel the tug of conservation more than before. I live in Fresno just west of about 4 million acres of forests and national parks. I have a ringside seat to observe what conservation efforts can do for the Sierra. Years from now, when my children are vacationing with their own families, I want them to have the same choice I do—indeed, the mountains first, then the beach.

—Mark Grossi

Acknowledgments

I need to thank a lot of U.S. Forest Service and National Park Service employees who stopped in the middle of their busiest seasons and helped me understand more than 11.5 million acres of public land I encountered in writing this book. These people often stayed after work or talked with me on the telephone from their homes; they went above and beyond.

The thanks should start with Matt Mathes, the regional public information officer for the Forest Service. He opened the agency's library to me. Lisa DeHart in the Stanislaus National Forest helped me understand the history in the Central Sierra. Ann Westling of the Tahoe National Forest, Renota Rich of the Sierra National Forest, and Jannette Cutts of the Inyo National Forest provided me with a lot of information about their parts of the mountain range.

Many folks read my drafts and straightened out my misguided passages. Without them, my shortcomings would have been far more noticeable. The list begins with Kris Fister at Sequoia-Kings Canyon National Park, who helped with words and photographs. Nancy Bailey at Lassen Volcanic National Park gave me her guidance and photographs of her Northern California park. Readers from the Forest Service providing their expertise were Sue Exline, Don Lane, Jeanette Ling, Pat Kaunert, Lee Anne Schramel Taylor, and Frank Mosbacher. From the federal Bureau of Land Management, Al Franklin contributed informed guidance. Steve Medley from the Yosemite Association helped make the Yosemite National Park section more accurate.

BEAVER
(Castor canadensis)

SPOTTED OWL
(*Strix occidentalis*)
The spotted owl is identified by its large, dark eyes and white spots on the head, back, and underparts.

Thanks also to author-historian Gene Rose, whose many books, deep Sierra background, and friendship have been an inspiration for me. He read and critiqued two large portions on the Eastern Sierra and the Southern Sierra.

Others may have been unaware of how valuable they are as sources of information and guidance. Among them are author-naturalist Bill Tweed and biologist David Graber, both of Sequoia-Kings Canyon National Parks; ecologist and California spotted owl expert Jared Verner; Yosemite public information officer Scott Gediman; Sierra Foothills Conservancy advocate Chuck Peck; and Richard Kunstman of the Yosemite area Audubon Association has long been a valued source of information. Conversations and time spent with each of them have added such depth to my understanding of the Sierra.

The Pacific Crest Trail Association was helpful in steering me to author-geologist Jeffrey Schaffer, whose prolific work and insights were an inspiration. A debt is also owed to Jeffrey Mount, geologist and professor at the University of California, Davis, whose study of California rivers has proven so valuable in this and other writing I have done. Jay Watson, regional director of the Wilderness Society, also helped me sort out many complex issues.

Thanks to Jay's wife, Kathleen Watson, for her lovely photographs of Lake Tahoe and the Central Sierra. Many thanks to editors Pam Holliday and Richard Lenz at Lenz Design and Communications for their tireless pursuit of proper English, accurate detail, and clearer writing. This book is so much better because of their work.

Finally, I must thank my wife, Sue. Without her patience, support, hard work, and encouragement, I could not have written this. My love and hope are always with her and our three children, Kristin, Joseph, and Nicholas, as well as my parents, Rocky and Lee Grossi.

—Mark Grossi

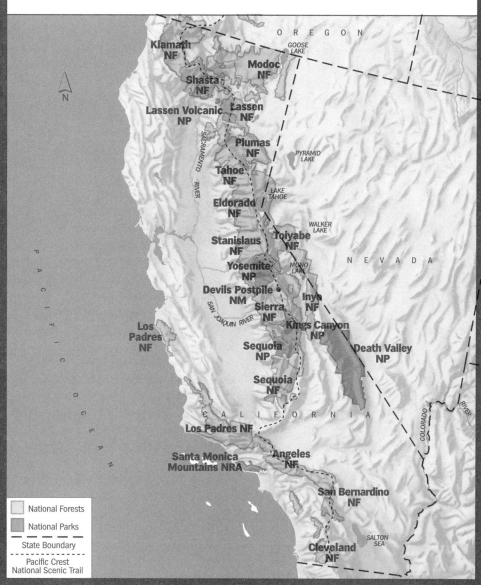

National Forests of California

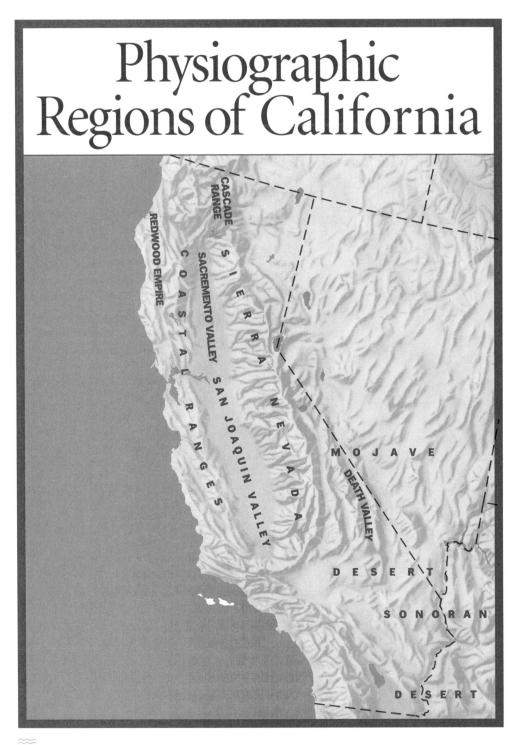

Physiographic Regions of California

The Natural History
of the Sierra Nevada

Perched on Half Dome in Yosemite National Park after the climb of your life, you might spend an indolent hour imagining glaciers occupying the steep, granite canyons of this breathtaking vista. On your way up the dome, you touch places that were scraped by a glacier in the past 1 million years.

Venture to the edge of Half Dome and peer down 4,000 feet to Yosemite Valley. You can see where the rock cracked and broke as smaller glaciers flowed at the foot of the dome.

But it's not so easy to imagine what this scene looked like before glaciers and granite. From the top of Half Dome, you probably will not find a hint of an ocean in the eroded cleavages of Yosemite's cliffs. Even if you know the history of the Sierra Nevada, it is difficult to imagine coral, starfish, and coiled cephalopods in salt water where Yosemite Valley is now. Yet, if you were looking back about 400 million years

[*Above:* A cinder cone in Lassen Volcanic National Park]

Geologic Time Scale

Era	System & Period	Series & Epoch	Some Distinctive Features	Years Before Present
CENOZOIC	**Quaternary**	Recent	Modern man.	11,000
		Pleistocene	Early man; northern glaciation.	1/2 to 2 million
	Tertiary	Pliocene	Large carnivores.	13 + 1 million
		Miocene	First abundant grazing mammals.	25 + 1 million
		Oligocene	Large running mammals.	36 + 2 million
		Eocene	Many modern types of mammals.	58 + 2 million
		Paleocene	First placental mammals.	63 + 2 million
MESOZOIC	**Cretaceous**		First flowering plants; climax of dinosaurs and ammonites, followed by Cretaceous-Tertiary extinction.	135 + 5 million
	Jurassic		First birds, first mammals dinosaurs and ammonites abundant.	181 + 5 million
	Triassic		First dinosaurs. Abundant cycads and conifers.	230 + 10 million
PALEOZOIC	**Permian**		Extinction of most kinds of marine animals, including trilobites. Southern glaciation.	280 + 10 million
	Carboniferous	Pennsylvanian	Great coal forests, conifers. First reptiles.	310 + 10 million
		Mississippian	Sharks and amphibians abundant. Large and numerous scale trees and seed ferns.	345 + 10 million
	Devonian		First amphibians; ammonites; fishes abundant.	405 + 10 million
	Silurian		First terrestrial plants and animals.	425 + 10 million
	Ordovician		First fishes; invertebrates dominant.	500 + 10 million
	Cambrian		First abundant record of marine life; trilobites dominant.	600 + 50 million
	Precambrian		Fossils extremely rare, consisting of primitive aquatic plants. Evidence of glaciation. Oldest dated algae, over 2,600 million years; oldest dated meteorites 4,500 million years.	

ago into a Paleozoic panorama, you would see the Pacific Ocean and small sea creatures.

In the 4.5-billion-year history of earth, you would not be looking back very far. The 400-mile-long and 60-mile-wide Sierra Nevada is a young mountain range, and it is still rising. The origins of the Sierra—the longest continuous mountain range in the United States—can be traced to the Pacific Ocean before California existed.

The North American West Coast was well east of the present-day Sierra, perhaps in Utah. The evidence of an ocean covering present-day California is still in the Sierra. Geologists have found marine sedimentary rocks—carbonates, such as limestone—dating back about 400 million years in the Eastern Sierra around Convict Lake and other places. Sediment from the North American continent had been eroding into the ocean for millions of years during a relatively quiet and stable geologic time. As the sediment layers cemented together, the continent was slowly extending into shallow sea floor.

But the quiet time was coming to an end. In the tumult to come, many of the sedimentary seabeds would be pushed vertical or squashed together in ways that seemed impossible to understand when geologists studied them in the nineteenth century. Today, scientists believe Plate Tectonics—the theory that continents drift on pieces of the earth's crust—set many changes in motion, including volcanoes, earthquakes, and mountain-building episodes.

Starting 400 million years ago, the volcanoes erupted sporadically for many millions of years off the coast of the North American Plate. Arc islands, similar to the environment of present-day Japan, began forming. Then, a mountain-building episode began around 230 million years ago, which some scientists believe marks the beginning of the White Mountains east of the Sierra. The activity occurred at the beginning of the Mesozoic Era as the earth's continents began to break apart from the single super continent known as Pangea. The North American Plate separated from Africa and Europe along the Mid-Atlantic Ridge. The North American Plate drifted west, colliding with the Pacific Plate.

These plate collisions develop belts called cordillera at the fringes of continents. On the western edge of the North American Plate, the Sierra today exists in a vast cordillera running south from Alaska to Tierra del Fuego. Its origins can be traced to the Mesozoic collision between the North American and Pacific Plates.

The thinner Pacific Plate was forced to dive below the North American Plate in the collision. On the upper side of the Pacific Plate, many miles of rocks melted and became magma. Some magma rose to the sea floor and erupted as volcanoes. But some magma remained below the surface, cooling and crystallizing into the granite that later was uplifted to become the White Mountains, which are east of the Sierra and Owens Valley.

About 80 million years later, the North American Plate began moving faster and forcing a larger piece of the Pacific Plate to submerge. Chunks of the ocean floor and the continental plate were violently broken, folded, and forced upward to create an ancestral Sierra range, which rose perhaps 15,000 feet above sea level. Remnants of the ancestral range can still be seen in rock pendants today, but this early-day Sierra is not the massive batholith now visible.

The current Sierra batholith was forming below the earth's surface in huge plumes of magma that were created by the accelerating collision of tectonic plates. Much of this magma did not surface. Instead, it cooled and crystallized into giant blobs of granite that would rise millions of years later. From about 150 million years ago until about 80 million years ago, such granite magma pulsed dozens of times to create this batholith. It subsided and remained below the earth's surface until erosion and uplifting episodes began raising it about 30 million years ago.

During the time the batholith cooled, rich veins of gold and silver were laid down in the large cracks and crevices of the granite. As the granite cooled, heated quartz solutions rose and filled the fissures. Besides gold and silver, the quartz contained jade, copper, and other minerals. These large veins of quartz would later be bared through erosion. Gold and other metals were washed into streams, as any gold miner in the 1840s would attest. Huge deposits of the quartz remained buried in hillsides where miners would excavate it in the nineteenth century.

But the gold and the granite magma of today's Sierra were still beneath the earth 120 million years ago when tremendous erosion began on the 15,000-foot-high ancestral Sierra. The range was lowered to about 3,000 feet at its crest 60 million years ago. At about the time the dinosaurs went extinct, the Sierra was a collection of gently rolling hills in an area with a tropical climate. Much of its rock settled as alluvial deposits in the 400-mile Central Valley, which was still covered by the ocean.

The Mesozoic rocks of the ancestral Sierra are classified as metamorphic because they have changed, or metamorphosed, over time. They changed from such rocks as sandstone and shale to slate and schist. They are similar to their Paleozoic predecessors, but they can often be distinguished in the Sierra high country by the color on their exposed surfaces. These types of rock are usually gray, while the exposed Paleozoic rocks are reddish. One of the better places to find the Mesozoic rocks is in the Eastern Sierra on the John Muir Trail near Shadow Lake.

Sierra rocks are tougher to identify than it sounds, though. A lot of volcanic and earthquake activity took place from 30 million years ago until about 12,000 years ago, and parts of the Sierra are a virtual mosaic of different rocks. In the Northern Sierra, for instance, geologists found Cenozoic volcanic rock along with Paleozoic and Mesozoic metamorphic rock. Some of the oldest rock is on top of the younger rock.

There is plenty of debate about what happened to push the Sierra into its present-day configuration. It is generally agreed that volcanoes and uplifting episodes, which include massive earthquakes and other forces, worked together. The two did their most dramatic work over the last 10 million years, but they began to shape the present Sierra about 30 million years ago.

Violent volcanic eruptions began in the Northern Sierra as magma pushed up from the diving Pacific plate. The process produced three types of volcanic rock—andesite, basalt, and rhyolite. Andesitic lava has light and dark minerals in it, and is thick, so it tends to flow only short distances. Basaltic lava, filled with iron and magnesium, flows easily and travels greater distances but it normally is not associated with explosive eruptions. Rhyolitic lava is similar to granite, and resists flowing. Rhyolite is the type of rock found around explosive volcanoes, such as Mammoth Mountain.

Rhyolite can be found north of Yosemite National Park throughout the Sierra, where explosive volcanoes erupted about 30 million years ago. The explosions died down after about 10 million years, but another dramatic explosion took place in more recent times at Long Valley Caldera, a 19-mile-long and 10-mile-wide depression still visible today. During the explosion about 700,000 years ago, rhyolitic ash rained on the countryside, as the explosion flashed at perhaps 100 miles per hour. Scientists believe the temperature in the middle of the caldera was between 600 and 750 degrees Fahrenheit.

The Sierra landscape also displays andesite, especially in the Central and Northern Sierra. Andesitic eruptions followed the Northern Sierra rhyolite events about 20 million years ago and produced rough, chunky rock formations. In the Central Sierra, thick andesite features can be seen at the Dardanelles Cone in the Stanislaus National Forest. Donner Summit in the Tahoe National Forest also contains similar features.

Basalt remnants can be seen on the Eastern Sierra. In the Mammoth Lakes area, a 600- to 700-foot basalt flow moved down the ancient San Joaquin River about 100,000 years ago. The flow created the Devils Postpile—bizarre-looking vertical columns that are considered one of the most geometrically regular remnants in the world.

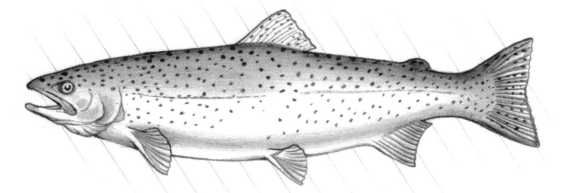

RAINBOW TROUT
(Oncorhynchus mykiss)

During the volcanic fireworks, how did the huge Sierra batholith rise? The possible answers to that question cause a lot of arguments. In general, scientists believe erosion of the ancestral range and episodes of earthquakes explain the appearance of the newer granite. The most imaginative arguments usually focus on where and when the uplifts occurred. But there is no argument about the power of earthquakes to lift the mountain range.

In 1872, Lone Pine in the Owens Valley, just east of 14,497-foot Mount Whitney, was virtually destroyed, and 27 people were killed in a quake that raised part of the Southern and Eastern Sierra 13 feet. If only one such quake happened every 1,000 years, the Southern and Eastern Sierra would grow 13,000 feet higher in just 1 million years. Between the sinking Owens Valley and the rising Sierra over the last several million years, there has been a displacement of about 19,000 feet from the crest to the Owens Valley block. Only about 11,000 or 12,000 feet of it can be seen because the rest extends beneath the soil to the valley block.

The Northern Sierra is a slightly different story. It had risen close to its present height about 2 million years ago. The rise came mainly on the eastern side of range as faulting tilted the Sierra to the west. The western edge of the Sierra's subsurface block disappears beneath the Central Valley floor where it encounters the block from the Coastal Range. Like the rest of the Sierra, it is still rising.

How high could the Sierra rise? The simple math is staggering. Erosion takes about 18 inches from the mountains every 1,000 years. If the range is rising 13 feet or more every thousand years, the Sierra could one day be the world's tallest mountains.

Add Ice

About 30,000 years ago, the Grand Canyon of the Tuolumne River was on ice—actually, under ice, about 4,000 feet of it. The canyon is just north of the world-famous Yosemite Valley, which also was buried in ice at the time. This was the height of Sierra glacial advances in the Ice Age, and the Tuolumne River had the biggest Sierra glacier of them all. In addition to being 4,000 feet deep, it was 60 miles long, creating a monumental, low-speed battering ram moving only inches or feet per year. This and other Sierra glaciers transformed V-shaped valleys into U-shaped valleys with all the urgency of a tortoise taking a morning stroll. It could take centuries for a glacier to move 0.5 mile.

But, in geologic time, this mountain-altering process moved at the speed of a frightened deer compared to the Sierra's previous history. The granite that began forming in the earth 150 million years ago was drastically changed in less than 3 million years. It would be like catching the last three minutes of a 2.5-hour movie and seeing some of the most exciting developments.

The Sierra, like the Rocky Mountains and the Cascades, was high enough

3 million years ago to stop great glaciers advancing from Canada and the rest of North America. But because it was so cold in summer, the Sierra formed its own glaciers. Over many years, snow began melding together into what some geologists consider a metamorphic rock made of hardened ice. It is called "firn," which is pre-glacial ice that does not thaw in summer. Today in the Sierra, scientists refer to the "firn limit" as the lower edge of compacted snow that does not melt.

The Mokelumne Wilderness in the El Dorado National Forest features more than 100 miles of trails.

To build a glacier, about 100 feet of snow must accumulate and harden to start downhill in a canyon already cut by a stream. The glacier is not a solid block of ice, however. The upper levels of a glacier can be fractured with cracks that can develop into crevasses. Large crevasses can be as deep as 200 feet. Crossing any large glacier can be hazardous because overhanging snow can mask a crevasse, though the small Sierra glaciers today probably do not present the same hazards as those in Alaska and other parts of the world.

The largest glaciers in the Sierra occurred from Donner Pass south to the Kern River canyon. Major watershed basins, such as the San Joaquin, Kings, and Kaweah in the Southern Sierra, had extensive ice fields and glaciers. There were four periods of glaciation and long periods of interglacial warmth in the Sierra.

The massive glaciers did a lot of grinding, scraping, and polishing on the Sierra granite. In the process, the heavy ice would gouge the bedrock, picking up pieces of rock and carrying them. As the glacier moves, it would leave debris on either side in a pattern called a "lateral moraine." When glaciers melted, they also would drop the debris heaps called terminal moraine. Visitors to Yosemite Valley can see a well-defined terminal moraine in Bridalveil Meadow.

Yosemite Valley contains many of the most spectacular effects of glaciation, including large waterfalls. Bridalveil Fall, for instance, was created when a glacier shaved off the mouth of Bridalveil Creek at the place where it entered Yosemite Valley. The creek was left suspended high above the valley floor, forcing it to take a misty plunge now enjoyed each spring and summer by millions who visit Yosemite National Park.

Other glacial signatures, such as erratics or rocks left behind in odd places, can be seen in the Sierra. Fallen Leaf Lake, next to Lake Tahoe, is a glacial remnant. It is a moraine-dammed body of water created when a departing glacier dropped its granitic debris along a stream.

The last Ice Age ended about 12,000 years ago, and the large Sierra glaciers departed some time later. The 65 or 70 small glaciers now occupying the Sierra are not more than 4,000 years old, and none are more than 1 mile long. The largest are on Mount Lyell in Yosemite and the Palisades in the Eastern Sierra.

Rivers and Rainfall

Rivers, the conduits of glaciers and carriers of sediment from eroding landscapes, have been around longer than the Sierra. Flowing from North America west to the Precambrian ocean, rivers have been doing their job for about 1 billion years on this part of the globe, although rivers have existed for a much longer period.

Rivers are important in the Sierra, as in any mountain range, because they are quite literally the main drains for anything washed off the landscape—common sediment, gold, boulders, trees, and other material. They also do the heavy work of cutting canyons in granite.

If not for such erosion processes, the range would have grown much taller in the last 5 million years. Mount Whitney might be higher than Mount Everest, which is more than twice Whitney's present height of 14,497 feet. Oxygen and water in the atmosphere simply wear down the mountains, chemically assailing the rocks. Rivers are collectors of the water and the debris dislodged in the erosion process. The erosion and the rivers depend on California's winter storm cycle.

The western slope of the Sierra is usually battered by winter storms from November through April. The name *Sierra Nevada* literally means "snowy mountain range" in Spanish. The Sierra is one of the snowiest places anywhere in the United States. Locations above 8,000 feet in the Central Sierra routinely record more than 35 feet of snow annually, and big winters can produce more than 70 feet in many high-elevation meadows.

The storms incubate in the Pacific Ocean and move east into the Pacific Northwest and California. When a moist ocean air mass—a storm front—reaches the Sierra's western slope, it must begin climbing or rising to get over the mountains. As it rises, the air mass cannot hold as much moisture, so it must drop moisture as rain. This can sometimes be orographic precipitation, or rainfall that occurs in the mountains but not down in the Central Valley. Once a Sierra storm rises to about 7,000 feet, it begins to drop snow.

But, by the time the storm clears the Sierra crest and begins descending the sheer east side of the range, it begins to quickly warm up, lose altitude, and stop dropping precipitation. The Eastern Sierra receives much less precipitation than the western slope. Generally, the major streams on the western slope are much longer and flow more consistently than the Eastern Sierra streams.

The western-slope rivers can sometimes be intimidating. During a 1950 storm, the 265-mile American River in the Central Sierra had a peak discharge of 180,000 cubic feet per second or 90,000 acre-feet of water in one day. That single-day runoff would be enough water to supply a California city of 100,000 people for a year. The American River drains about a 2,000-square-mile watershed. In contrast on the east side of the crest during the same 1950 storm, the 60-mile Truckee River peaked at about 17,500 cubic feet per second.

Between 1 billion and 400 million years ago, such peak flows amounted to little more than a deep cleansing on the western edge of North America. In the early Paleozoic Era, plants began to appear, and peak-flowing rivers meant fresh sediment would be washed into new areas to help spread and renew vegetation. Boulders would be rolled downstream and shattered to create gravel where trout would later spawn. Many other benefits would accrue for the ecosystem.

But, in the last 100 years, as people began to dam the major rivers of the Sierra, the peak flows became destructive floods. Dams cannot tame the biggest floods on the Sierra, and a large amount of water occasionally must be released from the dams during large storms. The result is billions of dollars in damages to homes and down-stream land where people build and farm too close to rivers. Ultimately, many have died in floods. The floods are still a boon to the ecosystem, but people sometimes tragically underestimate Sierra rivers.

The Life Zones

Imagine traveling north from the great southwest deserts of the United States to northern Canada. The vegetation, animal life, and landscape would change remark-ably for several reasons, including precipitation, temperature, soil, and geological features affecting the wind currents. But you wouldn't need to travel thousands of miles to see similar kinds of changes. Different elevations of the Sierra exhibit most of the same shifts in response to climate changes. As you ascend the Sierra and the air temperature drops, you find differences in the plants and animals. You pass through the Sierra's life zones.

American zoologist C.H. Merriam first noted the different zones of life that appear as he ascended the mountains of northern Arizona. Scientists do not suggest that the same vegetation and animals found in life zones of one mountain range would be found in others. The life within the different elevation zones of the Rocky Mountains differs from those in the Sierra Nevada. There are differences even from the Eastern Sierra to the western slopes of the Sierra. But the concept of life changing from zone to zone holds true for any mountain range.

The Sierra life zones have been sliced and parcelled a number of different ways, but one of the more universal views is that there are five distinct zones determined by elevation. For the western slope, they are the foothill, lower montane, upper montane, subalpine, and alpine zones. The eastern slope zones are the same except for the lowest zone, which is called pinion-sagebrush. The pinion-sagebrush zone is an adaptation to a drier climate, and it is ranges up to 7,000 feet compared to the 3,500- to 4,000-foot high point for the western slope foothill zone.

On the western slope, the lower montane ranges from about 3,500 feet to 6,000 feet. The upper montane runs from 6,000 to about 8,200 feet. The subalpine goes from 8,200 to about 10,500. The alpine is designated from 10,500 to above 13,000 feet. The elevations are similar on the Eastern Sierra, but slightly higher in elevation. The lower montane is compressed between 7,000 to 8,000 feet. The upper montane is between 8,000 and 9,000 feet. The subalpine is 9,000 to 11,000 feet. The alpine is 11,000 to above 13,500.

The higher the life zone, the shorter the growing season for plants. In the highest life zones, the subalpine and alpine, plants may only be able to grow seven weeks of the year. The rest of the year, prolonged freezes make plant growth difficult or impossible. Larger mammals, such as bears or mountain lions, do not generally live in the higher zones because there is not enough plant life to sustain prey or forage for them. Much of the Sierra's animal diversity and numbers are found from the montane down to the foothill or pinion-sagebrush life zones. The lower in elevation, the more animals you will find.

ALPINE

This stark, cold part of the Sierra is wind-blown and beautiful beneath the deepest blue skies in California—there's no smog up here. This life zone is above the timberline, meaning trees generally cannot survive at this elevation. The plants at California's rooftop are often divided into meadow and rock communities. They must survive in the tiny window of six or seven weeks during the summer when the snow finally disappears.

The alpine soil is rocky and well drained. Since the summers are often sunny and arid, plants must adapt to wind, dry conditions, and rocky soils. Plants do not grow large. Instead, they often grow close to the ground and send down deep taproots.

In the alpine meadows, there are grasses and sedges, such as alpine sedge (*Carex subnigricans*). The wildflowers also are low-growing species, including primrose monkey-flower (*Mimulus primuloides*). Few shrubs grow at this elevation, but dwarf huckleberry (*Vaccinium nivictum*) and a few others can adapt to the various wet places where snowmelt lingers.

Alpine rock plants are among the toughest vegetation in the Sierra. They generally must survive in even rockier soils than the meadow plants. The alpine spring locoweed *(Astragalus kentrophyta)* is a good example. The mountain sorrel *(Oxyria digyna)* is a smaller shrub that can survive in rock crannies.

Very few animals are year-round residents in the alpine zone. The yellow-bellied marmot *(Marmota flaviventris)* is one of them. There are visitors from lower elevations, and they include the white-tailed jackrabbit *(Lepus townsendii)* and the Clark's nutcracker *(Nucrifraga columbiana)*.

SUBALPINE

The highest forests of the Sierra are found here. If you hike up to the timberline anywhere from Kings Canyon National Park up to Lake Tahoe, you will probably see the distorted, heavy trunks of the whitebark pine *(Pinus albicaulis)* along ridgelines and in windy passes. Other trees near the timberline include the mountain hemlock *(Tsuga mertensiana)*, the foxtail pine *(Pinus balfouriana)*, and the lodgepole pine *(Pinus murrayana)*.

Soils in the subalpine are not usually filled with nutrients, and the winter storms leave 250 to 400 inches of snow annually. With the heavy snowfall, high winds, and low temperatures, trees near the timberline are not very large, nor do they grow very fast.

Many types of shrubs and wildflowers occupy the subalpine as well. This vegetation often can be found in both the upper and lower montane zones as well. Shrubs such as greenleaf manzanita *(Arctostaphylos patula)* can be found in a wide range of elevations from the subalpine all the way down to the lower montane. The Sierra primrose *(Primula suffrutescens)* is a wildflower that can usually be found in rocky subalpine areas.

The animal communities are larger in the subalpine areas compared to the alpine zone. Birds, reptiles, amphibians, and mammals live and visit subalpine elevations in the Sierra. There are not a lot of predators at this elevation because prey is more abundant in the montane and foothill areas. The American badger *(Taxidea taxus)* and the gray fox *(Urocyon cinereoargenteus)* often hunt for food in the subalpine zone.

YELLOW-BELLIED MARMOT
(Marmota flaviventris)
At the approach of danger, including predators such as the eagle, the yellow-bellied marmot retreats toward its burrow, usually located beneath rocks.

UPPER AND LOWER MONTANE

The heart of the Sierra's conifers is between 3,000 feet and about 8,500 feet in elevation—the upper and lower montane.

11

Biologists separate this part of the forest into elevation belts where certain types of trees dominate the landscape. For instance, the red fir *(Abies magnifica)* forest occupies the upper montane in well-drained soils between 6,500 and 8,500 feet. The white fir *(Abies concolor)* ranges from 4,000 to 8,000 feet. The ponderosa pine *(Pinus ponderosa)* is found from 2,800 feet to about 6,500 feet.

Notice the overlap. The forest belts contain more than a dozen different conifers and many broadleaf trees, and the boundaries are not at all distinct. Four or five different species of conifers, including those from different life zones, can be found in a single stand. You might find both the white and red fir in the same area. One of the more common trees throughout the upper and lower montane is the black oak *(Quercus kelloggii)*, which is found on open, dry ridges from the foothill life zone all the way to 8,000 feet in some areas of the Sierra's western slope. There is not as much variety on the Eastern Sierra, but the mixed conifer forests can be found there between 6,000 and 8,000 feet.

The general rule on the western slope is that the various forest belts extend to higher elevations as you travel south. The phenomenon is largely a function of precipitation and temperature. The Northern Sierra is wetter and cooler than the Southern Sierra because Pacific storms often enter California from the northwest and lose moisture before they reach the Southern Sierra. A shrub that could be found at 3,500 feet in the Northern Sierra can sometimes be found at 5,000 feet or even higher in the Southern Sierra. The same is true for wildflowers. More than 100 miles north of the Southern Sierra, the Fendler's meadow rue *(Thalictrum fendleri)* can occur all the way down to 3,500 feet. But in the Southern Sierra, it can be found all the way up to 10,000 feet.

The animals in the montane life zones include the larger mammals, such as the mule deer *(Odocoileus hemionus)*, mountain lion *(Felix concolor)*, and black bear *(Ursus americanus)*. Many animals, such as bighorn sheep *(Ovis canadensis)* will move with the seasons to find food. In winter, the sheep will move down into lower meadows when the snowpack begins to cover their higher elevation feeding grounds.

▓ FOOTHILL

The foothills of the Sierra can range from 500 feet to 4,000 or even 5,000 feet, based solely on plant species and climate. Other than vegetation and weather, there is no other physical or geological quality that distinguishes this zone from the rest of the range. But foothill vegetation is quite distinctive, including woodland, chaparral, and grassland ecosystems. These plant communities are specially suited to the often dry conditions of foothills, which receive as little as 12 to 15 inches of rainfall a year in the Southern Sierra.

Probably the most dominant woodland tree is the oak, specifically the blue oak *(Quercus douglasii)*. But there are other kinds of oak, including the stately valley oak *(Quercus lobata)* and interior live oak *(Quercus wislizenii)*. The digger pine *(Pinus sabiniana)* can be found in many stands of woodland oaks.

Chaparral is found in abundance along the Southern Sierra, but not as much to the north where damper conditions favor the woodlands. Chaparral grows on hot, dry slopes in brush thickets, and there are many plant species in the community. They include common buckbrush *(Ceanothus cuneatus)* and chaparral pea *(Pickeringia montana).*

The lower foothills are dominated by grassland species. Bunch grasses are the dominant plants, though the natives have been largely replaced by such exotics as foxtail fescue *(Festuca megalura).* Grassland wildflower displays in spring are quite extraordinary in heavy rainfall years.

Though the deciduous trees drop their leaves and some other vegetation goes dormant during winter, the foothills come alive in the winter months. Many creatures, including migrating birds, come down from the montane zones to warm up and find food. But many animals, such as the red-tailed hawk *(Buteo jamaicensis)* and the bobcat *(Lynx rufus),* live here year-round.

PINION-SAGEBRUSH

The high desert conditions of the Eastern Sierra create a pinion-sagebrush life zone from 7,000 feet down to about 4,000 feet, which is the elevation of the Owens Valley floor. This life zone is quite different from the western slope foothills because it is far more arid and higher in elevation. Rainfall totals can average as low as 6 inches annually on the valley floor, and perhaps 18 inches at 7,000 feet. Western slope totals are easily twice as high at comparable elevations.

The lower plant communities are filled with Great Basin sagebrush *(Artemisia tridentata),* which grows well in sandy soil. The Eastern Sierra is known for the sagebrush fragrance that is carried by the wind. But there are many other interesting plants, such as the desert peach *(Prunus andersonii).*

The upper part of the pinion-sagebrush zone is dominated by the pinion pine *(Pinus monophylla)* and associated plants, such as mountain mahogany *(Cercocarpus betuloides).* Quaking aspen *(Populus tremuloides)* is also found in the higher elevations of the upper pinion-sagebrush zone. The most common streamside tree in this upper area is water birch *(Betula occidentalis).*

The largest mammals in the pinion-sagebrush zone are deer and bighorn sheep, which eat the shrubs and herbs at these elevations. Many desert animals are found here, too. Birds and small mammals are lighter in color here than elsewhere in the Sierra because the lighter color reduces body heat and provides a better camouflage. These animals include the desert horned lizard *(Phrynosoma platyrhnos),* sagebrush chipmunk *(Eutamias minimus),* and pinion jay *(Gymnorhinus cyanocephalus).*

PEOPLE IN THE SIERRA

Volcanoes, earthquakes, glaciers, and rivers shaped the Sierra over the last 400 million years. Over the last 10,000 years, Native Americans have been making small, beneficial changes to the landscape. But during the last 150 years, European-American settlers have moved in and made some less than positive and rather astonishing alterations.

The transformations began in the late 1840s when gold mining mania brought a wave of development that resulted in roads, settlements, lumber harvesting, and river damming. Later in the century, thousands of acres were clear-cut by loggers, entire ridges were destroyed by hydraulic miners, and meadows were trampled by grazing livestock. Indeed, gold mining spawned massive commercial and industrial development and a half century of unrestricted resource extraction and ecosystem alteration. Mining, grazing, logging, and transportation came to dominate these mountains.

A conservation backlash followed. In the twentieth century national parks were established, and many thousands of acres were protected. But even with their good intentions, the conservationist thinking—which helped spur the federal government to snuff out as many fires as possible in the Sierra—was not informed enough to avoid another tragic mistake. In removing fire from the forest, the Sierra lost its most effective natural limit on the growth of the forest. People unknowingly created a boon for thick brush, smaller trees, and other vegetation. Now there is enough vegetation, or fuel, to turn many ordinary, natural fires into catastrophic wildfires that could consume thousands of forest acres, choke inland valleys with smoke, and threaten people.

Federal managers and scientists all over the 20 million acres of the Sierra are struggling to figure out the best protections for the range. The job is complicated because 36 percent of the land is in private hands. The rest is held by public agencies, such as the U.S. Forest Service, the Bureau of Land Management, the state of California, the National Park Service, and others. These agencies, private individuals, and commercial interests do not always agree on how to manage the forests.

How differently the pre-nineteenth century inhabitants, the Native Americans, saw the Sierra. Instead of relentless development or rigid preservation, they seemed to understand how to coexist with the ecosystem and maintain it. Evidence of their Sierra lifestyles has been traced back thousands of years in parts of the range. Before the nineteenth century, Native Americans numbered more than 50,000 individuals and spanned the Sierra, ranging from the Tubatulabal in the southern Kern River basin to the Northern Sierra tribes of the Maidu.

The Tubatulabal, Maidu, Yokuts, Miwok, Mono, Paiute, Washoe, and others practiced land management that would sustain plant diversity and maintain their cultural and agricultural pursuits. Their chief tool was fire, which was used to burn meadows, clear vegetation in wooded areas, and disperse seeds. They also transplanted native vegetation and weeded to promote its growth. They pruned, irrigated, and selectively harvested. In many recent discussions with tribal elders about the Sierra, the Native Americans say the range's decline is no mystery: No one is caring for areas the way they did many centuries before Europeans arrived.

Jedediah Smith is believed to be the first person of European background to cross the Sierra during an expedition in 1826 and 1827. He came from the south, trekking along the foothills from the Southern Sierra to the Central Sierra, and he saw many large mammals including vast herds of tule elk *(Cervus elaphus nannodes)*. He eventually crossed west to east at Ebbets Pass in the Central Sierra. Brigades of fur trappers and hunters soon followed, taking elk, bear, deer, antelope, beaver, and other creatures.

Twenty-one years after Smith passed through the Central Sierra, James Marshall found tiny gold nuggets in the South Fork of the American River, just west of present-day El Dorado National Forest. About 500,000 people flooded into California in search of riches. Saw mills sprang up to cut timber for houses and other buildings. About $750 billion of gold was produced over the next several decades. The ecosystem suffered as miners devised hydraulic mining, using strong blasts of water to strip away soils from hillsides and reveal veins of gold.

But as the gold and silver booms ended, loggers became the focus of commercial expansion in the Sierra. The lumber industry provided the timbers, ties, and other products for the Central Pacific and other railroads. California needed lumber to build homes and businesses. However, there were less than 100 lumber mills in the 1850s. By the late 1800s, historians believe the figure had more than tripled and more than a third of the Sierra's forests were taken. Some logging operations removed 70 million board feet annually, decimating the Sierra tree stock in some areas—especially yellow or ponderosa pine *(Pinus ponderosa)*. Many mature giant sequoias *(Sequoia giganteum)*, some 2,000 years old, were cut down in the Southern Sierra. The brittle wood was almost useless in construction, except as fence posts and roof shingles.

At the same time, sheep and cattle grazing affected the foothills, montane, and even subalpine in the Sierra. In the decades between 1860 and 1900, millions of sheep overgrazed Sierra meadows, though no one knows for sure how many animals there were. Because dairy cattle herds needed higher quality rangeland, they were often kept at the lower elevations where they damaged the grasslands.

Government regulation began to grip the Sierra after 1900. In a 40-year period, the U.S. Forest Service, the California Division of Forestry, the National Park Service, and other agencies regulated public lands and had an influence on private land. Dam construction for irrigation and hydroelectric purposes began under the auspices of government regulation, though the agencies and their regulations would become far more restrictive as scientific knowledge evolved during the twentieth century.

By the latter part of the twentieth century, people began to move into the mountains in droves. The population grew from about 300,000 in 1970 to 650,000 in 1990. Almost three-quarters of the people live on the western slope in the foothills. By 2040, projections show the population will grow to about 2 million. Federal officials and scientists are vigorously pursuing plans to protect the range and the people. With all these concerns, officials must plan for a problem nobody faced in 1950: recreation run amok. They must find a way to let millions of people hike, fish, boat, horseback ride, camp, photograph, and see the sights in the Sierra's backcountry playgrounds— yet they must somehow protect these pristine areas as well.

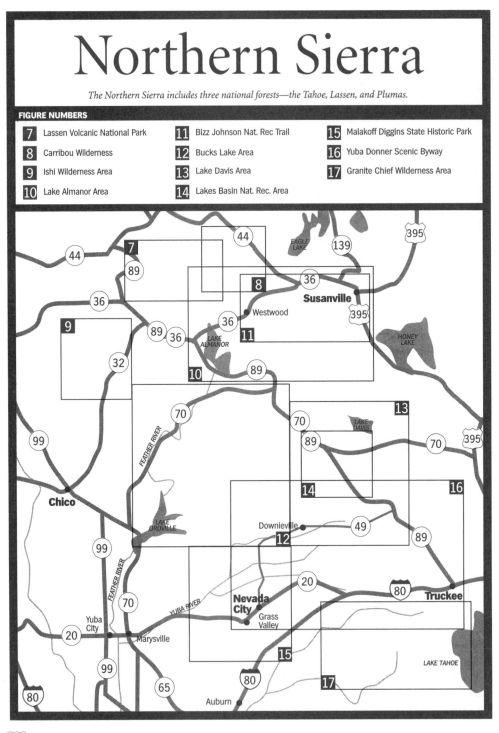

Northern Sierra

The Northern Sierra includes three national forests—the Tahoe, Lassen, and Plumas.

FIGURE NUMBERS

7 Lassen Volcanic National Park

8 Carribou Wilderness

9 Ishi Wilderness Area

10 Lake Almanor Area

11 Bizz Johnson Nat. Rec Trail

12 Bucks Lake Area

13 Lake Davis Area

14 Lakes Basin Nat. Rec. Area

15 Malakoff Diggins State Historic Park

16 Yuba Donner Scenic Byway

17 Granite Chief Wilderness Area

Northern Sierra

Volcanic activity of the last 50,000 years in the Northern Sierra created the basalt and andesite ridgelines and features that spread across the northern part of the batholith anchoring this mountain range. The farther north the visitor travels, the lower the peak elevations, as the batholith submerges beneath the earth's surface. Mountaintops can still reach higher than 9,000 feet in the Northern Sierra, but people do not come to this part of the mountain range for a high country experience. They come for the fishing, the sight-seeing, the rivers, and the camping.

While the porous volcanic surfaces allow water to seep into the ground much easier than granite, thus preventing the formation of many lakes, places such as the Plumas National Forest have become known as meccas for trout fishing. The lakes on the Plumas are formed by hydroelectric projects and are well-stocked with trout and other freshwater fish.

[*Above:* Lassen Peak in Lassen Volcanic National Park last erupted in 1915]

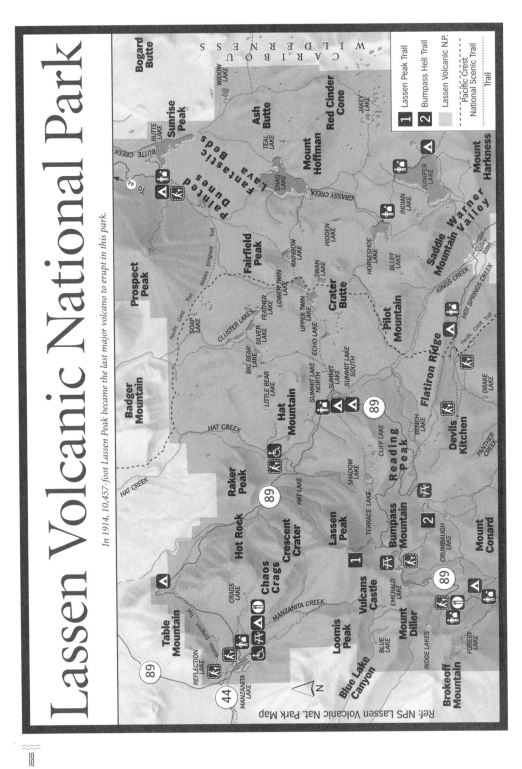

Lassen Volcanic National Park

In 1914, 10,457-foot Lassen Peak became the last major volcano to erupt in this park.

Ref: NPS Lassen Volcanic Nat. Park Map

Legend:
1 Lassen Peak Trail
2 Bumpass Hell Trail
Lassen Volcanic N.P.
Pacific Crest National Scenic Trail
Trail

The Northern Sierra is also known for weather. The precipitation gauge runs a bit deeper here; the forests appear greener, the temperatures cooler. The Feather River, for instance, can carry as much water as several Southern Sierra rivers combined because there is simply more rain and snow in the Northern Sierra.

The increased precipitation is part of the regional weather flow in the western United States. Storms coming in from the Pacific Ocean generally drop a lot of their moisture in the Northern Sierra and begin to taper off as they encounter atmospheric high pressure areas in the central and southern portions of the mountain range.

This weather pattern promotes forests that are greener in the Northern Sierra than in the more arid Southern Sierra. The green forests, rich in nutrients and insect life, make a wonderful habitat for diverse wildlife, particularly birds.

Geologists say the Northern Sierra ends roughly around Lake Almanor in the Lassen National Forest, where the batholith subtly disappears beneath the younger rocks of the Cascades. Indeed, the Sierra proper does not include Lassen Volcanic National Park, the spectacular show of volcanism in the Cascade Range just a few miles from Almanor. But the volcanic southern edge of the Cascades is so close that visitors to the Northern Sierra will also want to view the park.

The three forests of the Northern Sierra—the Tahoe, Plumas, and Lassen—do not include Lake Tahoe for the same reason that the lake is not lumped in with the Northern Sierra in this book. Lake Tahoe, much like Yosemite National Park, is literally in a class by itself as an outdoor destination and a natural location. The U.S. Forest Service considers the lake to be a separate entity, supervising it with the Lake Tahoe Basin Management Unit.

Even without Lake Tahoe, the three northern forests have quite a recent history of their own. Gold mining, grazing, logging, railroad building, hydroelectric project construction, and logging fill the area with remnants and scars that define the mountain and foothill communities. As a distinct area of the Sierra, these forests have characteristics not found anywhere else in the range.

Lassen Volcanic National Park

[Fig. 7] Just north of the Sierra Nevada, the Cascade Range's southernmost volcanic formations make the perfect bookend to the Sierra's granite. The showcase in the southern Cascades is Lassen Volcanic National Park where 10,457-foot Lassen Peak was active less than a century ago.

Though it is not a part of the Sierra, this national park is well worth the slight detour. Its explosive past and its current volcanic features should not be missed in any tour of Northern California.

The last major eruption at the park occurred when Lassen Peak began explosions at irregular intervals in 1914. By May 19, 1915, lava rose in the summit crater, spilling

Lassen Peak, part of the Cascade Range, is 10,457 feet high.

over the northeastern and southwestern sides. The glowing lava cooled and hardened before it reached the Sacramento Valley, but it caused a stir.

The lava melted snow and cut a fiery swath through forested land. On May 22, 1915, people from the valleys to the mountains could see a 40,000-foot-high volcanic cloud rising. A massive explosion had blown a new crater in the mountain. People in towns such as Redding were in a panic.

Today, the volcano is quiet, except for steam occasionally rising from the summit and flanks of the mountain. Light streaks of dacite and dark markings of andesite are prominent in the pumice that was ejected from the 1915 blast.

In Lassen, hot springs remain as reminders of the molten past. Temperatures as high as 230 degrees Fahrenheit have been recorded at some springs. The springs are called Bumpass Hell, Sulphur Works, Little Hot Springs Valley, Cold Boiling Lake, and Devil's Kitchen in Warner Valley.

Gases in the hot springs contain carbon dioxide and steam. Surrounding rocks usually contain sulphur, iron pyrite, quartz, and other substances. Four types of lava are found in the park, including rhyolite and dacite (light-colored lavas) and basalt and andesite (both of which are darker).

Lassen Peak, a Pelean-type plug dome volcano, pushed its way up about 27,000 years ago. The "plug" simply refers to the hardened magma lodged in the eroding cone. "Pelean" is the type of volcanic eruption that occurred in 1915, which scientists believe was similar to the 1902 eruption of Mont Pelée on Martinique, Lesser Antilles. Incandescent lava fragments were blown out of a central crater. In this type of eruption, a tongue-like, glowing avalanche then moves downslope at velocities as great as 100 miles per hour.

Such volcanic activity has been happening for 70 million years, dating back to the time the area was still covered by the Pacific Ocean. The volcanic activity was stimulated by the collision of the North American and Pacific tectonic plates, which began about 200 million years ago.

Lassen Peak and the other 16 major volcanoes of the Cascades are part of the "ring of fire" surrounding the Pacific Ocean. The "ring of fire" is a series of volcanoes that circle the Pacific tectonic plate spreading thousands of miles, including Hawaii and other parts of the South Pacific as well as the Pacific Northwest. The eastern side of the Sierra is also included in the circle.

The Cascade Range, where the park is located, is younger than the nearby Sierra by more than 100 million years. The range began in the Lassen Strait, a depression that broadened millions of years ago and eventually rose to separate the Sierra Nevada and the Klamath Mountains, which were believed to be one continuous range at one time.

Touring the park's main road, Lassen Park Road, which connects with Highway 89, people can see Lassen's 106,000 acres of volcanic beauty. The 150 miles of hiking trails include 17 miles of the Pacific Crest Trail.

Lassen's varied landscapes—volcanic, high altitude, meadow, rocky canyon, and others—provide support for more than 700 flowering plant species and 250 vertebrates. In the forests above 7,000 feet, the park's red fir *(Abies magnifica)* belt supports fewer species of animals because there is not enough plant life and other food sources for such creatures as the striped skunk *(Mephitis mephitis)*, which prefers grasshoppers, beetles, and other surface insects that are not as abundant at high elevation as they are farther down the mountains.

At elevations above 8,000 feet, the whitebark pine *(Pinus albicaulis)* can be found in drier, south-facing parts of the park. The mountain hemlock *(Tsuga mertensiana)* lives in similar elevations, but it grows best in shady, moister conditions, thriving in places where the snow lingers well into summer.

The Douglas fir *(Pseudosuga menziesii)* is perhaps the tree most associated with the national park and with the forest surrounding it. Blue grouse *(Dendragapus obscurus)* and mule deer *(Odocoileus hemionus)* eat its long, dark, yellow-green needles. The tree can grow up to 200 feet. In logging areas outside the national park, it is a favorite for use as a Christmas tree.

The midelevations, between 5,000 and 7,000 feet, are home to old-growth trees ranging from ponderosa or yellow pine *(Pinus ponderosa)* to the firs, including the white fir *(Abies concolor)* and the Douglas fir. These trees are important in the ecosystem as habitat for such rare creatures as the spotted owl *(Strix occidentalis)*, considered a sensitive species that must be protected in California. The owl nests in cavities of old-growth trees with diameters of 40 inches and bigger.

Old-growth tree stands contain trees that are centuries old and sometimes 200 feet tall. Most often, the stands contain downed trees that have fallen over time because of insect infestation, lightning strikes, or age. The trees can often remain in the ecosystem for hundreds of years, decomposing and providing places for wildlife to live or find refuge. As trees decompose, they also add nutrients to the soil.

Such stands of trees are becoming rare in California because many of them have been heavily logged. In Lassen National Park, as in Yosemite and Sequoia and Kings Canyon national parks, logging has been forbidden for many decades, so the national parks have the largest remnants of old growth.

In the lower elevations near pools of water along streams, look for the thumb-sized leaves of the Douglas spiraea *(Spiraea douglasii)* and the greenish-gray leaves of the western blueberry *(Vaccinium uglinosium* ssp. *occidentale)*. The edible fruit of the western blueberry may be found in late spring.

MULE DEER
(Odocoileus hemionus)

Plan any trip to Lassen with the weather in mind. The roads into the park can be closed due to snowy conditions.

Directions: Located 50 miles east of Red Bluff on Highway 36, and 50 miles east of Redding on Highway 44. Follow the signs. The three access roads into various areas of the park are Butte Lake Road (6 miles on gravel); Juniper Lake Road, The Lassen Chalet and Manzanita Lake (13 miles on gravel); and the Warner Valley Road (14 miles of paved road, then 3 miles of gravel). The Warner Valley and Butte Lake roads are usually open June through late Oct.

Facilities: Visitor centers and exhibits and the Loomis Museum are near Manzanita Lake at the northwest entrance via Highway 44 from Redding. The Drakesbad Guest Ranch is located 17 miles northwest from Chester on County Road 312. There are 8 campgrounds in the park. Reservations for the group campgrounds are required and must be made in advance. All others, first-come, first-serve. The Camper Store operates daily in the summer months and offers food and gifts. The Loomis Museum offers information and publications in the summer months. Both the Camper Store and Loomis Museum are near Manzanita Lake on Highway 44 at the northwest entrance.

Activities: Hiking, camping, nature walks, sight-seeing, bicycling, and snowshoeing.

Dates: Park is open year-round. Campgrounds generally open May through Sept. The Juniper Lake road is usually open early July to late October.

Fees: There is a charge to enter the park.

Closest town: Mineral, 9 miles.

For more information: Superintendent, Lassen Volcanic National Park, PO Box 100, Mineral, CA 96063-0100. Phone (530) 595-4444. Phone (530) 595-4444 ext. 5155 for group fees. The Drakesbad Guest Ranch, phone (530) 529-9820.

LASSEN PEAK TRAIL

[Fig. 7(1)] The volcano may have blown its top early this century, but it is not active now. The four-hour day hike to Lassen Peak is a strenuous trip, but it is well worth the view of this volcano, which was formed on a vent of Mount Tehama. There is no water, so carry your own.

From the Lassen rim at more than 10,450 feet, the views are spectacular. See Chaos Crags, Reading Peak, and Brokeoff Mountain. In the distance to the north, there is the Modoc Plateau. Lake Almanor is quite clear to the south. And, it seems like the whole Northern Sierra spreads in view for perhaps 100 miles on a clear day.

Large animals, such as the California black bear *(Ursus americanus)*, do not generally climb much beyond the tree line, which is about 9,000 feet. Still, hikers will see animal life above 10,000 feet on Lassen Peak Trail. Look for the yellow-bellied marmot (*Marmota flaviventris*), the largest ground squirrel in the park. It prefers the higher elevations, which provide refuge from large predators.

In the warmer months, hikers need only take a deep breath to smell the coyote mint or pennyroyal (*Monardella villosa*). High elevation winds waft the mint aroma from bunches of these white flowers, which often provide the only color at the higher elevations of this trail. Native Americans ingested mild doses of this flower to relax.

Directions: Drive 9 miles north of the Highway 36 and Highway 89 junction on Highway 89. You will enter the Raker Memorial Gateway at the southwest entrance. Drive north another 7 miles to the trailhead parking. Signs mark it.

Trail: 5 miles round-trip.

Elevation: 8,500 feet to 10,453 feet.

Degree of difficulty: Strenuous.

Surface: Barren, volcanic.

Splatter Cones

In areas such as Lassen Volcanic National Park and Lassen National Forest, visitors will sometimes see craters known as splatter cones. They were created thousands of years ago when lava poured from fissures along a rock formation. Gaseous pressures built up near the fissures and caused the lava to spew upward like a fountain. Chunks or clots of lava landed, flattened, and plastered themselves to the ground. Craters were left behind where the fountains had appeared. Together with the flattened chunks of lava, these craters came to be known as splatter cones.

BUMPASS HELL TRAIL

[Fig. 7(2)] The trail to Bumpass Hell goes to Cold Boiling Lake and Crumbaugh Lake. At Cold Boiling Lake, bubbles are often seen rising to the surface from the release of gas underground beneath the lake.

But the real show is at Bumpass Hell, where groundwater seeping into an underground magma chamber heats and rises. Walk the boardwalk and watch the mud pots and steam vents in this eerie place.

Directions: Drive about 17 miles north of the Highway 36 and 89 junction into Lassen National Park. Drive 6 miles to Road Post 30, turn right, and drive 0.3 mile to the trailhead at Kings Creek Picnic Area. The trailhead is at the southside of the parking lot.

Trail: 3 miles round-trip, can be done in four hours.

Elevation: 1,500-foot gain, high point 8,350 feet.

Degree of difficulty: Moderate.

Surface: Dirt pathway with some volcanic rocks as trail narrows.

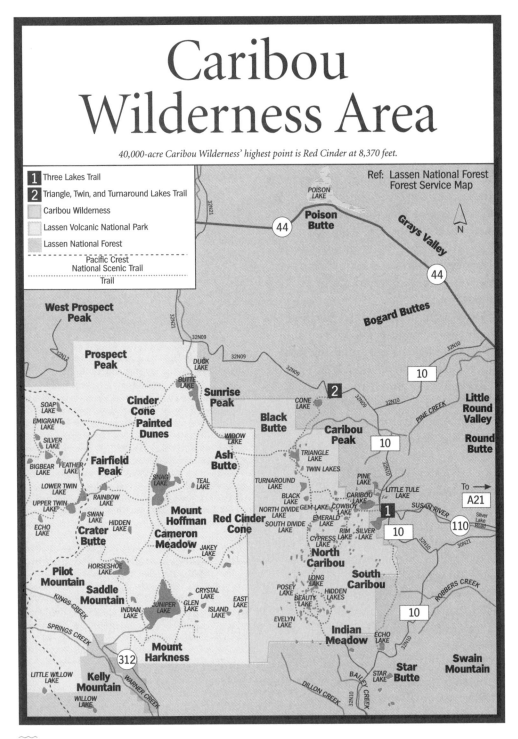

Caribou Wilderness Area

40,000-acre Caribou Wilderness' highest point is Red Cinder at 8,370 feet.

Ref: Lassen National Forest
Forest Service Map

1 Three Lakes Trail
2 Triangle, Twin, and Turnaround Lakes Trail
Caribou Wilderness
Lassen Volcanic National Park
Lassen National Forest
Pacific Crest
National Scenic Trail
Trail

Lassen National Forest

[Fig. 8, Fig. 9, Fig. 10, Fig. 11, Fig. 12] The 1.2 million-acre forest, established in 1905, is a kind of California crossroads where the Sierra Nevada's northern boundary meets the Cascade Range from the Pacific Northwest and the Great Basin from the East. The southern part of Lassen is in the Sierra, and the central and northern portions are in the Cascades. The eastern Lassen forest areas are in the Great Basin, which is on the more arid eastern side of the Sierra.

Visitors have the opportunity to learn the story of the last survivor of the Yahi Yana Native American tribe in the Ishi Wilderness, which contains about 41,000 acres. The forest in the wilderness has high granite countryside as well as lava-covered geologic ridges and meadows. The granite supports some lakes, but the volcanic soil is porous and cannot hold enough water for lakes.

Lassen National Forest surrounds 106,000-acre Lassen Volcanic National Park. In the park, 10,457-foot Lassen Peak erupted in the early part of the century with a spectacular blast seen for miles around.

Just east of the park, the Caribou Wilderness stretches for 40,000 acres and includes high-country lakes, wildlife, and wildflowers in midsummer.

CARIBOU WILDERNESS

[Fig. 8] Just east of the national park, the Caribou Wilderness is a gentle, rolling plateau with crater peaks, cinder cones, and large depressions that have evolved to timber-lined lakes. The headwaters of the Susan River begin in the Caribou, percolating up through the porous volcanic aquifer.

The volcanic peaks include Swain Mountain, Bogard Buttes, Prospect Peak, Ash Butte, Red Cinder Cone, and Mount Harkness. Red Cinder is the highest point at 8,370 feet.

The obvious large natural features—volcanic ridges, conifer tree groupings, and streams—sometimes overshadow the smaller parts of the ecosystem in Caribou and other California wildernesses. One of the more interesting microcommunities is on the forest floor where fungi grow.

As the sanitary agents of the forest that consume dead organic matter, fungi spread on the floor of a conifer area. The cup fungus (*Sacrosphaera coronaria*), for instance, can be found in the Caribou, along with man's hair (*Boletus edulis*) and narrow-headed morel (*Morella angusticeps*). Fungal spores blow in on the winds and take up residence at the foot of trees.

Along some trails in the Caribou, hikers will see a timber-destroying pore fungi called the red-belt fomes (*Fomes pinicola*). Look for the white and yellow fungi on the bark of such trees as the white fir (*Abies concolor*).

Though susceptible to fungal infection, white firs have developed an ability to exist in shaded, crowded conditions. Look for them in dense stands where they grow slowly

WHITE-HEADED WOODPECKER

(Dendrocopus albolarvatus)
White-headed woodpeckers have white heads and throats and males have a red patch on the back of their heads.

until larger trees fall aside and allow the sunshine to peek through. Scientists believe the shade adaptation occurred over thousands of years as the tree competed for sunlight with other conifers.

Snow stays late in spring in this wilderness. Often, the Caribou, which is about 40,000 acres, does not open until July, and the area is still marshy after the snowmelts, meaning mosquitoes are out in the morning and evening.

Directions: Drive 9 miles north of Westwood on Highway 44, turn southwest on Road A21 and go 4.5 miles. Turn west on Silver Lake Road and drive 6 miles. Turn right at Forest Road 10. Drive 1 mile to the Caribou Lake Trailhead.

Activities: Hiking, camping, fishing, boating, wildlife viewing.

Facilities: No campgrounds in the wilderness.

Dates: Mid-June to mid-Oct.

Fees: None.

Closest town: Westwood, 10 miles.

For more information: Almanor Ranger District, PO Box 767, Chester, CA 96020. Phone (530) 258-2141.

THREE LAKES TRAIL

[Fig. 8(1)] Emerald, Rim, and Cypress lakes may be the most beautiful attractions in the Caribou. Campsites are not developed at Rim Lake and in much of this area, but Cypress Lake does have many places where people can camp. This hike to all three lakes can easily be done in half a day, so camping may not be necessary.

Vistas of Lassen Volcanic National Park and other parts of the surrounding mountains can be enjoyed from nearby

North Caribou Peak, which is less than 1 mile from Cypress Lake. Swimming, camping, and nature walks are popular activities in this area.

Directions: Drive 9 miles north of Westwood on Highway 44, turn southwest on Road A21 and go 4.5 miles. Turn west on Silver Lake Road and drive 6 miles. Turn right at Forest Road 10. Drive 1 mile to the Caribou Lake Trailhead, which leads to the Three Lakes Trail.

White-headed Woodpecker

The white-headed woodpecker *(Dendrocopus albolarvatus)* is a common sight in the Northern Sierra, perching in ponderosa pine *(Pinus ponderosa)* and white fir *(Abies concolor)*. The only tree it will avoid is the lodgepole pine *(Pinus murrayana)*, for reasons not known. It nests in the stubbed trunks of dead trees, laying up to a half dozen eggs, and pecking out a cavity inside the tree. Both adults find food for the young. Full-grown, the bird is less than the size of a robin, with black feathers on its body and a white head. When it is flying, a white patch can be seen on its wing.

Trail: 7.4 miles round-trip

Elevation: 700-foot gain, high point 7,100 feet.

Degree of difficulty: Easy.

Surface: Footpath; open and easy to follow.

TRIANGLE, TWIN AND TURNAROUND LAKES TRAIL

[Fig. 8(2)] This trail has a high immediate-gratification factor. It is not long before hikers reach Triangle Lake and the cool water that can be so refreshing on a warm day in the Cascades.

The first lake, Triangle, is only about 2 miles from the trailhead. The loop trail around the lake is a little more than 1 mile and well worth the extra time. The pine and fir belt in the area makes it an eye-catcher.

The smaller Twin Lakes are less than 1 mile away, beyond a lush meadow. Turnaround Lake is about another mile. With modest ridges in the backdrop, the lake offers many places where campers can stay and another trail to circle the lake.

Directions: Drive about 20 miles northwest on Highway 44 from the Highway 44 and Highway 89 junction, which is about 35 miles northwest of Susanville. Turn west from Highway 44 on Forest Road 10, go 6 miles and turn right on Road 32N09. Drive 2.6 miles to the trailhead and registry at Cone Lake.

Trail: 8 miles, round-trip

Elevation: About a 500-foot gain.

Degree of difficulty: Easy.

Surface: Footpath, marshy in some spots.

Ishi Wilderness Area

This 41,000-acre wilderness is named for the last of the Yahi Yana Indians who died in 1915.

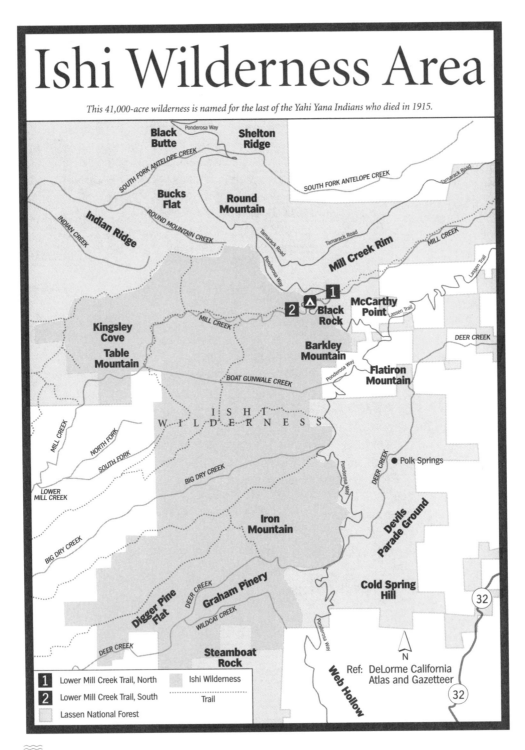

Black Butte

Ponderosa Way

Shelton Ridge

SOUTH FORK ANTELOPE CREEK

SOUTH FORK ANTELOPE CREEK

Tamarack Road

Bucks Flat

Round Mountain

INDIAN CREEK

Indian Ridge

ROUND MOUNTAIN CREEK

Tamarack Road

Ponderosa Way

Tamarack Road

Mill Creek Rim

MILL CREEK

Lassen Trail

1 McCarthy Point

2 Black Rock

Lassen Trail

DEER CREEK

MILL CREEK

Kingsley Cove

Table Mountain

Barkley Mountain

Flatiron Mountain

BOAT GUNWALE CREEK

Ponderosa Way

I S H I
W I L D E R N E S S

MILL CREEK

NORTH FORK

SOUTH FORK

BIG DRY CREEK

DEER CREEK

● Polk Springs

LOWER MILL CREEK

Ponderosa Way

BIG DRY CREEK

Iron Mountain

Devils Parade Ground

Cold Spring Hill

32

Digger Pine Flat

DEER CREEK

Graham Pinery

WILDCAT CREEK

Ponderosa Way

N

Ref: DeLorme California Atlas and Gazetteer

DEER CREEK

Steamboat Rock

Web Hollow

32

1 Lower Mill Creek Trail, North

2 Lower Mill Creek Trail, South

Ishi Wilderness

Trail

Lassen National Forest

ISHI WILDERNESS

[Fig. 9] The 41,000-acre Ishi Wilderness is in the Cascade foothills, just north of the Sierra batholith. Basaltic outcroppings and pillar lava formations are common here. It is about 8 miles southwest of Lassen Volcanic National Park, and it is another mostly volcanic feature that will interest geologists and other visitors alike.

East-west ridges abound with river canyons slicing through the countryside. Dense islands of ponderosa pine *(Pinus ponderosa)* grow on terraces left after rivers cut the canyons. The ponderosa also is known as the yellow pine, referring to the pale color of bark on the mature tree. Black oak *(Quercus kelloggii)*, sugar pine *(Pinus lambertiana)*, and white fir *(Abies concolor)* also are found with the ponderosa.

Below the terraces and ridgelines this is foothill territory with chaparral communities—dense groupings of plants with deep root systems that can survive where moisture is limited.

The chaparral communities of the Ishi have some manzanita *(Arctostaphylos)* and spice bush *(Calycanthus occidentalis)*. They are not as common here as they are south of Yosemite National Park because these plants adapt to drier conditions. Northern Sierra forests are generally wetter than the southern forests.

There are two types of manzanita found on dry, south-facing slopes in Ishi. They are the white-leaf manzanita *(A. viscida)*, which has white branches and sticky, rose-colored flowers, and the Indian manzanita *(A. mewukka)*, which has a deep red bark and smooth gray-green leaves. The porous volcanic soils are conducive to growth, allowing the root systems of these and other foothill plants to develop extensively.

More common shrubs in Ishi include bitter gooseberry *(Ribes amarum)*, silver lupine *(Lupinus albifrons)*, and coyote brush *(Baccharis pilularis)*. The more common wildflowers, seen in spring and summer, are Carolina geranium *(Geranium caroliniana)*, tower mustard *(Arabis glabra)*, and miner's lettuce *(Montia perfoliata)*.

Ishi is named for a Yahi Yana Indian who was the last survivor of a tribe that flourished in the area more than 3,000 years ago. European settlers killed most of the Yahi after 1850. *Ishi*, which means "man" to the Yahi, hid for many years in this wild and desolate place with only a few people as company.

After becoming separated from his companions, Ishi walked out of the woods into civilization in 1911. No one spoke his language. A University of California at Berkeley professor heard about Ishi and knew enough of the language to communicate with him. The professor moved Ishi to Berkeley. Ishi died four years later of tuberculosis after living in a basement in a Berkeley museum where he was a janitor.

The Tehama deer herd, the largest mule deer *(Odocoileus hemionus)* herd in California, spends winters in this foothill area. The herd is estimated to number between 40,000 and 60,000 deer. The deer spend winters in the area to forage for food; vegetation usually is not available in higher elevations. Such winter migrations are common for deer and many other animals in the Sierra.

The mountain lion *(Felis concolor)*, coyote *(Canis latrans)*, and black bear *(Ursus americanus)* are also inhabitants. Rock cliffs are nesting sites for raptors such as hawks, eagles, falcons, and owls.

Directions: From Red Bluff, travel about 10 miles east on Highway 36 to Road 232A (past the Ponderosa Sky Ranch, but before the California Department of Forestry fire station), turn south. Go almost 1 mile and take the right fork on Road 202. Drive about 0.5 mile, and turn left onto a gravel road called Road 7078. Stay on this winding road for about 3 miles. It turns into a dirt road and winds into Black Rock Campground, where parking is available.

Activities: Horse packing, camping, backpacking, photography, wildlife viewing.

Facilities: Black Rock Campground on the edge of the wilderness.

Dates: Open year-round, but it is best to visit from May to Oct.

Fees: None.

Closest town: Mineral, 9 miles.

For more information: Almanor Ranger District, PO Box 767, and Chester, CA 96020. Phone (530) 258-2141.

LOWER MILL CREEK TRAIL, NORTH

[Fig. 9(1)] The foothill wildflowers and the lava-rock canyon are the main attractions. This walk will take visitors through areas that have burned in the last decade, showing how fire is essential to California forests by helping to clear excess brush and regenerate.

When the brush is burned back from fire beneath the understory of trees, more room is made for flowers and low-growing vegetation. This pattern is familiar throughout the Sierra and is discussed in detail on page 14.

Wildflowers along the trail include California milkmaids *(Dentaria californica)*, fan violet *(Viola sheltonii)*, and Chinese caps *(Euphorbia crenulata)*. The Chinese caps are particularly interesting because they have no petals. They were named Chinese Caps because they have glands that resembling devil heads or ancient Chinese caps. They can be found in partial shade.

Mill Creek is a year-round stream with meadows and cool water. The rock in the area is basaltic, probably part of lava flows that occurred about 20 million years ago.

Directions: Trail starts at Black Rock Campground *(see* directions 14*)*.

Trail: 15 miles.

Elevation: 1,000-foot gain, high point 2,100 feet.

Degree of difficulty: Moderate.

Surface: Footpath with signs.

LOWER MILL CREEK TRAIL, SOUTH

[Fig. 9(2)] The steep Mill Creek Canyon is a sight-seeing delight, but poison oak *(Toxicodendron diversiloba)* can ruin a visit quickly. This hike is simply the south side of the canyon mentioned in the Lower Mill Creek Trail, north.

In the foothill areas, there is always the problem of poison oak, which can cause skin irritations for many people. It is pervasive in the Sierra from 100 feet to 5,000 feet in elevation, but it can be literally everywhere at elevations around 2,000 feet, which is about the elevation of this hike. The main lesson is to learn what it looks like and stay on the trail when approaching big thickets of underbrush. Wear long pants.

Directions: Trail starts at Black Rock Campground (*see* directions page 30). This trail goes into the wilderness.

Trail: 9 miles round-trip.

Elevation: 450-foot gain, high point 2,150 feet.

Degree of difficulty: Moderate.

Surface: Footpath, signs, not a steep grade.

LAKE ALMANOR NATIONAL RECREATION TRAIL

[Fig. 10(1)] Some of the best wildlife viewing in the Lake Almanor basin can be found along the Lake Almanor National Recreation Trail, which runs 9.5 miles along Lake Almanor. The trail is 10 feet wide and paved, so it is not a typical forest trail. It is on the west side of the lake, and begins at Humbug and Humboldt roads, running south to the Lake Almanor Campground. Expect to find people riding bikes or roller blading along the trail. The slopes are gentle and the hiking is easy.

Look for osprey (*Pandion haliaetus*), the fish hawk that lives around water and hunts by plunging feet-first into the water for fish. Bald eagles (*Haliaetus leucocephalus*), the white-headed emblem of the United States, occasionally can be seen from the western shore. Eagles are known to steal meals from osprey or other wildlife.

On the shore and in low, marshy meadows around the lake, the English sundew (*Drosera anglica*), northern bugleweed (*Lycopus uniflorus*), buckbean (*Menyanthes trifoliata*), and tofieldia (*Tofieldia occidentalis* ssp. *occidentalis*) can be found. Among these herbs, the English sundew is relatively rare in California because it requires more rainfall and cooler weather than the Sierra normally receives in many parts of the range.

The geology around the lake is fascinating as well, because the lake is actually over the northern boundary of the Sierra Nevada. Without close geological examination of the rocks, it would be difficult to see that the Sierra's northern boundary cuts through this trail and right into Lake Almanor. The Sierra block submerges below the younger Cascade volcanics.

The boundary, well-known to

OSPREY
(Pandion haliaetus)

Lake Almanor Area

Lake Almanor is 13 miles long, 6 miles wide, and as much as 90 feet deep, and it covers 28,000 acres.

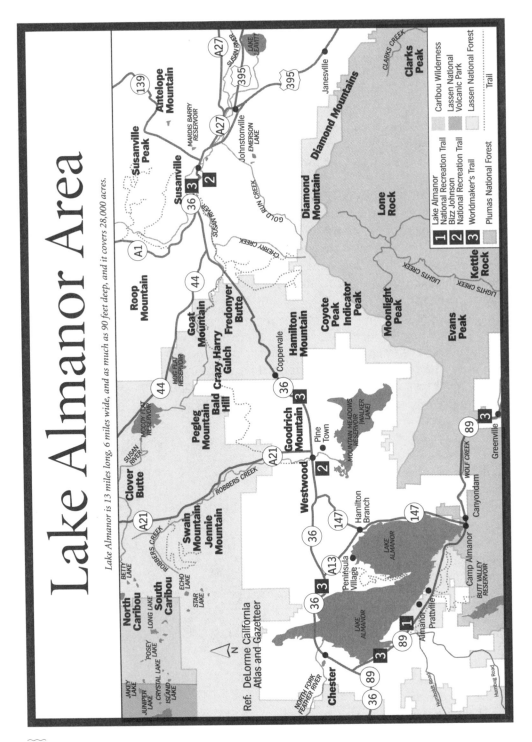

Ref: DeLorme California Atlas and Gazetteer

geologists but not easy for visitors to spot, runs just north of Oroville and continues through Almanor—the only hint being the change from ancient sedimentary rocks to younger volcanic rocks.

The lake, on the other hand, is easy to distinguish from natural lakes. It forms behind a concrete dam. The dam was built after the turn of the century when a power company built this hydroelectric facility.

It is a bit of an understatement to call Lake Almanor just another hydroelectric facility. The lake was made in 1914 by the Great Western Power Company at a time when hydro was the futuristic power source. It was named by combining the names of the three daughters of the company's vice president, Guy C. Earl. His daughter's names were Alice, Martha, and Elinore. The first two letters of Alice and Martha were joined with three letters of Elinore.

But this lake is something more than a hydro facility named after three daughters of a power company executive. It is a recreation area filled with swimming beaches, fishing spots, and wildlife viewing.

The lake is 13 miles long, 6 miles wide, and about 90 feet deep at its deepest, covering about 28,000 acres. By California standards, it is a larger-than-average reservoir with 1.3 million acre-feet of water. (An acre-foot of water is about 326,000 gallons.) To qualify as large in California, a reservoir should hold between 2 and 3 million acre-feet of water.

Directions: From Chester, drive Highway 36 west about 2.7 miles to the Highway 89 junction. Turn south on Highway 89 and drive 3.5 miles to a dirt road where the northern trailhead starts. The turn is directly across from a sign that says Humbug-Humbolt Road.

Activities: Open to hikers and nonmotorized vehicles, including bicycles and inline skates (preferably experienced and skilled skaters).

Facilities: More than 250 campsites are available first-come, first-serve. Some of these campsites are owned by the Forest Service and some are owned by Pacific Gas & Electric Company. A large overflow camping area is available at the Almanor North and South Campgrounds. The Almanor campgrounds have a swimming beach as well as a boat ramp and courtesy dock. Resorts are available. All national forest lands on the west side of Lake Almanor are closed to overnight camping except for developed recreation sites, such as the campgrounds, group camp, and overflow area. Reservations can be made for the Almanor Group Campground, Gurnsey Creek Group Campground, and Almanor North and South Family Campgrounds (campsites 1 through 9) by calling (877) 444-6777.

Dates: Facilities begin to open Apr. 1 and remain open through Nov. 1.

Fees: There is a charge for camping.

Closest town: Chester, 5 miles.

For more information: Almanor Ranger District, PO Box 767, Chester, CA 96020. Phone (530) 258-2141.

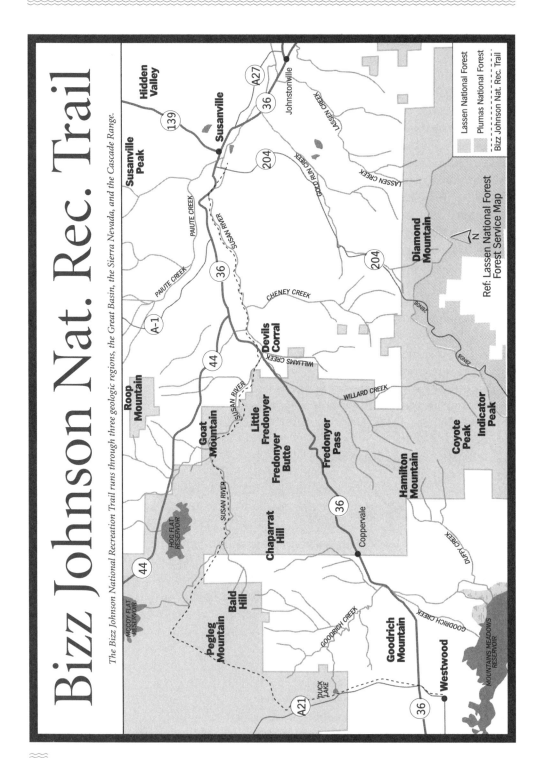

Bizz Johnson Nat. Rec. Trail

The Bizz Johnson National Recreation Trail runs through three geologic regions, the Great Basin, the Sierra Nevada, and the Cascade Range.

Lassen National Forest

Plumas National Forest

Bizz Johnson Nat. Rec. Trail

Ref: Lassen National Forest
Forest Service Map

Trail: 9.5 miles.
Elevation: 50-foot gain, 4,550-foot peak.
Degree of difficulty: Easy.
Surface: Paved with gentle slopes.

THE BIZZ JOHNSON NATIONAL RECREATION TRAIL

[Fig. 10(2)] People use the Bizz Johnson National Recreation Trail for bicycling, hiking, horseback riding, and cross-country skiing. It is the outdoor recreation corridor between Susanville and Westwood, giving people the chance to go more than 25 miles or take smaller trips.

As it winds through the rugged Susan River Canyon, the trail crosses the river 12 times on bridges and trestles and passes through two tunnels. The trail runs through three geologic regions, the Great Basin, the Sierra Nevada, and the Cascade Range. Along the way it passes through a semi-arid canyon to a dense forest of pine and cedar.

The flora changes as you move through the three geologic areas. The dense pine and cedar are part of the Sierra Nevada and the Cascade Range, which receive more rainfall on their western slopes. The precipitation is caused as storms traveling west to east gain altitude to clear the mountains.

The coniferous trees include the grey pine *(Pinus sabiniana)*, the aromatic incense cedar *(Libocedrus decurrens)*, and the Jeffrey pine *(Pinus jefreyi)*. Watch for the pygmy owl *(Glaucidium gnoma)*, the smallest Sierra owl. Unlike many other owl species, this owl calls and moves around by day. After a meal, it will perch in the open and groom itself.

Things change dramatically on the eastern side of the Sierra crest. This is the Great Basin. More arid conditions result from less rain because storms have dropped much of their moisture on the western side of the mountains. In the Great Basin area, the flora includes the huckleberry oak *(Quercus vaccinifolia)* and bush chinquapin *(Castanopsis sempervirens)*, which adapt to the drier conditions and high elevation. The dusky flycatcher *(Empidonax oberholseri)* and the green-tailed towhee *(Chlorua chlorua)* can be seen among the sagebrush and bitterbrush on the eastern side of the Sierra, too.

Along the Bizz Johnson, the human-made sights are interesting as well. One of them is the 25-foot carved redwood statue of Paul Bunyan near the Westwood side of the trail, which follows an old Southern Pacific Company rail line.

The statue is a monument to the 1930s' boomtown business called the Red River Lumber Company of Westwood, the largest pine mill in the world. At Westwood trailhead's railroad station kiosk, interpretive displays of the Westwood museum bring back an era when the woods and the town of Westwood bustled with the sounds and activities of logging and railroading.

As for the trail following the historic rail line, it runs from Susanville to Mason Station. For the first dozen miles, the trail follows the Susan River.

The old rail line was built in 1914 to serve the newly developed logging community of Westwood. The Fernley and Lassen Railroad was heavily used to haul logs and transport passengers for more than four decades.

The western half of the Fernley and Lassen Branch line was alive with logging camps, spur lines, and switching stations. The features can now be seen along the trail marked by replicas of station signs and explained in interpretive signs.

The rail line was first operated by Central Pacific, and later by Southern Pacific. It provided a much-needed connection from the Westwood mill in Lassen County to the railroad's main line in Fernley, Nevada. From Fernley, the milled lumber products were shipped to markets throughout the country and around the world.

The Westwood Mill gradually declined and the railroad died. The last trains ran on the Fernley and Lassen branch line in 1956. For 20 years the railroad lay unused.

In 1978, Southern Pacific obtained legal permission to abandon the line. The Bureau of Land Management, with the support of the U.S. Forest Service and many community groups, then started the rails to trails conversion. The name Bizz Johnson was attached to the trail to honor Congressman Harold "Bizz" Johnson, who worked on this and other public projects during his 22-year tenure in Congress.

Directions: From Lassen Volcanic National Park, take Highway 36 east to Westwood or Susanville. The trail connects the towns. Westwood: From Highway 36 at Westwood, follow County Road A-21 approximately 1 mile south into Westwood. Park at the Bizz Johnson Trail kiosk in front of the Westwood Community Center and next to the Paul Bunyan statue. Begin by following A-21 back through town, the way you came. Cross Highway 36 and continue on A-21 approximately 3 miles to County Road 101 (just before the railroad tracks). Follow County Road 101, 0.5 mile to Mason Station trailhead. Follow path past kiosk 0.25 mile to abandoned railroad grade. Follow the railroad grade 25 miles to Susanville. To reach the Susanville trailhead, drive to the west side of town on Highway 36. Turn south from Highway 36 onto Richmond Road and drive 0.5 mile south to Cypress Street where trailhead begins.

Activities: Hiking, mountain biking, horseback riding (for those who own or bring their own horse), cross-country skiing (in winter), fishing, snowmobile riding (west of Devils Corral only), wildflower viewing, wildlife viewing, bird-watching.

Facilities: A shuttle bus that will carry bikes runs between Susanville and Westwood Monday through Friday. For a current schedule and bus stops, call Lassen Rural Bus at (530) 257-5697. On weekends or at times not served by the bus, you may be able to arrange for a van shuttle. Phone Mount Lassen Cab and Shuttle Service at (530) 257-5277. The trail is mostly undeveloped. Bring your own water or filter your water.

Dates: Open year-round.

Fees: None. Campfire permits are required, but are free.

Closest town: Susanville and Westwood, at the trailheads.

For more information: Eagle Lake Ranger District, 477-050 Eagle Lake Road, Susanville, CA 96130. Phone (530) 257-4188. Bureau of Land Management, Eagle Lake Field Office, 2950 Riverside Drive, Susanville, CA 96130. Phone (530) 257-0456. For a list of area lodging, call the Lassen County Chamber of Commerce at (530) 257-4323.

Trail: 25 miles.

Elevation: About 900-foot gain, 5,200-foot peak.

Degree of difficulty: Moderate.

Surface: Gravel and dirt.

WINTER ACTIVITIES ON THE LASSEN NATIONAL FOREST

There are places to cross-country ski—especially on the Bizz Johnson Trail. In other sections of this Northern Sierra forest, snowmobiling is very popular. There are at least six areas where the brisk breeze and the fresh snow are sampled most often by people on snowmobiles.

The six places to snowmobile include Fredonyer and Bogard snowmobile areas in the Eagle Lake Ranger District in the northeast part of forest; Morgan Summit, Jonesville, and Swain Mountain snowmobile areas in the Almanor Ranger District in the central part of the forest; and Ashpan Snowmobile Area in Hat Creek Ranger District to the north of Lassen Volcanic National Park.

Each area has its own groomed and ungroomed areas. The Bogard area, for instance, has 80 miles of trails, and the groomed trails are considered easy to follow because they follow forest roads. There is one 38-mile trip that ends near Eagle Lake where bald eagles *(Haliaetus leucocephalus)* are sometimes sighted. Some routes are shared with cross-country skiers.

For cross-country skiing, the best areas along the Bizz Johnson Trail are on the upper 18.5-mile segment, west of Highway 36, and on the Devils Corral area. Elevations from 4,760 feet to 5,500 feet, northern exposures, and shading provide the most reliable snow conditions.

A segment of the Bizz Johnson Trail recommended for cross-country combines snowed-in road skiing from Highway 44 to Goumaz (3 miles) with trail skiing from Goumaz to Highway 36. This 9-mile segment affords a gentle downhill slope with good views of the Susan River and Diamond Mountain.

The lower 7 miles of trail from Highway 36 east to Susanville can be skied after major storms; the lower elevations and southern exposures cause the snow conditions to decline quickly in this section. The section also has two tunnels (800 and 450 feet), which require walking.

 Directions: From Highway 36 at Westwood, turn north on A-21 and drive 3 miles to the Mason Station trailhead. Drive about 7 miles west on Highway 36 from Susanville to the Devils Corral trailhead.

Dates: Nov. through Mar.

Fees: None.

For more information: Almanor Basin Snowmobile Coalition, phone (530) 258-3856; Butte Meadows Hillsiders, phone (530) 934-7111; Lake Almanor Snowmobile Club, phone (530) 596-3822; Sierra Cascade Snowriders, phone (530) 257-3585; and Sno-Riders Inc., phone (530) 547-1162. Cross-country skiers call the Eagle Lake Field Office of the Bureau of Land Management. Phone (530) 257-0456.

WORLDMAKER'S TRAIL

[Fig. 10(3)] On an afternoon of driving, people can follow more than 67 miles of an ancient trail started by the Mountain Maidu Indians centuries ago. The trail runs from Quincy to Susanville through the Lassen National Forest, just at the northern edge of the Sierra Nevada.

As the Maidu legend goes, the mountain lands were created after a great flood. Following the flood, the "Worldmaker" started on a journey to look at the land. He followed the trail that would become the major artery for Maidu people.

The Worldmaker encountered rugged terrain and the mythical "coyote," a literary figure that put obstacles in the way of the Worldmaker. The Worldmaker had to overcome monsters and smooth the rugged mountain landscape for the Maidu people.

The driving tour takes visitors to places where it is obvious nature has conspired to bring this tale to life. The ridges, ravines, rugged countryside, and streams would have offered obstacles to the progress of the Worldmaker. The landscape, aided by the coyote's mischief, made a formidable challenge. There are 15 scenic locations with views of streams, waterfalls, rock features, and other sights. Most of them have convenient turnouts and places to park.

If driven without many stops, the tour could be completed in two hours, but there are several walks that are worth taking. Only 0.8 mile from Quincy, the Gansner Park-American Valley offers a walk through marshes and streams, giving visitors an idea of the swamps that once covered the area. The swamps were deep with native grasses and filled with insect life. Streams carrying sediment have filled many areas to the point that only shallow marshes now exist instead of swamps.

BALD EAGLE
(Haliaetus leucocephalus)

About 1.5 miles from Quincy, Indian and Spanish creeks meet the Feather River at a traditional Maidu campsite. The Maidu would collect salmon, crayfish, and eel each spring.

A short hike over fairly steep terrain is required to see Thundering Falls about 0.8 mile north of Soda Rock. A picnic table is available at the overlook. The turnout for this walk is north of Indian Falls, and parking is available on the east side of Highway 89.

Fifteen miles and several stops later, Wolf Creek and Whitegrass Mountain can be found near Highway 89. The area provides the rare habitat for bear grass plant or white-grass *(Xerophylum tenax)*, which the Maidu used to make white patterns in baskets. Bear grass still is gathered by Maidu people for their well-known basket weaving.

About 3.3 miles later on Highway 89 at Highway 147, turn north and drive 0.5 mile to the scenic overlook at Big Meadow in the Lake Almanor area. Prior to building this hydroelectric lake, Big Meadow was an open, grassy valley. The Worldmaker, as legend goes, encountered a giant frog monster and little devils, which were turned into boulders. Lassen Peak, in the neighboring Lassen National Park, is visible from here.

Drive another 11 miles on Highway 147, turn east on Highway 36 for 20 miles, make a few other stops on the way. Cross the Susan River Bridge, turn at the trailhead for the Bizz Johnson National Recreation Trail, and walk along an easy footpath to the Susan River Canyon rim. The Worldmaker found devilish imps here and called on mud or cliff swallows *(Petrochelidon pyrrhonota)* to seal all the cracks and crevices and trap the little devils.

Five miles later, Susanville is in sight. Stop at the Honey Lake Valley Overview where the mountain forests meet an arid sagebrush desert. The vegetation changes as the route goes from the Sierra into the Great Basin, where storms drop much less precipitation. The weather patterns are part of the typical circulation of Pacific Ocean storms that drop most of their moisture on the western slopes of the Sierra Nevada as the clouds climb higher in the atmosphere to clear the mountain range.

The desert lands in this area of the Great Basin were given away by the Maidu to the Northern Paiute and Washoe Indians. The Worldmaker reportedly passed through Susanville, the easternmost winter village settlement of the Maidu, and was last seen traveling north over Antelope Grade, the location of present-day Highway 139.

Directions: Start at downtown Quincy on Highway 89 at the intersection of Quincy Junction Road and Highway 70/89; travel north. From the other side, Susanville, start at the Highway 36-Highway 139 intersection (Main and Ash streets). Local traffic moves quickly, so drive carefully.

Trail: 67.3 miles by automobile, with many short hikes.

Degree of difficulty: Most hikes are easy.

Surface: Most trails are open footpaths.

For more information: Plumas County Museum, 500 Jackson Street, Quincy, CA 95971. Phone (530) 283-6320. The Chester-Lake Almanor Museum, Lassen National Forest, 200 First Avenue, Chester 96020. Phone (530) 258-2742.

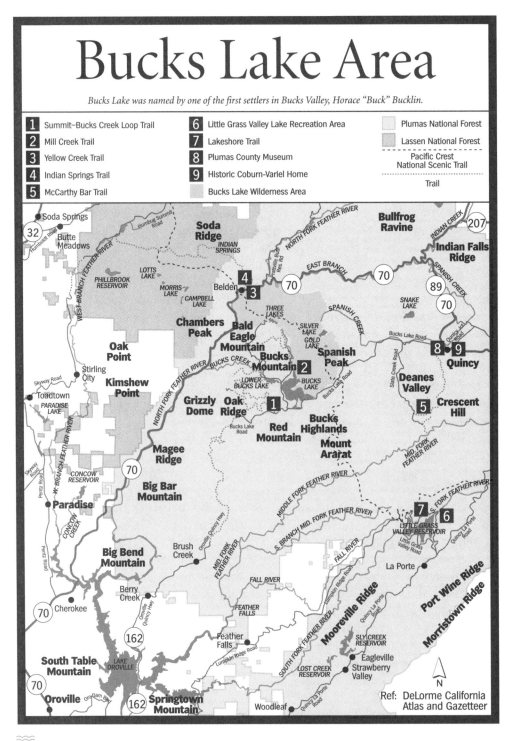

Bucks Lake Area

Bucks Lake was named by one of the first settlers in Bucks Valley, Horace "Buck" Bucklin.

1 Summit–Bucks Creek Loop Trail
2 Mill Creek Trail
3 Yellow Creek Trail
4 Indian Springs Trail
5 McCarthy Bar Trail

6 Little Grass Valley Lake Recreation Area
7 Lakeshore Trail
8 Plumas County Museum
9 Historic Coburn-Variel Home

Bucks Lake Wilderness Area

Plumas National Forest
Lassen National Forest
Pacific Crest National Scenic Trail
Trail

Ref: DeLorme California Atlas and Gazetteer

Plumas National Forest

[Fig. 10, Fig. 11, Fig. 12] The timber industry has shaped the Plumas National Forest's 1.1 million acres since it was established in 1905. For instance, in 1987 alone, loggers cut enough trees to build 19,000 three-bedroom homes. Plumas trees also help support another industry—Christmas tree sales. About a third of California's Christmas trees come from the Plumas. And they are white firs *(Abies concolor)*.

But logging is not common in every part of the forest. Bucks Lake Wilderness, for instance, does not have logging. Logging is forbidden in any wilderness. Federal law passed in the 1960s banned logging in designated wilderness areas. No mechanized activities are supposed to take place, including bicycle riding. Some exceptions are allowed for such activities as snow measurement, which involves the use of helicopters to reach snow fields.

The Feather River is the main stream in the Plumas. Its 100-mile Middle Fork is designated as wild and scenic, though the final third of the river above Lake Oroville is inaccessible to all but the bravest kayakers and hikers.

The North Fork of the river has eight hydroelectric powerhouses on it between Oroville and Bucks Lake Wilderness. The South Fork is probably the least known for natural beauty, draining smaller watersheds. It winds through Little Grass Valley Reservoir before joining the Middle Fork at Lake Oroville.

The lakes and streams of Plumas are well known for their abundance of fish. Several kinds of trout are found in these waters. Among them are rainbow trout *(Oncorhynchus mykiss)*, brown trout *(Salmo trutta)*, and the rarer golden trout *(Salmo aguabonita)*, a species that evolved in the Southern Sierra earlier this century after brown trout were planted in the Kern River and other places.

🦫 BUCKS LAKE WILDERNESS/RECREATION AREA

[Fig. 12] People come to the Bucks Lake Wilderness for the views. On a clear day, hikers can see Lassen Volcanic National Park, 40 miles away, somewhere near the northern edge of the Sierra Nevada. The sight is worth the considerable effort it takes to get many miles into this wilderness.

But the views of red fir *(Abies magnifica)*, brush fields, and delicate mountain meadows are also worth it. This small, 21,000-acre wilderness has a vibrant diversity of plant life, but not many lakes. Elevations range from 2,000 feet in the Feather River Canyon, to 7,017 feet at Spanish Peak.

Plant life includes the common horsetail *(Equisetum arvense)* and sago pondweed *(Potamogeton pectinus)*, both found in streams and bogs where the water moves slowly or stands still. The Sierra shooting star *(Dodecatheon jeffreyi)*, with its pink and crimson petals, is found throughout the lower elevations of the area along with the yellow and purple farewell-to-spring *(Clarkia viminea)*, which owes its name to its later appearance in the warmer months.

The red fir, occurring at ridgelines and rocky, high-elevation fields, thrives in Bucks Lake Wilderness in moist areas. The dark blue-green needles are aromatic and were used by early mountaineers as bedding.

In the high elevations of Bucks Lake, many red fir lose their tops in blizzards that batter the area during winter. The damaged trees will provide nesting cavities for chickarees *(Tamiasciurus douglasii)*, alpine chipmunks *(Eutamias alpinus)*, and martens *(Martes americana)*.

Because there are not many other food-producing plants at 7,000 feet, the red fir is also home to several kinds of woodpeckers, pygmy nuthatches *(Siita pygmaea)*, and brown creepers *(Certhia familiaris)* on its trunk. Seedeaters flock to the tree in autumn when cones mature.

The Bucks Lake Pluton, the massive granite formation beneath the area, is Cretaceous, or about 130 million years old. In this part of Plumas National Forest, the granite is striking in steep canyons and outcroppings.

At the southwestern edge of the wilderness, and about 10 miles west of Quincy, is Bucks Lake at 5,155 feet in elevation. The lake, a hydroelectric lake, has a surface area of 1,827 acres with 14 miles of shoreline.

Bucks Lake was named by one of the first settlers in Bucks Valley, Horace "Buck" Bucklin, who came into the area from New York in 1850. The lake is located in a valley known for almost 80 years as Bucks Ranch.

In 1925, the Bucks Creek Project was undertaken by the Feather River Power Company to produce electricity in the area. Part of the project, Bucks Dam, was completed in 1929. Title passed to the Great Western Power Company the same year, and later to Pacific Gas and Electric Company. About half of the shoreline is now owned by Pacific Gas and Electric and the other half is under the management of the Forest Service.

The recreation area is directly adjacent to the southwestern boundary of the wilderness. It is not included in the wilderness because it would be subject to restrictions that would not allow motorized vehicles or any other kind of mechanization.

Fishing, which is regulated by the California Department of Fish and Game, is a popular activity at the recreation area. Bucks Lake and surrounding streams and lakes support rainbow *(Oncorhynchus mykiss)*, brown *(Salmo trutta)*, and Eastern brook trout *(Salvelinus fontinalis)*. Bucks Lake is stocked with rainbow trout annually.

Directions: From Quincy on Highway 70, take the Buck Lake Road turnoff west. Drive 10 miles to the recreation area, which is marked with signs.

Activities: Hiking, backpacking, fishing, swimming, skiing, camping, sightseeing, and photography.

Facilities: The U.S. Forest Service operates six family campgrounds totaling 66 units. Whitehorse, Sundew, Mill Creek, Lower Bucks Lake, Grizzly Creek, and Hutchins Group Camp have a maximum stay of 14 days. The Lakeshore Resort includes a grocery store, gasoline station, restaurant, boat rental and launching area, swimming, and ski beaches. The Bucks Lake Lodge has a grocery store, gasoline, restaurant, boat rental and launching, swimming and ski beaches, and cabins. The Forest Service leases two areas on Lower Bucks Lake for organization use. These sites are now leased by a Boy Scout Council and a church group.

Dates: Open year-round, but the resort season is May through Oct.

Fees: There are fees for various activities. A campfire permit is required to have a campfire in the wilderness.

Closest town: Quincy, 10 miles.

For more information: Mount Hough Ranger District, 39696 State Highway 70, Quincy, CA 95971. Phone (530) 283-0555.

SUMMIT-BUCKS CREEK LOOP TRAIL

[Fig. 12(1)] The Summit-Bucks Creek Loop Trail provides the best views of the Bucks Lake Wilderness. It starts at Bucks Summit and leads 2 miles through meadows and forested areas.

When the trail reaches the pavement, turn right and take the Bucks Creek Trail 1.8 miles back to Bucks Lake Road and continue 0.25 mile to Bucks Summit. This trail goes through the Whitehorse Campground, and it can be used for hiking and mountain bicycling.

Directions: From Oroville take Oro Dam Boulevard east and turn right at Olive Highway, which becomes the Oro-Quincy Road. Drive 35 miles northeast to Bucks Lake Road. The trailhead is located east of Lake Oroville 14 miles west of Quincy, off Bucks Lake Road. Parking at either Bucks Summit parking area or Bucks Creek trailhead. Parking areas are marked.

Trail: 7.6-mile loop.

Elevation: 320-foot gain, 5,520-foot high point.

Degree of difficulty: Easy.

Surface: Clear pathway, some paved.

For more information: Quincy/Greenville Ranger Station, 39696 State Highway 70, Quincy, CA 95971. Phone (530) 283-0555.

MILL CREEK TRAIL

[Fig. 12(2)] The Mill Creek Trail leads to views of the Bucks Lake Wilderness. The trailhead and first mile are on Pacific Gas & Electric Company land, where recreation is permitted. Camping is allowed along the eastern shore of Bucks Lake, for those who want to stay the night by the lake after the hike.

For more adventuresome hikers, the trail continues into the wilderness for several miles. Horses are allowed on this trail, so hikers must keep their eyes open and yield.

Directions: From Quincy, drive west on the Bucks Lake Road about 14 miles (bear right and go around the west side of Bucks Lake) to the Whitehorse Campground. The trailhead is 0.5 mile west of the campground.

Trail: 5.5 miles one-way.

Elevation: 350-foot gain, high point 5,170 feet.

Degree of difficulty: Moderate.

Surface: Flat footpath, crosses streams.

For more information: Quincy/Greenville Ranger Station, 39696 State Highway 70, Quincy, CA 95971. Phone (530) 283-0555.

YELLOW CREEK TRAIL

[Fig. 12(3)] This is a good one for families. It is a short hike with some good fishing for the various kinds of trout. The box canyon has some nice picnic areas, but there are no developed facilities. It will take about 90 minutes to hike this trail.

Directions: Drive about 25 miles west of the Quincy Ranger Station on Highway 70 to Belden. The trailhead is to the right of the Elby Stamp Mill rest area, across from the town of Belden.

Trail: 1.4 miles one-way.

Elevation: About 500-foot elevation gain, highest point 2,800 feet.

Degree of difficulty: Easy.

Surface: Smooth, creekside pathway.

INDIAN SPRINGS TRAIL

[Fig. 12(4)] This one may be better as an overnight trip. The elevation gain alone is more than 0.5 mile, and it is also a long haul. The round trip is 13 miles—not that difficult for a fit, experienced hiker, but a challenge for most others.

The trail has excellent campsites along the way, along with splendid views. The sights include Lassen Volcanic National Park to the north.

Directions: The trailhead is marked by a sign very close to the Yellow Creek trailhead at the Elby Stamp Mill rest area.

Trail: 6.5 miles one-way.

Elevation: 3,700-foot gain, high point 6,000 feet.

Degree of difficulty: Strenuous.

Surface: Steep, rocky, sometimes narrow.

▨ FEATHER RIVER

[Fig. 12] The Feather River drains about 100 streams in the Plumas National Forest, stretching across most of the more than 1 million acres. The river is formed by three distinct branches—the North, Middle, and South forks.

The North and Middle forks are the focus of most recreation on this river. The North Fork is known for its hydroelectric powerhouses. About 100 miles of the Middle Fork have protection under the federal Wild and Scenic River Act. The South Fork does not carry the same volume of water and is not the same kind of attraction as the other two forks.

Though only the Middle Fork is considered wild and scenic, the North Fork could lay claim to being scenic as well. Along the North Fork of the Feather River, about 3 miles northwest of Oroville, anyone who has traveled through the Stanislaus National Forest or the Sierra National Forest will see a familiar site: a Table Mountain, created by a lava flow going down an ancient streambed.

Table Mountain is the proper name given to these geologic features. The lava flow near Oroville occurred about 50 million years ago, paving the streambed with basalt. The hardened basalt survived the erosion process over time and now stands as a flat-top mountain.

Along State Highway 70, there is evidence of rocks much older than the Table Mountain. Slates and schists, which probably were deposited as marine layers in the Pacific Ocean 200 million years ago, can be found along road cuts on Highway 70.

For a windshield tour of the upper watershed, the Feather River Scenic Byway offers spectacular views and countless points of cultural, geologic, and historical interest. The scenic byway begins 10 miles north of Oroville on State Highway 70, meanders east to US Highway 395, cuts through deeply carved canyons, tunnels through huge boulders, and races alongside the rugged North Fork of the Feather River. The Feather River Scenic Byway was officially dedicated in October 1998.

The Middle Fork is probably the most famous and revered by naturalists. It was one of the first nationally designated wild and scenic rivers in the United States.

The Middle Fork runs from its headwaters near Beckwourth to Lake Oroville, and it has three, distinct zones: recreation, scenic, and wild. Any part of the river or its canyon may be rugged and difficult to access.

In the wild zone, steep cliffs, waterfalls, and huge boulders discourage most people from trying to float or hike. While the scenic zone is less rugged, it still requires great preparation and skill. Even the recreation zone requires preparation and caution, especially in spring. In spring months, the volume of water coming down the Middle Fork alone would fill most of the streams in the southern part of the Sierra.

The lower part of the Middle Fork begins with Bald Rock Canyon Wild River Zone, extending from Lake Oroville (900 feet elevation) upstream for about 5.4 miles, through Bald Rock Canyon to the junction of an unnamed drainage on the east side of the river, about 7 miles south of Milsap Bar Campground (1,500 feet elevation). The wild and scenic lower parts of the Middle Fork should not be used for canoeing or rafting.

The next section of the Middle Fork begins as Milsap Bar Scenic River Zone, about 3.6 miles long, extending from the upper limit of Bald Rock Canyon Wild River Zone upstream to an area just below the English Bar Scenic Zone and Recreation Zone.

The English Bar Zone is more gentle. From Clio down to Quincy-La Porte Road, canoeing and rafting are possible during spring. When flow drops off later in the summer, air mattresses and inner tubes are the most common mode of travel. Whitewater rafting takes place downstream, below Lake Oroville. For more detailed information on the sights and dangers of rafting the Feather, contact the Plumas National Forest, phone (530) 283-2050.

Perhaps the most spectacular viewing is at the Feather Falls Scenic Area, near the old town site of Feather Falls. Granite domes and waterfalls are the big attractions. Visitors can see the sights from the Feather Falls National Recreation Trail, a challenging 10-mile round-trip hike (2,500-foot elevation gain). The hike will take several hours round-trip, and markers are provided every 0.5 mile to keep hikers aware of their progress.

There are no services along this trail—no refuse containers or restrooms. The trailhead has a vault toilet, water, and a refuse container. Otherwise, pack it in and pack it out is what the Forest Service advises. Carry food and lots of water. The reward at the end of the hike is the 640-foot high Feather River Falls, the sixth tallest waterfall in the United States. The falls are most accessible from early April to October.

Another attraction is Bald Rock, part of a granitic pluton formed about 140 million years ago. The rock is only 0.25 mile from a parking area. The views of the Great Central Valley are wonderful. Native Americans ground acorns on Bald Rock and legend has it that Uino, a Maidu monster, protected the Middle Fork of the Feather River from a vantage point high atop Bald Rock.

Take a little closer look around the river and see the California newt *(Taricha torosa)* and the Pacific treefrog *(Hyla regilla)* in the lower elevations. The only aquatic salamander found in the higher elevations is the long-toed salamander *(Ambystoma macrodactylum)*, and it lives around the Feather River, hiding under rocks in the quieter parts of the river.

The quieter water also allows insects, such as the water striders *(Gerris remingis)*, to develop and provide food for fish. Along the shore, the caddisflies (order Trichoptera), mayflies (order Ephemeroptera), and scorpionflies (order Mecoptera) provide food sources in their larval stages for many amphibians and other creatures.

Directions: Feather River Falls National Recreation trailhead: From Highway 70 in Oroville, take Highway 162 or Oroville Highway east to Olive Highway (also Highway 162) and drive 8 miles east to Forbestown Road. Then go north for 6 miles to Lumpkin Road, and drive 6 more miles on Lumpkin Road to reach the trailhead. Bald Rock: Take Olive Highway to Highway 162 north for 6 miles to Berry Creek; turn right on Bald Rock Road. Follow the signs. After pavement ends, take gravel road about 2 miles and look for parking lot.

Activities: Hiking, bicycling, horseback riding, bird-watching, camping, canoeing, rafting, river floating, scenic driving.

Facilities: Campgrounds, hiking trails.

Dates: Open year-round.

Fees: None.

Closest town: Oroville, 2 miles.

For more information: Feather River Ranger District, 875 Mitchell Avenue, Oroville, CA 95965-4699. Phone (530) 534-6500.

MCCARTHY BAR TRAIL

[Fig. 12(5)] It takes about 90 minutes of hiking on the McCarthy Bar Trail to get into some fine fishing. It is fast walking, though, because the trail goes downhill. It takes closer to three hours to hike out, because of the steep climb out of the canyon.

People often like to stop and camp along the river, sleeping to the sound of rushing water in one of Northern California's premiere rivers. The trout fishing is excellent in the cold water, which is rushing by after melting perhaps 24 hours earlier from a high Sierra snowpack at 7,000 or 8,000 feet.

Two other trails, the No Ear Bar and the Oddie Bar, are almost identical to the McCarthy Bar Trail. They may be a little easier to find, but they do not have as many campsites as McCarthy.

Directions: Drive Bucks Lake Road west from Quincy about 4 miles to Slate Creek Road (Road 24N28), turn left and drive 8.8 miles passing Dean's Valley Campground. Take the left fork of Road 23N99, go 1.5 miles to trail signs for Oddie and No Ear Bar trails. McCarthy Bar trailhead is to the left of the signs and about 1 mile beyond the signs. Four-wheel-drive vehicles are allowed on these roads closer to the canyon.

Trail: 1.7 miles one-way.

Elevation: Gain of about 1,900 feet, high point 5,500 feet.

Degree of difficulty: Strenuous.

Surface: Steep, rocky terrain; some narrow ledges.

LITTLE GRASS VALLEY LAKE RECREATION AREA

[Fig. 12(6)] Little Grass Valley Lake Recreation Area offers people a wide variety of outdoor experiences at an elevation of 5,046 feet. The lake covers a surface area of 1,615 acres and has a shoreline of 16 miles. The lake holds 93,000 acre-feet of water.

Besides fishing, boating, and camping—the three main attractions at many Plumas recreation spots—this area provides some bird-watching opportunities. Look for the common loon (*Gavia immer*), double-crested cormorant (*Phalacrocorax auritus*), and the Wilson's warbler (*Wilsonia pusilla*). All are known for nesting on the western slopes in this part of the Sierra, principally because of the water and cooler temperatures of the Northern Sierra.

The evening grosbeak (*Hesperiphona vespertina*) and other finches, such as the purple finch (*Carpodacus pupurens*) and the casin finch (*Capodacus cassini*), are found around Little Grass Valley Lake.

One of the unusual features of the area is the appearance of the brilliant red snow plant (*Sarcodes sanguinea*) during May, June, and July. These flowers grow at elevations between 4,000 and 8,000 feet and begin blossoming on the heels of melting snow. Against a carpet of pine needles, this saprophyte catches the eye instantly.

Before the arrival of European settlers, this valley was inhabited by migrating bands of Maidu Indians. They spent the summer in Little Grass Valley hunting and gathering berries and acorns away from the heat of the Great Central Valley to the west.

With the discovery of gold and the rush of miners into the gold-rich country, Little Grass Valley became a supply post. Ranchers began grazing sheep and cattle in the lush meadows, and they supplied meat and farm produce to the adjacent mining communities of LaPorte, Gibsonville, Howland Flat, Port Wine, and others.

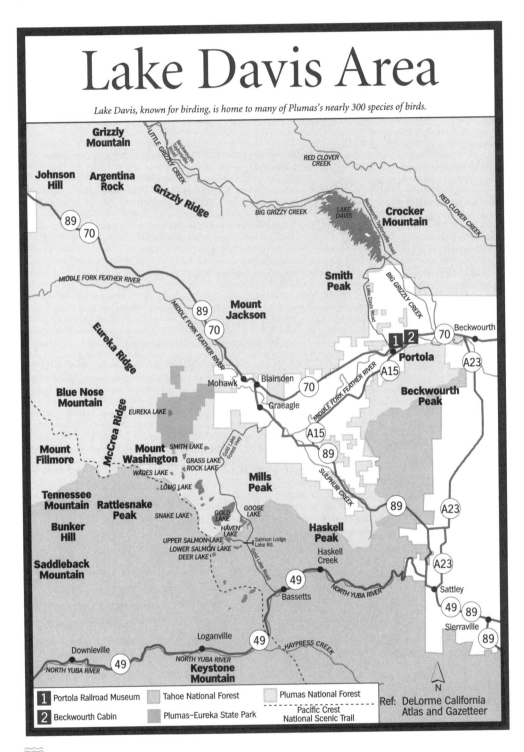

Lake Davis Area

Lake Davis, known for birding, is home to many of Plumas's nearly 300 species of birds.

Grizzly Mountain

RED CLOVER CREEK

Johnson Hill
Argentina Rock

LITTLE GRIZZLY CREEK

Beckwourth Taylorsville

Grizzly Ridge

BIG GRIZZLY CREEK

LAKE DAVIS

Beckwourth Taylorsville Road

RED CLOVER CREEK

Crocker Mountain

89 70

MIDDLE FORK FEATHER RIVER

Smith Peak

BIG GRIZZLY CREEK

Eureka Ridge

MIDDLE FORK FEATHER RIVER

89 70

Mount Jackson

Lake Davis Road

1 2
70 Beckwourth

A15 Portola

A23

Blue Nose Mountain

EUREKA LAKE

Mohawk Blairsden

70

MIDDLE FORK FEATHER RIVER

Beckwourth Peak

Graeagle

A15

Mount Fillmore

Mount Washington SMITH LAKE
GRASS LAKE
ROCK LAKE
WADES LAKE

Gold Lake Forest Hwy

89

SULPHUR CREEK

89 A23

LONG LAKE

Mills Peak

Tennessee Mountain
Rattlesnake Peak
SNAKE LAKE

GOLD LAKE

GOOSE LAKE

Bunker Hill

HAVEN LAKE

UPPER SALMON LAKE
LOWER SALMON LAKE
DEER LAKE

Salmon Lodge
Lake Rd.

Haskell Peak

Haskell Creek

A23

Saddleback Mountain

Gold Lake Road

49

Bassetts

NORTH YUBA RIVER

Sattley

49 89

Sierraville

Downieville

49

Loganville

49

HAYPRESS CREEK

89

NORTH YUBA RIVER

Keystone Mountain

NORTH YUBA RIVER

N

Ref: DeLorme California Atlas and Gazetteer

1 Portola Railroad Museum
2 Beckwourth Cabin

Tahoe National Forest
Plumas–Eureka State Park

Plumas National Forest
Pacific Crest National Scenic Trail

Directions: From Oroville take Olive Highway 8 miles east to Forbestown Road, then go north for 6 miles to Lumpkin Road. Turn onto Lumpkin Road, continue about 18 miles, and follow the signs into Little Grass Valley Recreation Area.

Facilities: About 290 camping sites with tables, water, and toilets. Boat launches, hiking and horse trails. Picnic sites at Blue Water Beach and Pancake Picnic Area. There is also a horse camp.

Activities: Camping, picnicking, fishing, water skiing, swimming, boating, hunting, bird-watching, wildflower photography, hiking, sight-seeing, and winter sports such as snowmobiling and cross-country skiing.

Dates: Facilities open Memorial Day weekend through Oct. 31. Lake is open year-round.

Fees: None.

Closest town: LaPorte, 2 miles.

For more information: Feather River Ranger District, 875 Mitchell Avenue, Oroville, CA 95965-4699. Phone (530) 534-6500.

LAKESHORE TRAIL

[Fig. 12(7)] Horseback riders, bicyclers, and hikers are likely to encounter each other on this trail, which runs along the north shore of Little Grass Valley Lake. People are encouraged to yield to larger, faster modes of transportation—namely, the bicyclers and the horseback riders.

No off-road vehicles are allowed on this trail.

Directions: See Little Grass Valley Lake directions. Follow signs in the parking lot to the trailhead.

Trail: 17.5 miles

Elevation: 5,100 feet.

Degree of difficulty: Easy.

Surface: Footpath, gravel and dirt.

LAKE DAVIS

[Fig. 13] Fishing, boating, camping, bike riding, and hiking are all available at Lake Davis, but this lake is also known for birding. Many of Plumas's nearly 300 species are at Lake Davis.

Birds such as the warbling vireo (*Vireo gilvus*) are best observed by listening first. They're found in the lodgepole fir belts and in such trees as the Lemmon willow (*Salix lemmonii*), which are near the water. The vireo's throaty "zree" can be sustained and repeated many times.

The red-breasted nuthatch (*Sitta canadensis*) is another that can be heard before being seen. It can be heard repeating its high nasal "na," faster and faster when it becomes agitated. It sounds like a small trumpet.

Other birds worth watching are the hairy woodpeckers (*Denrocopus villosus*), American white pelicans (*Pelicanus erythrorhynchus*), osprey (*Pandion haliaetus*),

Northern Pike

Lake Davis in the Plumas National Forest was poisoned in October 1997 with 60,000 pounds of powdered chemicals and 16,000 gallons of liquid chemicals, killing every fish in the 7-mile-long lake. The state Department of Fish and Game decided to poison the lake because it was infested with the voracious game fish called the northern pike *(Esox lucieus)*. The pike is a toothy, bony, non-native fish that eats trout and salmon.

But the poisoning was not the end of the story. The fish began appearing again in 1999. By May 1999, 36 had been caught at the lake. Officials believe rogue fishermen, who prefer the pike's fighting ability once it is on the hook, planted the fish in the lake.

State officials are worried the pike will migrate to the sensitive Sacramento-San Joaquin River Delta, next to the San Francisco Bay. The pike can easily begin destroying fish runs, such as the winter-run chinook salmon *(Oncorhynchus tshawytscha)*, currently a protected fish under the federal Endangered Species Act.

Nevertheless, Lake Davis was stocked with 1 million trout in 1999 and tourists flocked to this trout-fishing haven. Biologists have considered local shock treatments to the water so pike the pike could be stunned and removed, but local residents fear that someday the lake will be poisoned again.

western tanager *(Pranga ludoviciana)*, and, of course, the seemingly ubiquitous wood duck *(Aix sponsa)*. For a free list of birds common to the area, contact the Plumas Audubon Society, PO Box 3877, Quincy, CA 95971, or phone (800) 326-2247.

Biking is another favorite activity around Lake Davis. In many parts of the Plumas, including Lake Davis, cyclists can use abandoned logging roads, areas designated for off-highway vehicles, and some backcountry roads. These areas are open to bikers and provide a good cross-section of terrain and topography. Stay on the roads, and don't cut the switchbacks.

The Lake Davis Loop is perhaps the best-known bicycling trip in the area,

NORTHERN PIKE
(Esox lucievs)
Northern pikes occur in North America, Europe, and Asia, making it one of only two freshwater fishes definitely known to live on these three continents.

featuring a flat, easy loop around Lake Davis. Points of interest include Jenkins Sheep Camp and lake vistas. Cyclists can also enjoy bird and wildlife viewing. Vehicle traffic may be heavy on weekends.

The loop is 18.4 miles at an elevation just below 5,800 feet. Average riding time is two hours. The surface is gravel for 6.1 miles and paved for 12.3 miles. To reach the trailhead, from Highway 70 near Portola take Lake Davis West Street (County Road 126) 7 miles to Lake Davis Dam. Park at the information kiosk.

But bird-watching and bicycling are not the only attractions. Fishing may be more popular. The lake is stocked and some natural trout occur in this 84,000-acre-foot body of water. The dimensions of the lake—maximum depth, 105 feet; surface area, 4,000 acres; and shoreline, 32 miles—make it small enough for anglers to learn quickly. Yet it is large enough to allow a lot of water recreation, which does not include water skiing.

Varieties of trout include rainbow (*Oncorhynchus mykiss*), brown (*Salmo trutta*), and Eagle Lake (*Salmo eagllia*). Brown bullhead (*Ictalurus nebulosus*) also are found in this cold-water lake. Fishing is regulated by the California Department of Fish and Game, not the U.S. Forest Service.

Directions: From Highway 70 near Portola take Lake Davis West Street (County Road 126) 7 miles to Lake Davis Dam. An information station is nearby.

Activities: Camping, fishing, boating, hiking, bird-watching, bicycling, wildlife photography.

Facilities: Campgrounds with 165 sites, flush toilets, fire rings, tables, grills, potable drinking water.

Fees: A fee is charged for camping. Call (877) 444-6777, toll free for reservations.

Dates: Campgrounds are generally open from Apr. through late Oct. The lake is open year-round. Tributary streams are open only from July 1 to Sept. 30 because of spawning cycles.

Closest town: Portola, 4 miles.

For more information: Beckwourth Ranger District, 23 Mohawk Road, PO Box 7, Blairsden, CA 96106. Phone (530) 863-2575.

PLUMAS-EUREKA STATE PARK

[Fig. 13] The Plumas-Eureka State Park offers gold-rush history, cross-country skiing, and natural history.

The geologic history runs back 400 million years. About 400 yards south of the entrance to the campground of this state park is evidence of volcanic silicic ash and breccia, which are probably predated only by 400-million-year-old slates and sandstones in the area. This is truly a geologic time capsule for those patient enough to inspect the rock formations.

At 7,447-foot Eureka Peak, hikers can see where dolomite flowed into uplifted folds of older rock. The older rock, such as chert and limestones, is also present in

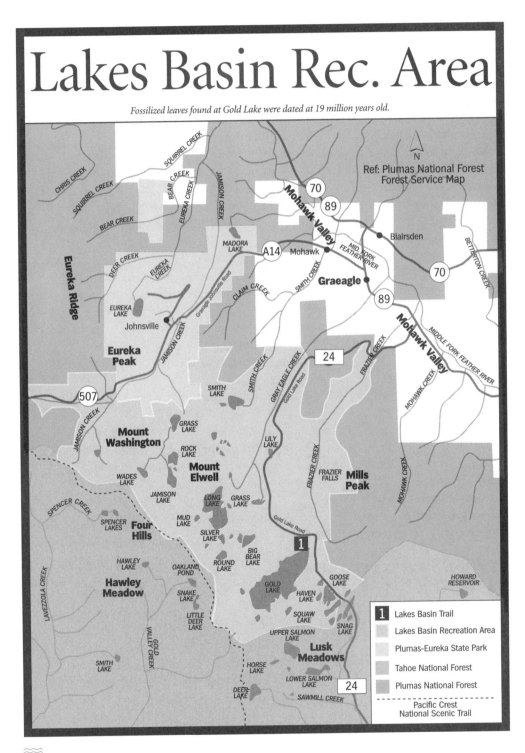

Lakes Basin Rec. Area

Fossilized leaves found at Gold Lake were dated at 19 million years old.

Ref: Plumas National Forest
Forest Service Map

Legend:
1	Lakes Basin Trail
	Lakes Basin Recreation Area
	Plumas-Eureka State Park
	Tahoe National Forest
	Plumas National Forest
- - - - -	Pacific Crest National Scenic Trail

formations that probably originated as marine sediments more than 400 million years ago.

But, like many places in this part of the Sierra, this area is more known for its recent history—the gold rush. Gold was found on the east side of Eureka Peak on May 23, 1851, when the mountain was known as Gold Mountain.

The discovery by nine miners triggered widespread gold fever. Several operators and many companies dug 62 miles of shafts. British mining experts figured ways to remove the rich ore from within the mountain.

At one point, three stamp mills were in operation at various locations on the mountainside, but the Mohawk Stamp Mill became the main mill of the time. Built in 1876 at a cost of approximately $50,000, the Mohawk contained 60 stamps, each weighing from 600 to 950 pounds. The stamps could crush more than 2 tons of ore every day.

Today, visitors can go to the main museum, originally the miners' bunkhouse, to learn about natural and cultural history of the park. Across the street, the old Mohawk Stamp Mill still stands.

Along with the history, the park offers a variety of wildlife viewing opportunities. In the 5,500 acres of the park, visitors may see the pileated woodpecker (*Dryocopus pileatus*), the largest woodpecker in the Sierra. It most likely would be found in a fir tree—generally a Douglas fir (*Pseudotsuga menziesii*) or a white fir (*Abies concolor*)—pounding while swinging its head in an exaggerated, 8-inch arc.

The lavender feathers of the smallest hummingbird in North America, the calliope hummingbird (*Stellula calliope*), also can be seen. The best viewing months are between May and August when the hummingbirds visit white-leaf manzanita (*Arctoostaphylos viscida*) or currants (*Ribes*) for nectar.

Madora and Eureka lakes, as well as Jamison Creek, offer fishing opportunities. Rainbow trout (*Salmo gairdinerii*) and brown trout (*Salmo trutta*) can be found at Madora. Eureka has only brook trout (*Salvelinus fontinalis*). The creek has mostly rainbow trout. Various smaller alpine lakes have species of golden trout (*Salmo aguabonita*). The golden trout developed into a separate species in the Southern Sierra several decades ago after rivers and lakes were planted with brown and rainbow. The golden trout were then planted in other areas.

Cross-country skiing is another favorite activity in the park. There is one developed ski trail and numerous other alternatives for those who like to combine mountaineering and skiing.

Directions: From Highway 70, drive 5 miles west of Blairsden on County Road A-14 into the park.

Activities: Hiking, sight-seeing, camping, fishing, and skiing.

Facilities: The Plumas Ski Bowl, the downhill facility at the park; most runs are intermediate in difficulty. To contact the concession, phone (530) 836-2317. The Upper Jamison Creek campground at the foot of Eureka Peak has 67 sites, each with a table and fire pit. Hot showers are located within the campground. For a little more privacy, there are 14 walk-in sites, available on a first-come, first-serve basis. The maximum trailer length is 24 feet, motor homes 30 feet. A specially designed handicapped-accessible campsite is also available.

Dates: Park is open year-round. Campgrounds open from May to Oct. 15.

Fees: None, but there is a charge to enter the museum or use the campgrounds.

Closest town: Blairsden, 2 miles.

For more information: Plumas-Eureka State Park, 310 Johnsonville Road, Blairsden, CA 95103. Phone (530) 836-2380.

LAKES BASIN RECREATION AREA

[Fig. 14] Take your pick: Gold Lake, Squaw Lake, Haven Lake, Long Lake, Rock Lake, Jamison Lake. There are more than a dozen lakes with fishing, boating, swimming, and camping being the main attractions.

Lakes Basin is where many outdoor enthusiasts have seen nesting bald eagles (*Haliaetus leucocephalus*), endangered birds known to do their share of fishing.

Around the lake, hikers will find an interesting and characteristic feature of the Northern Sierra—solifluction terraces. They are saturated parts of the soil that are creeping downslope and become hung up on small terraces. The soil begins folding and piling up.

Plants, such as sedges and alpine willow (*Salix petrophila*), begin growing and solidifying the saturated soil. Small ponds form in the depressions of these terraces, usually as the snow melts.

The basin area is a gem of the Plumas National Forest, archaeologists say. It may have been the summer hunting and fishing ground of a tribe related to the prehistoric Martis people or the Great Basin or Central California native Americans. Visitors can see petroglyphs—some dating back as far as 10,000 years—near the Lakes Basin Campground.

The area's natural history has been studied extensively. Fossil leaves found in Gold Lake were dated at 19 million years old, and experts have concluded the area climate was tropical at the time. A summer rain season, which does not exist now, contributed to the 35 to 40 inches of annual rainfall at the time. Trees that are now common in the southeastern United States were found in this area at that time.

For anyone interested in the volcanic history of the area, Frazier Falls is a place where the top of a 2-mile-thick formation of volcanic rock begins. While most folks may be absorbed in the 176-foot vertical drop of the falls, just northeast of Gold Lake, the volcanic sandstone and andesite can be seen just west of the picnic grounds at the falls. Since the depth of this widespread formation varies so greatly, some geologists believe it might have been a massive volcanic eruption that was tilted on its side by the active California geology of the past.

The Lakes Basin hike is the tour of choice for most hikers, though it is strenuous.

It features the Sierra's northernmost glacial basins. For those who are not interested in taking their families on a long, arduous walk, many shorter trails branch from this one and wind up at scenic lakes.

Directions: The trip to the Lakes Basin hike trailhead will get visitors into the vast recreation area. Drive south on Highway 89 from Graeagle for 2 miles, turn south on Gold Lake Road. Drive 5 miles to the Lakes Basin Campground. For Gold Lake, drive another 2.5 miles, turn southwest on a road designated "Gold Lake Lodge."

Activities: Fishing, hiking, camping, bird-watching, sight-seeing, cross-country skiing.

Facilities: Twelve campgrounds with vault toilets, resort hotels, 4 picnic areas.

Dates: Open year-round.

Fees: There is a charge for camping.

Closest town: Graeagle, 5 miles.

For more information: Beckwourth Ranger District, Mohawk Road, PO Box 7, Bairsden, CA 96103. Phone (530) 863-2575.

LAKES BASIN TRAIL

[Fig. 14(1)] **Directions:** At the Gold Lake parking area, walk to the marked road where the trailhead begins.

Trail: 9.5 miles one way.

Elevation: 1,475-foot elevation gain; trailhead starts at 6,600 feet.

Degree of difficulty: Strenuous.

Surface: Rocky but easily distinguishable.

MUSEUMS OF THE PLUMAS NATIONAL FOREST

Plumas County Museum, 500 Jackson Street, Quincy, CA 95971. Phone (530) 283-6320. [Fig. 12(8)] Cultural and home art displays are featured, as well as agriculture, mining, logging, and railroad history. Collections include Maidu Indian basketry and pioneer weaponry. The outdoor area has a miner's cabin and mining implements. A carriage and buggy along with a blacksmith shop are also featured.

Historic Coburn-Variel Home, 137 Coburn Street, Quincy, CA 95971, located next to the Plumas County Museum. Phone (530) 283-6320. [Fig. 12(9)] This is a restored, three-story Victorian home furnished from the museum collection.

Portola Railroad Museum, PO Box 608, Portola, CA 96122. Phone (530) 832-4131. [Fig. 13(1)] The Feather River Rail Society established the museum in downtown Portola in 1983 to preserve equipment, photographs, and artifacts of rail travel. During summer, train rides are offered on a 1-mile track.

Indian Valley Museum, Mount Jura Gem and Mineral Society Building, PO Box 165, Taylorsville, CA 95983. Phone (530) 284-6511. The museum, at the corner of Cemetery and Portsmouth roads, features an 1850s to present collection to represent the settling of the Indian and Genesee valleys. There are also mining and mineral displays.

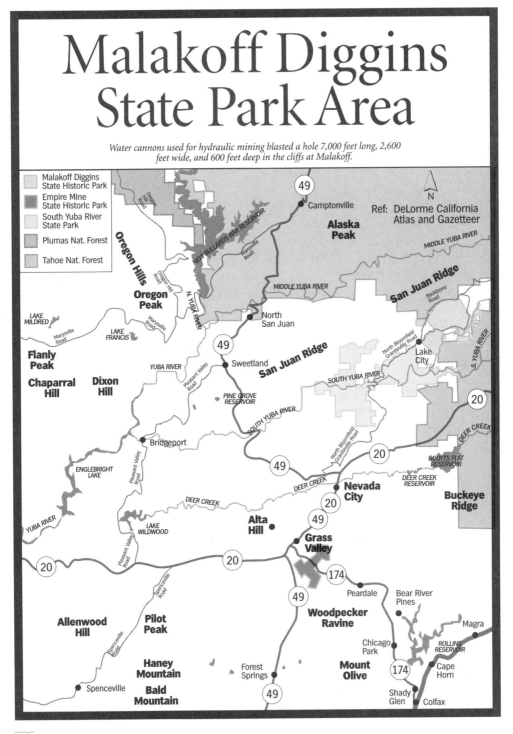

Malakoff Diggins State Park Area

Water cannons used for hydraulic mining blasted a hole 7,000 feet long, 2,600 feet wide, and 600 feet deep in the cliffs at Malakoff.

Malakoff Diggins State Historic Park

Empire Mine State Historic Park

South Yuba River State Park

Plumas Nat. Forest

Tahoe Nat. Forest

Ref: DeLorme California Atlas and Gazetteer

Beckwourth Cabin, 2180 Rocky Point Road, Portola, CA 96122. Phone (530) 832-4888. [Fig. 13(2)] Viewing by appointment only. This is the refurbished hotel and trading post opened by Plumas County pioneer Jim Beckwourth, one of the few pioneer leaders who was African-American.

Tahoe National Forest

[Fig. 15, Fig. 16, Fig. 17] The Tahoe National Forest, designated in 1907, has 400 miles of hiking trails in 1.2 million acres and a cultural history that includes gold miners, hydroelectric power companies, timber companies, and pioneering families in California. The Tahoe is where the ill-fated Donner party spent the harsh winter of 1846, and many of the settlers died in the Sierra's frigid grip.

A few years after the Donner disaster, frontier families streamed through Donner Pass to pursue the gold rush. Their lives and their work are detailed in foothill-area museums and other attractions.

The American River, the main watershed in Tahoe, has been dammed at several places to provide hydroelectric power for growing cities, such as Sacramento. The alpine areas of the Granite Chief Wilderness overlook the forest from the east. The granite peaks of Mount Mildred at 8,398 feet and Granite Chief at 9,006 feet bear the scratches and scrapes of passing glaciers.

On the map, the Tahoe National Forest has a checkerboard appearance—some private ownership, some public ownership. Its history is filled with private land ownership by railroads, power companies, and logging firms. The legacy continues today with many acres of land still privately held within the forest boundaries.

STATE PARKS
MALAKOFF DIGGINS STATE HISTORIC PARK

[Fig. 15] The cliff at Malakoff gives dramatic evidence of the hydraulic mining done in years past. The cliff's sediments were stripped with powerful streams of water as gold miners searched for precious metal. The cliff is preserved, and state officials are trying to revegetate it slowly.

Visitors can still see a 7,847-foot bedrock tunnel that served as a drain for all the water. The miners used the tunnel as a drain for water brought in from Bowers Lake 15 miles away. More than 50 miles of canals were built to take advantage of the water.

A lot of natural habitat was lost in the hydraulic mining. From the beauty of the trees in the area today, it is not difficult to imagine what was lost. Visitors will find blue oak (*Quercus douglasii*), valley oak (*Quercus lobata*), redbud (*Cercis occidentalis*), California buckeye (*Aesculus californica*), digger pine (*Pinus sabiniana*), and canyon live oak (*Quercus chrysolepis*).

The digger pine is particularly well suited to serpentine soils often found in the area. It also is able to survive in dry conditions, growing sometimes in rocky conditions that would not work at all for oak trees.

Long before the hydraulic mining and before the time of the trees, volcanic ash showered the gold-bearing streams in the Sierra from 60 million years ago until about 9 million years ago. The ash came first from rhyolite explosions that began to subside about 20 million years ago. They were followed by andesite eruptions along vents in the Northern Sierra, such as Castle Peak and Mount Lincoln.

Lava flows rolled down the streambeds, creating layers above the gold and other minerals as well as diverting streams in foothill areas of the gold country.

The ancient streambeds and the volcanic activity that altered them are important in the story of Malakoff. The lava made the streambeds less resistant to erosion. With time and weathering, especially from 60 million years ago to 33 million years ago when the climate was more tropical in California, everything around the streambeds eroded, and the streambeds became elevated.

The elevated ancient streambeds became targets for enterprising miners between the 1860s and the 1880s. Using water cannons, the miners blasted through millions of years of sediments to find $3.5 million worth of gold at Malakoff. The effort produced 50 million tons of tailings that washed down the Yuba River.

Farmers downstream finally stopped the miners from the practice of washing away mountains. The farmers filed a successful legal action, which limited hydraulic mining by requiring containment of the tailings.

The water cannons left a hole 7,000 feet long, about 2,600 feet wide, and 600 feet deep in the cliffs at Malakoff. In all, similar hydraulic mining took more than 1 billion tons of sediment, rock, and debris from Sierra foothills.

Directions: Drive 17 miles northeast from Nevada City on North Bloomfield Road. The road is winding and unpaved for 9 miles, so allow extra travel time.

Facilities: Wheelchair accessible bathrooms are available.

Dates: Open year-round.

Fees: There are fees for day use and camping.

Closest town: Nevada City, 26 miles.

For more information: Malakoff Diggins State Park, 23579 North Bloomfield Road, Nevada City, CA 95959. Phone (530) 265-2740.

EMPIRE MINE STATE HISTORIC PARK

[Fig. 15] For more than 100 years, Empire Mine in Grass Valley was one of the largest, deepest, longest operating, and richest gold mines around, producing nearly 6 million ounces of gold. The park contains many of the mine's buildings, the owner's home and restored gardens, as well as the entrance to 367 miles of abandoned and flooded mine shafts. There are 10 miles of trails in the park.

In June 1850, George McKnight discovered a gold-bearing quartz outcropping about 1 mile from St. Patrick's Church in downtown Grass Valley. Then, in October 1850, a lumberman named George Roberts found flecks of gold in a surface outcropping of quartz where the park's main parking lot is now.

The mine claim changed hands several times in the coming years, finally winding up in the hands of William Bourn Jr., the son of a capitalist. Bourn pursued the expansion of the mine.

The most important factor in the success of hard-rock mining in California was the immigration of skilled miners from Cornwall, England, where hardrock tin and copper mining had been carried on for more than 1,000 years. Cornish miners drilled, blasted, and mucked out most of the 367 miles of tunnels—some of which angled downward into the earth some 11,000 feet, nearly a full vertical mile below the surface.

By the time the mine shut down in 1956, the mine had produced more than $2 billion worth of gold at 1990s prices.

Directions: Drive about 24 miles north of Auburn on Highway 49 to the Empire Street Exit in Grass Valley. The park is at 10791 East Empire Street.

Facilities: Interpretive information, restrooms.

Fees: There are fees to enter.

Dates: Open year-round.

Closest town: Grass Valley, 2 miles.

For more information: Empire State Historic Park, 10791 East Empire Street, Grass Valley, CA 95945. Phone (530) 273-8522.

SOUTH YUBA RIVER STATE PARK

[Fig. 15] The longest single-span covered bridge in the United State can be seen at South Yuba River State Park. The bridge is more than 230 feet long. The parkland runs for miles along the steep, rugged canyon of the South Yuba River, providing beaches and picnic areas. The park also offers the Independence Trail, which is wheelchair accessible.

Docent-led history, nature, and gold-panning tours take place at various times of the year. More than 600,000 people visit the park each year.

Anyone who walks through the foothills in wild areas such as the South Yuba River should be aware of the western rattlesnake (*Crotalus veridis*). Though sightings of it are not common, particularly this far north in the Sierra, the snake is present in this area. Most often, the rattlesnake is seen in springtime.

The rattlesnake, the only poisonous reptile in the Sierra, usually is either hibernating or hidden beneath rocks or in grasslands along trails. It is cold-blooded, meaning it has no internal heat regulation. In spring, it warms itself in the sunshine when temperatures reach 65 to 70 degrees Fahrenheit.

The rattler is known for its tail, which can rattle into a buzz when the snake is provoked. It does not always rattle its tail, however. The snake's 2-inch fangs normally do not strike higher than 1 foot off of the ground, because the snake cannot jump. High leather boots are advised, especially in spring. Stay on the trails and watch where you step if you must leave the trail.

Directions: Drive north on Highway 49 to Highway 20 west. Drive 9 miles to Pleasant Valley Road. Turn left on Pleasant Valley Road, then 8 miles to Bridgeport. Follow the signs.

Activities: Swimming, hiking, viewing wildflowers, and touring historic sites.

Facilities: Picnic tables, restrooms.

Dates: Open year-round.

Fees: None.

Closest town: Penn Valley, 8 miles.

For more information: South Yuba River State Park, 17660 Pleasant Valley Road, Penn Valley, CA 95946. Phone (530) 432-2546.

WINTER RECREATION AT TAHOE NATIONAL FOREST

Winter is probably the biggest reason people live in Truckee and other cities in the Tahoe National Forest. People enjoy the milder months, but most cannot wait for downhill and cross-country skiing, snowboarding, and snow play.

It is not apparent to most visitors until they look at a map, but the winter recreation areas are not all in the national forest. The map looks like a checkerboard of public and private property.

Of the 1,208,993 acres within the boundary, 811,740 acres, or 67 percent, are National Forest System lands. The other 397,253 acres are owned by private individuals, corporations, or other governmental agencies. In most cases, these lands have been privately held since before the creation of the national forest.

The large, downhill ski complexes include **Alpine Meadows**, 3 miles west of Highway 89 south of Truckee, (530) 583-4232; **Boreal Ski Area**, on Interstate 80, (530) 426-3666; **Soda Springs Ski Area**, Interstate 80, (530) 426-3663; **Donner Ski Ranch**, Norden, (530) 426-3635; **Sugar Bowl**, Norden, (530) 426-3651; and **Squaw Valley**, 2 miles off Highway 89 South, (530) 583-6985.

Squaw Valley has the most ski facilities with 10 double chair lifts, 9 triple chairs, 4 high-speed detachable quads, a gondola, and 3 pony tows. The other ski complexes vary in their operations, with Alpine, Boreal, and Sugar Bowl offering more facilities than the others.

Privately operated cross-country ski facilities and tours include **Alpine Skills International**, Norden, (530) 426-9108; **Eagle Mountain Resort**, Interstate 80 at the Yuba Gap, (530) 389-2254; **Royal Gorge**, Soda Springs, (530) 426-3871; and **Lakeview Cross Country**, Tahoe City, (530) 583-9353.

Most of the cross-country operations, as well as the downhill resorts, offer groomed trails, lessons, and rentals. Lakeview Cross Country also has cross-country skating lanes. For snowmobilers and cross-country skiers who want to get away from the resorts, there are four areas designated by the state as Sno-Parks. A $5-per-day permit allows winter enthusiasts to snowmobile, cross-country ski, or build snowmen, ride sleds, and throw snowballs.

The areas include **Yuba Pass**, **Yuba Gap**, and **Donner Summit**, all of which are along Interstate 80 west of Truckee. For information about any of them, call the California Department of Parks and Recreation, (916) 324-1222.

In the southern part of the forest, **China Wall Off-Road Vehicle Staging Area** doubles as a kickoff point for winter recreation. The area, 14 miles east of Foresthill on Foresthill Divide Road, has plenty of parking, vault toilets, and trailhead access.

Cross-country skiers will not find groomed trails, but the skiing is easy because the terrain is level. The trails from the staging area will take skiers to the Mitchell Mine, Humbug Ridge, or Mumford Bar trailhead.

For snowmobiles, there is a 16-mile route up the divide corridor to Robinson Flat. From there, the trip winds north toward Soda Springs and Norden, which is about 40 miles away. At intermediate distances—12 to 14 miles away from Robinson Flat—are American Hill, Tadpole Meadow, and Sailor Flat. These destinations are along unplowed roads.

For those interested in the beginnings of skiing in this area of California, the **Western Skisport Museum** is at the Boreal Ridge Ski Area, 9 miles west of Truckee on Interstate 80. There is no fee, and films about the development of the sport in the northern Sierra are shown by request. The museum is open Tuesday through Sunday during the ski season and Wednesday through Sunday during summer.

The displays guide visitors through the early resorts and skiing in the area, dating back to the 1930s. The winter of 1932-33 was the first season that Highway 40 was kept open after lobbying by the Auburn Ski Club.

OVERLAND EMIGRANT TRAIL

[Fig. 16(5)] Elisha Stevens, an old trapper, led a party of 46 men, women, and children out of Council Bluffs, Iowa, in 1844 on the first wagon trail through the Sierra Nevada, traveling through the present-day Tahoe National Forest. They traveled the Overland Emigrant Trail, where visitors today can drive and hike to see what the pioneers saw.

The drama of Stevens's journey was somewhat obscured by the tragedy that unfolded two years later when the Donner party trekked the same route and encountered an October blizzard. The Donner party was split up and stranded, and many died.

The Stevens party came through the area—Tahoe Forest's portion of the 2,000-mile Emigrant Trail—at a time when no one was quite sure how to cross the Sierra in a wagon train. Scaling granite escarpments and wooded slopes of the eastern Sierra, Stevens's group struggled through a series of canyons and rugged ridges on the western slope.

The group was guided by a Paiute Indian named Truckee, for whom the city of Truckee is named. The travelers established the forerunner of the major routes built through this part of the Sierra, including Interstate 80 and old Highway 40.

WESTERN HEMLOCK
(Tsuga heterophylla)

Even though about half of the Donner party died in the winter of 1846-1847 at Donner Camp, just north of Truckee, wagon trains poured through the area. More than 500 wagons came through the year after the Donner party. In 1852, more than 50,000 emigrants passed through Big Bend, about 15 miles west of Truckee.

Emigrant John Markle wrote about the trail in 1849, calling it "the damedest [*sic*], rockiest, and roughest road I ever saw." Travelers had to spend days unhitching their teams and carefully letting the wagons down over massive granite boulders as well as fording cold, rushing streams.

This trail later became the blueprint for a portion of the transcontinental railroad. In the 1860s, the Central Pacific Railroad charged a toll on an improved Emigrant Trail, which had been renamed Dutch Flat and Donner Lake Wagon Road.

By 1870, the railroad was constructed, and the wagon road was abandoned. Forty-three years later, in 1913, the Lincoln Highway opened as the first paved automobile route across the country, and it passed through the Emigrant Trail corridor. In 1930, it was replaced by Highway 40, or "Old 40" as it was called. By the mid-1960s, the modern, high-speed Interstate 80 emerged to replace "Old 40."

With all the transportation history, it might be easy to overlook the geologic background of this northern Sierra area. The granitic surface around Donner Summit, which is more than 7,000 feet high, dates back more than 80 million years.

Cretaceous river channels are preserved at Donner and at Paradise Lake, north of Donner. A pluton beneath Emigrant Gap, west of Donner Summit, has been estimated to be 10 miles across and more than 160 million years old.

Some of this rich geologic history can be traced on the road cuts along the modern interstate. The tilted layers of metamorphic rock between Auburn and the Emigrant Gap are believed to have been part of the ancient Sierra before the final pulses uplifted the mountain range over the last several million years. The metamorphic rock is representative of a time about 60 million years ago when the Sierra's climate was more humid, and the low, rolling hills were crossed by large rivers.

Road cuts at Dutch Flat, just west of Blue Canyon along Interstate 80, reveal gold-bearing gravels. They stand out even to motorists passing at 65 miles per hour, because the gravels have been turned red by weathering processes.

Beyond Emigrant Gap, granite is the main story. The granite, scarred by glaciers that passed through over the past 2 million years, is dotted in places with parts of older rocks that were caught in the plutons as they rose through the earth's crust.

Ridgelines on the eastern side of Donner Pass are coated with volcanic debris from eruptions that took place over the last 20 million years. The weathering processes have opened windows into a more distant geologic past, revealing other metamorphic layers that are perhaps more than 150 million years old.

Mingled with the geology is a diverse mixed conifer forest and wildlife. The forest varies from ponderosa pine *(Pinus ponderosa)* and white fir *(Abies concolor)* to mountain hemlock *(Tsuga mertensiana)* in the higher, subalpine belt on ridgetops around Donner Pass.

The wildlife includes the acrobatic mountain chickadee *(Parus gambeli)*, a bird that curiously hangs upside down to capture insects for nourishment. The chickadee spends all day searching for food in the open woods around evergreens and oaks. Other birds include the winter wren *(Troglodytes troglodytes)*, black-backed three-toed woodpecker *(Picoides arcticus)*, junco *(Junco oreganus)*, and purple finch *(Carpodacus pupurens)*.

The area is also known for migrating birds. The Hammond flycatcher *(Empidonax hammondi)*, the calliope hummingbird *(Stellula calliope)*, and the hermit thrush *(Hylocichla guttata)* fly south to places such as Guatemala to spend the winter. They leave because the cold weather would deprive them of their insect diet. Look for them in summer, but they are gone by October when the nights cool down.

The Interstate 80 corridor is the best place to start exploring this area. The historic Overland Emigrant Trail is shown on a map sold by the U.S. Forest Service. The trail is about 35 miles long and suitable for driving in several places, but some sections must be hiked. It could take two days to complete.

The trip is broken into four distinct segments with a total of 19 stops, so it is

PONDEROSA
PINE
(Pinus ponderosa)

not necessary to traverse the entire trail. It begins with the Ascent, between Dog Valley to the east of the Sierra crest, and the Donner Memorial State Park and Museum. The second segment contains three main passes over the crest. The third runs from Summit Valley to Alpha-Omega Rest Stop. The fourth is the run to the foothills from Deadman's Flat to Steephollow Crossing.

Plan before attempting the trip. It is best to find overnight accommodations at campgrounds or motels in Truckee, Colfax, or Soda Springs, which are along the route. Buy a map from the Truckee Ranger Station of the Tahoe National Forest.

Directions: To start the Emigrant Trail from the east, drive 12 miles east of Truckee on Interstate 80, exit at Verdi, Nevada, and go to the business section of town. Turn left on Dog Valley Road (Bridge Street), and cross the Truckee River. Drive 3 miles, turn left at the Y in the road onto Road 027, west toward Truckee. Park in the turnout 50 yards from the turn. Follow the map to the next stop.

Activities: Hiking, scenic driving, camping, sight-seeing, and picnicking.

Facilities: Museums, interpretive signs, restrooms, picnic areas, and campgrounds.

Dates: Open year-round.

Fees: None.

Closest town: Truckee, 1 mile.

For more information: Truckee Ranger Station, 10342 Highway 89 North, Truckee, CA 96161. Phone (530) 587-3558.

HIGHLIGHTS ON THE OVERLAND EMIGRANT TRAIL

The **George and Jacob Donner Picnic Site**, which can be reached by turning north onto Highway 89 from Interstate 80 and driving 2.5 miles, is where 14 people died in the cruel winter of 1846-1847. The first blizzard of the season caught the weary travelers in October, long before they expected to see snow fly.

George and Jacob had turned off the Emigrant Trail into the Alder Creek valley to repair wagons. A larger contingent of their party moved on, though they were hit just a few miles farther down the trail by the same blizzard.

The 25 people in Alder Creek valley quickly ran out of food and had no chance of moving through the deep snowdrifts. They had little chance to even build crude structures. They huddled in tents and cut trees to burn for warmth. Tree stumps found in later years were measured at 12 feet, indicating the depth of the snow.

Jacob was dead by December. George and many of the adults also died, denying themselves food so their children would survive.

The interpretive signs on the 400-yard walk around the area say the emigrants boiled the hides of their dead animals and ate the gluey mess. They do not confirm rumors of cannibalism, but they do raise the question.

At **Donner Memorial State Park and Museum**—return to Interstate 80, drive 4 miles west to the Donner Lake turnoff—the story of the rest of the wagon train is told. Those travelers, too, were caught in the blizzards of 1846-1847, and they suffered many deaths as well. A slide show and exhibit at the museum tell the whole story.

The park is near a prime recreation spot: Donner Lake. The park has no boat-launching ramp, but a public ramp operated by the Truckee Donner Recreation and Parks District is available in the northwest corner of Donner Lake. A fee is charged for boat launching. For information, call (530) 582-7720. The lake is open to both power and sail boats. **Donner Lake Village Resort**, 15695 Donner Pass Road, Truckee, CA 96161, has lakeside rooms. For information, call (800) 621-6664.

The park also has over 3 miles of frontage on Donner Lake and Creek. Fishing is not usually spectacular, though there are rainbow trout *(Oncorhynchus mykiss)* and some brown trout *(Salmo trutta)* in the lake. The lake is stocked with trout and a fishing license is required.

Other activities at the park include camping and hiking. The campground has 150 sites and a day-use area along the lake with picnic tables, restrooms, a beach, and a lakeside interpretive trail that has 18 panels that discuss the nature and cultural diversity of the area.

The **Emigrant Trail Museum** at the park takes about an hour to visit. It depicts the history of the area and the people who came into this part of the Sierra. Postcards, posters, maps, and books about the human and natural history of the area are for sale at the museum. There is an entrance fee.

Near the museum are the **Pioneer Monument** and the **Murphy family cabin site**. Also starting from the side of the museum is a self-guiding nature trail that is a 0.5-mile loop. Nature trail guides are available at the museum and campground entrance station. Guided hikes, ranging from one to two hours, start at the museum at 10 a.m. The hikes, special feature shows, and campfires start in late June and continue until late September. For specific information on any of the activities, call the park at (530) 582-7892.

Several miles west of the Donner park, **Big Bend** is another historic part of the Emigrant Trail where visitors can actually see rust marks that wagon wheels left on the granite. Captain John Fremont led a U.S. Army mapping detachment through Big Bend in 1845, the year before the Donner tragedy. Though this was still a Mexican territory at the time, Freemont was scouting for valuable resources.

To find Big Bend, drive west on Donner Pass Road from the state park for 2.25 miles, about 0.3 mile past Rainbow Lodge. Pull into a gravel turnout on the right just short of a granitic knob and walk 70 yards toward Interstate 80, which should still be well within earshot. Dozens of faint rust marks are apparent in the area.

Some of the most obvious rust marks from the iron wagon wheels can be found at Loch Leven trailhead, 0.25 mile east of the Big Bend Visitor Center on Donner Pass Road, farther down the road from the granitic knob. Walk down toward the Truckee River and you will find an iron "T" marker placed by Trails West. You are on the Emigrant Trail at that point. To contact the Big Bend Visitors Center, call (530) 426-3609. Tours of the Emigrant Trail can be arranged on weekends between Memorial Day and Labor Day.

Just a few yards upstream of the marker, walking east, you can find rust marks on the side of the rocks, caused by side scraping from thousands of wagon wheels. The rusted spots feel smoother because of the polishing done by the many passing wheels.

MOUNT JUDAH LOOP TRAIL

[Fig. 16(4)] The views from the Sierra crest are magnificent, and this trail is not a difficult day for many hikers. It allows hikers to quickly get to the top of the mountain range where views stretch seemingly forever.

The red face of 7,841-foot Red Mountain is apparent from the rooftop at Mount Judah. The reddish color comes from the metamorphic rock. In the distance is Mount Rose, the volcanic peak that, at 10,776 feet high, rivals the granitic domes in this Northern Sierra region.

Hikers can look for evidence of winter in the trees on the ridgetops and near the peaks on this trail. For instance, winds up to 50 miles per hour regularly whip through the canyons and over the summits in the Sierra, stripping the needles and branches on the windward side of lodgepole pine *(Pinus murrayana)* or white fir *(Abies concolor)*.

The lodgepole particularly will sprout from granite cracks and crevices in a ridge, then bend as young saplings. When the saplings grow into mature trees, often their trunks will have a curved or "pistol butt" appearance.

Directions: Take Interstate 80 from east or west of the Sierra crest, exit at Soda Springs, drive about 4 miles east along former Highway 40 to Donner Pass. Drive another 0.3 mile from the pass and park along an old turnout or wide spot to the side of the road. The trailhead begins down a pole-line road that goes east for less than 50 yards, then forks right.

Trail: 11.5-mile loop.

Elevation: About 1,100-foot elevation gain, 8,242-foot summit at Mt. Judah.

Degree of difficulty: Moderate.

Surface: Rugged, granite with trail ducks as markers. Steep.

KYBURZ FLAT

[Fig. 16(2)] Two thousand years ago, the Washoe Indians lived in this small Northern Sierra valley. Their simple, unobtrusive lives had little impact on the ecosystem. Though the tribe is still in the area, a majority of the Washoe departed the area in 1850.

They left behind petroglyphs similar to the ancient carvings found in other parts of the northern Sierra. The rock carvings contain a type of petroglyph called *cupules*, small round pits that have been forced into the rock.

Cupules are believed to be part of the many ceremonial rituals of Native Americans. The rituals involved weather control or fertility rites.

For best viewing, see the cupules in the late afternoon. The lower light picks up the subtleties in the rock. Visitors will notice the cupules rock has been cracked in three sections. Do not touch it or attempt to make casts of it.

The cupules rock is the first stop on a walking or driving tour of the Kyburz Flat Interpretive Area. Signs give direction and history in a 3-stop tour that should take less than an hour to drive.

The second stop illustrates a typical 1860s stage stop. The Gold Rush changed the face of transportation in the area in the mid-nineteenth century. Entrepreneurs built a network of roads and started stage and freight companies to serve new mining communities.

The archaeological remains of More's Station—occupied by Lysander More and his family—are visible at this site. Signs mark different features of the 320-acre

**LODGEPOLE
PINE**
(Pinus murrayana)

site, which was complete with a hotel, barn, and stables. The signs, interestingly, locate a root cellar used for cold storage.

The last stop in the interpretive area is Wheeler Sheep Camp, where visitors can see the brick oven where bread and stews were made as long ago as 1927. The oven is a reconstruction of the old equipment that collapsed in the 1980s.

Fresh bread—sheepherder's bread—was supplied to the herders every five days. Decades later, this type of bread is a popular item found in many grocery stores in the western United States.

The camp, with a three-bedroom cabin and tent platforms, was built by the Wheeler Sheep Company, which grazed sheep in the high Sierra during the summer. The camp was owned by John Martin Gallues, a Basque immigrant. He and his brother, Felix, built several of the structures themselves. The camp included sheep corrals, chutes, and livestock scales.

Directions: From Interstate 80 at Truckee, drive north about 12 miles on Highway 89. Turn right on Sierra County Road S450. The petroglyphs begin about 1 mile down the road. Follow the signs.

Activities: Driving or hiking the interpretive trail.

Facilities: Parking, restrooms, and interpretive signs.

Dates: Open year-round.

Fees: None.

Closest town: Sierraville, 3 miles.

For more information: Sierraville Ranger District, PO Box 95, Highway 89, Sierraville, CA 96126. Phone (530) 994-3401.

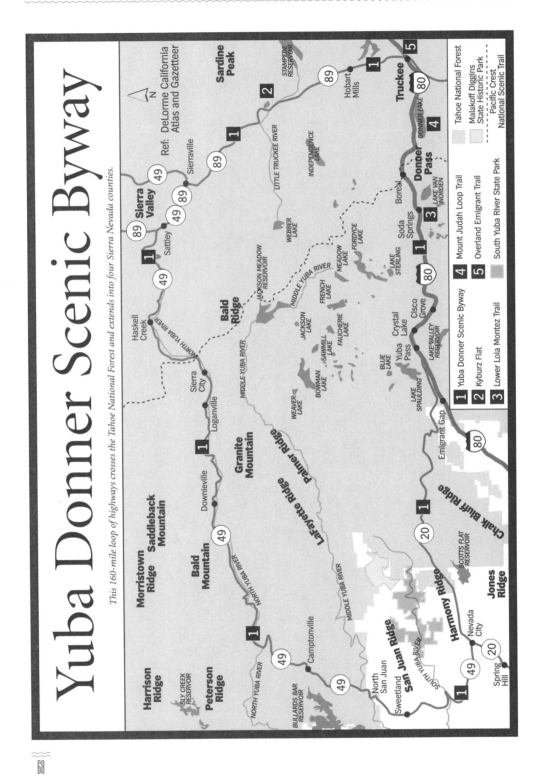

Yuba Donner Scenic Byway

This 160-mile loop of highways crosses the Tahoe National Forest and extends into four Sierra Nevada counties.

Ref: DeLorme California Atlas and Gazetteer

Legend:

Tahoe National Forest
Malakoff Diggins State Historic Park
Pacific Crest National Scenic Trail

4 Mount Judah Loop Trail
5 Overland Emigrant Trail
South Yuba River State Park

1 Yuba Donner Scenic Byway
2 Kyburz Flat
3 Lower Lola Montez Trail

YUBA DONNER SCENIC BYWAY

[Fig. 16(1)] Historic Kyburz Flat is only one stop on the **Yuba Donner Scenic Byway**, a 160-mile loop of highways crossing the Tahoe National Forest. The transportation history, recreational opportunities, and sites of interest extend into four Sierra Nevada counties—Nevada, Placer, Sierra, and Yuba.

The scenic byway takes visitors to gold and silver mining museums and railroad sites. It goes north from Truckee on Highway 89 to Highway 49 where it turns west and then south to Highway 20. From there, it continues east to Interstate 80 and back to Truckee.

Along the byway are many towns, museums, and walking tours. For walking tours, call individual cities: Forest City, (530) 288-3231; Downieville, (800) 200-4949; Grass Valley, (530) 273-4667; Nevada City, (530) 265-2692, and Truckee, (530) 587-2757.

Call individual museums for more information: **Firehouse Museum**, Nevada City, (530) 265-5468; **Grass Valley Museum**, Grass Valley, (530) 272-4725; **Historic Library**, Nevada City, (530) 265-5910; **Nevada County Historical Society Video History Museum**, Grass Valley, (530) 274-1126; **North Star Mining Museum**, Grass Valley, (530) 273-4255; the **Downieville Foundary**, (530) 289-3261; the **Alleghany Mining Museum**, Alleghany, (530) 287-3330; **Kentucky Mine Museum**, Sierra City, (530) 862-1310; **Loyalton Museum**, Loyalton, (530) 993-6754; and **Pelton Wheel Exhibit**, Camptonville, (530) 288-3231.

LOWER LOLA MONTEZ TRAIL (BICYCLING)

[Fig. 16(3)] Though private property seems to be everywhere in the Tahoe National Forest, there are bike trails where it is acceptable for the public to go. One such trail is off of Interstate 80, along the Yuba Donner Scenic Byway. It is called the Lower Lola Montez Trail, and it is moderately difficult.

From the trailhead, bikers follow the trail north for 0.25 mile to a road and turn right. The road goes to lower Castle Creek crossing. The creek is lined with mesh wire, so be careful to avoid a flat when crossing.

The trail goes up and down, passes through an open mountain meadow, and winds past Lower Lola Montez Lake, a wonderful swimming and camping location. There are a lot of hikers on weekends, so control the speed of descent on this trail. Because there is private property in the area, bicyclers are advised to stay on the trails.

Directions: Drive about 15 miles west of Truckee on Interstate 80, exit on the north side of the freeway at Soda Springs, and follow the paved road east for 0.3 mile to the parking and trailhead area.

For more information: Truckee Ranger District, 10342 Highway 89 South, Truckee, CA 96161. Phone (530) 587-3558.

Trail: 3 miles one-way.

Degree of difficulty: Moderate.

Elevation: 6,640 to 7,200.

Surface: Some dirt road, but mostly single-track trail.

Granite Chief Wilderness

The name Granite Chief comes from a 9,006-foot mountain on the northern shoulder of the wilderness.

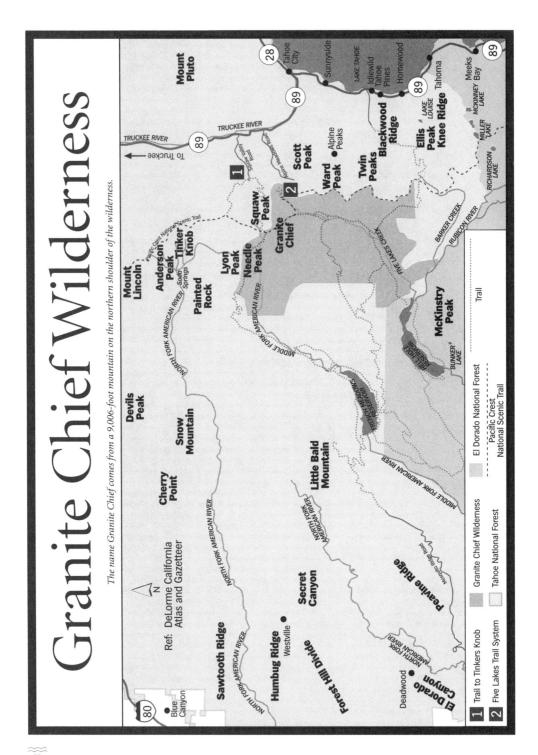

Ref: DeLorme California Atlas and Gazetteer

1 Trail to Tinkers Knob
2 Five Lakes Trail System

Granite Chief Wilderness
Tahoe National Forest
El Dorado National Forest
Pacific Crest National Scenic Trail
Trail

GRANITE CHIEF WILDERNESS

[Fig. 17] This not the best place to find a lake for fishing or simply admiring. The reason, oddly, is that the Granite Chief Wilderness is not dominated by granite, despite the name. Much of the terrain is volcanic in nature. Lakes do not form as readily in volcanic settings.

The Granite Chief, at a little more than 25,000 acres, is considered a smaller and less-crowded wilderness, by California standards. It is not as easily accessible as some wildernesses, but it also can be hiked in a day or two by experienced hikers.

For those who venture into this wilderness, there are rewards. The forest contains the primitive headwaters of the American River where evidence of vast glaciation is noticeable in granite canyons. So, actually, there are some granite attractions. Alpine meadows and volcanic formations are also big attractions.

Some of the Granite Chief area was privately held by one of California's biggest landowners—Southern Pacific Land Company—until the 1980s when it became a wilderness. The area was logged through this century. The logged areas have grown back with dense groupings of trees, including the yellow pine *(Pinus ponderosa)*, lodgepole pine *(Pinus murryama)*, and Douglas fir *(Pseudotsuga menziesii)*.

Stands of 100-year-old trees and the brush beneath them make U.S. Forest Service officials nervous about fires. The Forest Service for decades extinguished every fire it found, allowing the thick growth to develop. Without periodic fires to clear out understories of brush and smaller trees, if a fire sparked, great expanses of the forest could be incinerated by wildfires burning the thick vegetation out of control. The blazes could be similar to those that blackened hundreds of thousands of acres in Yellowstone National Park in the late 1980s.

The thick growth of trees promotes another danger to the forest: fungal damage. Root rot *(Heterobasidion annosum)* spreads on the forest floor on the seasonal winds. The spores that land at the base of trees germinate and kill tree roots. The fungus will spread to other trees nearby. Trees die in a circle around the infection, and hikers will notice the circles of dead trees periodically near many trails in the Granite Chief.

The name, Granite Chief, comes from a 9,006-foot mountain on the northern shoulder of the wilderness. Unfortunately, Granite Chief Peak did not wind up in the wilderness, yet another oddity about this place. Nearby landowners, worried about a great influx of hikers and outdoor enthusiasts in a nearby corridor, successfully lobbied to exclude it from the wilderness.

Despite the volcanic nature of the area and the relatively low number of lakes compared to other wildernesses, the popular Five Lakes area in the wilderness is well worth visiting. Several hikes in the Granite Chief offer panoramics of the high Sierra. But, on the whole, the Granite Chief is not overrun with people because it offers more solitude than breathtaking views.

Yet, some of the main trails off of Highway 89 can be heavily used. Whenever visitors are on the Pacific Crest Trail, they should remember bicycles or motorized vehicles are not allowed. The Pacific Crest Trail is one of the ways into the Granite Chief Wilderness. To get there, hikers must start at the Granite Chief trailhead and walk to the Pacific Crest Trail, which will lead them into the wilderness.

Directions: From Truckee, drive Highway 89 south to the Squaw Valley Road. Turn right and go 3 miles. Look for the Squaw Valley Fire Station on the right. The Granite Chief trailhead is just behind the fire station. Park across the street in a ski area parking lot. No roads go into the wilderness.

Activities: Hiking, backpacking, camping, photography.

Facilities: There are none in this wilderness.

Dates: Open year-round.

Fees: None.

Closest town: Tahoe City, 12 miles.

For more information: U.S. Forest Service, 631 Coyote Street, Nevada City, CA 95959-6003. Phone (530) 265-4531.

Trail: 5 miles to the Pacific Crest Trail and the wilderness.

Elevation: About 2,300-foot gain, 8,550-foot peak.

Degree of difficulty: Moderate.

Surface: Rocky, broken. No blaze, but trail is easily followed by watching for trail ducks (piles of rocks).

FIVE LAKES CREEK TRAIL SYSTEM

[Fig. 17(2)] The popular Five Lakes Creek Trail is a major artery running through the Granite Chief Wilderness, and many destinations can be reached from it. To find the trail, hike in from Barker Pass on the southeastern side of the wilderness.

Follow the Powderhorn Trail about 4 miles to the Diamond Crossing where the Five Lakes Creek Trail begins. From there, hikers can choose several trails for the walk northeast toward Whiskey Creek.

The Bear Pen Trail junction is 0.1 mile north of Diamond Crossing, and 1.7 miles north of that is the trail to Big Springs, which makes a pleasant 1-mile detour. From this junction the trail bends to the left, crosses Five Lakes Creek, and then heads north again to the Shanks Cove Trail intersection.

The Shanks Cove Trail is one of the connecting links to the Western States Trail. The Five Lakes Creek Trail continues north on the west bank of the creek climbing moderately up the crest of a lateral glacier moraine until it reaches Whisky Creek where the trail ends.

Other trails accessible from this point—the Pacific Crest Trail, Five Lakes, Western States, and Tevis Cup—make Whisky Creek a popular crossroad in the wilderness.

Directions: From interstate 80 in Truckee, take Highway 89 south and drive to Tahoe City. Continue south on Highway 89 from Tahoe City for another 4.2 miles to Kaspian Picnic Area. Turn west on Blackwood Canyon Road. The road follows Blackwood Creek for 2.3 miles, crosses the creek, and then climbs 4.8 miles to Barker Pass. Pavement ends at the summit. The Powderhorn trailhead is 2.3 miles down the road from where the pavement ends.

For more information: Truckee Ranger Station, 10342 Highway 89 North, Truckee, CA 96161. Phone (530) 587-3558.

Trail: 5 miles one-way.

Elevation: About a 900-foot gain, 6,920-foot peak.

Degree of difficulty: Moderate.

Surface: Footpath, sometimes narrow, sometimes sandy.

TRAIL TO TINKERS KNOB

[Fig. 17(1)] Wildflowers and granite are at play along this trail. This is a rugged day hike, but well worth the views in this glacially influenced landscape just north of the Granite Chief Wilderness.

The sights include the headwaters of the North Fork American River, Granite Chief Peak, and even Lake Tahoe. Hikers might want to think about camping a night to take it all in. Otherwise, it is a full day of hiking.

Campers along this and many other Northern Sierra trails have reported being startled on summer evenings by a huge, brown beetle. The spiny woodborer or pine sawyer *(Ergates spiculates)*, one of the largest beetles in the West, will fly directly into flashlights, lanterns, and other lights. At 2 inches long, the beetle makes some people feel as though they've been struck by a rock.

Along with the eyed elater *(Alaus melanops)*, another big beetle, the spiny woodborer, can do a lot of tree damage. The eggs that these two beetles lay in the crevices of such trees as the Douglas fir *(Pseudotsuga menziesii)* can hatch into larvae that chew into the wood.

Directions: Take the Highway 89 South Exit off of Interstate 80 in Truckee, and drive 8.5 miles south to the Squaw Valley junction. Drive 2.2 miles west on the Squaw Valley access road, past the Olympic Village Inn, and park near the fire station on the right. The trailhead is marked nearby.

Trail: 17 miles, one-way.

Elevation: 2,700-foot gain, high point at 8,949 feet.

Degree of difficulty: Strenuous.

Surface: Rugged, steep granite bedrock with trail ducks. Sometimes difficult to follow.

DOUGLAS FIR
(Pseudotsuga menziesii)

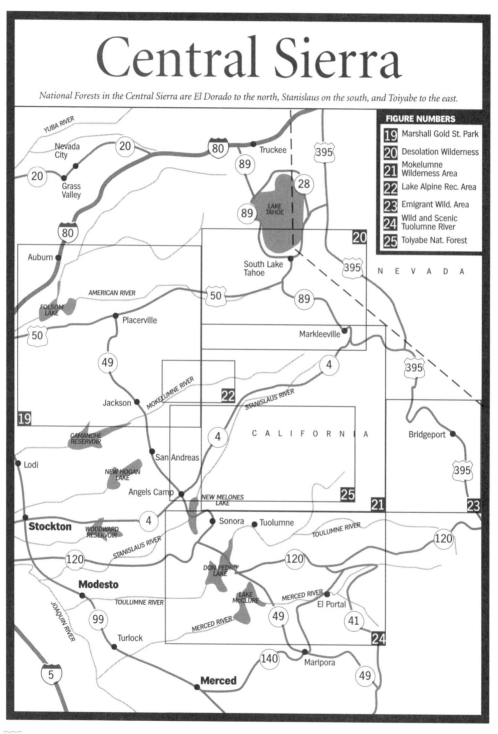

Central Sierra

National Forests in the Central Sierra are El Dorado to the north, Stanislaus on the south, and Toiyabe to the east.

FIGURE NUMBERS

19 Marshall Gold St. Park
20 Desolation Wilderness
21 Mokelumne Wilderness Area
22 Lake Alpine Rec. Area
23 Emigrant Wild. Area
24 Wild and Scenic Tuolumne River
25 Toiyabe Nat. Forest

Central Sierra

The western slope of the Sierra Nevada rolls gradually from foothills up to the jagged pinnacles of volcanic and granite high country, creating a cross-section of the elevations, animal life, and vegetation. Then it drops dramatically on the East Side, where a more arid climate supports a different landscape and volcanic influences are quite apparent.

More than any other area of this mountain range, the Central Sierra defies boundaries. Many naturalists consider Yosemite National Park to be part of it, even though Yosemite is an entity unto itself in the Sierra and California in general. Many naturalists lump the El Dorado National Forest into the Northern Sierra, which understates its importance as a central regional transportation hub in the Sierra.

The center part of this 400-mile range is best defined as El Dorado on the north, Stanislaus National Forest on the south, and the Toiyabe National Forest to the east—

[*Above:* Desolation Wilderness includes 150 alpine and subalpine lakes]

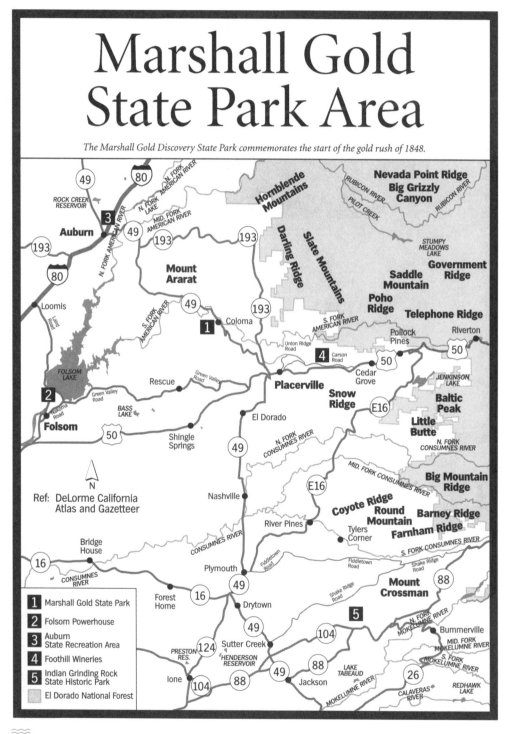

Marshall Gold State Park Area

The Marshall Gold Discovery State Park commemorates the start of the gold rush of 1848.

Nevada Point Ridge
Big Grizzly Canyon
RUBICON RIVER
PILOT CREEK
RUBICON RIVER

ROCK CREEK RESERVOIR

Hornblende Mountains

N. FORK AMERICAN RIVER

Auburn

N. FORK LAKE

MID. FORK AMERICAN RIVER

Darling Ridge

Slate Mountains

STUMPY MEADOWS LAKE

Government Ridge

Saddle Mountain

Poho Ridge

Telephone Ridge

Loomis

Laird Road

S. FORK AMERICAN RIVER

Mount Ararat

Coloma

S. FORK AMERICAN RIVER

Pollock Pines

Riverton

Union Ridge Road

Carson Road

Cedar Grove

JENKINSON LAKE

FOLSOM LAKE

Rescue

Green Valley Road

Placerville

Snow Ridge

Baltic Peak

Folsom

Natoma Road

Green Valley Road

BASS LAKE

El Dorado

Little Butte

N. FORK CONSUMNES RIVER

Shingle Springs

N. FORK CONSUMNES RIVER

MID. FORK CONSUMNES RIVER

Big Mountain Ridge

N

Ref: DeLorme California Atlas and Gazetteer

Nashville

Coyote Ridge

Round Mountain

Barney Ridge

River Pines

Tylers Corner

Farnham Ridge

S. FORK CONSUMNES RIVER

Bridge House

CONSUMNES RIVER

Plymouth

Fiddletown Road

Fiddletown Road

Shake Ridge Road

Mount Crossman

CONSUMNES RIVER

Forest Home

Drytown

Shake Ridge Road

Bummerville

N. FORK MOKELUMNE RIVER

MID. FORK MOKELUMNE RIVER

PRESTON RES.

Sutter Creek

HENDERSON RESERVOIR

S. FORK MOKELUMNE RIVER

Ione

Jackson

LAKE TABEAUD

MOKELUMNE RIVER

CALAVERAS RIVER

REDHAWK LAKE

1 Marshall Gold State Park

2 Folsom Powerhouse

3 Auburn State Recreation Area

4 Foothill Wineries

5 Indian Grinding Rock State Historic Park

El Dorado National Forest

about 3 million acres of the Sierra Nevada and all its natural charms along with a considerable wealth of natural and cultural history.

The three national forests include vast wild areas such as the Hoover Wilderness and the Emigrant Wilderness with high country lakes and volcanic features such as The Dardanelles and a Table Mountain. Yet these forests are known for so much more—skiing, fishing, bicycling, and bird-watching, among other activities.

The gold rush of the late 1840s happened here more than anywhere in the Sierra. The state parks in the foothills display vestiges of that past in museums, preserved structures, and artifacts. Hydraulic mining, the use of water cannons to blast sediment away from ancient riverbeds and reveal gold, left scars that tell perhaps as much about the time as the artifacts.

Driving the west-east arteries across the crest of the Sierra is perhaps the fastest and most revealing method of inquiry. Highways 88, 108, and 4 wind through some of the wildest high country, while Highway 50 is faster and more like a freeway.

El Dorado National Forest

[Fig. 19, Fig. 20, Fig. 21] The 1.2-million-acre Eldorado National Forest was created in 1905 for the Forest Service to manage the timber and grazing resources. The forest has the Desolation Wilderness, about 63,500 acres to the northeast, and the 105,000-acre Mokelumne Wilderness to the southeast. Both have hiking trails, wildflowers, and wildlife viewing.

The foothills in the forest and just west of the El Dorado are filled with recreation opportunities, natural history, and cultural richness. James Marshall's discovery of gold occurred just west of the forest. Some of the finest whitewater runs in California can be found on the American River, within and just outside forest boundaries. And foothill wineries just outside the western boundary of the forest are slowly making a name for themselves along Highway 50, which was once the route of the Pony Express.

The El Dorado also was known as a trans-Sierra corridor for pioneers in the nineteenth century. After Marshall's gold discovery, wagon trains came through regularly between 1850 and 1870.

One of the more interesting attractions is Robbs Hut, a rebuilt fire lookout. People can rent it and spend days in an area where the Forest Service once searched the horizon for any hint of smoke. For high Sierra sights, the El Dorado has the 10,380-foot Round Top, a granite spire that lives up to its name: It is quite round and barren on top.

▨ MARSHALL GOLD DISCOVERY STATE PARK

[Fig. 19(1)] A good piece of California history resides at Marshall Gold Discovery State Park, which commemorates the area where James Marshall found gold and started the gold rush in 1848. Museums and exhibits tell Marshall's story. Visitors can

Western Pine Beetle

Short, cylindrical beetles can be as destructive to conifer forests in the Sierra as any wildfire. The beetles are most devastating during drought when trees are weakened. Areas particularly hard hit by the western pine beetle *(Dendroctonus brevicomis)* are the Tahoe National Forest and other Northern California areas. Its favorite target is the ponderosa pine *(Pinus ponderosa)*. In spring, the beetle bores winding holes for its eggs between the bark and sapwood, weakening and eventually killing the tree. To combat a beetle infestation, forest managers usually have to chop down the afflicted tree and get it out of the forest.

WESTERN PINE BEETLE
(Dendroctonus brevicomis)
In 1917 and 1943, this beetle destroyed about 25 billion board feet of ponderosa pine along the Pacific coast, an amount of devastation that is seldom matched by any pest.

even pan for gold here.

Gold-bearing quartz veins often came in groupings, which were dubbed "lodes." The Northern Sierra foothills contain a metamorphic belt that produced about three-quarters of a billion dollars worth of gold in less than 20 years. It is still known as the "Mother Lode." Marshall Gold Discovery State Park today marks the birthplace of the Mother Lode in Coloma, just northeast of Sacramento and just west of present-day El Dorado National Forest.

Researchers are trying to piece together the mining history of Coloma. In the 1990s, scholars in search of gold rush-era building foundations found a late-1800s mining operation. Sometime in the 1890s, long after the 49ers had given up on their dreams of instant riches and returned home, a group of hopeful miners worked over the abandoned land in anticipation of finding a previously undiscovered vein of gold.

They tore down the decaying buildings and dug up the land beneath them. Teams of men forced the dirt through long sluices tossing large cobbles behind them as they worked. Fifty years after the discovery of gold, Coloma still remained a popular spot for eager gold seekers.

Archaeologists also recovered a lot of relatively undisturbed Chinese artifacts, which may indicate the ethnicity of the miners and the location of their temporary living site. Researchers also uncovered several postholes in this lot that indicate the existence of a post-mining era structure. In recent years, the archaeologists have set up tables at the Marshall park and invited the public to observe the activities of the excavators and talk to crew members.

The history of Marshall's discovery is well known. On January 24, 1848, Marshall found what erosion and the elements had been slowly revealing over the past 20 million years: gold. Marshall and his work crew were camped on the South Fork American River at Coloma. The crew was building a sawmill for John Sutter.

A few tiny gold nuggets, heavier than most other rocks, washed down and Marshall found them on that chilly January morning. Thus began the migration of half a million people from around the globe in search of gold and riches.

Gold began forming in these foothills a long time before Marshall, Sutter, and all the miners came. Between 80 million and 200 million years ago, 100 massive plutons (named after Pluto, the Roman god of the underworld) intruded into metamorphic marine layers beneath the Pacific Ocean.

Over many millions of years, magma, from which the pluton rocks were formed, continued to heat, cool, and crystallize into pyroxene, amphibole, biotite, and olivine. Later in the process, plagioclase feldspars and quartz formed. These minerals sealed veins in the sheets of granite and other rock, forming concentrations of asbestos, chromite, iron, silver, gold, and others.

Less than 50,000 years ago, the surrounding foothill areas began to fill with the many grasses of Central California. Though native grasses can be found, California's foothills and grasslands are now dominated by alien grass species. Many of them are native to the Mediterranean region and were transported to California by Spaniards and Mexicans. The seeds were meant to feed livestock. Others were probably carried in on the coats of animals.

By the mid-1800s, the alien varieties had a stranglehold on the grasslands. Some of the native bunchgrasses still exist. They include the foothill bluegrass (*Poa scabrella*) and the purple needlegrass (*Stipa pulchra*).

Directions: Drive 7 miles north on Highway 49 from Placerville at the junction of Highway 49 and Highway 50 east of the El Dorado National Forest.

Facilities: Museum, with exhibits that tell the story of the Gold Rush, a replica of the sawmill, and a number of historic buildings. Visitors also have the opportunity to pan for gold in the river or enjoy a picnic under the trees. A statue marks the gravesite of Marshall, who died in 1885.

Dates: Open year-round.

Closest town: Coloma, 0.5 mile.

For more information: Marshall Gold Discovery State Park, PO Box 265, Coloma, CA 95613. Phone (530) 622-3470. Or the Placerville County Visitor Information Center, phone (530) 887-2111.

FOLSOM POWERHOUSE

[Fig. 19(2)] Get a tour of the old powerhouse and a dose of history at the Folsom Powerhouse. Visitors can also see such natural sights as meadowfoam (*Limnanthes alba*), a white flower with white hairs on the stems. It is found in low areas where moisture accumulates. Wildflower lovers should also look for Fremont's tidytips (*Layia fremontii*), a stunning yellow flower that blooms in May in the Folsom area.

Gold mining created the town of Folsom and contributed the momentum to build the historic Folsom Powerhouse on the American River east of Sacramento. The sons of Horatio Livermore embraced the idea of hydroelectric power in the early 1890s, when experiments had been successfully completed on a limited basis in Germany and New York. Nothing had been attempted that was on the scale of the Livermore project.

They built a canal 9,500 feet long, which provided water to power four large electrical generators that had been built up the stone dam across the American River. The water also powered the bulkhead and headgates for the canal. The canal itself was finished in 1893. Folsom State Prison was the first to benefit from the dam when it put its own hydroelectric powerhouse into operation, also in 1893.

By 1895, the main powerhouse complex was completed and was ready to transmit power to Sacramento. It consisted of four 750-kilowatt electrical generators (also called "dynamos"), each more than 8 feet high, weighing more than 57,000 pounds. The General Electric Company manufactured them. The concept was simple: Turbines were driven by water surging through four 8-foot diameter penstocks. The generators have been altered a little over the years. The basic equipment is still where it was when the plant shut down in 1952. The plant closed because other sources of power became available, and owners decided not to continue this comparatively small project.

The state Department of Parks and Recreation acquired the Folsom Powerhouse project area, along with about 0.5 mile of the canal, as a donation from Pacific Gas & Electric Company in 1958. In the late 1960s or early 1970s, interpretive panels and displays depicting the history of the Folsom Powerhouse were installed in the garage at the north end of the office/shop building.

The Folsom Powerhouse is listed on the National Register of Historic Places (1981) as being significant in the areas of engineering and industry. It has been said that it represented a momentous advance in the science of generating and transmitting electricity. It is also a National Historic Civil Engineering Landmark (1975) and a National Historic Mechanical Engineering Landmark (1976), and it is designated as a California Registered Historical Landmark.

Directions: Drive Highway 50 about 10 miles east from Sacramento to the first City of Folsom Exit (Folsom Boulevard), turn left at the light and continue on Folsom, which will turn into Leidesdorf Street. At the light, turn right on Riley Street. The powerhouse is on the left-hand side. Turn left into the parking lot just past the first light (Scott Street) and before reaching the Rainbow Bridge.

Activities: Powerhouse tours, viewing displays.

Facilities: Powerhouse, historic displays, interpretive center.

Dates: Open year-round.

Closest town: Folsom, 2 miles.

For more information: Folsom Powerhouse, 7806 Folsom-Auburn Road, Folsom, CA 95630-1797. Phone (916) 988-0205 or (916) 988-0206.

AUBURN STATE RECREATION AREA

[Fig. 19(3)] The 35,000-acre Auburn State Recreation Area stretches along 40 miles of the North and Middle Forks of the American River where thousands of gold miners swarmed in the 1850s. Now, it is a recreation area for more than 500,000 visitors annually.

More than 100 miles of hiking and horse trails wind through the steep American River canyons and along the American River. The most famous trail is the Western States Trail, which runs 100 miles from Lake Tahoe to Auburn, with over 20 miles in the recreation area. A map showing the trails is available from the recreation area office.

Mountain bicycling is a popular activity as well. The maximum speed on all trails is 15 miles per hour. The maximum speed is 5 miles per hour when passing pedestrians and equestrians and when approaching blind curves.

The historic Stagecoach Trail from Russell Road in Auburn to the Old Foresthill Road Bridge on the North Fork of the American River connects with the fire road to the West End of the big Foresthill Bridge.

The recreation area offers a 9.5-mile run on the North Fork American from the Iowa Hill Bridge to Ponderosa Bridge. Several difficult rapids are encountered, most notably these: Chamberlin Falls, Staircase Rapids, and Bogus Thunder. Trips down this river are typically made in one day.

Boating the North Fork requires a sound background in technical whitewater skills. The most desirable flow range is between 1,500 and 3,000 cubic feet per second (3,000 to 6,000 acre-foot flows per day).

In the recreation area, one-, two-, or three-day trips are available on the challenging Middle Fork American River. The 15-mile run from Oxbow put-in to Greenwood take-out features several very fast rapids, as well as numerous slower rapids. Most notable are the Tunnel Chute and Kanaka Gulch.

Where the water does not run so fast, the riparian woodland has a variety of vegetation worth seeing. White alder (*Alnus rhombifolia*) and the bigleaf maple (*Acer macrophyllum*) are among the most common sights in the recreation area.

Riparian or riverside vegetation is reduced to a thin ribbon around the river in steeper, rocky terrain. But as the river reaches more gentle inclines farther down the mountain, nearer to the Central Valley, the soils become looser, more saturated with nutrients, and able to support more plant life.

Shrubs include California pipe vine (*Aristolochia californica*), osoberry (*Osmaronia cerasiformis*), and California wild grape (*Vitis californica*). All are fairly uncommon shrubs in the Sierra foothills, except alongside streams such as the American River.

Sierra Juniper

The Western or Sierra juniper (*Juniperas occidentalis*) is known for size and longevity, especially in the Stanislaus National Forest. One of the oldest known Western junipers known in the world is named Bennett after the naturalist Clarence Bennett, who devoted much of his life to the study of the tree.

The juniper can rival the famed bristlecone pine (*Pinus aristata*), which is known to be almost 5,000 years old. The Bennett juniper in Stanislaus is estimated to be more than 3,000 years old, though no one is certain. A fallen branch 3 inches in diameter contained 550 annual rings. It took close to 1,000 years for the tree to add the outer foot to its trunk.

With its deep, heavy root system, the juniper can withstand the hostile Sierra winters. The tree clings to granite and can be found on rocky summits, where it is often scarred by lightning.

The juniper's short, conical, and often-twisted trunk is particularly photogenic. To find the Bennett juniper, drive east on Highway 108 in Tuolumne County 43 miles from Sonora. Turn right on Forest Road 5N01 and follow the signs.

Sometimes, natural history is easiest to find just a few feet from an interstate highway. On the way to Auburn State Recreation Area, the edges of an eroded granite pluton perhaps 50 million years old are apparent along Interstate 80. It was a single bubble of granite that somehow separated from the main plutons many miles away.

Black Mariposa slate can be seen just beyond the pluton to the east. A small ridge farther east is actually a former rolling hill that was part of the Sierra more than 50 million years go, long before the range's uplift tilted the ridge. To the west, visitors can find younger sediments from Sierra erosion over the past 20 million years.

Directions: Drive east on Interstate 80 about 12 miles from the city of Auburn, northeast of Sacramento. Turn right on the main access route, the Auburn-Foresthill Road, which leads to the recreation area. Follow the signs.

Activities: Hiking, swimming, boating, fishing, camping, mountain biking, whitewater boating, and gold panning.

Dates: Open year-round.

Fees: None.

Closest town: Auburn, 1 mile.

For more information: State Parks Management District: American River, PO Box 3266, Auburn, CA 95604-3266. Phone (530) 885-4527. For boating information, contact the Whitewater Management Office of the district, phone (530) 885-5648.

FOOTHILL WINERIES

[Fig. 19(4)] When people think of California wineries, they're usually thinking about the ones in Napa. But the Central Sierra foothills are slowly becoming known for the fruit of the grape. People make a brief tour of the wineries along Highway 50, west of Lake Tahoe, and enjoy tasting wines in an area that actually has a bit of history in wine-making.

In the nineteenth century, when Napa was known for prunes, Sierra Nevada foothill communities had several dozen wineries. The wineries sprang up in El Dorado County after the 1849 Gold Rush. Miners needed to diversify their work as the mining craze died out.

But population in the gold mining areas began to dwindle. By the beginning of the twentieth century, there were fewer wineries. Then Prohibition snuffed out whatever was left of the winery business. Soon, El Dorado County became more known for timber.

The 1970s brought new interest when a member of a Napa wine family invested in a Placerville pear orchard and replanted it with wine grapes. The buyer, Greg Boeger, a descendent of the Nichelini family of Napa, realized the climate in the foothills was very close to the Napa climate—warm summers, dry autumns, and cool, wet winters.

WESTERN OR SIERRA JUNIPER
(Juniperas occidentalis)
This is a small tree, 20 to 60 feet tall and 1 to 3 feet in diameter, found on rocky slopes.

Others saw Boeger's success and began moving into El Dorado County. Now almost two dozen wineries are flourishing in this area. The highest is at 3,000 feet in elevation. Some of the more popular types of wines include chardonnay, cabernet sauvignon, and zinfandel. The Boeger spread, about 50 acres, grows 25 different kinds of wine grapes.

Wine tasting and touring is slowly becoming a tradition in the Central Sierra foothills. The wineries are generally located along Highway 50 about an hour west of Lake Tahoe just east of Placerville. Most open on weekends for tasting and some are open daily. Picnic areas are available for those who wish to bring a basket and purchase a bottle of wine.

The wineries also benefit from the multitude of apple orchards in the area. Each autumn, people take the turnoff near Placerville—Schnells School Road from the west or Carson Road from the east—to visit the apple orchards to sample the fruit. People usually like to pick their own. And, right next door to the largest orchards, they find wineries.

Other wineries are scattered throughout the foothills all the way down to Mariposa County near Yosemite. According to many wine experts, the foothill wineries are gaining on the prestigious the Napa-area wineries.

People are beginning to mark their calendars for April because the El Dorado wineries get together to present Passport Weekend. On the first and second weekends of April, people can buy a two-day pass to 18 wineries to eat gourmet food and cheeses as they sample wines. About 2,500 people attended in 1999.

Directions: From Lake Tahoe, drive about 50 miles east on Highway 50 to Carson Road, and exit to the north. Drive 3 miles to begin seeing wineries.

Activities: Picnics, wine tasting, wine purchasing.

Facilities: Wine tasting rooms, picnic tables, restrooms. A partial list of wineries includes the following: Boeger Winery, 1709 Carson Road, Placerville, CA 95667, phone (530) 622-8094; Coulson Winery, 3550 Carson Road, Camino, CA 95709, phone (530) 644-2854; Fitzpatrick Winery, 7740 Fairplay Road, Somerset, CA 95684, phone (530) 620-3248; Granite Springs Winery, 5050 Granite Springs Winery Road, Somerset, CA 95684, phone (530) 620-6395; and Venezio Winery & Vineyard, 3520 Overton Road, Cool, CA 95614, phone (530) 885-6815.

Dates: Open year-round. Passport Weekend in April.

Fees: There are fees for wine.

Closest town: Placerville.

For more information: El Dorado Winery Association, PO Box 1614, Placerville, CA 95667. Phone (800) 306-3956.

ROBBS HUT

[Fig. 20(3)] A stay at Robbs Hut is a chance to get away from it all for several days and sample the rustic, simple living of fire lookouts. The views are magnificent if you don't mind a little hiking to get to Robbs Hut. This slice of outdoor life was made possible by the U.S. Forest Service's change in thinking about fires.

The U.S. Forest Service began spotting Sierra fires and snuffing them quickly in the early part of the twentieth century, building many lookouts such as Robbs Hut in the El Dorado National Forest. The mountain hut, constructed in 1934 and decommissioned from active status in 1978, is a midelevation Sierra vantage point at 6,686-foot Robbs Peak, and it is a delight for outdoor enthusiasts who can now rent it for overnight use.

Just as the Forest Service's use for Robbs Hut has changed, its practice of extinguishing forest fires on sight has been altered. One person would reside in lookouts such as Robbs Hut from late June until early September, watching for fires all day and, in very dry conditions, seven days a week.

The practice of suppressing the fires led to overgrown brush at many elevations in the Sierra. Biologists, ecologists, and the Forest Service had no idea that thick brush would set up the ecosystem for huge wildfires that would climb to canopies of even the highest trees. Such a fire burned hundreds of thousands of Sierra woodland acres in 1978.

Finally, officials began to understand why the Miwok and other tribes many centuries ago regularly burned understories of brush. The Native Americans knew the forest ecosystem relied on fire to thin out areas and create places where natural competition would allow a diverse biotic community.

Fire promoted the basic forest health that Native Americans needed. It also opened clear areas through which tribes could see surprise attacks and defend themselves.

Now, the Forest Service and the National Park Service allow some areas to burn naturally when lightning sets off fires. It is still important to spot the fires, but now government agencies are using fire as a forest management tool to protect resources.

The resources being protected around Robbs Hut are typical of the 3,000- to 7,000-foot elevation on the Central Sierra's west slope. In some tree stands around Robbs Hutt there are five different conifers. The white fir *(Abies concolor)* is at somewhat higher elevations. The yellow or ponderosa pine *(Pinus ponderosa)* is more acclimated to the lower end, more easily adapting to drier conditions. Other trees include the sugar pine *(Pinus lambertiana)*, incense cedar *(Calocedrus decurrens)*, and the black oak *(Quercus kelloggii)*.

Robbs Hut is not for the inexperienced hiker or outdoors person. Access to the Robbs Peak Lookout during winter and early spring is by foot, skis, or snowmobile, depending on snow conditions. At the bottom of the road to the hut there is a gate, which is always locked in the winter. The Forest Service will provide combinations to the locks for anyone who rents the cabin.

The road into the area is passable in a regular automobile during summer, but it is not plowed in the winter. At times, a four-wheel drive vehicle is required to get up the road.

The elevation gain from the parking area to the bunkhouse is more than 1,000 feet. The trip from the car to the hut can take from two to six hours to complete.

Directions: Drive east on Highway 50 to Riverton, 20 miles east of Placerville. Turn left on Ice House Road (Forest Road 3) and go 23 miles to the Robbs Peak Road turnoff and turn left. Drive about 20 miles to Forest Service Road 13N31 and turn left. In the winter, there is a locked gate at this road. In summer, it is unlocked. Park and follow the road on foot or on skis for 3 miles. The road (trail) to Robbs Hut is intermittently marked with blue diamonds; however, do not rely on the markings alone. A map and compass skills may be necessary to locate the hut under certain conditions. A detailed Forest Service map is suggested.

Activities: Backcountry skiing, mountain biking, hiking, and backpacking.

Facilities: Bunkhouse sleeps six and is equipped with a gas fireplace as the sole source of heat, a two-burner propane cooking stove, three sleeping platforms, mattresses, six wool blankets, an axe, a shovel, a bucket, cleaning gear, and a fire extinguisher. The stove and permanently mounted propane lights are served by piped-in propane.

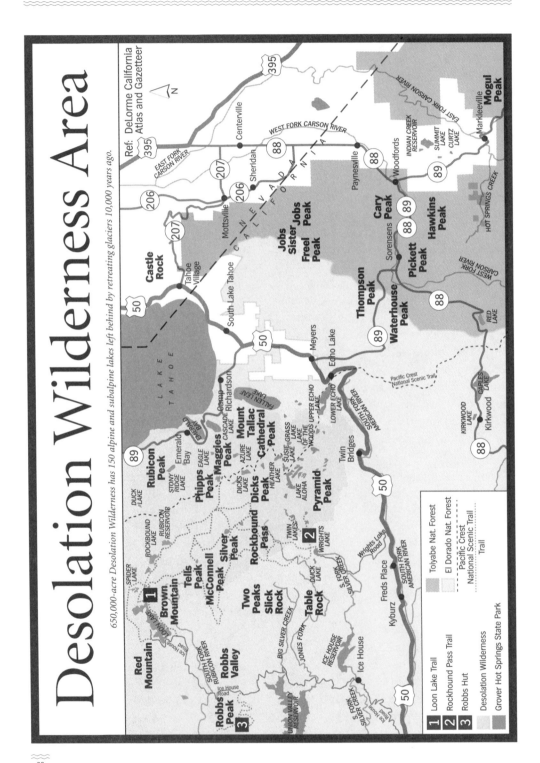

Desolation Wilderness Area

650,000-acre Desolation Wilderness has 150 alpine and subalpine lakes left behind by retreating glaciers 10,000 years ago.

Ref: DeLorme California Atlas and Gazetteer

Dates: The road and hut are open year-round.

Fees: There is a fee for overnight stays.

Closest town: Riverton, 4 miles.

For more information: Eldorado National Forest Information Center, 3070 Camino Heights Drive, Camino, CA 95709. Phone (530) 644-6048.

DESOLATION WILDERNESS

[Fig. 20] Visitors can see what the retreating glacial age left behind 10,000 years ago in the 63,500-acre Desolation Wilderness—150 alpine and subalpine lakes in the ancient, high-elevation granite. Unfortunately, there are sometimes so many people hiking here that it feels less desolate and less like wilderness than almost any other Sierra wildlands.

The lakes, the glacial remnants, and the sights make it one of the most popular wildernesses in California. It is also popular because it is so conveniently located on the busy corridor between Lake Tahoe to the east and San Francisco and Sacramento to the west.

In Glen Alpine Valley, the signs of a glacier's passing are apparent on the *roche moutonnée* found there. The granite feature was fashioned by a glacier that wore away a massive boulder in a gradual plane on one side and in a sharper, more jagged way on the other. About 20,000 years ago, a glacier created these landmarks in Glen Alpine Valley as well as in Desolation Valley to the southwest.

The name "*roche moutonnée*" came from Horace Benedict de Saussure. When he saw the features at Tuolumne Meadows in present-day Yosemite National Park, he called them *roche moutonnée*, meaning they looked like a flock of "rock sheep" at a distance.

Driving up Highway 50 to the Desolation Wilderness, the road cuts reveal a deep history of the Sierra in the Eldorado National Forest. At one point, before reaching Echo Summit, visitors will see a low spot between Pollock Pines and Riverton at the South Fork of the American River. Through erosion of the volcanic ash, perhaps 5 to 10 million years old, the oldest sedimentary rocks on the western slope of the Sierra are exposed. The sedimentary rocks date back to 200 to 300 million years ago before the sea floor began descending.

Within the wilderness, the granite batholith peeks out from beneath the volcanic rock as well. Elevations range from 6,500 feet to more than 10,000.

The elevations create interesting habitats that attract an array of wildlife. The lower elevations of the Desolation Wilderness provide cedar and fir trees that seed-eating creatures prefer. California ground squirrel (*Citellus beecheyi*), deer mouse (*Peromyscus maniculatus*), bushy-tailed wood rat (*Neotoma cinerea*), and Steller's jay (*Cyanocitta stelleri*) are good examples.

Visitors also may encounter the California mountain king snake (*Lampropeltis zonata*), a 20- to 40-inch snake with red, white, and black bands circling its body.

This is a very secretive snake, but it is also extremely common, so visitors might see one in the moist forest near rocks or along a stream with fallen timber nearby. Don't distressed. This snake is completely harmless.

In the subalpine meadows of the wilderness, the volcanic soils are loose and filled with nutrients to grow such plants as the subalpine shooting star *(Dodecatheon subalpinum)*, which requires moisture and soils that allow its root system to easily develop. When soils become soggy—especially in meadows where the snowmelt is considerable in June and July—the greater elephant's head *(Pedicularis groenlandica)* is found, growing a beautiful pink to deep rose-colored flower.

The Desolation Wilderness also has numerous migratory birds that visit the upper-elevation forest, known as the red fir *(Abies magnifica)* and lodgepole pine *(Pinus murrayana)* belts. The common merganser *(Mergus merganser)*, olive-sided flycatcher *(Nuttallornis borealis)*, Brewer's blackbird *(Euphagus cyanocephalus)*, chipping sparrow *(Spizella passerina)*, and the pine siskin *(Spinus pinus)* are among the seasonal visitors that nest and nurture their young in the wilderness.

The crowds gather at Wrights, Echo, Fallen Leaf, and Eagle Falls trailheads. Lighter use occurs in northwest portions of the wilderness. Open wood fires are not allowed, but portable stoves are.

This wilderness has a 700-person limit for overnight use between June 15 and Labor Day. Group size limit is always 15, and smaller groups are recommended for some heavily used trails. As with other wildernesses, travelers may hike or ride on horses or llamas. In Desolation Wilderness there are no buildings or roads. The wilderness can be entered by 15 trailheads; a detailed map is available from the U.S. Forest Service.

Directions: From Lake Tahoe, take Highway 89 south along the eastern edge of the wilderness to one of several trails of the wilderness. The trails include Eagle Falls, Bayview, Tallac, Cathedral, Glenn Alpine, and Echo Lake. Most are within 2 to 4 miles of the wilderness.

Activities: Hiking, camping, swimming, backpacking.

Facilities: Some campgrounds.

Dates: Open June through Sept.

Fees: There are fees for wilderness permits.

Closest town: Twin Bridges, 2.5 miles south of the wilderness off of Highway 50.

For more information: Eldorado National Forest Information Center, 3070 Camino Heights Drive, Camino, CA 95709. Phone (530) 644-6048.

LOON LAKE TRAIL

[Fig. 20(1)] People who want to stay out in the Desolation Wilderness for two or three days will probably camp out along this trail and go all the way to Blakely Trail. Most day hikers will start at Pleasant Campground, hike in 6 or 8 miles to Rock-hound Lake or Rubicon Reservoir and turn around.

The sights include the South Fork Rubicon River and Loon Lake, where campsites can be found at Loon Lake Campground. Brown Mountain, to the southeast, may have been a basaltic volcano at some point.

Loon, Rockhound, and Rubicon lakes are all part of a system that feeds water to Sacramento. If they begin to look a little puny in late summer, it's because the water is being siphoned to the Central Valley.

An amphibian of interest in this area is the ensatina *(Ensatina eschscholtzi)*, about 2 inches in length with orange spots. This creature is not found at the higher elevations of this trail, so look for it early in the hike. It lives around rotting wood near streams, and it is more common below 6,000 feet. But the ensatina, active between April and September, has been seen in places along this trail. If startled, it will arch its back and swing its tail.

Directions: Drive about 25 miles east of Placerville on Highway 50, turn left on Ice House Road. Drive 22 more miles on Ice House Road (Forest Route 3) until reaching Loon Lake Road, then branch right. Drive 5 miles to a fork, take the right fork, and go 0.5 mile to an equestrian campground. Continue on the same road and fork right, curving counterclockwise around a group camp. Enter the trailhead parking area where day wilderness permits are available.

Trail: 13.8 miles, one-way.

Elevation: 800-foot gain, high point 7,210 feet.

Degree of difficulty: Moderate.

Surface: Rocky footpath with outcroppings, occasional narrowing, and stretches of abandoned roads.

ROCKHOUND PASS TRAIL

[Fig. 20(2)] Glaciers receding about 17,000 years ago left their calling cards not far from Beauty Lake on the Rockhound Pass Trail to Pearl Lake. There are some huge boulders or erratics remaining. The hiking is easy, but the trail is also a place four-wheel-drive vehicles are known to frequent in the summer months.

By the time hikers reach Pearl Lake, they have crossed glacial sediments and moraines that have deep, rich histories in the last Ice Age. Campsites are easily found, but it's always best to take a hard look at any cliff or overhang first. Exfoliation and rockfall continues in much of the Sierra. This place is no different.

Directions: Drive about 25 miles east of Placerville on Highway 50, turn left on Ice House Road. Drive 33 miles on Ice House Road (Forest Route 3) to Forest Route 32 and turn right. Drive 9 more miles, passing three campgrounds, and meeting Forest Route 4 or Wrights Lake Road. Turn left and drive 1.9 miles to another branch in the road, and go right. It will take you past Wrights Lake Horse Camp. Continue less than 0.5 mile to the Wrights Lake Information Kiosk for a wilderness permit. Past the kiosk, bear left and drive for about 0.25 mile and there is parking on the left. Follow signs for the Rockhound Pass trailhead from Wrights Lake to the first stop, Beauty Lake.

Trail: 4.7 miles, one-way.

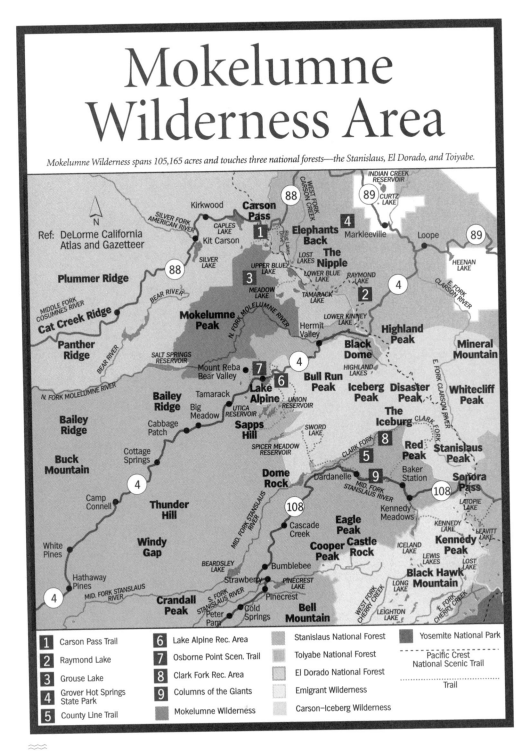

Mokelumne Wilderness Area

Mokelumne Wilderness spans 105,165 acres and touches three national forests—the Stanislaus, El Dorado, and Toiyabe.

Ref: DeLorme California
Atlas and Gazetteer

1	Carson Pass Trail	6	Lake Alpine Rec. Area		Stanislaus National Forest		Yosemite National Park
2	Raymond Lake	7	Osborne Point Scen. Trail		Toiyabe National Forest	- - -	Pacific Crest National Scenic Trail
3	Grouse Lake	8	Clark Fork Rec. Area		El Dorado National Forest		
4	Grover Hot Springs State Park	9	Columns of the Giants		Emigrant Wilderness	......	Trail
5	County Line Trail		Mokelumne Wilderness		Carson–Iceberg Wilderness		

Elevation: 500-foot gain, high point 7,350 feet.
Degree of difficulty: Moderate.
Surface: Footpath with outcroppings, marked with occasional trail ducks (piles of rock).

MOKELUMNE WILDERNESS

[Fig. 21] The 9,334-foot Mokelumne Peak stands high above the steep walls of the Mokelumne River canyon. The peak is probably 50 million to 65 million years old, meaning dinosaurs once treaded upon its eroded granite features.

It is not generally a destination for day hikers or the casual visitor in the Mokelumne Wilderness, which spans 105,165 acres and spreads across the Sierra crest to touch three national forests, the Stanislaus, El Dorado, and Toiyabe. But it is characteristic of the steep and primitive landscape that can be seen in this area when hiking the more than 100 miles of trails.

As with many areas in the Central Sierra, the Mokelumne was covered with volcanic eruptions in the past 20 million years and glaciated in the last 2 million years. Glacial moraines dammed lakes in the Bear River-Tanglefoot Canyon area.

On the southern border of the wilderness, just inside the Stanislaus National Forest, is 8,600-foot Mount Reba, the site where a rare fossil was found. This floral fossil dates back about 7 million years and was preserved in the volcanic flows that occurred during a time of faulting and uplifting in the Sierra. Scientists believe the flora in the fossil could only have survived in temperatures colder than tropical weather, which had dominated the Sierra about 33 million years ago. The fossil helps establish that Sierra weather was cooling down from the tropical patterns and slowly approaching the Ice Age that began 2 million years ago.

In the nineteenth century, the Mokelumne Wilderness was used for early emigrant routes of travel from Lake Tahoe to Calaveras Big Trees and for mining and grazing. Other routes slowly became more heavily used in the twentieth century; the area came to be protected as part of the National Wilderness Preservation System in 1964. Boundaries were expanded in 1984.

Besides the Sierra's white fir (*Abies concolor*) and lodgepole pine (*Pinus murrayana*) as well as other familiar trees, the Mokelumne has spectacular wildflowers. The selection includes Lemmon's wild ginger (*Assarum lemmoni*) and the alpine aster (*Aster alpigenus*). The aster is particularly noticeable with its pink to purple flower head peeking out of mountain meadows in the Mokelumne.

Varieties come and go as the warmer weather begins at lower elevations and moves to the higher elevations in late June, July, and August. In that way, spring seems to be blooming somewhere all through the summer. Such signature western slope flowers as the Sierra lupine (*Lupinus grayi*) are also characteristic of the dry wooded areas when summer warms up the Central Sierra.

In August around the Mokelumne, such mammals at the gray fox (*Urocyon cinereoargenteus)* are feeding on manzanita (*Arctostaphylos*) or coffeeberries (*Rhamnus rubra*). The fox are active day and night. They are more plentiful and easier to spot than the red fox (*Vulpes fulva*), which live in the higher elevations, occasionally straying down to about 6,000 feet.

Mokelumne is not known for its lakes as much as it is for its rocks. But Frog Lake, Winnemucca Lake, Round Top Lake, Fourth of July Lake, and Emigrant Lake are considered interesting attractions. The wilderness can be entered from 29 trailheads.

Directions: The wilderness is bordered by Highway 4 on the south and State Highway 88 on the north. Drive 45 miles east of Pioneer on Highway 88 to the Kirkwood Ski Area and Caples Lake, where northside trailheads can be found. Drive 40 miles east on Highway 4 to Hermit Valley, where more southeast trailheads can be found.

Activities: Hiking, backpacking, camping, swimming, and boating.

Dates: Open June through Sept.

Fees: There is no fee for hiking permits, but fees are charged for day-use parking at Carson Pass and Meiss trailheads off of Highway 88.

Closest town: Kirkwood, on Highway 88, about 2 miles from the wilderness.

For more information: Eldorado National Forest Information Center, 3070 Camino Heights Drive, Camino, CA 95709. Phone (530) 644-6048. Amador Ranger Station, 26820 Silver Drive, Pioneer, CA 95666. Phone (209) 295-4251.

CARSON PASS TRAIL

[Fig. 21(1)] Though the wilderness has no roads and motorized travel is prohibited, visitors can see panoramics from several short hikes. All are accessible from Highway 88, which runs east and west just north of the wilderness. On the western side, Highway 88 goes through the El Dorado National Forest; on the east, it passes through Toiyabe National Forest.

Once visitors travel beyond the Sierra crest at Carson Pass, vegetation and soils will change visibly. The east side is drier because of prevailing weather patterns and the influence of the Sierra itself (*see* page 203 for further explanation of Eastern Sierra weather). The soils are more porous. There are fewer lakes, and plants become sparser, with Great Basin sagebrush (*Artemesia tridentata*) dominating the ecosystem.

On the western side, there are several lakes with glacial histories. Many are easy to reach and provide opportunities to photograph wildflowers, alpine and subalpine plant species. The hikes include Woods Lake trailhead to Winnemucca Lake, Woods Lake trailhead to Round Top

RED FOX
(Vulpes fulva)

Lake near the Lost Cabin Mine Trail, and the Caples trailhead to Emigrant Lake.

An easy-to-find trail, which passes through an area representative of the landscape in the Mokelumne, is the Carson Pass Trail to Winnemucca Lake. As with many trails in California, it is a well-worn route, established without blazes. Along the way, according to U.S. Geological Survey maps, the trail passes directly over a large fault that runs east toward Hope Valley.

Perhaps the first people to use this trail were the various Native Americans who inhabited the area for 10,000 years. The most recent inhabitants, the Miwok from the west slope and the Washoe of the Great Basin, spent the warmer months hunting in the high country and trading with each other.

Explorers such as Jedediah Smith (1826) and John C. Fremont and Kit Carson (1844) were the first Euro-Americans to visit the Mokelumne Wilderness. In 1848, the Mormon Battalion successfully pioneered a trail just south of present day Carson Pass in a trek from Sutter's Fort to Salt Lake City, and later, thousands of emigrants followed this route on the way to the gold fields of California. Shepherds later grazed stock in the spring and summer.

Directions: Drive to Carson Pass, about 100 miles east of Highway 99 on Highway 88, or about 20 miles south of Highway 50 from the Lake Tahoe area on Highway 88. Go to the Carson Pass Visitor Center at the south end of the long turnout to find the trailhead.

Trail: 2.5 miles one-way to Winnemucca Lake.

Elevation: 8,590 feet to 7,700 feet.

Degree of difficulty: Moderate.

Surface: Rocky, steep in places but easy to follow.

RAYMOND LAKE

[Fig. 21(2)] Take two or three days to enjoy a hike along the Pacific Crest Trail to Raymond Lake, passing volcanic pillars, domes, and all kinds of streams. But be careful. This trail crosses Highway 4 near Ebbetts Pass. That's probably about as much danger as most hikers will see.

The trail passes Upper Kinney Lake, Pennsylvania Creek and Reynolds Peak before reaching Raymond Canyon. The up-and-down hike at this elevation—mostly over 8,000 feet—will make most backpackers sleep at night. Small campsites are available at Raymond Lake.

Directions: Drive Highway 4 to Ebbetts Pass at the crest of the Sierra and park about 0.5 mile east of the pass in the Pacific Crest Trail parking lot.

Trail: 21.2 miles round-trip.

Elevation: 1,250-foot gain, high point 9,000 feet.

Degree of difficulty: Moderate.

Surface: Bedrock granite, footpath, trail ducks (small piles of rocks as markers).

GROUSE LAKE

[Fig. 21(3)] For those who do not want to put in an eight-hour day to complete this hike, there are campgrounds all along this trail. Whether you camp or day hike, the trip to this tarn is an eventful route filled with meadows and subalpine vegetation.

After crossing three basins and ascending a rocky ridge, the views of the Mokelumne Wilderness are stunning. The ridge tops out at more than 9,000 feet, but the reward is a swift descent to the lake and campsites at 8,400 feet where the Sierra air is a little thin but definitely clear.

Directions: From the west, drive 6.5 miles past Carson Pass on Highway 88, and turn right on Blue Lake Road. Drive 12 miles on Blue Lake Road until you reach an intersection at Lower Blue Lake. Turn right, and drive about 2 miles on a Pacific Gas & Electric Company road. Park at the base of Upper Blue Lake Dam. Trailhead is on the left side of the parking lot.

Trail: 12 miles, round-trip.

Elevation: 1,300-foot gain, high point 9,200 feet.

Degree of difficulty: Moderate.

Surface: Granite pathway, sometimes difficult to follow. Look for trail ducks (small piles of rocks).

INDIAN GRINDING ROCK STATE HISTORIC PARK

[Fig. 19(5)] In the foothills west of the El Dorado National Forest, there are 1,185 grinding holes in outcroppings of marbleized limestone made by Native Americans who lived here for many centuries and still live here today. It is the largest collection of bedrock mortar holes found anywhere on a single stone in North America.

The Miwok Indians pounded acorns from the abundant valley oak *(Quercus lobata)*, the stately California oak that grows to 9 feet in trunk diameter and has wide, drooping branchlets. The tree, which is found on the Sierra's western slope below 4,000 feet, provides acorns to the California woodpecker *(Melanerpes formicivorous)*. The flora include a number of flowering plants, such as the monkey-flower *(Mimlus torrey)*, white mariposa lily *(Calochortus venustus)*, and Sierra iris *(Iris hartwegii)*.

In the surrounding woodland near this valley, visitors can hear the calling of a hermit thrush *(Catharus guttata)* nesting in the nearby foothills. The thrush, like many birds of the wooded foothills, prefers living near the ground under a canopy of leaves. The 135-acre park has many bird species, much as it did when the Miwok first inhabited it.

To the Miwok, the place is known as *Chaw'se*, the pounding stone. The Miwok would slowly pound seeds and acorns into meal, leaving the distinctive cup-shaped impressions that survive today. The Miwok's daily activities here included weaving baskets, making flour from acorns, and processing other plants for food, fiber, and medicines. Along with all those mortar holes, there are many decorative carvings in the rock—spokes, human tracks, wavy lines. These petroglyphs are thought to be 2,000 to 3,000 years old. This is the only place where such mortar holes and petroglyphs occur together.

The marbleized limestone rock is quite fragile and susceptible to breaking and fracturing with time and weathering. Many petroglyphs are fading, and visitors in future generations will not be able to see this historic artwork.

Directions: From the junction of Highway 49 and Highway 88, east of Stockton, drive 8 miles to Pine Grove, turn left on Pine Grove-Volcano Road. Go 1 mile to the park on the left side of the road.

Facilities: Campground with 23 sites, picnic area, bathrooms, museum, and replica village.

Dates: Open year-round.

Fee: There is an entrance fee.

Closest town: Pine Grove, 2 miles west on Highway 88.

For more information: Indian Grinding Rock State Historic Park, 14881 Pine Grove-Volcano Road, Pine Grove, CA 95655. Phone (209) 296-7488.

Stanislaus National Forest

[Fig. 21, Fig. 22, Fig. 23, Fig. 24] Created in 1891, the 900,000-acre Stanislaus National Forest is one of the oldest national forests in California and the U.S. Two mammoth wildernesses spread across the upper elevations of the Stanislaus. The imposing granite of the 160,000-acre Carson-Iceberg Wilderness is on the east flank of the forest, while the volcanic-dominated Emigrant Wilderness covers 113,000 acres to the northeast.

Highway 108 passes between the two wildernesses through a 5-mile gap. At the Sierra crest, Highway 108 crosses the Sierra crest through Sonora Pass to the dry, high-desert conditions on the east side of the mountain range. The area around the pass is where the Sierra shows off its high elevation. At Carson Pass, the 11,750-foot Leavitt Peak stands to the north and the 11,462-foot Sonora Peak stands to the south. Leavitt is in the Emigrant Wilderness; Sonora is in the Carson-Iceberg.

A little farther west down the slope, the Wild and Scenic Tuolumne River runs for 28 miles in the southern part of the forest. Though the river is dammed to the east—forming Hetch Hetchy Reservoir in Yosemite National Park—there are no other dams on the river through Stanislaus National Forest. The river is considered a challenge even for the most experienced rafters and kayakers.

Recreation areas include Pinecrest Lake on Highway 108 and Lake Alpine along the Highway 4 corridor. There are also ski resorts, including Dodge Ridge Ski Area and Mount Reba Ski Area. In the foothills, east of Stanislaus, there are historic sites, such as the Colombia State Historic Park. The nearby Red Hills also provide a nature preserve that tells visitors about the soils in California.

❧ CARSON-ICEBERG WILDERNESS

[Fig. 22] Glacial history can be a consuming fascination in the 160,000-acre Carson-Iceberg Wilderness. Straddling the crest of the Sierra, with one foot in the Toiyabe National Forest and one in the Stanislaus, the Carson-Iceberg displays evidence of a glacier that existed about 26,000 years ago. Hiking, camping, backpacking, and sight-seeing are the reasons people come to this backcountry. And the glacial past is what created the sights.

In places such as Disaster Creek and Arnot Creek canyons, two glaciers flowed down to meet another larger body of ice flowing down the Stanislaus River. The one on the North Fork Mokelumne River was 1,300 feet deep, covering such present-day features as Highland Lakes. It was 500 feet thick even over Ebbetts Peak, more than 10,000 feet high.

The granite glacial basins are only part of the fascination, though. Between 10 and 20 million years ago, volcanic eruptions created lahars, or volcanic mudflows. They continued sporadically until just about 100,000 years ago, and they may occur again some day because the magma has not completely cooled.

Many lava flows rolled down rivers, such as the Stanislaus River, where they bonded with the granitic rock. As in other Sierra locations where this happened, the processes of erosion lowered the surrounding landscape, leaving a flattop or Table Mountain in the ancient stream beds. Such an andesite remnant, a 9 million-year-old Table Mountain, can be seen in the lower elevations at the junction of Highway 108 and Highway 120.

The Dardanelles is considered the most striking volcanic feature of this wilderness, and it is a prime example of this upside-down geology. A lava flow of perhaps 2,000 feet in depth swallowed this area about 10 million years ago, forming the Dardanelles palisade at the bottom of a canyon. Because of the erosion all around it, the Dardanelles today stands 3,000 feet above the Stanislaus River.

Lava flow also is associated with the 150,000-year-old basalt formation known as Columns of the Giants, near Sonora Pass on Highway 108, one of two main routes to Carson-Iceberg. The northerly route, Highway 4, runs between the Mokelumne Wilderness to the north, and the Carson-Iceberg to the south.

The Carson-Iceberg's higher elevations are considered alpine—9,900 feet and higher in this part of the Sierra. Only the hardiest vegetation can survive the long, cold winters and the eight-week growing season in the warmer weather. Scientists refer to this region as the dwarfed timberline belt, where trees and shrubs do not reach their full height.

The rocky soil is thin and the surface is blasted by freezing winds, even in May and June. The cutleaf daisy *(Erigeron compositus)* adapts by spreading along the granite surfaces and wedging roots into cracks and crevices. The sky pilot *(Polemonium eximum)* is another example, using its leaves to insulate the flowering stock.

Flowers in these harsh conditions are formed by buds that grew the previous year.

So, a cold Sierra summer could mean few flowers a year later. Examples of flowers include the alpine buttercup *(Ranunculus eschscholtzii)*, alpine paintbrush *(Castilleja nana)*, rosy stonecrop *(Sedum rosea)*, and alpine goldenrod *(Solidago multriadiata)*.

Visitors will not find a lot of animals in these forbidding conditions. Occasionally a rare red fox *(Vulpes fulva)* may wander through the talus in high elevation areas. The yellow-bellied marmot *(Marmota flavientris)*—an inspired thief around any hiker who leaves food unsupervised—and the alpine chipmunk *(Eutamias alpinus)* are about the only companions that high-elevation travelers will find up here.

The Carson-Iceberg gets its name from the Carson River, named after adventurer and explorer Kit Carson, and the distinctive granite formation called The Iceberg in the southern part of the wilderness near Clark Fork Road. As the mining boom of the 1840s became the bust of the 1860s, grazing took hold in the area. Along the Driveway Trail in the Silver Valley area, hikers will see something the Basque sheepherders called an *arri mutillak* or stone boy, basically a pile of rocks the sheepherders made to pass the time.

More than 100 miles of trails are spread throughout, giving visitors the opportunity for long backpacking tours or short jaunts. Motorized travel is not allowed.

Directions: For entrance on the north side of the wilderness, drive Highway 4 about 35 miles east of Calaveras Ranger Station at Hathaway Pines to the east side of Lake Alpine to find trailheads for Duck Lake and Rock Lake. Or continue east on Highway 4 another 10 miles to the Highland Lakes turnoff, then go 6 miles to reach trailheads. For entrance on the south side, drive 40 miles east of Sonora on Highway 108 and bear left or north on Clark Fork Road to pick up trailheads at Fence Creek, Clark Fork, and Iceberg Meadow. From the east side of the Sierra, Highway 108 through Sonora Pass can be reached from Highway 395 about 40 miles north of Bishop. Highway 4 can be reached from Lake Tahoe to the north on Highway 89. Another branch of Highway 89 also connects to Highway 4 from Highway 395 to the east.

Activities: Hiking, backpacking, fishing, camping, horseback riding and packing, and boating.

Facilities: About 50 campgrounds, varying in size from a few campsites to more than 100. Some are equipped for recreational vehicles, but most are not. Surrounding areas, such as Pinecrest, have resort hotels.

Dates: Open May to mid-Oct.

Fees: None for wilderness permits; a camping fee is required.

For more information: On the East Sierra: Carson Ranger District, 1536 South Carson Street, Carson City, NV 89701. Phone (702) 882-2766. On the north or Highway 4 side: Calaveras Ranger District, PO Box 500, Hathaway Pines, CA 95233. On the south or Highway 108 side: Summit Ranger District, No. 1 Pinecrest Lake Road, CA 95364. Phone (209) 965-3434.

Lake Alpine Recreation Area

Lake Alpine is a 45–foot–deep lake that is stocked annually with more than 20,000 rainbow trout.

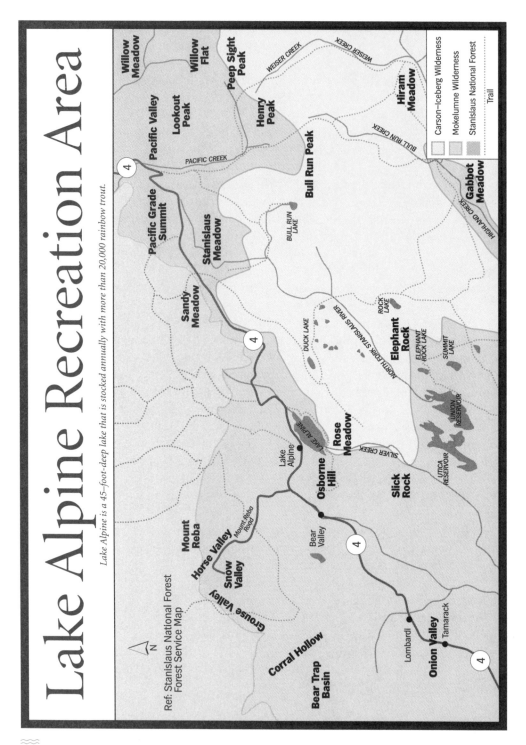

Ref: Stanislaus National Forest
Forest Service Map

N

Carson–Iceberg Wilderness
Mokelumne Wilderness
Stanislaus National Forest
Trail

Willow Meadow
Willow Flat
Peep Sight Peak
Pacific Valley
Lookout Peak
Henry Peak
Hiram Meadow
PACIFIC CREEK
WEISER CREEK
WEISER CREEK
BULL RUN CREEK
Bull Run Peak
Gabbot Meadow
HIGHLAND CREEK
Pacific Grade Summit
Stanislaus Meadow
BULL RUN LAKE
ROCK LAKE
Sandy Meadow
DUCK LAKE
NORTH FORK STANISLAUS RIVER
Elephant Rock
ELEPHANT ROCK LAKE
SUMMIT LAKE
UNION RESERVOIR
Rose Meadow
LAKE ALPINE
SILVER CREEK
Lake Alpine
Osborne Hill
Slick Rock
UTICA RESERVOIR
Mount Reba
Horse Valley
Mount Reba Road
Snow Valley
Bear Valley
Grouse Valley
Corral Hollow
Bear Trap Basin
Lombardi
Onion Valley
Tamarack

4
4
4
4

COUNTY LINE TRAIL

[Fig. 21(5)] This hike can be done as a backpack, but many people consider it a day hike. The views of the Dardanelles, an ancient lava flow that engulfed the area many thousands of years ago, are spectacular, and many people enjoy taking their time with this hike.

There are places such as Lost Lake to stop and swim. Don't miss the views of Donnel Lake and Sword Lake.

Look for the porcupine *(Erethizon dorsatum)*. They nest in tree cavities and rock crevices near this trail. Porcupines are fine tree climbers, but their sharp, protective quills allow them to be slow of foot and wit. About the only predator that seems to have no trouble with the quills is the fisher *(Martes pennanti)*. But most other predators prefer their prey to be a little less complicated. Hikers should likewise look but not get close enough to touch.

Directions: From Sonora, drive 50 miles east on Highway 108, turn west at the Clark Fork turnoff. Drive about 1 mile on Clark Fork Road. Cross the Middle Fork Stanislaus River and Clark Fork. Turn left on unpaved Road 6N06. Pass Fence Creek Campground and Wheats Meadow Trail before reaching County Line trailhead about 6 miles beyond the Clark Fork and Road 6N06 junction.

Trail: 11.6 miles round-trip.

Elevation: About a 600-foot gain, high point 7,590 feet.

Degree of difficulty: Moderate.

Surface: Footpath along granite, some meadow, and some swampy areas.

LAKE ALPINE RECREATION AREA

[Fig. 21(6), Fig. 22] The sights in the warmer season at Lake Alpine are likely to include fishing boats. This heavily timbered section of the Stanislaus National Forest is the backdrop for fishing in a 45-foot deep lake that is stocked with more than 20,000 rainbow trout *(Oncorhynchus mykiss)* annually.

Motorized boats are not allowed to go faster than 10 miles per hour. Overnight mooring is prohibited and so are motorized boats after sundown.

Along with nearby Emigrant Trail, the 3.5-mile Lakeshore Trail is where the tourists go. It's an easy walk on an established trail with only brief ascents next to this body of water at 7,350 feet in elevation. The lake is a hydroelectric facility built by Pacific Gas and Electric Company.

Directions: Drive 50 miles east of Angels Camp on Highway 4. Follow the signs.

Activities: Hiking, boating, fishing, swimming, and cross-country skiing.

Facilities: Boat launch ramp, campgrounds, and restrooms.

Dates: Open year-round.

Fees: There are fees for camping, fishing permits, and skiing permits.

Closest town: Bear Valley, 3 miles.

For more information: Calaveras Ranger District, PO Box 500, Hathaway Pines, CA 95232. Phone (209) 795 1381.

OSBORNE POINT SCENIC TRAIL

[Fig. 21(7)] The granite boulders on Osborne Point indicate a glacier that probably stood about 500 feet above the Lake Alpine Basin in the last 26,000 years. Those visitors with a geologist's eye will note the exposed layers of volcanic sandstone deposited many millions of years ago by an ancient stream.

This hike is an easy, half-hour walk for most people. The walk rewards visitors with views of wildflowers in the dark volcanic soil.

Looking up from the geology and the wildflowers, visitors will see the Dardanelles and the Dardanelles Cones, features created by lava flows 10 million years ago.

Directions: Drive about 50 miles east from Angels Camp on Highway 4. The trailhead is about 0.25 mile east of Silvertip Campground and .03 mile west of Road 7N17. There is no trailhead parking, so hikers normally park along the side of the road.

Trail: 2.3 miles one-way.

Elevation: From about 7,300 feet to 7,600 feet.

Degree of difficulty: Easy to moderate.

Surface: Some granite, some volcanic, generally well established.

CLARK FORK RECREATION COMPLEX

[Fig. 21(8)] Clark Fork, on the southwest side of the Carson-Iceberg Wilderness, provides a camp with 13 sites where campers can keep horses. There's even a watering trough for horses. So decisions about whether to pack the extra food, the more comfortable sleeping pad, and the heavier tent are rendered much simpler for those who ride horses. Horses can easily carry items that backpackers consider to be too heavy to carry—such as a bulky but protective tent.

Outside of the horse camp, there's nothing particularly intriguing about this camping complex, except that the facilities are an impressive platform from which to launch into the wilderness. At 5,600 to 6,100 feet in elevation, it is a little cooler in the summer. The area has more than 150 campsites, including a recreational vehicle dump station and showers.

The Dardanelles and other volcanic features wait in the distance. For those perceptive enough to see it, the end of a massive moraine can be detected where the Clark Fork and the Middle Fork of the Stanislaus River meet. It is evidence of a glacier that extended all the way from the Dardanelles Cones, several miles northeast.

Fishing is also a passion in this area. Clark Fork River is stocked annually, and the Cottonwood Creek day-use area is 3.5 miles from the Highway 108 and Clark Fork junction. Barbecuing is allowed, but no overnight camping or campfires.

Directions: From Sonora, drive 49 miles east on Highway 108, take the left fork onto Clark Fork Road. Drive another 6 miles. The Clark Fork campgrounds as well as the horse camp are to the right.

Activities: Fishing, hiking, horseback riding, swimming, and picnicking.

Facilities: About 180 campsites, flush, pit, vault toilets, picnic grounds.

Dates: Open mid-May through Oct., or until snow closes Highway 108.

Fees: There is a charge for showers, campsites, and horse facilities.

Closest town: Dardanelle, 10 miles.

For more information: Summit Ranger District, No. 1 Pinecrest Lake Road, Pinecrest, CA 95364. Phone (209) 965-3434.

COLUMNS OF THE GIANTS TRAIL

[Fig. 21(9)] Columns of the Giants is a basalt formation that is probably 400 feet thick. It formed more than 100,000 years ago in the Middle Fork Stanislaus River canyon, where wildflowers now bloom on the riverbanks.

Adventurous travelers will climb to the top of the basalt and see the fine polishing of previous glacial ages and the erratics the ice flows deposited. But be careful crossing a steep gully to the left side of the ancient volcanic flow.

The walk to the columns is far less eventful. Most people will traverse it in minutes and enjoy a short nature tour on the way to the basalt formation. The U.S. Forest Service has provided information about the formation at the end of the trail.

Directions: From the junction of Highway 108 and Clark Fork Road, drive 5 miles on Highway 108 to Pigeon Flat Picnic Area. Take the right fork on the entrance road to the picnic area. Trailhead is marked.

Trail: 0.4 mile one-way.

Degree of difficulty: Easy to moderate.

Elevation: About 100-foot drop at the 6,000-foot elevation.

Surface: One bridge and developed trail easily followed.

For more information: Summit Ranger District, No. 1 Pinecrest Lake Road, Pinecrest, CA 95364. Phone (209) 965-3434.

CROSS-COUNTRY SKI AREAS AROUND LAKE ALPINE

The Lake Alpine Basin is above 7,000 feet, so it often receives more than 30 feet of snow in winter. Several recreation opportunities are available for skiers, snowmobilers, and those who just want to play in the snow.

The Lake Alpine Basin offers a 3.5-mile loop trail around Lake Alpine. The trailhead is marked on the south side of Highway 4. This trail can be slick and difficult. Only intermediate to advanced skiers are encouraged to use it.

But there are other opportunities for skiers of all skill levels at nearby **Lake Alpine Sno-Park**. There are 8 miles of groomed snowmobile trail along Highway 4 from the park to Mosquito Lakes. The trail is separated into three distinct sections.

First, beginners can use the 0.75-mile trail to Lake Alpine. Do not ski on the frozen lake. Ice is unsafe in this area. In 3 miles, skiers reach Cape Horn Vista, a slow, easy uphill climb from Lake Alpine. It will take intermediate skiers about half a day, and the 300-degree view is spectacular.

The last 4-mile segment is an all-day affair in a gradual climb to Mosquito Lakes. Stay to the right as snowmobiles come through.

The trail to Pine Marten and Silver Valley campgrounds is about 0.5 mile of flat, groomed snowmobile trail along the east end of Lake Alpine. The unmarked trails are easy to follow and provide a good course for beginners.

About 0.5 mile west of Lake Alpine on the highway, **Bear Valley Cross Country Area** has an extensive trail system with 30 separate, groomed courses. Trailside huts, picnic tables, and food service are available as well as ski rentals and instruction.

About 5 miles west of Lake Alpine along Highway 4, **Big Meadow Nordic Ski Trails** offer ungroomed Nordic courses. Snowmobiles are prohibited. Beginner trails wind through the campground. The intermediate and advanced trails follow the rugged, scenic rim of the Stanislaus River Canyon.

For information on any of these trails, contact the Calaveras Ranger District at (209) 795-1381. Maps and brochures are available, as well as information about other cross-country skiing areas on snow-bound forest service roads.

Farther west, about 12 miles, some trails can be found at the **Calaveras Big Trees State Park**. For information about the trails, call (209) 795-2334.

PINECREST LAKE

[Fig. 23] This is one of the Sierra's better examples of a lake with a short but busy past. Cradled in a meadow that emigrants called Strawberry Flat and rimmed with granite outcroppings, Pinecrest Lake is the last in a series of dams constructed on the South Fork of the Stanislaus River for mining and hydroelectric power. The Tuolumne County Water and Power Company built the first dam called Big Dam 7.5 miles upstream of the present one in 1856.

The purpose was to divert water via ditches and flumes to the mining claims in and around Columbia, California. The second, called Middle Dam and sometimes called Upper Strawberry Lake Dam, was also built in 1856. The third, located 0.5 mile upstream from the present, was also built in 1856.

The present dam at Pinecrest, previously called Lower Strawberry Reservoir Dam, was built by Sierra and San Francisco Power Company (to whom Tuolumne County water and Power had sold the dam in 1916 for the purpose of providing cheap hydroelectric power).

Pinecrest's history goes back a little further. Jedediah Smith made the first recorded crossing of the Sierra by white men in early spring 1827 at the Stanislaus River in what today is known as the Stanislaus National Forest. Smith's party veered from the northern banks of the Stanislaus—not far from present-day Pinecrest—and climbed the foothills up into the pines. Eventually, they found the granite and packed snow of ridgelines. They passed through the high Sierra, exiting the west side near the current site of Ebbetts Pass on Highway 4.

At the time Smith passed through, the area was inhabited by Native Americans (Miwok). The trail emigrants followed past Pinecrest was called the West Walker Route later to be called the Emigrant Trail. The emigrants called Pinecrest's meadow Strawberry Flat because of the wild strawberries (*Frageria virginiana*) that grew there.

Situated just above the foothills at 5,600 feet, the Pinecrest area is painted in wildflowers at a time when lower elevations are beginning to swelter. The area's mid-July wildflowers include such plants as aster *(Aster alpigenus)*, water hemlock *(Douglassi)*, wild strawberry, buttercups *(Ranunculus)*, clover *(Trifolium)*, and elderberries *(Sambucus)*.

The wildflowers accent the thick coniferous forest surrounding the area, typical of Sierra elevations just above the foothill level. Trees in the area include white fir *(Abies concolor)*, incense cedar *(Calocedrus decurrens)*, and sugar pine *(Pinos lambertiana)*.

By Sierra standards, Pinecrest is a small lake, with 18,000 acre-feet of water. (One acre-foot is 325,900 gallons, or enough to supply the average California family for 18 months.)

The U.S. Forest Service's Summit Ranger District station, on Highway 108 about 1 mile from Pinecrest Lake, has information about a replica village of the Central Sierra Miwok, the most recent Native Americans to inhabit the area over the last 9,000 years. The replica is across the street from the ranger station and open to forest visitors at no charge. Visitors can walk along the 0.25-mile Shadow of the Miwok Trail, which is a loop through the replica village with interpretive signs posted along the way.

Directions: Drive 30 miles east on Highway 108 from Sonora and turn off at Pinecrest Road. The U.S. Forest Service's Summit Ranger District office is on the corner. Drive another mile down Pinecrest Road to find the lake.

Activities: Camping, fishing, boating, and hiking.

Facilities: Several restrooms, picnic grounds, nearby motels.

Dates: Open year-round.

Fees: There is a fee for camping.

Closest town: Pinecrest, 0.25 mile.

For more information: Summit Ranger District, No. 1 Pinecrest Lake Road, Pinecrest, CA 95364. Phone (209) 965-3434.

BOURLAND TRESTLE

[Fig. 23(2)] The Bourland Trestle is considered a one-of-a-kind narrow-gauge logging railroad trestle because it is the last still standing in the western United States. Built in 1922, it was located 43 miles from the mill in Tuolumne City. The Westside Lumber Company system owned and operated it until 1960.

The trestle, 75 feet high and 315 feet long, was so vital to loggers that a watchman was posted at all major bridges to watch passing trains and check for sparks. Fire was a big concern. Ironically, a watchman's cabin remained right beside the trestle until it burned in the 1980s.

Today, the goal is to convert the trestle into a safe pedestrian bridge. It was partially stabilized in 1995, but a lot of work is still necessary. Recent storms have caused further damage to the trestle. Still, the trestle is a nice picnic spot at the end of a drive, hike, or bike.

Directions: Drive east 24 miles from Sonora on Highway 108 to the second Long Barn exit and turn right. Drive 0.1 mile to Forest Service Road 3N01 and continue

17.9 miles to Forest Service Road 2N14 and turn right. Drive 2.8 miles to Forest Service Road 2N29 and turn left. The trestle is 2.5 miles from the junction of 2N14 and 2N29. Note Road 2N29 overlays the old railroad grade and is very narrow.

Activities: Hiking, picnicking.

Facilities: None.

Dates: Open May through mid-Oct.

Closest town: Mi-Wuk Village on Highway 108.

For more information: Mi-Wuk Ranger District, PO Box 100, Mi-Wuk Village, CA 95364. Phone (209) 586-3234.

DODGE RIDGE SKI AREA

[Fig. 23(1)] Dodge Ridge skiing provides 1,600 feet of vertical drop from 8,200 feet at the ridgetop to 6,600 feet at the base. The terrain accommodates three levels of skiers: beginner (20 percent of the runs), intermediate (40 percent), and advanced (40 percent).

There are 60 trails, the longest being 2 miles. A Nordic 11-kilometer cross-country course is designed for beginner to intermediate skiers. A new fixed grip quad chairlift has 159 chairs moving at 450-500 feet per minute, making it the fastest chair at Dodge. The entire Dodge Ridge lifts system has recently increased its carrying capacity of 13,600 per hour to 15,700. It is served by 12 lifts total.

Other skiing opportunities in the Stanislaus National Forest include 22.8 miles of Nordic skiing on U.S. Forest Service trails. That skiing is free. Call the Summit Ranger District, (209) 965-3434, for more details.

Directions: From Sonora, drive east on Highway 108 approximately 30 miles to Pinecrest. Follow the signs.

Activities: Downhill and cross-country skiing, snowboarding.

Facilities: Ski rentals, restaurants at the ski area.

Dates: Open Nov. to Apr.

Fees: There are fees for skiing at Dodge Ridge.

For more information: Dodge Ridge Ski Area, PO Box 1188, Pinecrest, CA 95364. Phone (209) 965-3474.

THE RED HILLS

[Fig. 24(2)] In California, where exotic vegetation has taken over much of the open range and foothills, the Red Hills area stands as important stronghold of native perennial bunchgrasses. The unusual soils that provide a refuge for these bunchgrasses also support a unique plant community with many rare species. The federal government so valued the vegetation, soil, and animals that the Red Hills were set aside as an Area of Critical Environmental Concern or a "biological island."

The secret is the serpentine soils. The Red Hills Management Area is in the western tectonic block of the Sierra Nevada metamorphic belt. The hills contain much of the Tuolumne ultramafic complex, one of the largest exposures of serpentine rocks in the Sierra Nevada metamorphic belt. Nearly the entire area is underlaid by dunite, a variety of peridotite consisting of dark green olivine and minor chromite, which has been partly or entirely serpentinized to antigorite magnesite-magnetite.

In many similar foothill areas without the serpentines, the native perennials have been mostly replaced by exotic annuals. The important native perennial species include California oniongrass *(Melica californica)*, big squirreltail *(Sitanion jubatum)*, and pine bluegrass *(Poa secunda)*.

Hikers in the Red Hills will be able to identify virtually the only tree species—foothill pine *(Pinus sabiniana)*, which is found throughout the Red Hills in low densities. Buckbrush *(Ceanothus cuneatus)* comprises a majority of the shrub cover. Other shrubs include toyon (Heteromeles arbutifolia), coffeeberry *(Rhamnus tomentella,)* chamise *(Adenostoma fasciculatum)*, hollyleaf redberry *(Rhamnus ilicifolia)*, California yerbasanta *(Eriodictyon californicum)*, and manzanitas *(Arctostaphylos spp.)*.

Visitors also will be able to see California verbena *(Verbena californica)*, a Red Hills endemic, meaning it is found nowhere else in the world. It is confined to short stretches of the mostly intermittent streams that run through the Red Hills. These stretches of the creeks remain moist year-round due to groundwater seepage. Permanent pools in these riparian zones support the rarest animal found in the Red Hills, a minnow called the Red Hills roach. These tough little fish can survive the elevated temperatures and low oxygen levels of these small pools in summer.

California verbena and Layne's butterweed are two plants that grow in the Red Hills that are listed under the federal Endangered Species Act. In addition, the Red Hills put on a spectacular display in the early spring when the annual wildflowers bloom.

Visitors can see most of the Red Hills on various loop trails, which total about 17.3 miles. The hiking is easy on open footpaths and gentle slopes.

The Red Hills Management Area includes 7,100 acres of public land located near the intersection of Highways 49 and 120 just south of the historic town of Chinese Camp in Tuolumne County. The Red Hills came into federal ownership along with most of California with the signing of the Treaty of Guadalupe Hidalgo in 1848 to officially end the war with Mexico.

The area is still in federal ownership simply because no one wanted the land in the days when it was government policy to dispose of public property. There was little or no gold associated with the serpentine rocks, and crops wouldn't grow properly in the serpentine-derived soil.

The Red Hills are mostly used for recreation and education. Important activities include wildflower viewing, nature study, hiking, horseback riding, and amateur prospecting. To protect the fragile resources of the area, in 1991 target shooting and off-road vehicle use were prohibited on public land in the Red Hills.

Directions: From Sonora, take Highway 49 south 10 miles to Chinese Camp, then drive southwest on Red Hills Road for 1 mile.

Activities: Horseback riding, hiking, wildflower viewing, and bird-watching.

Facilities: Overnight camping is discouraged. Target shooting and off-road vehicle use are prohibited. Lodging is available in Jamestown, approximately 5 miles north on Highway 49, and in Sonora, about 10 miles in the same direction. Food and supplies are available at the Kiwi Store in Chinese Camp.

Dates: Open year-round.

Fees: None.

Closest town: Chinese Camp, about 0.5 mile.

For more information: Bureau of Land Management, Folsom Field Office, 63 Natoma Street, Folsom, CA 95630. Phone (916) 985-4474.

COLUMBIA STATE HISTORIC PARK

[Fig. 23] Once known as the "Gem of the Southern Mines," gold miners hauled out $500 million worth of gold (at today's value) between 1850 and 1870. Columbia, at the time, was California's second largest city.

Columbia is so well preserved today because it was never completely deserted. Since 1945, when the state decided to protect the old buildings, the town's old Gold Rush-era business district has remained intact with shops, restaurants, and two hotels. Proprietors do their business in period clothing.

There are opportunities to ride a mud wagon (which is a replica of the ones used in the 1800s), hire a "fine steed" for a horseback ride through the area where prospecting took place, pan for gold, or tour an active gold mine. The two-story brick schoolhouse and cemetery still overlook the town.

Visitors also can take a short stroll on trails in the area where it is common to see mule deer (*Odocoileus heminous*). Though these creatures are usually quite good at hiding in brushy cover, some have become acclimated well enough to the people in the area that they do not hide themselves very well. Mountain lions (*Felis concolor*), chief predators of the deer, have benefited greatly, thinning many herds.

Visitors are advised not to feed the deer and not to allow small children to stray very far from adults.

Directions: From Sonora, drive 2 miles north on Highway 49, turn off on Parrots Ferry Road, and drive 1 mile to Columbia.

Activities: Sight-seeing, horseback riding, adjacent 1897 rail town park exhibit in nearby Jamestown, short hikes.

Facilities: Two historic hotels, museum, theater.

Dates: Open year-round, though hours for businesses change seasonally. Closed Christmas and Thanksgiving.

Fees: None.

Closest town: Columbia.

For more information:
Columbia State Historic Park, 22708 Broadway Street, Columbia, CA 95310. Phone (209) 532-0150.

MOUNTAIN
LION
(Felis concolor)

CALAVARAS BIG TREES STATE HISTORIC PARK

[Fig. 23] The largest redwood in Calaveras Big Trees State Park is the Louis Agassiz Tree in the South Grove. It is one of many large, historic reasons to visit this park along Highway 4. Agassiz Tree is 250 feet tall—not a record-setter—but its diameter is 25 feet at a height of 6 feet above ground level. The diameter is not a record-setter either, but the tree is about 2,000 years old and is a lot of wood.

The largest tree in the North Grove is the Empire State Tree, which is 18 feet in diameter 6 feet above the ground. The size of these giant sequoia *(Sequoiadendron giganteum)* is a little difficult to comprehend, even standing in the parking lot looking at them. It is not a bad idea to have a friend or family member stand fairly close to one of the fallen giants along the many short trails in the park to put the trees in perspective.

How did these trees get here? About the time of Christ, some slender seedlings, looking very much like blades of grass, reached out of the soil in the Central Sierra Nevada. The radicle or root also reached down into the soil. After a few days, the empty shell of the seeds popped off, and several little giant sequoia, the largest living thing on earth, began life. Though germination is rare under ordinary, natural conditions, hundreds of these redwoods spread through midelevations of the Sierra's western slopes, but only a few stands survived logging in the nineteenth century. Two of these groves are found at the Calavaras Big Trees State Historic Park where some of the largest giants in the world still survive.

Around the Calaveras trees, as in many places on the western slope, wildflowers appear on the sunnier, south-facing slopes first, then in lightly shaded or moister areas. Rangers remind people not to pick the flowers. Some of the more popular flowers include five spot *(Nemophila maculata)*, Sierra lupine *(Lupinus grayii)*, manzanita *(Arctostaphylos manzanita)*, Mariposa lily *(Calochortus)*, and western wall flower *(Erysimum capitatum)*.

The giant sequoias, also known as Sierra redwoods, are the largest trees in the world, often ranging between 250 and 300 feet tall. The tallest has been measured at about 325 feet. But people also pause at the trees' width. They are measured at about 5 or 6 feet from the ground. Their diameters range to 30 feet and more. Their circumferences, the distance around the tree, can be more than 90 feet, or about 30 yards on a football field.

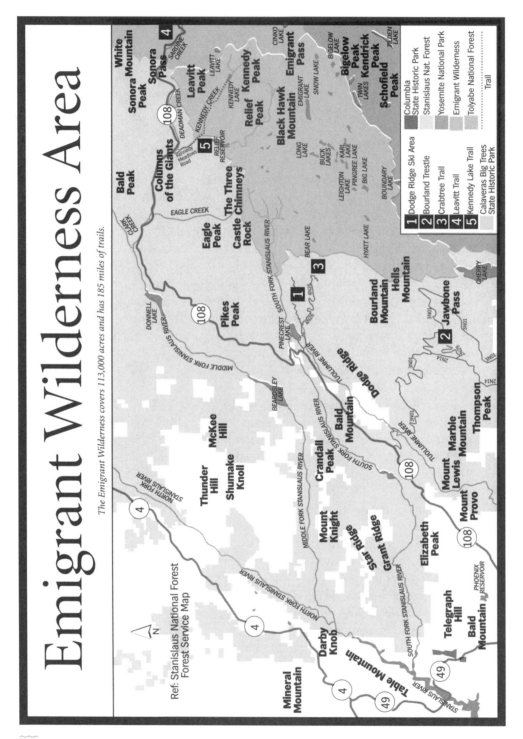

Emigrant Wilderness Area

The Emigrant Wilderness covers 113,000 acres and has 185 miles of trails.

Ref: Stanislaus National Forest
Forest Service Map

1	Dodge Ridge Ski Area
2	Bourland Trestle
3	Crabtree Trail
4	Leavitt Trail
5	Kennedy Lake Trail

Columbia
State Historic Park
Stanislaus Nat. Forest
Yosemite National Park
Emigrant Wilderness
Tolyabe National Forest
Trail

Calaveras Big Trees
State Historic Park

The largest tree in the world—which refers to volume, not just height—is the General Sherman Tree in Sequoia-Kings Canyon National Parks. It is 272 feet tall and is 36 feet in diameter at its base. A Sierra redwood of similar dimensions may contain enough wood to build 40 five-room homes, weigh 4,000 tons, and be as tall as the Statue of Liberty.

The giant sequoias, or "big trees" as they are known, are scattered between 4,500 feet and 8,000 feet on unglaciated ridges. They are found as far north as Placer County, west of Lake Tahoe, and as far south as the Southern Sierra in Sequoia-Kings Canyon National Parks, site of the largest remaining groves in the world. The Calaveras park groves are the next largest.

The trees need moist conditions, but they do not develop in areas of extreme cold. The trees can survive thousands of years because of the tannin in their bark. The tannin stops wood-boring insects and fungi.

But the bark itself is also a formidable defense. It is a dry, tough bark that is between 2 and 4 feet wide. It has no sap, which is flammable. Even when fire somehow gets through the bark, the tree remains alive and standing as long as some living wood is still present.

Directions: Drive northeast of Stockton on Highway 4. The park is 4 miles northeast of the town of Arnold on Highway 4.

Activities: Hiking, fishing, and picnicking.

Facilities: Restrooms, self-guided tour information on signs and kiosks, wheelchair accessible.

Dates: Open year-round.

Fees: There is an entrance fee.

Closest town: Arnold, 4 miles.

For more information: Calaveras Big Tree State Park, PO Box 120, Arnold, CA 95223. Phone (209) 795-2334.

EMIGRANT WILDERNESS

[Fig. 23] Walking through the Emigrant Wilderness is a stroll through the many stages of the Sierra's past. People hike, camp, and see the geologic sights in this wilderness.

The metamorphosed pendant jutting out from the batholith at Bigelow Peak near the Yosemite National Park line gives a hint of the pre-Sierra history. About 10 percent of this wilderness contains visible Paleozoic sedimentary rocks such as shales, limestones, and siltstones.

Volcanic terrain—in the form of rhyolite, basalt, andesite tuffs, and latite—is apparent as well. But, like much of the Sierra, granite is the main feature here. In the last 2 million years, glaciation honed the salt-and-pepper coloration. The quartz monzonite and granodiorite are common.

SUGAR PINE
(Pinus lambertiana)
This is the tallest
American pine,
reaching heights
of 175 to 200
feet, and it has
the longest cones
of any American
conifer, 10 to 26
inches long.

The Emigrant, with its drainage basins and life zones, is a typical 113,000-acre slice of the Central Sierra. The wilderness ranges in elevation from about 5,000 feet, about as high as one would find foothill vegetation, at Cherry Reservoir at the southwestern edge of the wilderness to 11,750-foot Leavitt Peak on the northeast shoulder of the Stanislaus National Forest.

The vegetation belts start with the dominant tree species. Sugar pine *(Pinus lambertiana)*, Douglas fir *(Pseudotsuga menziesii)*, white fir *(Abies concolor)*, incense cedar *(Calocedrus decurrens)*, and black cottonwood *(Populus trichocarpa)* are abundant, many gathered in almost unnaturally close quarters in the elevations between 5,000 and 7,000 feet in the wilderness.

Fire suppression stopped the natural thinning process of burning for most of this century. Historically, fires have burned intermittently in this and other Sierra forests. Fires vary in intensity depending on the amount of vegetation available to burn, weather conditions, and the season.

If fires remain "cool"—smaller flames burning brush and understory vegetation without reaching the thick canopies of mature trees—they are actually very beneficial and necessary in the Sierra. By clearing excess vegetation, the fire bares the soil needed by plant seedlings.

In a cool fire, burned material still carries potassium, phosphorus, magnesium, and nitrogen, which are necessary for plant growth. The soil benefits from such fires. Hot fires, which burn intensely and destroy soil organisms, are not as beneficial, though they serve the purpose of clearing out the forest.

In hiking the Emigrant, look for previously burned areas where plants are beginning to colonize. Among the plants in the open forest will be the huckleberry oak *(Quercus caccinifolia)*, bush chinquapin *(Castanopsis sempervirens)*, and Fresno mat *(Ceanothus fresnensis)*.

Burning vegetation was part of life for the Miwok Indians who controlled parts of the Stanislaus River and Tuolumne River when European explorers passed through the area in the 1830s. The Washoe and Mono tribes from the eastern Sierra were also known to claim territory in the area. The Native Americans were intense gatherers of food and plants, trading regularly with each other.

They knew the area well, devising overland trails that were most difficult to discern. Sometimes a bent piece of brush or a scrape on a granite slab were the only indications of which direction the trail would lead. When all else failed, the Miwok would conveniently mark a trail with a dead skunk, making sure no one would miss their message.

Europeans made some of their first Sierra crossings on the flanks of the Emigrant. Joseph Reddeford Walker pioneered a future wagon trail between the headwaters of the East Walker River and the Tuolumne River and continued down into the Hetch Hetchy Valley, which is in present-day Yosemite.

The wilderness was used for cattle grazing in the 1860s. Today, there are 15 valid mining claims in the Snow Lake area and the East Fork of Cherry Creek above Huckleberry Lake. The areas are highly mineralized with scheelite, a source of tungsten. The mines are largely unsuccessful.

But the Emigrant has become quite a success story for outdoor lovers. The U.S. Forest Service reports 18,000 people a year backpack, hike, ride horseback, and fish in the wilderness. Permits are required for overnight stays. And most people stay overnight if they walk these trails, which can consume a lot of time and energy. There are 185 miles of trails. As in any Sierra wilderness, no mechanized travel is allowed, including bicycles.

Directions: Drive east about 45 miles beyond Sonora on State Route 108, 9.4 miles west of Sonora pass summit to Kennedy Meadows Road. Go south 0.6 mile, then turn left to trailhead parking at an elevation of 6,380 feet.

Activities: Hiking, camping, backpacking, horseback riding, and fishing.

Facilities: Few primitive campsites. There are not established campsites or services in the wilderness. Camp at least 100 feet from streams.

Dates: Open year-round, but the best hiking time is June through Sept.

Fees: None.

Closest town: Groveland, 12 miles.

For more information: Groveland Ranger District, 24525 Old Highway 120, Groveland, CA 95321. Phone (209) 962-7825.

CRABTREE TRAIL

[Fig. 23(3)] The granite domes and canyons of the Emigrant Wilderness are probably best seen on a longer trail, though visitors may not need more than a day hike to get into the high country sights. The Crabtree Trail system climbs from about

Sugar Pine

The sugar pine (*Pinus lambertiana*) has the largest cone of the pine trees in the Sierra. It is often more than 15 inches long and 5 inches in diameter with thin, open scales. In the Northern Sierra, the sugar pine occurs at 3,500 to 6,500 feet in elevation. The tree is also found in the Southern Sierra at higher elevations, from 4,500 to 9,000 feet. The sugar pine, which can grow to 175 feet tall, is normally outnumbered by other types of pine and fir trees in the conifer belts of the Sierra. But when it is present, it can be recognized for its huge cones.

6,800 feet to almost 8,000, and many people prefer to camp out a night or two to take in the intoxicating geology that includes some stunning, unnamed basalt towers.

At some points on the granitic ascent, hikers will find stair steps carved into the rock, courtesy of the federal government. The government, at one time or another in the past 60 years, has carved similar stair steps in many popular places along the Southern Sierra as well as the Central.

The six-hour, 13-mile haul on this loop trip is not a strain for experienced hikers, but novices and the inexperienced should be aware of the demands when ascending 1,000 feet on a hike that begins higher than 6,000 feet. Some people prefer to arrive a day early, spend the night near the trailhead at around 7,100 feet to acclimate a bit to the elevation—though the overnight stay probably will not make a big difference to some people. If you do choose to stay overnight, a wilderness permit is required.

This trail crosses Little Creek, so it is wise to find a suitable log. Also, during spring runoff, Sierra creeks can be docile creatures in the mornings, but raging beasts in the afternoon when the snowmelt picks up. Take care in afternoon crossings.

Directions: From Sonora, drive east on Highway 108 for 30 miles and take the Pinecrest Lake turnoff. Take the Pinecrest Lake Road 0.4 mile to an intersection and turn right toward the Dodge Ridge Ski Area for 3.1 miles. Stay right at the divide, and follow the signs to Aspen Meadow for 0.5 mile. Make a left at the next intersection. At 1.6 miles, the road forks, but continue straight on Forest Service Road 4N26 through Aspen Meadows. After 2.8 miles, the Crabtree trailhead will appear and a parking lot is right next to it.

For more information: Summit Ranger District, No. 1 Pinecrest Lake Road, Pinecrest, CA 95364. Phone (209) 965-3434.

Trail: 13-mile loop.

Elevation: Gain of 1,300 feet.

Degree of difficulty: Moderate to strenuous.

Dates: July through Sept.

Surface: Well-maintained, granite surface along much of the trail. Some large puddles, streams.

KENNEDY LAKE TRAIL

[Fig. 23(5)] The picture seems a little off kilter: The remnants of winter snow slowly melt on the windswept ridges framing a herd of cows munching on the seasonal grasses near Kennedy Lake. The cows may seem more appropriate at lower elevations, but there is little for them to eat farther down the hill in July. So they are herded here as they have been for more than a century in the Sierra, particularly in the central and southern parts of the range.

The cattle mingle now with hikers, horse packers, and the occasional wild animal. This can be a little like rush hour during the summer. The cattle grazing started in 1861 when W. F. Cooper ranged cattle in the northwest corner of the Emigrant Wilderness, and other ranchers soon followed during the frequent and often intense droughts that continue to plague California.

Cowboys often blazed trails, creating many of the trails in the system today between mountain meadows. The term "blazing" or marking trees to designate the trail was established. Blazing continues today, although many of the mainstream trails in the Sierra do not require it simply because they have become so well worn.

Visitors could get lost here, but they don't ever seem to be very far from someone on this trail. The views of the volcanic and granitic past are the main reasons everyone is so attracted to this place.

Visitors need to plan for this trip because it will require camping for at least a night. Get in shape, too. Work crews years ago blasted the trail into steep and perpendicular hillsides. The unnamed waterfalls, Kennedy Lake, and the geology are enough to keep most visitors interested.

There are detours for the more adventurous and experienced hikers. Night Cap Peak Trail would prove a challenge to many. A good map and some preparation for extra climbing and boulder scrambling would bring hikers to a quieter place called Relief Reservoir. A call to the ranger's station is advisable before trying it.

Directions: Drive Highway 108 from Sonora for about 48 miles east to Kennedy Meadows Road. Turn south on Kennedy Meadows Road for 0.7 mile. Park and walk up the valley dirt road called the Huckleberry Trail for about 4 miles to find the Kennedy Lake Trail.

For more information: Summit Ranger District, No. 1 Pinecrest Lake Road, Pinecrest, CA 95364. Phone (209) 965-3434.

Bald Eagle

Of the estimated 50,000 bald eagles (*Haliaetus leucocephalus*) in North America, about 80 percent are found in Alaska. But many bald eagles migrate to California during the colder months and nest, particularly in the Northern Sierra.

Finding bald eagles in California was becoming difficult in the 1970s. Bald eagle populations had dwindled since the late 1950s. The federal government officially considered the bald eagle to be an endangered species in 1976, and authorities have recognized the bird's dwindling population since the late 1960s.

Pesticides, such as DDT, probably caused most of the eagle's problems. The pesticides were sprayed on plants eaten by invertebrates, which were then eaten by eagles. The poison accumulated in the birds, hampering their abilities to produce viable eggs.

But after more than two decades, the eagle's population is on the rebound. Federal officials in July 1999 recommended the bird to be removed from protection under the Endangered Species Act.

An adult bald eagle grows to about 3 feet in length with a wingspan of 7 to 8 feet. The bird weighs 10 to 14 pounds. Wild bald eagles may live as long as 30 years, but it is more common for them to live about 20 years. They normally mate for life, and the female usually lays two eggs that hatch in about 5 weeks.

Wild and Scenic Tuolumne River

The Tuolumne River whitewater run covers 18 miles as it winds toward Don Pedro Reservoir from Hetch Hetchy Reservoir.

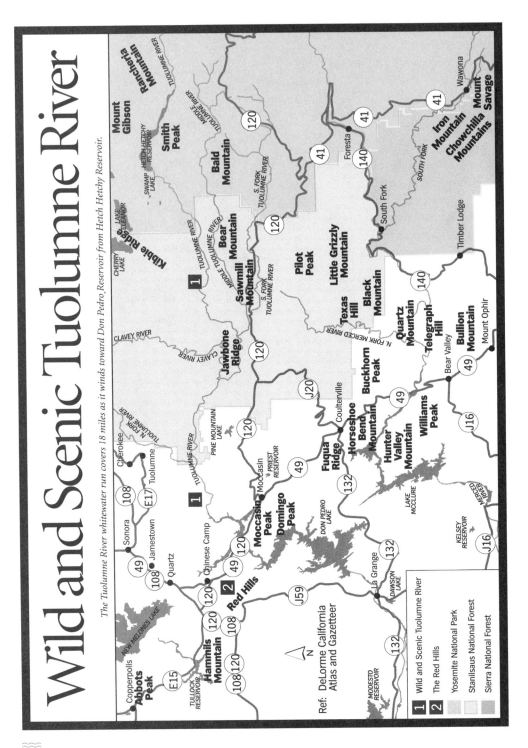

Ref: DeLorme California Atlas and Gazetteer

1	Wild and Scenic Tuolumne River
2	The Red Hills
	Yosemite National Park
	Stanislaus National Forest
	Sierra National Forest

Trail: 15-mile loop, two days of hiking.

Elevation: 3,300-foot gain to a high point of 9,600 feet.

Degree of difficulty: Moderate.

Surface: Rocky, sometimes narrow, but generally well worn and easy to find.

LEAVITT TRAIL

[Fig. 23(4)] For those who want to backpack over three days and see a lake at 9,230 feet in elevation, this hike will provide views of the eastern Sierra. Campsites are available all around the lake. Don't forget the camera on this one.

Directions: From the west side of the Sierra, drive east on Highway 108 to Sonora Pass, then continue about 8 miles to the Leavitt trailhead parking, where toilets and trash facilities are available. Leavitt Meadow Campground is about 100 yards away. Go through the campground, and bear left until you come to day-use parking near West Walker River. Trail starts on the other side of the river.

Trail: 30 miles round-trip to Cinko Lake.

Elevation: 2,000-foot gain, high point 9,450 feet.

Degree of difficulty: Strenuous.

Surface: Footpath in granite, easy to follow.

WILD AND SCENIC TUOLUMNE RIVER

[Fig. 24(1)] One of the most challenging whitewater river runs in the Sierra is several miles south of 268,000-acre-foot Cherry Lake, the large body of water on the southwest flank of the Emigrant Wilderness. The Tuolumne River whitewater run covers about 18 miles as it winds, leaps, and rushes toward Don Pedro Reservoir in the foothills to the west.

The river is one of two major streams leaving Yosemite National Park, south of the Emigrant. The river's glacial ancestry is apparent in the granite canyons carved deep into the Sierra batholith over the last 2 million years.

The whitewater run is a virtual slalom course of boulders. It escalates in intensity with staircase rapids, chutes, and pools by the score as it comes down the mountain. Few people would challenge it until the mid-1970s when the U.S. Forest Service counted 1,200 boaters making the trip in 1975. Now, the federal government limits noncommercial rafters to 90 persons per day between May and October. The art of river rafting has progressed and most rafters have far more expertise now than they did 20 years ago. But there are also a lot more rescues because there are also a lot of people who do not understand how wild the river is. This river is considered Class IV to V rapids. A Class I is a fairly flat, placid stream, and a Class VI is steep, treacherous, and not navigable. Most people boat the Tuolumne with a recognized commercial rafting company, and there are eight.

The Tuolumne is a prime water source for the city of San Francisco. The water coming out of Hetch Hetchy Valley in Yosemite on the Tuolumne is so pristine that San Francisco has been one of the largest cities in America that does not treat its river water before sending it to the taps. Visitors might look at the streamside areas where the river's rapids calm down and become gentler. Amphibians can be found there. They

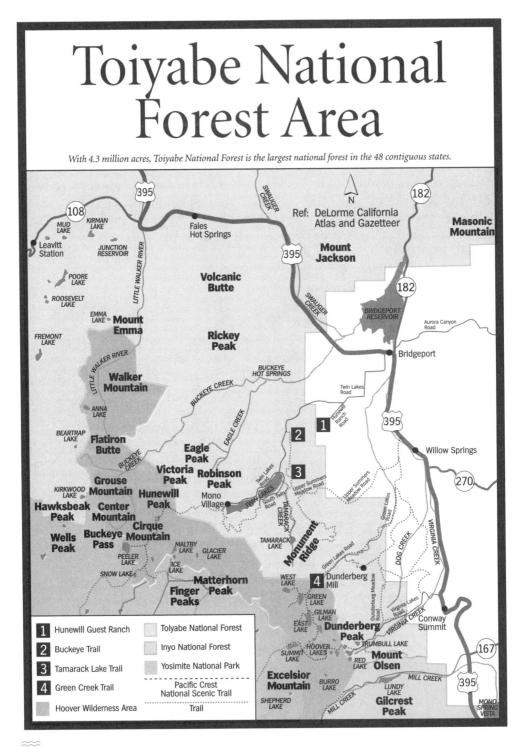

Toiyabe National Forest Area

With 4.3 million acres, Toiyabe National Forest is the largest national forest in the 48 contiguous states.

Ref: DeLorme California Atlas and Gazetteer

1	Hunewill Guest Ranch	Toiyabe National Forest
2	Buckeye Trail	Inyo National Forest
3	Tamarack Lake Trail	Yosimite National Park
4	Green Creek Trail	Pacific Crest National Scenic Trail
	Hoover Wilderness Area	Trail

include the red-legged frog *(Rana aurora)* and the California newt *(Taricha torosa).*

The newt feasts on earthworms, snails, and slugs, which are found in abundance around the Tuolumne River in the loose soils at lower elevations. The newt spends most of its time out of the water. Look for the reddish-brown color on top and a yellow-orange color below on the body of the newt. Reptiles are also all around. Look for the Gilbert's skink *(Eumeces gilberti),* southern alligator lizard *(Gerrhonotus multi-carinatus),* and striped racer *(Masticophus lateralis).*

If visitors hear a distinctive "oooah, coo, coo" in the distance, they will know they have happened upon a common bird that is hunted in the woodlands and sometimes around streams such as the Tuolumne. It is the mourning dove *(Zenaida macroura),* a seed-eating bird often found around the river year-round. The dove's call is the best way to identify it, but if in doubt, watch the bird walk. If the head bobs back and forth in an almost comical gait after the "oooah, coo, coo," the bird probably is a dove.

Directions: Drive about 15 miles from Sonora on Highway 49 South to Highway 120 east. Go past Groveland about 7.5 miles to Ferreti Road, then a short distance to Lumsden Road, and Lumsden campground is just off the road. Many people put in at Merals Pool Lumsden Campground and take out at Wards Ferry Bridge.

Activities: Whitewater rafting, kayaking, picnicking, hiking, and sight-seeing.

Facilities: Some vault toilets at restrooms.

Dates: Rafting is done May through Oct.

Fees: There is a fee for the boating permit.

For more information: Groveland Ranger District, 24525 Old Highway 120, Groveland, CA 95321. Phone (209) 962-7825. Rafting companies include: Ahwahnee Whitewater in Columbia, (209) 533-1401 or (800) 359-9790, e-mail: fun@ahwahnee.com; O.A.R.S. Inc. in Angels Camp, (209) 736-4677 or (800) 346-6277, e-mail: reservations@oars.com; All Outdoors Whitewater Rafting in Walnut Creek, (925) 932-8993 or (800) 247-2387, e-mail: rivers@aorafting.com; Sierra Mac River Trips in Sonora, (209) 532-1327 or (800) 457-2580, e-mail: smrt@mlode.com; ARTA River Trips in Groveland, (209) 962-7873, or (800) 323-2782, e-mail: arta-info@arta.org; Whitewater Voyages in El Sobrante, (510) 222-5994 or (800) 488-7238, e-mail: fun@wwvoyages.com; ECHO: The Wilderness Co. in Oakland, (510) 652-1600 or (800) 654-3246, e-mail: echo@echotrips.com; Zephyr Whitewater Expeditions in Columbia, (209) 532-6249 or (800) 431-3636, e-mail: zephyr@goldrush.com.

Toiyabe National Forest

[Fig. 25] A glance at the size of the Toiyabe National Forest, established in 1964, makes one wonder if it is not the dominant natural area in the Sierra Nevada. The forest is 4.3 million acres, making it the largest national forest in the contiguous 48 states. But most of Toiyabe's acreage is in Nevada or along the California/Nevada line, outside the Sierra geological province.

Still, the forest offers spectacular hiking, wildlife viewing, and camping on the Sierra's stark east escarpment. The 48,000-acre Hoover Wilderness contains glacial lakes that have been stocked with trout. Yosemite National Park is just west of the wilderness. Hikers can easily go from Hoover Wilderness to one of the 10,000- or 11,000-foot passes into the park.

When crossing the crest of the Sierra on Highway 108, through Sonora Pass, motorists will watch the lush alpine vegetation switch over in a matter of minutes to the high desert vegetation that is characteristic of the arid east side. Anyone traveling through Sonora Pass or any of the other high Sierra passes should remember that the roads are usually closed in winter under heavy snowfall.

Volcanic features are also a part of the landscape on the east side. Aside from the views, volcanic activity leaves the residual benefit of hot springs. There are many on the east side, and Grover Hot Springs State Park is one of the more popular ones.

GROVER HOT SPRINGS STATE PARK

[Fig. 21(4)] A dip in mineral water at 102 degrees Fahrenheit is probably the best reason to visit Grover Hot Springs State Park, especially in the late fall or early winter. The biggest season is August, because that's when the tourist season is in full swing. But the cooler off-season is among the best times to visit.

Just be sure to check the weather report before going to Grover. Weather in the Sierra—or any high mountain range—is always worthy of watching and respecting because it can change so quickly. On the arid eastern side of the Sierra, weather is especially capricious.

Pristine, clear, warm days can be followed by cold, stormy nights. The eastern crest of the Sierra is a drier version of the west slope because of its steep slope, with a relatively gentle upslope on the west compared to the sudden and almost severe drop on the east side. Storms tend to drop a lot of precipitation on the west side, lose moisture before they get to the east side, and still pack a lot of wind energy. Thunderstorms are especially violent on the east side of the Sierra in August.

At Grover Hot Springs, which is at the edge of the Great Basin Province, the open pine forest and sagebrush belt are pummeled by everything from major blizzards to violent thunderstorms to dry, scorching winds. Winter temperatures can drop to minus 5 degrees Fahrenheit, and summer temperatures can climb up to 95 degrees.

The two pools at Grover Hot Springs will close during major thunderstorms whenever lightning strikes come within 1 mile (about five seconds between the sighting and the thunder). The thunderstorm season reaches its height in July and August. The weather supports pinion-juniper woodland, mixed with a coniferous forest. But the park's most interesting characteristic is Great Basin sagebrush (*Artemesia tridentata*). The smell of sagebrush in the eastside woodland is noticeable, especially in spring. Many miles down the road from mountain passes, people can smell this aromatic shrub.

It is the dominant plant over hundreds of miles on the eastern Sierra. It is home and protection to many kinds of insects and small animals. Many trails around the park will lead visitors to vast acreages of this ecosystem. It can be found in well-drained soils on outwashes, alluvial fans, and upland flats.

The sagebrush can be seen around the Grover Hot Springs area, along with wildlife such as deer mouse *(Peromyscus truei)*, black-tailed jackrabbit *(Lepus californicus)*, and sagebrush chipmunk *(Eutamias minimus)*. But sagebrush and wildlife are not the main attractions for most visitors at the 700-acre Grover park. More than 100,000 people visited this place each year in the mid-1990s, and most were here for a dip in the pools. To achieve a comfortable temperature, state authorities combine cold water with the 148-degree stream, heated by the magma hundreds of feet below the ground level. The temperature in the hot pool runs between 102 and 104 degrees year-round, even in snowstorms.

The hot springs were formed thousands of years ago when a fault below ground level moved and diverted an underground stream through a heated, magmatic area. Many kinds of minerals, such as salt and calcium carbonate, are dissolved in the water at the higher temperatures. This spring is relatively low in sulfur content, so it does not have a powerful odor.

One of the more common questions about the hot springs is, "Why do they look green?" The main reason is the oxidation between the mineral salts and the sanitizing agent (Bromine) used in the pool. Viewed from a distance, the light tends to fall in the yellow and green parts of the spectrum.

Directions: From Lake Tahoe, drive about 35 minutes south on Highway 89 to Markleville. Turn right on Hot Springs Road, and drive 4 miles to the park.

Activities: Hiking, camping, sitting in hot springs.

Facilities: Campgrounds (some large enough for trailers or motorhomes), potable water, restrooms (1 is handicapped accessible), showers (no hot showers during winter months).

Dates: Open year-round, though campgrounds close down through winter.

Fees: There is a park entrance fee.

Closest town: Markleville, 4 miles to the east.

For more information: Grover Springs State Park, PO Box 368, Bridgeport, CA 93517 (530) 694-2248. For pool information, phone (530) 694-2248.

HUNEWILL GUEST RANCH

[Fig. 25(1)] Many people enjoy visiting a working Western cattle ranch. At the Hunewill Guest Ranch, near Bridgeport at 6,500 feet on the eastern Sierra, visitors learn cowboy skills and share the workload involved in caring for 1,200 head of cattle. Visitors here often gather and sort cattle for vaccinating or branding.

Special events are scheduled to challenge the more advanced horse riders. Visitors learn to rope, part out a cow, track a cow and not get lost, and explore "cow logic."

There's also a 60-mile cattle drive to move the herd into the Nevada acreage each fall.

Activities include talent night, family dance night, barbecues on the creek, or watching as young foals and yearlings are nurtured. There is world-class trout fishing in the nearby East Walker River and in the many lakes and streams in the adjacent Toiyabe National Forest.

The ranch was founded in 1861 by Napoleon Bonaparte Hunewill and his wife, Esther. In the 1930s, LeNore and Stanley Hunewill started the Hunewill Guest Ranch. Hunewill Ranch is still a working cattle ranch with 1,200 cows and 120 horses, as well as 60 sheep, 35 llamas, and 4 pigs.

Directions: Drive about 100 miles south of Lake Tahoe on Highway 395 to Bridgeport. Turn right off Highway 395 on to Twin Lakes Road. Drive 4 miles southwest on Twin Lakes Road and follow the signs into the ranch.

Activities: Horseback riding, learning cowboy skills, fishing, and hiking.

Facilities: About 4,500 acres of land with corrals and barns. Guest facilities include cabins and Victorian ranch house rooms.

Dates: Open May through Sept. for the summer. Fall cattle gathering in Sept. and Oct. Annual cattle drive in Nov.

Fees: There are fees for overnight accommodations. Guests stay for several nights. People can visit during the day, but accommodations are not available for visitors who want to drop in for one night.

Closest town: Bridgeport, 4 miles.

For more information: Hunewill Circle "H" Ranch, PO Box 368, Bridgeport, CA 93517. Phone (760) 932-7710 (summer), (775) 465-2201 (winter). E-mail hunewillranch@tele-net.net.

HOOVER WILDERNESS

[Fig. 25] With 48,000 acres of wild and rugged high Sierra between the elevations of 7,000 and 12,000 feet, the Hoover Wilderness is a favorite place for backpackers and day hikers. Long hikes can be taken at any time of the year, but the best time to travel in this wilderness is July through September. Though rain, blizzards, extreme cold, and strong winds can occur in any season, the summer months are the mildest.

Firewood is scarce, and no wood fires are permitted in 20 Lakes Basin, which is among the most heavily used areas. For those who want solitude, the least used area is in the northern part of the wilderness.

Wildlife viewing is one of the big reasons to hike this wilderness. Of the thousands of places in the Sierra to see mule deer *(Odocoileus hemionus)*, this is probably one of the best because it is so remote. But the deer are adept at hiding themselves in brush, so hikers must be very patient and vigilant to catch a glimpse.

For birders, the soaring red-tailed hawk *(Buteo jamaicensis)* is common in this and other parts of the Toiyabe National Forest. This hawk's binocular vision allows it to find mice, rabbits, and ground squirrels to eat. These hawks have been known to attack rattlesnakes when other prey is not available.

In this part of the Sierra, campers may also encounter the California black bear (*Ursus americanus*), which can grow to 300 pounds and eat everything in ice chests for miles. Though they are called black bears, they are often cinnamon brown in the Sierra. They are omnivores, eating vegetation, honey bees, fish, small mammals, birds, and, unfortunately for campers, anything remotely smelling like food in ice chests, garbage cans, and cars.

Visitors can easily scare off bears by banging pots and pans, yelling, or blowing whistles. They are not usually dangerous or aggressive, though there is always a danger when a mother bear and her cubs are in the area. The mother bear could misinterpret any movement as a threat to her cubs and defend them. This is a very rare situation and injuries from bears or bear attacks are uncommon in the Sierra.

The Hoover's many backcountry locations are an advantage, because black bears in the backcountry do not have as many opportunities to raid camps as those in busy places such as Yosemite National Park to the west. They simply do not learn to become as bold as bears in busier places. Usually, campers can hang their food from a tree limb about 20 feet high and thwart any nighttime bear raids.

Campers should be warned, however: Do not keep food in the tent with you. Bears have entered tents for food. Do not leave the food in the car where a bear might see it or smell it. Bears can easily peel a window or door off the car for something as small as a gum wrapper.

Campers need to obtain permits in the Hoover Wilderness, but day hikers do not need a permit. The wilderness is on a quota system, which allows only a certain number of backpackers and overnight visitors to camp each day. The exact number changes from year to year. The quota system has been adopted because summer crowds were beginning to damage meadows, trails, and other features in the wilderness.

Directions: Drive Highway 395 about 100 miles south of Lake Tahoe to Bridgeport and turn right at Twin Lakes Road to access trailheads for the central and northern parts of the wilderness. For the southern part of the wilderness, drive another 10 miles south beyond Bridgeport to County Road 021 and turn right or southwest. Continue about 4 miles to the Virginia Lakes area where southern wilderness trailheads can be found.

Activities: Hiking, backpacking, camping, fishing, wildlife viewing.

Facilities: Campgrounds at various places outside of the wilderness, but there are no campgrounds inside the wilderness.

Dates: Open year-round, but the hiking season is May through Sept.

Fees: There is a fee on trails with a quota system. Because some trails are so crowded, the U.S. Forest Service has imposed a quota or a limit on the number of hikers to maintain the wilderness experience and protect the wilderness. The fee is for day use and for overnight stays.

For more information: Bridgeport Ranger District, PO Box 595, Bridgeport, CA 93517. Phone (760) 932-7070.

BUCKEYE TRAIL

[Fig. 25(2)] The trail follows Buckeye Creek up a canyon that leads to splendid wildflower displays in June and July. Alder and fir trees mix near mountain meadows with paintbrush (*Castilleia pinetorium*) and lupine (*Lupinus*). Be prepared to hike most of the day. As the trail climbs, there are increasing numbers of aspen (*Populus tremuloides*) whose leaves will turn to gold in autumn. Even higher, granite peaks are visible as hikers come to the sign marking "Buckeye Trail," which indicates the boundary of the proposed addition to the Hoover Wilderness. The trail crosses three very small creeks as it climbs a bit then drops down to a wash.

There is no way to cross Buckeye Creek without getting wet. In September, it's shallow and easy to wade, but it could be a difficult crossing earlier when the creek is higher. Climbing along the west side of the canyon, hikers will see evidence of major washouts from snowmelt runoffs in recent years. Rock, dirt, and water came down the mountainside. Take this trail slow and easy. The trail will take hikers into the Hoover to Buckeye Forks.

Directions: Take the Twin Lakes Road turn (right) from Highway 395 at Bridgeport. Drive southwest on Twin Lakes Road to Doc & Al's Resort, about 5 miles. Turn right at the resort and follow the signs for Buckeye Campground. Drive past the campground and park near the trailhead, which is clearly marked.

Trail: 9.2 miles round-trip

Elevation: 7,000 to 8,200 feet.

Degree of difficulty: Moderate.

Surface: Rugged footpath, some rocky places. Marked in places by small stacks of rocks.

TAMARACK LAKE TRAIL

[Fig. 25(3)] The trail is accessible to stock animals in addition to hikers, and both Tamarack Lake and the pond about 1 mile below it are nice spots to go for some trout fishing. On the way to the lake, look for wildlife including deer, lizards, and birds. Fall is a prime time to observe raptors, especially red-tailed hawks (*Buteo jamaicensis*), and possibly bald eagles (*Haliaetus leucocephalus*) and golden eagles (*Aquila chrysaetos*) around Twin Lakes.

Be sure to bring plenty of water (at least two quarts), as the trail is exposed to the sun for most of the way, and climbs steeply. From the trailhead, climb a steep grade to the northeast up to a bench, where the trail doubles back to the southeast. There are good camping spots on this bench. The trail switchbacks up over another bench, then to the top of the moraine. There are good views of Twin Lakes on the way up. On top is Upper Summers Meadows.

The trail follows along the top of the moraine south for about 0.25 mile, then meets and crosses the creek. It then begins to climb pretty steeply again southward past aspens (*Populus tremoloides*), sage (*Salvia columbariae*), and bitterbrush (*Purshia tridentata)* into a dry, open, alpine environment.

Scattered around the creeks are some pines and juniper mixed among the aspens. After crossing the creek and beginning to climb, the trail turns into a gravel/sand mixture, still easily discernible. Not more than 1.5 miles after topping out, there is an easy 1-mile walk through trees, across the creek, along the south side of a grassy meadow, up through more trees, and finally across a dry alpine meadow to Tamarack Lake.

There are lots of camping spots to the north and west sides of the lake. Tamarack Lake is shallow but pretty, bounded on two sides by Monument Ridge, and on the third by Crater Crest. The ridges hold several small snowfields, and just about a 1-mile scramble up to Hunewill Lake brings you to the base of some of them.

Directions: From Highway 395 at Bridgeport, turn right onto the Twin Lakes Road. Drive west for approximately 10 miles to where the road enters a 25-mph zone, and turn left onto a dirt road at the "Forest Service Campgrounds" sign. Travel over a bridge and past the Lower Twin Campground to the trailhead parking lot on the right-hand side of the road (about 0.5 mile). To reach the trailhead, walk about 50 yards back down the road and you'll see the trailhead signs up to your right (the east side of the road).

Trail: 4 miles one-way.

Elevation: About 2,600-foot gain in elevation from about 7,100 feet to about 9,700 feet.

Degree of difficulty: Strenuous.

Surface: Clear path that turns sandy and sometimes gravely.

GREEN CREEK TRAIL

[Fig. 25(4)] The trail leads to Hoover Lakes, and the hike is exceptional because it contains so much of the East Sierra's stark beauty. It begins at Green Creek Campground, which is equipped with a toilet, garbage can, and running water—not a bad combination to find at 8,000 feet in elevation.

This is a good two-day hike because of the lakes along the way. Green Lake, East Lake, and Gilman Lake provide wonderful stops along the way. Campsites can be found in most areas.

Directions: From Bridgeport, drive about 4.2 miles south on Highway 395, and turn right on Green Creek Road (a gravel road). Drive 3.6 miles to the Virginia Lakes Road junction. Turn right, and drive another 5 miles to the trailhead.

Trail: 12.8 miles round-trip.

Elevation: About an 1,800-foot elevation gain, high point 9,860.

Degree of difficulty: Moderate.

Surface: Granite with small piles of rocks as markers.

COYOTE
(Canis latrans)

Lake Tahoe

Lake Tahoe has 71 miles of shoreline—42 in California and 29 in Nevada.

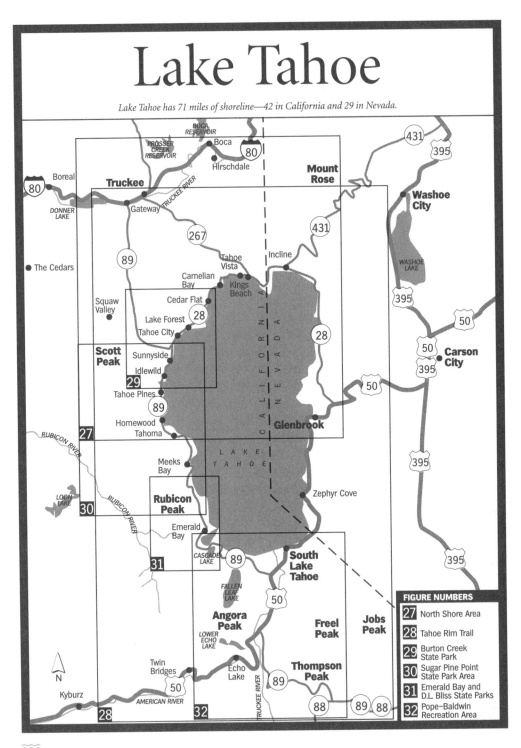

FIGURE NUMBERS

27 North Shore Area

28 Tahoe Rim Trail

29 Burton Creek State Park

30 Sugar Pine Point State Park Area

31 Emerald Bay and D.L. Bliss State Parks

32 Pope–Baldwin Recreation Area

Lake Tahoe

The Lake Tahoe Basin has been a recreational gathering place for many decades this century because millions of people are attracted to Lake Tahoe, one of the larger, clearer, high-elevation lakes in the world. People come here to hike, boat, camp, gamble, bicycle, and take photographs. Lake Tahoe and Yosemite National Park are the busiest outdoor recreation places in California, but Tahoe offers something Yosemite does not: Nevada casinos.

Lake Tahoe is at the California/Nevada state line. A visitor can spend time at a large Nevada casino where gambling and entertainment continue round-the-clock. Yet, within minutes, the same visitor can walk a mile to a spot near the lake and see an osprey *(Pandiion haliaetus)* fighting a Cooper's hawk *(Accipiter cooperi)* over a salmon.

Speedboats zoom along this 22-mile-long lake. Hikers and bicyclers navigate the 71 miles of shoreline—42 in California, 29 in Nevada. Parasails and hot-air balloons

[*Above:* 122.1 million-acre-foot Lake Tahoe is larger than any human-made reservoir in California.]

float across the sky. Motels crowd the shoreline.

Behind the recreational glitter, a deep geologic and cultural history surround this 122.1 million acre-foot lake. Though the lake's basin is adjacent to the Eldorado, Tahoe, and Toiyabe national forests, scientists consider it separate from other parts of the mountain range, for good reason.

For one thing, it is a pretty rare breed. Sixty-three streams flow into Lake Tahoe, but only one, the Truckee River, flows out past Reno and into Pyramid Lake. Tahoe's water never flows into the Pacific Ocean.

Tahoe's huge, natural collection of water dwarfs even the biggest human-made reservoirs in California. The water that evaporates from the lake every 24 hours could supply the city of Los Angeles for a day. At about 1,645 feet deep and 193 square miles, it is obvious that Lake Tahoe is not a body of water that would fit neatly into one administrative forest—or even one state. That's why the federal government set up the Lake Tahoe Basin Management Unit, rather than include it in a national forest.

The government clears up all kinds of misconceptions about the lake. Perhaps the biggest misunderstanding involves the lake's origins. Some people mistakenly believe the lake was formed by the collapse of a volcanic crater. Actually, plate tectonics had more to do with it in the beginning. The basin was formed 5 million to 10 million years ago when the Sierra crest began to lift on the west and the Carson Range did likewise to the east.

Volcanic eruptions entered the picture later. About 2 million years ago, an andesite lava flow from the north shore of Mount Pluto formed a barrier across the basin's northeastern outlet. Eventually, as the lake rose, the Truckee River was able to cut through these flows and flow around the volcanics to the lowlands of Nevada.

Glaciers downstream of the lake also dammed it between 20,000 years ago and 2 million years ago, causing the lake level to fluctuate as glacial periods came and went. At one point, the lake was almost 800 feet higher than its present level. Large sedimentary terraces perched above the lake remain as evidence of the old shore much closer to the natural rim.

It is believed that long-term drought—which has occurred periodically over the last several thousand years—is responsible for the lowering of the lake even farther below the current shoreline than it is today. Researchers have found tree stumps as deep as 16 feet below the surface of the current south shoreline and 40 feet deep along the east shore. The trees were about a century old when they died. A lake reduction of that magnitude in the last several thousand years suggests stream changes, wetland modifications, and a host of erosion and sediment problems that would have impacted the area.

Further back in time, three major periods of glaciation occurred in this part of the Sierra during the last Ice Age, which ended 10,000 years ago. Rather than featuring the regional "ice sheets" that covered much of North America, the Ice Age manifested itself as individual glaciers forming at the highest elevations. These glaciers carved out individual valleys during their downward movement. Emerald Bay on Lake Tahoe and nearby Fallen Leaf Lake have the elongated shapes characteristic of glacial valleys.

The ice dams across the Truckee River canyon floated several times and broke apart, releasing walls of water that carried immense boulders downstream, now found along the Truckee River canyon and in the Reno area. These floods also carved through the glaciers surrounding Truckee and eroded channels through their glacial debris.

Similar events took place around the lake; many are described in signs around the lake. The signs say Tahoe, at 6,225 feet in elevation above sea level, is the 3rd deepest lake in North America and 10th deepest in the world. The lake bottom is actually 92 feet below the level of Carson City, Nevada, to the east. Scientists estimate it would take 700 years to refill if it somehow emptied into the Pacific.

The tributaries deliver about 300,000 acre-feet of water to the lake annually to keep it deep and cold. Because of the lake's depth and circulation, it does not freeze. However, portions of Emerald Bay on the southwest shore have been covered with ice. Temperatures tend to stratify in the lake, with the shallower portions reaching temperatures as high as 68 degrees Fahrenheit. Below 600 feet, however, the water remains a fairly constant 39 degrees Fahrenheit.

The pristine mountains surrounding this high-elevation lake are filled with flora and fauna that have been studied for many years. Like the rest of California, the big swings in temperatures, precipitation, and terrain make it a place filled with endemics—plants that are found nowhere else on earth. Among them are the clarkias, sunflower family members, and buckwheats.

The animals include the black bear (Ursus americanus), which can grow to 500 pounds. Migrating birds, small terrestrial scavengers, and many types of fish are found around the lake. One interesting fish is the kokanee salmon, which does not migrate to the ocean and then return to fresh water to spawn. The kokanee instead spawns in surrounding streams and lives its life in Lake Tahoe's clear water.

The lake's water is known for being clear because of the high Sierra streams that empty snowmelt into it. In many places, people can see down 75 feet. But Lake Tahoe is in the process of filling up with sediments washed into it from slopes that are being cleared for construction. Each sediment particle carries nutrients that stimulate algae growth and could eventually ruin the famous clarity of the lake.

This is where the human activity and the ecosystem clash. Federal government scientists continue to study human impacts on water and air quality, and the delicate natural balances that keep Tahoe healthy. For instance, ozone, the invisible gas created in summer when chemical emissions from cars mix with sunlight, is actually being carried into the lake area through atmospheric winds from other parts of California.

The basin has long been considered a place where contaminants, smoke, and airborne matter could accumulate, even from limited sources. Smoke from natural lightning fires and fires set by the Washoe people occurred at the lake in historic times. The smoke is believed to have played an important role in limiting outbreaks of insect pests in the forest. The wood smoke, however, is not nearly as bad as emissions from automobile engines and other sources.

Until about the last half century, Lake Tahoe was quite a different place for people. Humans have been part of the ecosystem for about 8,000 years.

Centuries before explorers John Fremont and Kit Carson discovered Lake Tahoe in 1844, the Lake Tahoe Basin was a summer gathering place for three bands of peaceful Washoe Indians. Scientists believe the Washoe inhabited the area as long as 1,300 years ago. The lake held a spiritual meaning for the tribe and many sacred ceremonies were held along the southern shores.

The Indians hunted, fished, and gathered in this elegant ecosystem. Burning, weeding, and selective harvest were part of their manipulation of the ecosystem. Pinion pine *(Pinus monophylla)* and acorns from various trees provided winter staple foods.

But by the end of 1862, the tribe lost all its lands due to encroachment from European settlers. The California Gold Rush lured emigrants and fortune seekers to the rugged Sierra. Prospective miners used passes to the north and south to circumnavigate the Tahoe Basin.

The first west-to-east road across the mountains, the "Bonanza Road," was built to handle travelers eager to cash in on Virginia City's massive Comstock Lode, which was discovered in 1859. Highway 50 now covers this route. Way stations, stables, and tollhouses sprang up along the route. These stations were the basis for most development in the area, from Friday's Station at Stateline, which served as a Pony Express stop, to Yank's Resort in Meyers, which was built in 1851.

The discovery of the Comstock Lode not only increased traffic, but it also inflated the use of the Tahoe Basin's natural resources to a dangerous level. Wood was needed for fuel and to support the labyrinth of mines being constructed beneath Virginia City.

Between 1860 and 1890, two-thirds of Tahoe's forests were stripped of trees. During peak years, 72 million board-feet of lumber were milled. The Carson and Tahoe Lumber and Fluming Company produced 750 million board-feet and 500,000 cords of firewood between 1873 and 1898. And there were three other major companies. The decline of the Comstock Lode may have been the saving of the Tahoe forest.

About the time the Comstock mines opened in the late 1850s, the commercial fishing industry discovered the world-class trout fisheries at Lake Tahoe. Within a few years, San Francisco, New York, Chicago, and other cities were importing Lake Tahoe trout. In 1880, state records show commercial fishing took 70,000 pounds of the native cutthroat or black-spotted trout *(Oncorhynchus clarki)*. Commercial fishing was banned in 1917, just before the native trout population was fished out of existence.

Grazing also took place in the Comstock era. With commercial hay production reaching 800 tons each year, thousands of head of livestock were driven through the Lake Tahoe Basin to Virginia City where they were sold. Sheep were grazed for four decades after the Comstock era.

Washoe elders, who continue to gather basket materials and medicinal plants, say the sheep grazing probably destroyed the last of many important plant resources in the area. In some areas, the ubiquitous sheep grazing consumed every last shrub and patch of grass. Herders also burned many large, downed trees that they considered an obstruction. The large trees were key parts of the ecosystem, providing shelter and nutrition for insects and small animals.

Other attempts were made to control the ecosystem as well. In the late 1800s, dams were built on streams in the basin and water was diverted to Echo and Marlette lakes. The water was used for a variety of purposes, including irrigation.

At one point, U.S. Senator Francis G. Newlands pursued construction of a new dam at Lake Tahoe's outlet along the northern shore to ensure a constant water supply into Nevada for irrigation. His efforts resulted in the landmark Federal Reclamation Act of 1902, the law of the land in this century for parcelling water among users on federal projects. The Newlands Project—the dam at Tahoe's outlet to provide irrigation water for Nevada—remains the largest single appropriator of water from the Lake Tahoe Basin.

But the conservation backlash began almost at the start of the drain on Tahoe resources. The scenic qualities of Tahoe were not lost on the San Francisco newspapers, which reported the area's recreation potential as early as 1859.

A young Mark Twain wrote in 1861 of the beauty he saw at Tahoe: "As I lay there with shadows of the mountains brilliantly photographed upon its still surface, I thought it must surely be the fairest picture the whole earth affords."

These reports of Lake Tahoe's beauty did not go unnoticed by the wealthy families of San Francisco. By the turn of the century, the lake had become a haven for the well-to-do. Popular hotels of the era included the Tallac House, Tahoe Tavern, and the Glenbrook Inn. This period marked the heyday of steamship transportation around the lake, with boats providing mail and supply delivery and lavish transport for visitors.

In 1900, the Lake Tahoe Railway opened between Truckee and Tahoe City on the west shore, allowing wealthy San Franciscans to make the trip in nine hours. This melding of tourism and a wilderness ethic was established and carried through the twentieth century.

During the '20s and '30s, the roads through the mountains were paved, bringing in greater numbers of people and sparking growth of smaller, middle-class lodges. Development at Lake Tahoe began in earnest in the 1950s. Roads to the basin began to be plowed year-round, enabling permanent residence.

The growth took off with the emergence of the private automobile, the booming post World War II population, and the growing middle class. Casinos, conveniently

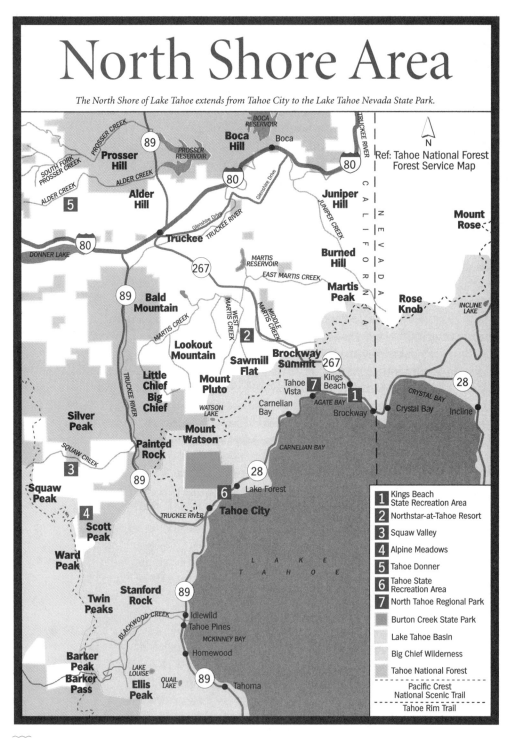

North Shore Area

The North Shore of Lake Tahoe extends from Tahoe City to the Lake Tahoe Nevada State Park.

Ref: Tahoe National Forest
Forest Service Map

Legend:

1. Kings Beach State Recreation Area
2. Northstar-at-Tahoe Resort
3. Squaw Valley
4. Alpine Meadows
5. Tahoe Donner
6. Tahoe State Recreation Area
7. North Tahoe Regional Park

- Burton Creek State Park
- Lake Tahoe Basin
- Big Chief Wilderness
- Tahoe National Forest
- - - Pacific Crest National Scenic Trail
- - - Tahoe Rim Trail

located just across the state line in Nevada, were an added attraction. In 1944, Harvey Gross started the casino trend by opening Harvey's Wagon Wheel Restaurant and Casino. Others followed. By 1955, William Harrah purchased the Gateway Club and opened Harrah's hotel and casino. Two years later, in 1957, he expanded from a summer-only business to year-round.

The 1960 Winter Olympics at Squaw Valley put Lake Tahoe firmly on the map as the skiing center of the western United States. In 1968, growing environmental concerns caused California and Nevada to form the Tahoe Regional Planning Agency to oversee environmentally responsible development in the basin. Work began on a master plan designed to improve the local tourism industry while protecting the fragile environment on which it is based.

Tourism has developed into a $1 billion-a-year industry at Lake Tahoe. On peak holidays, more than 200,000 people visit the basin. An estimated 15 million people see Tahoe each year.

The late twentieth century urbanization of Tahoe and the crush of visitors have prompted the Washoe people to focus on re-establishing a presence in the basin. The tribe's influence had slowly diminished after 1950. Now, the Indians have become vocal stakeholders in the process of protecting the Lake Tahoe Basin.

There are generally four sections of the Lake Tahoe Basin—North, West, South, and East shores. This chapter intentionally omits most of the East Shore because that side of Lake Tahoe is in Nevada. Also, the mountains on the Nevada side are generally the Carson Range, which is separate and distinct from the Sierra Nevada.

North Shore

[Fig. 27] The North Shore of Lake Tahoe extends from Tahoe City to the Lake Tahoe Nevada State Park—from California into Nevada. Some people also like to include the Truckee and Squaw Valley/Alpine Meadows areas to the west.

The North Shore seems a bit less busy than the South Shore, where historic sites, recreation, and casinos come together. But the North Shore has plenty of visitors.

Campgrounds, beaches, fishing holes, ski areas, and other facilities are used by thousands of people every year. Beaches are particularly popular. There are a half dozen within just a couple of miles around the Kings Beach State Park.

Fishing and boating are big attractions. A number of fishing guides, charter companies, and boating schools can be found on the North Shore.

All around the North Shore are views of ancient volcanoes, which helped dam the lake to create it. Andesite ridges of volcanic origin mingle with the granite of the Sierra. The volcanics and soils support many kinds of trees and brush along with brilliant wildflower shows.

Probably the most important volcano in the area is Mount Pluto, which was among the many volcanoes that erupted 25 millions years ago. Pluto ejected the lava plug that dammed Lake Tahoe. Mount Rose, on the Nevada side, is another example of a volcano that arose during the Miocene as the Pacific and North American tectonic plates collided. As with many other volcanic episodes in the Sierra and elsewhere in the world, geologists believe the collision of the tectonic plates caused magmatic unrest that resulted in the volcanics.

KINGS BEACH STATE RECREATION AREA

[Fig. 27(1)] This is the place to bring the children. The Kings Beach State Recreation Area has picnic tables, restrooms, and barbecues. Children enjoy the calm, shallow water. It is a safe place where families can recreate, but there is an entrance fee.

Kings Beach is not the only game in town for the North Shore, however. And other beaches have no entry fees, though they often do not have the facilities of the Kings Beach. The free beaches include National Avenue Beach, Moondunes Beach, Agatam Beach, and Secline Beach. They are all within about a mile of Kings Beach on the North Shore.

For those who are curious about all those trees just beyond the beach, tree identification is pretty simple matter around Kings Beach. The Jeffrey pine *(Pinus jeffreyi)* and the ponderosa pine or yellow pine *(Pinus ponderosa)* are common here.

Along the 700 feet of lake frontage at Kings Beach, the ponderosa pine displays a lighter or more pale color on mature trees, unlike any other conifer. The ponderosa pine was logged extensively and used in building materials. The fine, straight-grained wood is abundant in resin. This impressive tree can grow 200 feet tall in some areas, with a trunk width up to 8 feet. The bark on mature trees can be up to 4 inches thick, so this tree can withstand many forest fires.

In this area of the North Shore, giant hyssop *(Agastache urticifolia)* was used by Native Americans to make strong tea. The hyssop can still be seen today at the lower elevations around Kings Beach. The aromatic flower blooms in late June and July in clusters of spikes.

Directions: From Tahoe City on Highway 28, drive north about 12 miles to the junction of Highway 267. The entrance to the park is 0.25 mile east of

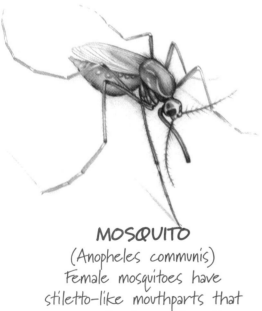

MOSQUITO
(Anopheles communis)
Female mosquitoes have stiletto-like mouthparts that are usually down when the insect is at rest.

the junction at Highway 28 and Highway 267. Follow the signs.

Facilities: Picnic areas, restrooms, and barbecue areas.

Activities: Swimming, walking, sight-seeing.

Dates: Open year-round, but the beach season is June through Sept.

Fees: There is a fee per vehicle.

Closest town: Kings Beach, 0.2 mile.

For more information: Kings Beach State Recreation Area, PO Box 266, 7360 West Lake Boulevard, Tahoma, CA 96142. Phone (530) 525-7232.

HORSEBACK RIDING

Four major stables operate in the North Shore area, including Tahoe Donner Equestrian Center, Northstar Stables, Squaw Valley Stables, and Alpine Meadows Stables. Each offers an array of rides. Tahoe Donner, for instance, has a "Horsemanship Camp" in which children learn equestrian skills.

Squaw Valley has one-, two-, and three-hour rides that leave on an hourly schedule. At Alpine Meadows, 5-year-olds are allowed on the rides. Most stables are closed for winter, but Northstar Stables offers sleigh rides when the snow flies.

For more information: Tahoe Donner Equestrian Center, phone (530) 587-9470, reservations recommended; Northstar Stables, phone (530) 562-1230, reservations recommended; Squaw Valley Stables, phone (530) 583-7433, reservations not necessary; Alpine Meadows Stables, phone (530) 587-9470.

FISHING, BOATING

Even for seasoned fishing enthusiasts, Lake Tahoe is an immense challenge. The deep-dwelling brown trout *(Salmo trutta)* and lake or Mackinaw trout *(Salvelinus namaycush)* can be trophy-sized, but it saves time to know where to fish.

Fishing is one of the big reasons people come to the North Shore. Many charter companies make it easier to find the best fishing areas. Boating and camping can often be part of a fishing trip to the North Shore, though they are certainly separate activities for many people.

For fishing enthusiasts, the kokanee salmon *(Oncorhynchus nerka)* can be an interesting and game catch. The silver and a bluish-black fish normally has a green

Mosquitoes

Anybody who has hiked the high Sierra in early July will tell you to consider another time for your hike. Mosquitoes—*Anopheles communis* and several other species—will greet July visitors in swarms. The insects hatch in the wet meadows and woodland areas where the snowmelt pools as it drains to streams and rivers.

Mosquitoes don't bite on cool or windy days, but they can be very persistent in the calm, early evening. Don't look for mosquito abatement authorities in the high Sierra. Your best bet is to come back in August or September. But if you must hike in July, bring a strong repellent and a tent with a good insect screen.

head. It has three layers of muscle—white, pink, and red or lateral muscle. The lateral muscle is found along sides, just under skin. It has high fat content used in steady, untiring swimming activity during migration from a lake to a fresh water stream nearby in September and October. Kokanee salmon require clean sand and gravel beds in streams to spawn, and the North Shore and the rest of Tahoe can provide those.

To fish for the kokanee or other Tahoe fishes, many visitors opt for the help of professionals. Fishing charter companies supply tackle and one-day licenses where they are needed. Any person, 16 years of age or older, must have a California or Nevada sport-fishing license to fish in Lake Tahoe. Surrounding lakes and streams require a license for the state in which the person is fishing.

After the fishing license, people need to know where they can find the best fishing—whether it's in the lake or in a nearby stream. That's where the charter fishing companies or guides come in. What other advice would they have? One example would be to avoid fishing during times of mirror-like calm, unless fishing deep for Mackinaw. Even a slight surface riffle will break up shadows cast on the bottom and will partially obliterate the angler from view.

There are many charter companies; here are a few: **Kingfish**, (530) 525-5360, at Homewood; **Reel Deal Sportfishing and Lake Tours**, (530) 581-0924, at Tahoe City; and **Mickey's Big Mack Charters**, (530) 546-5444, at Carnelian Bay.

For fly-fishing, try driving to Truckee in the nearby Tahoe National Forest on Highway 89 north. Among several companies, there's a place called Thy Rod and Staff, (530) 587-7333, which teaches the art of barbless-hook catching and releasing. At the end of the day, there's no fish to eat, but there's not a bunch of fish to clean out, either.

Fishing is not the only reason people flock to the water. Boating rates just as high for some people. They ski, kayak, or just tour the lake in either a tour boat or a rental. On the North Shore, check **Sierra Boat Company** in Carnelian Bay, (530) 546-2551; **North Tahoe Marina** in Tahoe Vista (530) 546-8248; or **Coon Street public launch ramp** in Kings Beach, (530) 546-7248.

Anyone interested in learning to water ski at the North Shore could contact **High Sierra Water Ski School and Sailing Center**, (530) 583-7417 in Sunnyside or **Goldcrest Resort Water Ski School** in Kings Beach, (530) 546-7412. Children as young as 4 years old have learned water skiing at such schools.

For budding sailors, **Tahoe Sailing Charters** offers skippered cruises, yacht charters, and sailing lessons. Up to six people can go on a tour for two hours. The company operates out of Incline Village on the Nevada side of the line. Phone (775) 832-1234, Ext. 51.

Some people just want to get out in the lake without getting wet or working at it. For those folks, it's easier to just sit back at the bar on the *Tahoe Gal*, a Mississippi paddle-wheeler, operated by **North Tahoe Cruises** in Tahoe City. Phone (530) 583-0141.

TAHOE STATE RECREATION AREA

[Fig. 27(6)] Tahoe State Recreation Area is one of the better choices for camping because it is very close to trails and beaches. It is also a favorite place for fishing enthusiasts. Once people have decided what they want to do around the water, they sometimes opt to camp instead of staying at motels. It generally saves money and brings people a lot closer to nature than a motel room. On the North Shore, as in other places on the lake, most of the campgrounds are open Memorial Day through October.

Most campgrounds charge a fee for extra vehicles or pets, if the pets are allowed. There are other campgrounds near Tahoe State Recreation Area. At nearby Lake Forest, a Tahoe City-owned campground, there are 20 campsites, and there are 44 at Sandy Beach, a private facility. Group sites, hookups for recreational vehicles, showers, restrooms, and boat ramps are available at each place.

Directions: From the junction of Highway 89 and Highway 267, drive south about 11 miles on Highway 89 to the sign for the recreation area. Turn left at the sign and enter the recreation area.

Activities: Camping, hiking, boating, bird-watching, and fishing.

Facilities: 38 campsites are at the park. Potable water, restrooms, showers, boat launch, picnic areas, hiking and bicycling trails.

Dates: Open June through Sept.

Fees: There are camping fees at all campgrounds.

Closest town: Tahoe City, 2 miles.

For more information: Tahoe State Recreation Area, PO Box 266, 7360 West Lake Boulevard, Tahoma, CA 96142. Phone (530) 583-3074.

BLACK BEAR
(Ursus americanus)
This bear grows to
300 pounds.

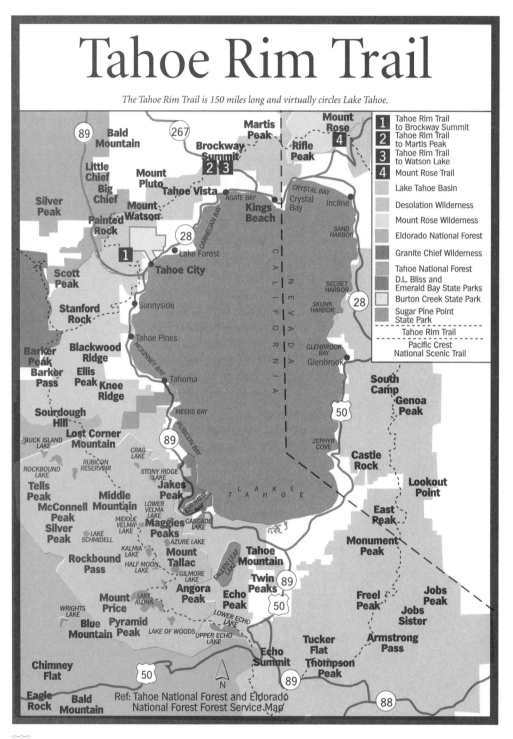

Tahoe Rim Trail

The Tahoe Rim Trail is 150 miles long and virtually circles Lake Tahoe.

Ref: Tahoe National Forest and Eldorado National Forest Forest Service Map

Legend:

1. Tahoe Rim Trail to Brockway Summit
2. Tahoe Rim Trail to Martis Peak
3. Tahoe Rim Trail to Watson Lake
4. Mount Rose Trail

- Lake Tahoe Basin
- Desolation Wilderness
- Mount Rose Wilderness
- Eldorado National Forest
- Granite Chief Wilderness
- Tahoe National Forest
- D.L. Bliss and Emerald Bay State Parks
- Burton Creek State Park
- Sugar Pine Point State Park
- Tahoe Rim Trail
- Pacific Crest National Scenic Trail

✇ HIKING

The North Shore is known for tough hiking trails that get up to the high Sierra quickly and provide views of the Northern Sierra, Nevada, and Lake Tahoe. The North Shore also has a number of stables to give visitors a chance to see everything without sweating so much.

One of the highlights of the North Shore hiking and equestrian areas is the Tahoe Rim Trail, the 150-mile route that can be used to virtually circle Lake Tahoe. It has two northern entry points on the California side of the lake. The entry points are at Tahoe City and Brockway Summit.

Two other trailheads—Mount Rose and Ophir Creek—also are on the North Shore across the state line in Nevada. The rim trail has a total of 11 trailheads, spread on the South, West, and East shores.

TAHOE RIM TRAIL, TAHOE CITY TO BROCKWAY SUMMIT

[Fig. 28(1)] People generally hike the Tahoe Rim Trail over many summer seasons, taking one section at a time. The high country views, the wildflowers, and the panorama of the lake are the reasons most backpackers need to hike this trail. On the North Shore, most people prefer the 18.5 miles between Tahoe City and Brockway Summit. Most people do not attempt the entire section in one day.

The Tahoe Rim Trail has not been around for very long. Construction on the single-track, 24-inch wide trail began in 1981. It has about 140 miles of completed trails and nine segments. The route gets a big boost from sharing the Pacific Crest Trail for 50 miles on the west side of the lake. Each segment is anchored by trailheads with information kiosks and parking.

This is high-country hiking. The trail elevations range from 6,300 feet to 9,400 feet, and the trail does not miss many peaks or ridgetops. The trail crosses six counties and passes through parts of both California and Nevada. It is a steady average grade of about 10 percent, so it is moderate in difficulty.

In these rugged conditions, the wildflower shows are remarkable. One of the more spectacular sights above 8,500 feet is the showy polemonium *(Polemonium pulcherrimum* var. *pulcherrimum)*. This light blue or sometimes violet flower blooms in open clusters. It can look like a fern with overlapping leaflets. Look for this tough little flower in the rocky outcroppings at higher elevations, ridgetops, and summits along the rim trail.

Another flower that may not be so common in other parts of the Tahoe Basin is the slender paintbrush *(Castilleja tenuis)*, known for its small yellow flowers. It needs enough moisture to grow in abundance and disappears quickly after July. The slender paintbrush was formerly called hairy owl's clover. The flower is more apparent on the North Shore because of slightly more moisture on this side of the lake.

In vernal pools below 6,800 feet, least navarretia *(Navarretia leucocephala* ssp. *Minima)* occurs along the trail in the North Shore area. It has long, outward bracts and linear petals. It is found in midseason as things are warming up and vernal pools begin to dry. The hairy leaf and rounded flower petals of the common plant, needle navarretia

WESTERN
TANAGER
*(Prianga
ludoviciana)*

(Navarretia intertexta ssp. *Propinqua)* can be found in many places throughout this area, but the least navarretia is not common anywhere but the North Shore.

Along this trail, migrating birds—birds that fly in for the summer to take advantage of plant life and warmer weather to nest—are apparent. The western tanager *(Prianga ludoviciana)* and the white-crowned sparrow *(Zonotrichia leucophrys)* prefer the higher elevations along the red fir and lodgepole pine forests, which provide the birds protection from predators as well as habitat for nesting in the high Sierra.

On this and other trails in the Sierra, hikers should carry water pumps or water purification pills to treat any water before it is ingested. Contaminants from the air, from human and animal waste, and from other sources create health hazards from such microscopic organisms as giardia and even the mysterious cryptosporidium. Anyone who does not have either the pump or the pills should boil water before drinking it.

It is also wise to be well armed with information. Anyone hiking any significant part of this trail should have a map and details. Brochures with trail information are available at trailhead bulletin boards, the Tahoe Rim Trail office, the Taylor Creek Visitors Center, and chamber of commerce offices around the lake. The Lake Tahoe Nevada State Park restricts camping to designated campsites.

Directions: From the junction of Highway 89 and Highway 267, drive south on Highway 89 about 12 miles to Tahoe City. Turn right on Fairway Drive in Tahoe City, and go about 0.125 mile to the Fairway Community Center.

Trail: 18.5 miles, one-way.

Elevation: About 1,500-foot gain, 7,700-foot peak.

Degree of difficulty: Moderate.

Surface: Developed trail with easy-to-follow path.

For more information: Tahoe Rim Trail Association, PO Box 4647, 297 Kingsbury Grade Suite C, Stateline, NV 89449. Phone (775) 588-0686.

TAHOE RIM TRAIL TO MARTIS PEAK

[Fig. 28(2)] It does not take long to reach a vantage point of more than 8,600 feet on the North Shore. The volcanic features and the panorama of Lake Tahoe make this hike on a portion of the Tahoe Rim Trail well worth the effort.

The grade is a steady 10 percent after about 0.5 mile on a south-facing slope. If hiked in summer, plenty of water should be carried.

On the way up, the views include Jeffrey pine and white fir. An andesite ridgeline around 7,700 feet opens views of the lower countryside. To the west, see Truckee and Donner Pass. About 1,000 feet above, Martis Peak awaits.

In the next 2 miles, look south along the Carson Range to see Genoa Peak in Nevada. It stands 9,150 feet high. To the southeast corner of Lake Tahoe, locate the highest parts of the Tahoe rim: Jobs Sister at 10,822 feet and Freel Peak at 10,881 feet. Make sure it's a clear day. The peaks are more than 30 miles away.

By the time the Martis Lookout is reached, the views take in a wider panorama to the west into the Tahoe National Forest, which include several reservoirs, such as Prosser. Expect to see other folks in this area. It is a short haul, and it accommodates bicyclers.

Directions: Drive north on Highway 267 about 3 miles from Kings Beach to Brockway Summit at about 7,000 feet in elevation. Park 0.5 mile past the summit on Forest Road 18N02.

Trail: 5 miles, one-way.

Elevation: About 1,600-foot gain, 8,700-foot peak.

Degree of difficulty: Moderate.

Surface: Narrow, curving with volcanic features.

For more information: Lake Tahoe Basin Management Unit, 870 Emerald Bay Road, Suite 1, South Lake Tahoe, CA 96150. Phone (530) 573-2600.

TAHOE RIM TRAIL TO WATSON LAKE

[Fig. 28(3)] Backpackers enjoy hiking to 6-acre Watson Lake for the scenery and the camping at a small, quiet lake. The glacier-carved basin displays sites of volcanic eruptions over the last 10 million years.

The lake itself rests completely on volcanic rock, which makes Watson Lake a one-of-a-kind body of water, some geologists say. Water normally percolates through porous volcanic bedrock, but Watson Lake formed on particularly dense formations of volcanic bedrock.

As in other places around the North Shore, wildflowers are worth the walk. In May, June, and July, look in the protected volcanic niches along this trail for the Sierra primrose *(Primula suffrutescens),* the only true primrose of California. Reproducing asexually through rhizomes, this bright pink flower lights up the mountainsides in the northwest area of Tahoe.

Up on the volcanic plateaus and slopes—and even along some ridgelines—the Corry broomrape *(Orobanche corymbosa)* blooms with up to two dozen pink and purple flowers. They are best seen in the middle of the warm season, perhaps July. This plant is a member of the nonphotosynthesizing, leafless parasite family. The roots adapt by piercing the root systems of neighboring plants and stealing the nutrients.

Directions: From Kings Beach, drive north on Highway 267 toward Brockway Summit for 3 miles to reach the Tahoe Rim trailhead. Turn right and drive 0.5 mile

Trout And Yellow-legged Frogs

You'll always know when you've run across the mountain yellow-legged frog *(Rana muscosa)* because they smell like garlic. These frogs live near streams at 7,000 feet around the Lake Tahoe area, but they are becoming quite scarce. Scientists theorize it has something to do with Eastern brook trout *(Salvelinus fontinalis)*, although they're not quite sure what is happening.

The trout have been planted in streams for many years, but their populations have grown so large that scientists believe they're simply running out of food in streams. Scientists finally realized that the fish are regenerating naturally and that the plantings were overpopulating streams.

As the habitat for the trout declines, the populations of frogs have disappeared in many streams. This is true on the Eastern Sierra as well as the Tahoe area. Scientists do not know if the trout are eating the frogs or if the decline of trout habitat is also affecting the frog population. Some scientists believe the two populations are unrelated. The federal government has cut back the planting of fingerlings and study continues on the dwindling frog population.

on Forest Route 56 and park on the right.

Trail: 6.6 miles, one-way.

Elevation: About 800-foot gain, 7,800-foot peak.

Degree of difficulty: Moderate.

Surface: Old, one-lane roads mixed with open paths, rocky and narrow in places.

MOUNT ROSE TRAIL
[Fig. 28(4)] The Mount Rose Trail is in Nevada, which is outside the focus of this book. But Mount Rose is certainly worth crossing the state line for if hikers like wildflowers and a summit above 10,000 feet. The trail is not the best for viewing Lake Tahoe, but there are desert views to the northeast.

The alpine meadow wildflowers are brilliant in late June, July, and August along this trail. They include the dwarf knotweed *(Polygonum minimum)*, alpine paintbrush *(Castilleja nana)*, Anderson's alpine aster *(Aster alpigenus*, var. *andersonii)*, Sierra saxifrage *(Saxifraga aprica)*, and alpine shooting star *(Dodecatheon alpinum)*.

Hikers will notice the weathered granite or granodiorite. It has been exposed for perhaps the last 70 million years, geologists estimate.

At the summit, the panoramic view from 10,776 feet includes Mount Tallac, jutting above the horizon to the south. Hikers also will be able to see Freel Peak to the southeast. At 10,881 feet, it is the tallest peak in the Lake Tahoe area. It is on the California side.

Directions: From Tahoe City, drive 10 miles northeast on Highway 28 to the Mount Rose Highway, or Highway 431. Turn left onto Mount Rose Highway and drive about 8.5 miles, past Tahoe Meadows, to the Mount Rose trailhead, which begins at a service road with a gate across it.

Trail: 5.9 miles one-way.
Elevation: About 1,950-foot gain, 10,776-foot peak.
Degree of difficulty: Moderate/strenuous.
Surface: Service road for 2.5 miles, and your choice of a road or a rocky trail beyond.

MOUNTAIN
YELLOW-
LEGGED FROG
(Rana muscosa)
This is the only frog in the high Sierra and it has a pungent, musky odor.

☸ SNOW SKIING AND SNOWPLAY

Some of the best downhill and cross-country snow skiing anywhere can be found around Lake Tahoe. North Shore has its share of skiing attractions. Early in the season, the snow is fluffy, with lower water content than the heavy, soggy snowfalls that often occur later in winter. But, even late in winter, many slopes and trails are groomed and well maintained.

The Sierra Nevada—which literally means "snowy mountain range" in Spanish—is one of the snowiest places in North America, and the Tahoe area is one of the snowiest areas of the Sierra. It is not uncommon for Tahoe to receive 20 feet of snow at 6,000 feet each year. Just south of Tahoe at the 8,000-foot level of Tamarack Peak, the average snowfall is near 40 feet a year. A few times this century, Tamarack has approached 1,000 inches of snow in a winter.

The snow is created as Pacific Ocean storms are forced to climb over the Sierra. The storms cool and drop their moisture as snow on the west slope. There usually is very little moisture left once the storms get over the crest, so the east side is quite arid by comparison.

On the west slope, particularly around Tahoe, snow accumulations make skiing available from November through May. In big winters, snow skiing takes place in June. Northstar-at-Tahoe Resort offers downhill and cross-country courses. They are normally well groomed and ready for lots of skiers because Tahoe is a ski destination for many San Francisco Bay area and Northern California residents.

NORTH TAHOE REGIONAL PARK

[Fig. 27(7)] North Tahoe Regional Park provides cross-country access on 5 kilometers of novice trails. It's a good family place to find snowplay areas. Saucers and sleds can be rented here. For those who prefer snowmobiling, the equipment can be rented at the North Tahoe Regional Park and used on a 0.25-mile course for beginners.

Directions: From Tahoe City, drive northeast on Highway 28 about 6 miles to Tahoe Vista. Turn left on National Avenue and drive about 1 mile. Follow signs into the park.

Activities: Cross-country skiing, snowplay, and snowmobiling.

Facilities: 5-kilometer cross-country ski route, snowplay areas, rental outlet, bathrooms, and parking.

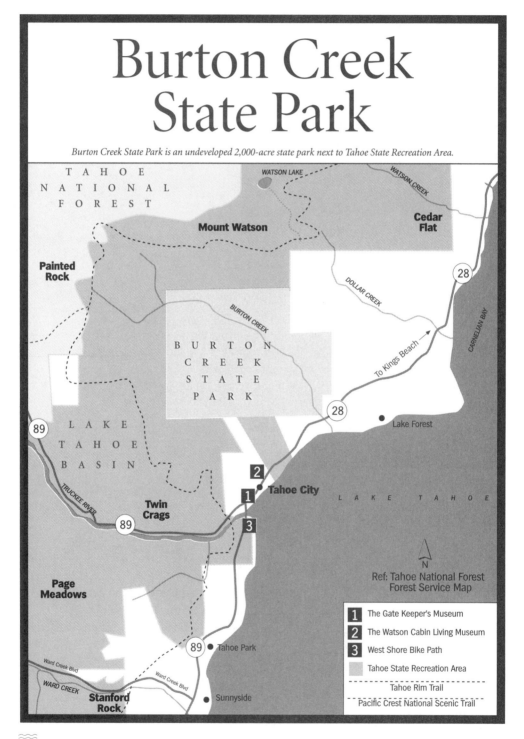

Burton Creek State Park

Burton Creek State Park is an undeveloped 2,000-acre state park next to Tahoe State Recreation Area.

TAHOE
NATIONAL
FOREST

WATSON LAKE

WATSON CREEK

Mount Watson

Cedar
Flat

Painted
Rock

BURTON CREEK

DOLLAR CREEK

28

CARNELIAN BAY

To Kings Beach

BURTON
CREEK
STATE
PARK

28

89

LAKE
TAHOE
BASIN

Lake Forest

TRUCKEE RIVER

2

1

Tahoe City

LAKE TAHOE

Twin
Crags

89

3

N

Ref: Tahoe National Forest
Forest Service Map

Page
Meadows

1	The Gate Keeper's Museum
2	The Watson Cabin Living Museum
3	West Shore Bike Path
	Tahoe State Recreation Area
	Tahoe Rim Trail
	Pacific Crest National Scenic Trail

89

Tahoe Park

Ward Creek Blvd

Ward Creek Blvd

WARD CREEK

Stanford
Rock

Sunnyside

Dates: Snow activities, Nov. through May.

Fees: There is a fee to enter the park.

Closest town: Tahoe City, 6 miles.

For more information: North Tahoe Regional Park, PO Box 139, 875 National Avenue, Tahoe Vista, CA 96148. Phone (530) 546-5043.

BURTON CREEK STATE PARK

[Fig. 29] Burton Creek State Park is an undeveloped 2,000-acre area next to Tahoe State Recreation Area (*see* page 135). There are no buildings or services of any kind. People use the 6 miles of unpaved roadways in the park for cross-country skiing. It is basically considered part of the Tahoe State Recreation Area.

Directions: From the junction of Highway 89 and Highway 267, drive south about 11 miles on Highway 89 to the sign for the recreation area. Turn left at the sign and enter the recreation area.

Activities: Cross-country skiing, snowplay.

Facilities: 6 miles of cross-country skiing, snowplay areas, bathrooms, and parking.

Dates: Snow activities, Nov. through May.

Fees: There is a fee to enter the park.

Closest town: Tahoe City, 0.25 mile.

For more information: Burton Creek State Park, PO Box 266, 7360 West Lake Boulevard, Tahoma, CA 96142. Phone (530) 525-7232.

NORTHSTAR-AT-TAHOE RESORT

[Fig. 27(2)] Here visitors can find ski classes, child care, and a slope that drops more than 1,800 feet. Northstar's runs are on Mount Pluto, which has courses for every skill level of skier.

Directions: Drive 6 miles north of Kings Beach on Highway 267. Turn left on Northstar Drive. Resort lodge is 1.5 miles from the turn on Northstar Drive. Continue about 1 mile to skiing areas.

Activities: Downhill and cross-country skiing, lessons, snowplay.

Facilities: Chairlifts, snowmaking machines, 2,000-foot intermediate run, free bus shuttles from area hotels, rentals, lodge, and restaurant.

Dates: Snow activities, Nov. to May. The resort is open year-round for many other activities.

Fees: There are fees for rentals and skiing.

Closest town: Tahoe Vista, 4 miles.

For more information: Northstar-at-Tahoe Resort, Highway 267 and North Star Drive, PO Box 129, Truckee, CA 96160. Phone (530) 562-1010.

▒ MUSEUMS OF THE NORTH SHORE
THE GATE KEEPER'S CABIN
[Fig. 29(1)] The cultural history of Lake Tahoe is told in the Native American exhibits, books, and artifacts in the Gate Keeper's Cabin. Washoe baskets and obsidian arrowheads are among the treasured items on display.

The cabin was the home for the official regulator of Tahoe's water level between 1916 and 1968, when control of the lake's levels was handed over to the Federal Watermaster's Office in Reno.

Agreements between Nevada and California allow a certain amount of water to be released from Lake Tahoe to irrigation projects on the Truckee River, which flows from the lake to Reno. The river empties into Pyramid Lake.

Directions: Drive about 6 miles south of Kings Beach on Highway 28 to the Tahoe City Y, where Highway 28 and Highway 89 meet. Turn left onto Highway 89, cross over Fanny Bridge, and park in the museum parking lot just to the right.

Activities: Touring, photography.

Dates: Open May 15 through June 15 and Labor Day through Oct. 1.

Fees: Donation only.

Closest town: Tahoe City.

For more information: The Gate Keeper's Cabin, PO Box 6141, 130 West Lake Boulevard, Tahoe City, CA 96145. Phone (530) 583-1762.

ENGELMANN SPRUCE
(Picea engelmanni)
This spruce grows up to 120 feet tall and is identified by four-sided blue-green needles and cones with wavy edges on the scales.

THE WATSON CABIN LIVING MUSEUM
[Fig. 29(2)] The only log cabin standing in the middle of Tahoe City makes an interesting place to have a museum. The cabin has been restored almost to its original condition; it was built around the turn of the century. Robert Watson, Tahoe City's first constable, built the cabin.

The Watsons were among the first families to live in Tahoe City on a year-round basis. Robert Watson was known throughout the area because people would see him patrolling on his horse.

The Watson Cabin was occupied until 1950 when the family's daughter, Mildred, moved out. The cabin was leased as a gift shop. In 1979, the North Lake Tahoe Historical Society bought the cabin and successfully petitioned to have it placed on the National Register of Historic Places.

Directions: Drive about 6 miles south of Kings Beach on Highway 28 to Tahoe City. The museum is on Highway 28, also known as North Lake Tahoe Boulevard, about 0.2 mile north of the Tahoe City Y, where Highway 28 and Highway 89 meet.

Activities: Touring, photography.

Dates: Open daily in summer, holiday weeks and weekends only the rest of the year.

Fees: Donation only.

Closest town: Tahoe City.

For more information: The Watson Cabin Living Museum, PO Box 6141, 560 North Lake Tahoe Boulevard, Tahoe City, CA 96145. Phone (530) 583-8717.

ASPEN
(Populus tremaloides)

West Shore

The West Shore runs from Tahoe City south along Highway 89 about 10 miles past three major state parks—Sugar Pine Point State Park, D.L. Bliss State Park, and Emerald Bay State Park. The three parks, along with Rubicon Bay and McKinney Bay, give visitors a lot to see and do.

People come here for fishing, hiking, backpacking, camping, and boating of all sorts. The sight-seeing includes the spectacular Vikingsholm Castle, which is modeled after Scandinavian-style architecture. It was built in 1929.

The Desolation Wilderness, one of the busiest wildernesses in the country, is just west of the Lake Tahoe Basin. Permits are required just to hike for the day. For overnight visitors, there are fees required by the Eldorado National Forest where the wilderness is located.

Sugar Pine Point State Park carries the name of a pine tree, the sugar pine *(Pinus lambertiana)*, known for its long pinecone. It was a useful tree in the life of the Native American tribes, which took the hardened fluid from within the tree bark for something schoolchildren could appreciate: They chewed the sugar sweet white nodules like gum.

On such routes as the Rubicon Trail, hikers will see volcanic pinnacles as well as evidence of glaciation, which took place sporadically over the last 2 million years in this area. Various hikes will pass granite spires and offer views of Lake Tahoe where glaciers receded only 10,000 years ago. At various elevations, there are bogs and wet meadows teaming with various kinds of wildlife.

Glacier impacts from about 1 million years ago are particularly interesting in Emerald Bay, where visitors can see the scouring effects that canyons of ice inflicted

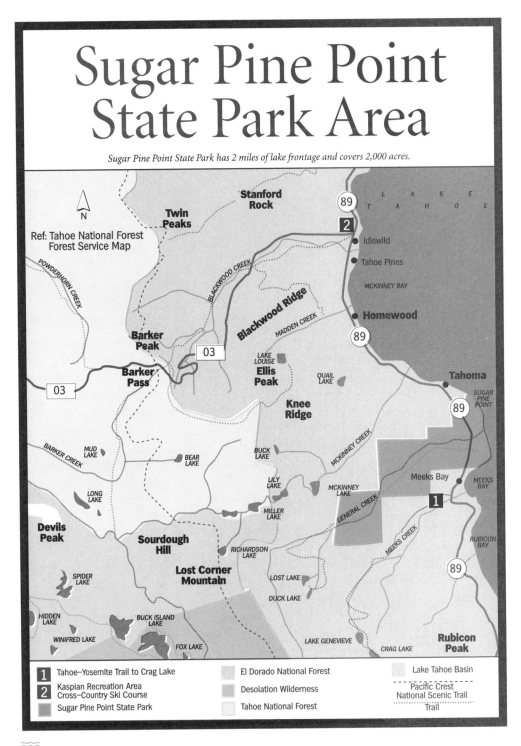

Sugar Pine Point State Park Area

Sugar Pine Point State Park has 2 miles of lake frontage and covers 2,000 acres.

on rock formations around the bay. Yet, amid the evidence of such power, people find the natural elegance of lilies, such as the Indian pond lily *(Nymphaea polysepala)* at Emerald Bay.

SUGAR PINE POINT STATE PARK

[Fig. 30] A deep cultural history brings people to Sugar Pine Point State Park where the Washoe Indians spent warm summers fishing along the peaceful banks of Lake Tahoe in the previous century. Bedrock mortars and grinding stones still can be seen at Sugar Point.

The park has 2 miles of lake frontage, filled with pine, aspen, and juniper. The park is named after a point of land where sugar pine stands congregate.

But the more impressive tree in this area may be the aspen *(Populus tremaloides)*, a slender tree with smooth, greenish-white bark. The oval leaves on this deciduous tree seem to tremble or quake in almost any breeze. Along the lake in Sugar Pine Point State Park, the trees light up the water's edge with golden yellow leaves in autumn.

Out in the water near Sugar Pine Point, brown trout *(Salmo trutta)* and lake or Mackinaw trout *(Salvelinus namaycush)* hide under ledges that can be 300 feet deep. People who fish for these trout need long lines and lots of patience. The General Creek provides the clearest water of any stream emptying into Lake Tahoe.

From the turn of the century to 1965, when it became a state park, the 2,000-acre area was owned by the Hellman family of San Francisco. I.W. Hellman, a financier, built a large summer home here in 1903. His daughter, Florence Hellman Ehrman, inherited the estate and entertained guests here until the family sold the Ehrman Mansion and the 2,000 acres to the state parks system. The three-story home, with 12 bedrooms and nine bathrooms, is now maintained and operated as a museum. It is another example of the early-century opulence at Lake Tahoe.

Directions: From Tahoe City, drive south about 10 miles on Highway 89. Follow the signs.

Activities: Fishing, hiking, swimming, boating, picnicking, cross-country skiing, camping, and touring.

Facilities: Restrooms, Ehrman Mansion museum, nature center with many displays, 12 miles of cross-country skiing, 175-site campground.

Dates: Skiing, Jan. through Mar.; other facilities open year-round.

Fees: There is an entry fee.

Closest town: Meeks Bay, 0.5 mile.

For more information: Sugar Pine Point State Park, PO Box 266, 7360 West Lake Boulevard, Tahoma, CA 96142. Phone (530) 525-7982.

TAHOE-YOSEMITE TRAIL TO CRAG LAKE

[Fig. 30(1)] The trail to Crag Lake will take hikers from the Lake Tahoe shore into the Desolation Wilderness to the west, so a day-use wilderness permit is required. The trail can be steep and warm. Take plenty of rest stops and drink a lot of water.

Look for wildflowers on the way to Crag Lake. The uncommon Shelton's violet (*Viola sheltonii*), which occurs only in deep, gravelly soils or in forests up to 8,000 feet, can be seen on this trail. The yellow flower may never have thrived in abundance around Tahoe, and it is a treasured find for any wildflower enthusiast. The more common variety, mountain violet (*Viola purpurea* ssp. *integrifolia*) is also found here. Recognize it from the dark green leaves and purple petals.

The Desolation Wilderness along this trail features granite spires and outcroppings along with an open forest of Jeffrey pine. Lake Genevieve is an inviting spot to rest, but keep going for about another 0.5 mile to find scenic Crag Lake.

The family might enjoy this outing. But make sure everyone is prepared for a full day of hiking, picnicking, swimming, and sunbathing.

Directions: From Tahoe City, drive about 11 miles south on Highway 89 to trailhead parking at Meeks Bay. Follow the signs into the parking lot.

Trail: 10 miles round-trip.

Elevation: 2,000-foot gain, 8,100-foot peak.

Degree of difficulty: Moderate/strenuous.

Surface: Dirt road, turning into granite trail, well-marked.

For more information: Wilderness permits are required. They can be obtained at the Lake Tahoe Basin Management Unit, 870 Emerald Bay Road, Suite 1, South Lake Tahoe, CA 96150. Phone (530) 573-2600. Day-use wilderness permits are available at the trailhead.

WEST SHORE BIKE PATH

[Fig. 29(3)] Families can enjoy short or long rides on the West Shore Bike Path because there are so many stopping places to picnic, see the sights, or simply stop to rest along Highway 89. The trail goes for about 10 miles to Sugar Pine Point State Park, but many people do not ride that far.

For instance, a nice brunch ride would take visitors about 4 miles to Sunnyside, a place with picnic tables and views of the lake with no fees. About 1 mile away Kaspian Recreation Area also offers picnic areas with no fees, along with beach access near campgrounds operated by the U.S. Forest Service.

About 5 miles farther is Sugar Pine Point State Park, where fees are charged for entry. For some people, this would be a morning ride, a picnic lunch, and an easy ride back in the early afternoon. For others who like to take it a little slower, it would be an all-day affair.

Directions: In Tahoe City, the trail starts about 0.2 mile south of the Tahoe City Y, where Highway 89 and Highway 28 meet. The trail is marked as the Truckee River Public Access Trailhead.

Trail: About 20 miles round-trip.

Elevation: 200-foot gain, 6,100-foot peak.

Degree of difficulty: Easy/moderate.

Surface: Mostly paved.

KASPIAN RECREATION AREA CROSS-COUNTRY SKI COURSE

[Fig. 30(2)] The trail is a gentle 4-mile round trip into the Blackwood Canyon to the west on Forest Road 3. It is a good beginner and intermediate cross-country skiing area.

The canyon, formed over the last 15,000 years by Blackwood Creek, becomes a challenging course beyond the road where more experienced skiers can ascend to Barker Pass at about 8,000 feet. Forest Service officials warn the area beyond the paved road is prone to avalanches.

Directions: From Tahoe City, drive about 4 miles south to Kaspian Recreation Area. Follow signs to the Sno-Park where the trail begins on the west side of Highway 89.

Activities: Cross-country skiing, snowplay.

Facilities: Restrooms with flush toilets, potable water, and trail.

Dates: Open Nov. through Mar., depending on the snow season.

Fees: None.

Closest town: Tahoe City, 3 miles.

For more information: Lake Tahoe Basin Management Unit, 870 Emerald Bay Road, Suite 1, South Lake Tahoe, CA 96150. Phone (530) 573-2600.

D.L. BLISS STATE PARK

[Fig. 31] Emerald Bay and D.L. Bliss state parks, two nearly adjoining parts of the state parks system, encompass 1,830 acres, and the core area of Bliss is about 750 acres. Many activities are common to both—fishing, swimming, boating, and hiking. But Bliss has a natural feature that distinguishes it from Emerald Bay: the Balancing Rock.

The 130 tons of granite in the northwestern part of the park are balanced on the slender base of two stone pedestals, which are eroding and cracking. Eventually, the supporting rock will crumble, and the large rock on top will come crashing down. The rock can be seen and photographed on a 0.5 mile, self-guided tour.

The thin granitic soil away from the shoreline allows only hardy trees with root systems that can spread for some distance along the ground to find nutrients. Often the trees, such as ponderosa pine, Jeffrey pine, and white fir, are gnarled and stunted.

Closer to the water, along stream banks and Tahoe's bank, the vegetation becomes lusher as the soils become deeper. Look for mountain alder (*Alunus tenuifolia*), aspen (*Populus tremaloides*), and creek dogwood (*Cornus californica*). The reddish-stemmed dogwood will blossom in white, round-topped clusters in April around Bliss park.

D.L. Bliss State Park is named for a pioneering lumberman, railroad owner, and banker of the region. His family donated 744 acres to the state parks system in 1929.

Directions: From Tahoe City, drive about 17 miles south on Highway 89 and turn left onto Emerald Bay Road. Follow the signs to the park.

Activities: Hiking, swimming, boating, scuba diving, bird-watching, fishing, and touring.

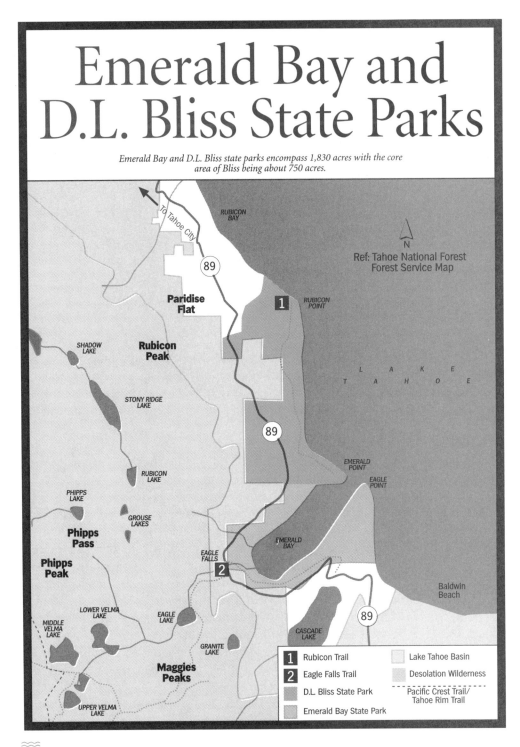

Emerald Bay and D.L. Bliss State Parks

Emerald Bay and D.L. Bliss state parks encompass 1,830 acres with the core area of Bliss being about 750 acres.

To Tahoe City

RUBICON BAY

N

Ref: Tahoe National Forest
Forest Service Map

89

Paridise Flat

1 RUBICON POINT

SHADOW LAKE

Rubicon Peak

STONY RIDGE LAKE

L A K E
T A H O E

89

RUBICON LAKE

EMERALD POINT

EAGLE POINT

PHIPPS LAKE

Phipps Pass

GROUSE LAKES

Phipps Peak

EAGLE FALLS

2

EMERALD BAY

Baldwin Beach

LOWER VELMA LAKE

EAGLE LAKE

MIDDLE VELMA LAKE

GRANITE LAKE

CASCADE LAKE

89

Maggies Peaks

UPPER VELMA LAKE

1	Rubicon Trail		Lake Tahoe Basin
2	Eagle Falls Trail		Desolation Wilderness
	D.L. Bliss State Park		Pacific Crest Trail/ Tahoe Rim Trail
	Emerald Bay State Park		

Facilities: Restrooms, picnic areas, campgrounds, boating launch.

Dates: The park is open year-round. Campgrounds operate May through Sept.

Fees: There is an entry fee.

Closest town: Meeks Bay, 1 mile.

For more information: D.L. Bliss State Park, 9881 Emerald Bay Road, PO Box 266, Tahoma, CA 96142. Phone (530) 525-7277.

RUBICON TRAIL

[Fig. 31(1)] The Rubicon Trail allows visitors to hike along the shore of Lake Tahoe between D.L. Bliss State Park and Emerald Bay State Park. On clear, calm days, people can see features 50 to 70 feet deep in the water—a bit different from 100-foot-plus depths people could see 30 years ago in the lake. As development continues around the lake, wastes contribute to large algae blooms and cloudy water.

The trail takes hikers past the Old Lighthouse. Unused today, the lighthouse is surrounded by conifers that partially block a once magnificent view of the lake.

Hikers will notice the aroma of the tobacco brush (Ceanothus velutinus) along the Rubicon. This shrub combines with other vegetation, such as alpine prickly currant (Ribes montgenum) and pinemat manzanita (Arctostaphylos nevadensis), to fill out the understory beneath pines in the area.

In spring and summer, hikers will see the osprey (Pandion haliaetus), an efficient fishing bird, nesting in nearby trees. The osprey is considered a species at risk in the Sierra. Development of wildlands and diminishing habitat are among the osprey's biggest problems.

Directions: From Tahoe City, drive about 17 miles south on Highway 89 to D.L. Bliss State Park. Park in the Calawee Cove parking lot at the edge of the lake.

Trail: About 9 miles round-trip.

Elevation: About 200-foot gain, 6,580-foot peak.

Degree of difficulty: Moderate.

Surface: Open, rocky footpath.

For more information: Lake Tahoe Basin Management Unit, 870 Emerald Bay Road, Suite 1, South Lake Tahoe, CA 96150. Phone (530) 573-2600.

EMERALD BAY STATE PARK

[Fig. 31] Boating, wildlife viewing, and scuba diving are all popular activities at Emerald Bay State Park. Vikingsholm Castle is a favorite for touring. The castle was built on the shore, and a smaller stone structure, called the "Tea House," is built on Fannette Island, the only island in Lake Tahoe.

Geologists believe Fannette survived a siege of glaciers over the last 1 million years. The granite island simply resisted the forces of glacial erosion and now rises about 150 feet above the water. It is sparsely populated with timber, mostly sugar pine.

Look for various migrating birds and shorebirds in this area, particularly the Wilson's warbler (Wilsonia pusilla). The warbler's sharp, staccato call can be heard

*Visitors to the Desolation Wilderness in El Dorado National Forest
can enjoy this view of Lake Tahoe.*

from the plant cover. The bird snatches flying insects near the water's edge. In this area, warblers and other birds feed on the stoneflies (order Plecoptera), Thirps (order Thysanoptera), and water striders (family Gerridae).

On the West Shore, biologists say wolverines *(Gulo luscus)* were once a big part of the ecosystem. Wolverines are considered quite rare in the Sierra Nevada now, victims of poaching and the encroachment of civilization. They were once abundant from Tahoe south to Giant Forest in Sequoia National Park.

Like the grizzly bear *(Ursus arctos)*, which disappeared completely from the Sierra in the 1920s, wolverines created a balance in the ecosystem by staking out territory that mountain lions *(Felis concolor)* and coyotes *(Canis latrans)* would routinely avoid. Grizzlies and wolverines had a habit of taking kills from the lions and coyotes.

With lions and coyotes avoiding certain territories, there were reasonably safe places for many creatures such as the mountain or bighorn sheep *(Ovis canadensis)*. Without the protection of the larger predators, the sheep population has dwindled to 100 on the East Side of the Sierra, and it is listed under the federal Endangered Species Act. Other smaller creatures, such as the southern grasshopper mouse *(Ony-chomys torridus)* and the panamint chipmunk *(Tamias panamintinus)*, are slowly disappearing, and many believe it is because of the ecosystem imbalance.

The human species has had no such trouble in Emerald Bay. In the 1920s, Lora Josephine Knight purchased Fannette Island and some land on shore. She commissioned the construction of Vikingsholm and the "Tea House." Only the stone shell of the Tea House remains today, but decades ago Mrs. Knight would entertain guests for tea in the 16-by-16-foot room.

On shore, touring the castle is like stepping back into medieval times. It has a sod roof over two sections, and several other parts of the structure have no nails or spikes. The castle also has six fireplaces. The second floor furnishings were constructed in detail to replicate Scandinavian design.

In 1994, Emerald Bay was also designated an underwater state park because of the artifacts that can be found on the bottom of the lake in this area. Scuba divers will find artifacts near the old Emerald Bay Resort on the north shore of Emerald Bay. One diver saw a Model A Ford. Other items from the past include telephone batteries, sinks, toilets, and an old pier. Divers are reminded not to remove or disturb artifacts.

Directions: From Tahoe City, drive south on Highway 89 about 22 miles. Follow the signs.

Activities: Hiking, swimming, boating, scuba diving, bird watching, fishing, and touring. Camping is prohibited on Fannette Island.

Facilities: Restrooms, picnic areas, boat camp with mooring buoys for 20 campsites, Vikingsholm Castle, and Tea House.

Dates: Vikingsholm is open year-round; the Tea House is open from Feb. through June 15.

Fees: There are fees to tour Vikingsholm and for park entry.

Closest town: South Lake Tahoe, 5 miles.

For more information: Emerald Bay State Park, PO Box 266, Tahoma, CA 96142. Phone (530) 541-3030.

EAGLE FALLS TRAIL

[Fig. 31(2)] This short walk up to Eagle Falls is surrounded with lush vegetation. Look for aquatic perennials such as the buckbean *(Menyanthes trifoliata)*, which roots from submerged rhizomes, as well as the yellow pond lily *(Nuphar lutea* ssp. *polysepala)* in calm pools of water, away from the falls.

The falls usually slow down in late summer as the snowmelt subsides in the high Sierra. For a good look at roaring falls, make this hike in May or June.

Directions: From Tahoe City, drive 18 miles south on Highway 89 to the Eagle Falls Picnic Area's parking lot entrance. Signs mark the trailhead.

Trail: About 0.25 mile round-trip.

Elevation: About a 400-foot gain, 6,630-foot peak.

Degree of difficulty: Easy.

Surface: Open footpath about 0.125 mile long.

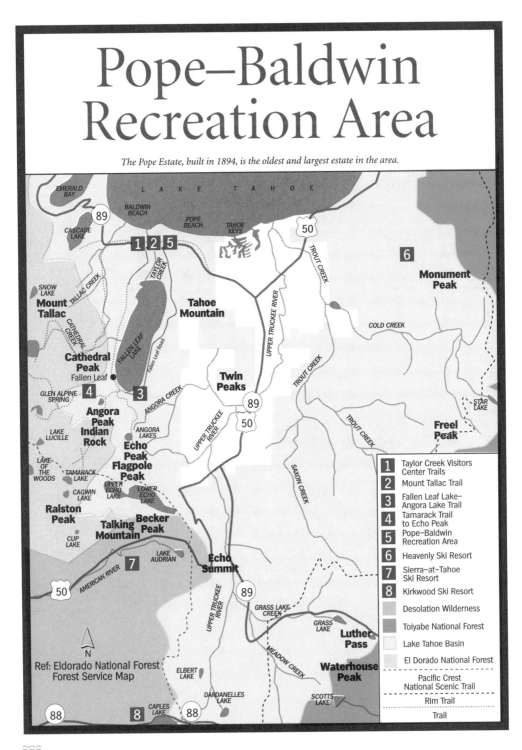

Pope–Baldwin Recreation Area

The Pope Estate, built in 1894, is the oldest and largest estate in the area.

1 Taylor Creek Visitors Center Trails
2 Mount Tallac Trail
3 Fallen Leaf Lake–Angora Lake Trail
4 Tamarack Trail to Echo Peak
5 Pope–Baldwin Recreation Area
6 Heavenly Ski Resort
7 Sierra–at–Tahoe Ski Resort
8 Kirkwood Ski Resort

Desolation Wilderness
Toiyabe National Forest
Lake Tahoe Basin
El Dorado National Forest

Pacific Crest National Scenic Trail
Rim Trail
Trail

Ref: Eldorado National Forest Forest Service Map

South Shore

A lot of people visit South Shore to enjoy the interesting combination of camping, boating, hiking, touring, and gambling. With large casinos, such as Harrah's, just across the state line in the city of South Lake Tahoe, outdoor recreation can be the second choice for some people.

Out on the lake, not more than 0.5 mile from the casinos, people boat, enjoy the sunshine, and swim. A little farther away from the bright lights, such places as the Pope-Baldwin Recreation Area beckon visitors to hike and visit historic sites. Tallac Historic Trail takes visitors to the beach and to self-guided tours of homes dating back to the early part of the century. Other trails lead to such wonders as Mount Tallac, the 9,735-foot peak visible from all parts of the South Shore. Tallac stands so close to the lake that hikers can actually see the currents moving. Tributaries adding water, wind blowing across the surface, and other factors create currents.

The migrating birds are exceptional at sites on the South Shore, as they are in many places around Lake Tahoe. Fishing, camping, and boating are all part of the attraction, though it can get a little crowded in August during the height of the tourist season. Snow skiing and snowplay are among the major reasons to visit the South Shore. Skiers can find about a half-dozen cross-country courses and several downhill locations. Snowmobiling and ice skating are part of the winter recreation on the South Shore.

In the South Shore area, the bedrock is like that in the rest of the basin, composed of a type of granite rock called granodiorite and a type of volcanic rock called andesite. The volcanic soils tend to hold more nutrients. The volcanic rock breaks down easier than granite, contains more clay, and makes a good place for plants to grow. The vegetation and wildlife are not hard to find on trails to the surrounding peaks. Freel Peak, at 10,881 feet, is the tallest and affords the most panoramic views of the lake and the Sierra. Echo Peak, at 8,895 feet, is less spectacular, but it is much closer to the lake than Freel and offers special views of nearby drainages into Tahoe.

POPE-BALDWIN RECREATION AREA

[Fig. 32(5)] Cultural history is almost everywhere for visitors to find in the recreation area. The Tallac Resort, the Pope Estate, and the Baldwin Estate are prime examples, but they are not the only attractions.

The natural features get a lot of attention from visitors, too. Though large animals are not common here, as they are in the wilderness and backcountry areas, there are squirrels burrowing under trees, water frogs, snakes, crayfish, and many species of birds.

Common California gray squirrels *(Sciurus griseus)* can be seen scampering in search of food. Don't feed them. Animals such as squirrels can become dependent on human food and abandon their natural foraging.

In the case of the gray squirrel, food and shelter come from the surrounding trees. Pine seeds and oak acorns are the usual fare. The squirrel has no cheek pouches, so it must eat whatever it finds instead of holding some food in its cheeks.

The gray squirrel nests high in pine trees, unlike the golden-mantled ground squirrel *(Citellus lateralis)*, which burrows beneath pine trees, such as the lodgepole pine. Visitors probably will encounter golden-mantled ground squirrels because most of them have little trouble approaching humans. They will rummage through campgrounds for food, even eating from the hand of a camper.

In the natural order of things, the squirrels are generally targets for the long-tailed weasel *(Mustela frenata)*, mountain coyote *(Canis latrans)*, and hawks of many species. The struggle for life among predators and prey sometimes continues almost unnoticed on South Shore because people can become preoccupied with the cultural and recreation attractions, especially along the flat, 2-mile Tallac Historic Site Trail. The trail begins at the Taylor Creek Visitors Center in the Pope-Baldwin Recreation Area.

A number of turn-of-the-century estates and an old resort site are within walking distance of each other at the Tallac Historic Site. They are on a 74-acre site that was transferred to the U.S. Forest Service about 30 years ago. Many of the buildings needed to be restored to give visitors a good idea of how wealthy Northern Californians vacationed in the past.

The Tallac Resort, dating back to 1890, is where the "Greatest Casino in America" once stood at Tallac Point. It was part of a resort owned by San Francisco real estate businessman Lucky Baldwin. Not much of the resort is left to see these days.

But the Pope Estate, built in 1894 by a prominent San Francisco Bay area family, is nearby, and it is intact. It is the oldest and largest estate in the area. Special programs and guided tours are available in the many buildings, gardens, and grounds. Each year in August, The Pope Estate is home for The Great Gatsby Festival, where people dress in early-twentieth century attire and celebrate. People can walk from the estate to Pope Beach, which is less than 100 yards away.

The Baldwin Estate dates back to 1921. It was the home of Lucky's granddaughter. Now it is the Baldwin Museum. The exhibits include Washoe Indian culture, Baldwin history, and the Baldwin House itself. The Heller Estate, built in 1923, is also known as Valhalla. It has a large lawn, hall, and fireplace, and is popular for public and private gatherings.

Directions: Drive 3.1 miles northwest on Highway 89 from the intersection of Highway 50 and Highway 89. Turn right at road sign for Tallac Historic Site. Follow signs.

Activities: Hiking, swimming, touring, picnicking, horseback riding, camping, boating, bicycling, fishing, and wildlife viewing.

Facilities: Campsites, bathrooms, picnic tables, barbecue pits, boat launches, horse rentals at Camp Richardson Corral on Highway 89 in the Pope-Baldwin area and Cascade Stables on Highway 89 near Cascade Lake, museums, and visitor center.

Dates: Open year-round.

Fees: There is a charge for camping, horseback riding, and Pope Estate tours.

Closest town: South Lake Tahoe, 2.5 miles.

For more information: Tahoe-Tallac Association, 1775 Sherman Way, South Lake Tahoe, CA 96151. Phone (530) 542-4166. Tahoe Heritage Foundation for Baldwin Museum, 870 Emerald Bay Road, Suite 1, South Lake Tahoe, CA 96150. Phone (530) 541-5227.

TAYLOR CREEK VISITORS CENTER TRAILS

[Fig. 32(1)] Interpretive trails have been constructed around the U.S. Forest Service's Taylor Creek Visitors Center to tell people about the natural history. They include the 1-mile Lake of the Sky Trail, the 0.6-mile Rainbow Trail, the 0.1-mile Smokey's Trail and the 0.2-mile Forest Tree Trail. A fifth trail, the Tallac Historic Site Trail, goes to the historic estates and sites around the area. It is about 2 miles long.

On the Lake of the Sky Trail, look and listen for the many pileated woodpeckers *(Dryocopus pileatus)* as they hunt through the trees for bugs, which could actually be destructive to the trees. Various kinds of bark beetles, such as the western pine beetle *(Dendroctonus brevicomis)*, burrow into pinewood to deposit larvae that emerge the next spring. The bark beetles are extremely destructive if they grow to epidemic infestations. Many acres of trees have been felled to clean out infestations that have occurred periodically during the twentieth century in the South Shore and many other places in the Sierra.

On the 0.5-mile Rainbow Trail, stop at the boardwalk and on the viewing bridge

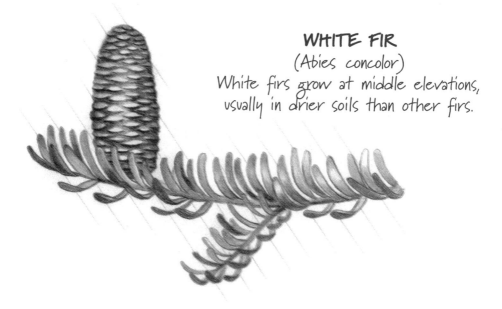

WHITE FIR
(Abies concolor)
White firs grow at middle elevations,
usually in drier soils than other firs.

over Taylor Creek to observe the water world: fish of all sizes; insects under, on, and above the water; frogs. Common garter snakes *(Thamnophis sirtalis)* are in this area. They are up to 4 feet long and harmless. Look for them near or in the water. Kokanee salmon *(Oncorhynchus nerka)* spawn in Taylor Creek before returning to Lake Tahoe to live.

At the end of the Rainbow Trail, there is a Stream Profile Chamber that allows 300,000 people annually to view the stream environment through aquarium-like windows built on a diversion of Taylor Creek. The chamber features floor-to-ceiling viewing windows, about 12 feet of viewing, and a 180-degree curved diorama along with interactive interpretive components.

Directions: Drive 3.2 miles northwest on Highway 89 from the intersection of Highway 50 and Highway 89. Turn right at road sign for Taylor Creek Visitors Center, just about 150 yards west of Fallen Leaf Road. Follow signs to the center.

Activities: Self-guided trail tours, hiking, bicycling, special events such as the Kokanee Salmon Festival (first weekend in October).

Facilities: Bathrooms; visitors center offering maps, brochures, wilderness guides, and interpretive programs.

Dates: Open year-round.

Fees: There are fees to purchase books. Other information and trails are free.

Closest town: South Lake Tahoe, 2.6 miles.

For more information: Lake Tahoe Basin Management Unit, 870 Emerald Bay Road, Suite 1, South Lake Tahoe, CA 96150. Phone (530) 573-2600.

MOUNT TALLAC TRAIL

[Fig. 32(2)] Mount Tallac is a magnet for hikers who want to get above 9,000 feet

GARTER SNAKE
(Thamnophis sirtalis)
Garter snakes have three stripes, one on back and one on each side. They're often found near water.

and stay close to Lake Tahoe. The views of the glacial moraines are stunning. The rocky borders where glaciers melted and dropped granite boulders outline Emerald Bay, Fallen Leaf Lake, and other landmarks.

Near Floating Island Lake, note the grass of Parnassus *(Parnassia fimbriata)* that lines the water's edge in a few damp, shady areas. Look for the large white flower. Also, look for the black fruit of the Sierra coffeeberry *(Rhamus rubra)*. It looks like a coffee bean, but this isn't something hikers will want in their coffee cup. It is not edible.

Floating Island Lake is named for large mats of bentgrass *(Agrostis)*, brewer's reedgrass *(Calamagrostis breweri)*, and various shrubs that seem to be floating in the shallow lake. As early as 1890, the lake was noted for its floating mats of vegetation.

At the summit of Tallac, hikers will see some interesting wildflowers in July and August. The flowers must maintain most of their growth below ground to protect themselves from the cold winds whipping over the mountaintop. Such flowers include the dwarf alpine daisy *(Erigeron pygmaeus)*, hairy paintbrush *(Castilleja pilosa)*, and butterballs *(Eriogonum ovalifolium)*. These plants must adapt to the colder, harsher conditions on ridgetops by simply growing lower and staying closer to their source of food.

Directions: Drive to the Taylor Creek Visitors Center (*see* directions, page 158) where the trailhead is designated.

Trail: About 10 miles round-trip.

Elevation: About 3,300-foot gain, 9,736-foot peak.

Degree of difficulty: Moderate/strenuous.

Surface: Steep with switchbacks, narrow in places.

FALLEN LEAF LAKE-ANGORA LAKE TRAIL

[Fig. 32(3)] The view of Lake Tahoe and Fallen Leaf Lake are wonderful on this hike. Stands of white fir line the trail. As hikers move higher in elevation the smell of tobacco brush *(Ceanothus velutinus var. velutinus)* greets them along with the distinctive white flowers with yellow stamens.

Swimming is a favorite activity at Angora or Fallen Leaf lakes. Wait until late August or September to take a dip, however. The fresh snowmelt earlier in the season makes the water very cool.

When hikers reach Angora Lake, amid stands of Jeffrey pine bent and stunted because of the wind, they will be almost within view of the Angora Resort, which was built in 1917. Many years ago, children called this place the Lemonade Lake because of the lemonade served at the resort.

Directions: Drive 3.1 miles northwest on Highway 89 from the intersection of Highway 89 and Highway 50 on the South Shore. Turn left onto Fallen Leaf Road and drive another 2 miles and park at the Marina parking lot. Walk along the frontage road along the shore for a few hundred feet until reaching a church where the trail begins.

Trail: 3 miles round-trip.

Elevation: 1,120-foot gain, 7,470-foot peak.

Degree of difficulty: Easy.

Surface: Rocky, open pathway.

TAMARACK TRAIL TO ECHO PEAK

[Fig. 32(4)] The Tamarack Trail is a wildflower hike in summer. Microclimates are created by the up-and-down topography that shields small nooks and crannies from the cold north winds. The result is sheltered benches and meadows filled with white thimbleberry *(Rubus purviflorus)* and purplish blue aconite monkshood *(Aconite columbianum)*.

Birds eat the thimbleberry fruit, the small dark berry. But animals and people alike do well to avoid eating any part of the monkshood, which contains an alkaloid called anconitine. One bite of this stuff and people start experiencing nausea and impaired vision, a bad combination on any high Sierra trek.

The hike also takes people past deep history in the granite. Metamorphic rock from a time well before the main Sierra uplift—perhaps 120 million years ago—can be seen with intrusions of younger granite. Look for the features before reaching and crossing Glen Alpine Creek on the Tamarack Trail.

After about 2 miles, hikers will be able to decide if they would like to visit Triangle Lake to the northwest or turn northeast to 8,895-foot Echo Peak. The hike can be reduced by about 1 mile by skipping the lake. Many people prefer to stop at the lake for a dip before turning around and hiking up to Echo Peak, which provides views of the lake and the Desolation Wilderness to the west.

Directions: Drive about 3.2 miles on Highway 89 from the intersection of Highway 89 and Highway 50. Turn left on Fallen Leaf Road, and drive about 5.5 miles through Fallen Leaf Lake's developed area and to the Tamarack trailhead. Park at the Glen Alpine trailhead just across the Glen Alpine Creek Bridge.

Trail: 7.3 miles round-trip.

Elevation: 2,300-foot gain, 8,895-foot peak.

Degree of difficulty: Strenuous.

Surface: Rocky, steep, well established.

FREEL PEAK

[Fig. 32] People who enjoy hiking the high country and want to see a 360-degree panoramic of Lake Tahoe, parts of Nevada, and even a piece of the Central Sierra should try this trail. It is a chance to see high-elevation wonders without the crowds. Though it requires a fit, strong hiker to make this day trip, it is well worth the work.

The Tahoe Rim Trail will take hikers close enough to make the 1-mile, 1,100-foot cross-country scramble to the summit. People leave the rim trail at its highest point, 9,728 feet, for the cross-country jaunt. Granite pinnacles and volcanic ridges are everywhere in view, including Mount Tallac to the northwest of the trail.

For wildflower lovers, the hike is a treat in July and August. The blue, bell-shaped flowers of Jacob's ladder *(Polemonium californicum)* are likely to be seen in this area, especially in the open forest below 9,000 feet as the hike begins. The stems have ladder-like leaves with several hairless lancelate leaflets.

The diamond clarkia *(Clarkia rhomboidea)* is a rare species in Tahoe, having been first cataloged near Fallen Leaf Lake on the South Shore many years ago. Now, the diamond-shaped petals can be seen only in dryer areas at the beginning of this hike. The genus is named for William Clark of the nineteenth century Lewis and Clark expedition.

Look for the dwarf alpine aster *(Aster alpigenus)*, the lavender flower that grows on the borders of meadows in September when other wildflowers have already faded. The deep purple flowers are the meadow penstemon *(Penstemon rydlbergii)*, which also grow in drying meadows.

The aster and the penstemon, as well as shrubs along this trail, adapt well to the thin, rocky soils. The plants use tap roots and dwarf characteristics—such as growing low to the ground—to survive.

Some plants adapt even to small cracks in the granite, created by freezing and thawing over time. Such hardy vegetation includes the alpine fescue *(Festuca brachyphylla)*, draba *(Draba densfolia)*, and alpine locoweed *(Astragalus kentrophyta)*. These plants can survive under snow cover during the winter, but they also can survive in extremely windy, dry conditions.

Not many large animals go above the tree line, which hikers will notice is at about 9,000 feet on this hike. The trees simply stop growing because the soil, elevation, sunlight, and other factors make it impossible for larger trees to survive. Hikers will notice some animals, such as the heather vole *(Phenacomys intermedius)* and the gray-crowned rosy finch *(Leucosticte tephrocotis)*. The finch forages for seeds in summer above 9,500 feet.

The frequent freezes and thaws at these elevations also create interesting geology. The bedrock along the slope to Freel Peak is littered with quartz and feldspar crystals. But most first-time hikers on this trail will be looking for a stable place to walk or stand so they can take in the views from the rooftop of Lake Tahoe.

Directions: Drive south 9 miles on Highway 89 from the intersection of Highway 89 and Highway 50 on the South Shore. About 1 mile after passing the Luther Pass sign, turn left on Willow Pass Road, also known as Forest Road 51. Drive north about 3.5 miles and take the left fork for another 0.5 mile and park at the end of the road.

Trail: About 9 miles round-trip.

Elevation: 2,400-foot gain, 10,881-foot peak.

Degree of difficulty: Moderate for the first 3.5 miles; strenuous to the summit.

Surface: Narrow, well-defined trail, but the last mile up to the summit is a generally safe cross-country scramble over boulders. The angle can be quite steep, so take it slowly.

SKI RESORTS OF SOUTH SHORE

The South Shore skiing, featuring some of the best skiing anywhere, is home to three major resorts, many cross-country skiing courses, and a long snow season. Sometimes the skiing goes all the way through June, particularly if the El Nino weather pattern has sent a lot of storms from the Pacific Ocean.

The history of skiing runs deep at Lake Tahoe, especially at the South Shore. Prior to the 1950s, skiers in the South Shore went to Echo Summit. Early in the century in Truckee near the North Shore, there was a winter carnival with skiing and jumping events. The first chairlifts in the West arrived at Tahoe in the late 1930s.

The Winter Olympics of 1960 put Tahoe's slopes in the spotlight. The downhill events were held at Squaw Valley, near the West Shore but technically in the Tahoe National Forest. People from all over the world began to visit Tahoe in the winter just to ski.

Now, people visit more than a dozen ski areas in the Tahoe area. People ride snowmobiles and sleds. When the weather does not cooperate, people can gamble at the nearby casinos or visit a museum.

For those who prefer cross-country skiing, Tallac Historic Site Trail and the Taylor Creek/Fallen Leaf trail system provide opportunities. The Tallac trail, located in the Pope-Baldwin Recreation Area (*see* page 158) is flat and well marked. It is perfect for beginners. The Taylor Creek/Fallen Leaf system, found around the Taylor Creek Visitors Center (*see* page 157), is also mostly flat and easy for beginners.

HEAVENLY SKI RESORT

[Fig. 32(6)] It's not hard to understand why a lot of people ski at Heavenly—more than two dozen chairlifts, 37 feet of snow each year, and about 4,500 acres of skiing over two states. This is one of the larger skiing operations anywhere, and it is in one of the snowiest places in the United States.

Monument Peak rises to more than 10,000 feet on the southeast and the drop is almost 4,000 feet to Heavenly Valley. The resort offers skiing hills for all levels as well as ski lessons.

Directions: From Highway 50 in South Lake Tahoe, turn east on Ski Run Boulevard and drive about 2 miles to a marked parking area where Heavenly ski buses transport people to the resort.

Activities: Skiing, outdoor photography, sight-seeing.

Facilities: 7 lodges, more than 2 dozen lifts, 5 bus lines for shuttles, rentals, repair, restaurants, lessons.

Dates: Open Nov. through May, and sometimes in June.

Fees: There is a fee for skiing, rentals, lessons, and accommodations.

Closest town: South Lake Tahoe, 2 miles.

For more information: Heavenly Ski Resort, 3860 Saddle Road, South Lake Tahoe, CA 96156. Phone (775) 586-7000.

SIERRA-AT-TAHOE

[Fig. 32(7)] The Sierra-at-Tahoe ski resort, sister of the Northstar-at-Tahoe on the North Shore, offers long runs for skiers of all skill levels. The resort, which was once called Sierra Ski Ranch, has one run that covers 3 miles.

The area has a more modest rise in elevation than Heavenly. It drops from about 8,850 feet to about 6,600 feet, but it has plenty of excitement and variety, according to the experts.

Though Sierra-at-Tahoe is actually in the El Dorado National Forest, it has traditionally been considered a feature of South Shore skiing.

Directions: Drive about 5 miles southeast on Highway 50 from the intersection of Highway 89 and Highway 50. Turn south on the Sierra-at-Tahoe Road turnoff and drive 0.8 mile south to the resort parking lot.

Activities: Skiing, snowboarding, tubing.

Facilities: Chairlifts, rentals, repair, restaurants, and lessons.

Dates: Open Nov. through May, and sometimes in June.

Fees: There is a fee for skiing.

Closest town: Twin Bridges, 1.5 miles.

For more information: Sierra-at-Tahoe, 1111 Sierra-at-Tahoe Road, South Lake Tahoe, CA 95735. Phone (530) 659-7453.

KIRKWOOD SKI RESORT

[Fig. 32(8)] Kirkwood gets some of the heaviest snowfall in the Tahoe region. Parts of this area have received more than 50 feet of snow a few times this century. Kirkwood has a reputation for having good snowpacks and long seasons, so skiers flock to this area.

The resort has a four-story lodge and 19 condominiums. People can just ski back to their rooms when they're finished on the slopes.

Kirkwood has about 2,000 acres of groomed slopes and runs for people of all skill levels. The highest elevation run starts at 9,825 feet.

Directions: Drive 30 miles south of South Lake Tahoe on Highway 89 to Highway 88. Turn southwest on Highway 88, and drive 10 miles to the turnoff marked for Kirkwood. Drive 0.4 mile to the parking lot.

Activities: Skiing, sight-seeing.

Facilities: Chairlifts, rentals, repair, restaurants, retail stores, lodge, and lessons.

Dates: Open Nov. through May, and sometimes in June.

Fees: There is a fee for skiing, rentals, classes, and accommodations.

Closest town: Kirkwood, 1 mile.

For more information: Kirkwood Ski Resort, PO Box 1, 1501 Kirkwood Meadows Drive, Kirkwood, CA 95646. Phone (209) 258-6000.

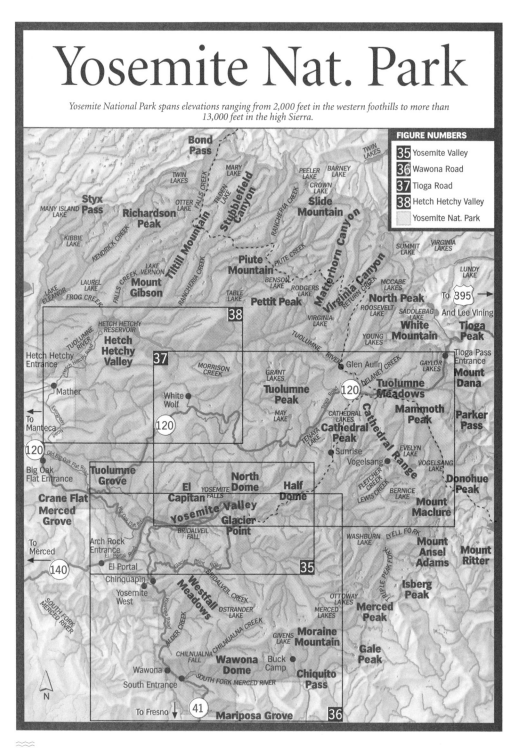

Yosemite Nat. Park

Yosemite National Park spans elevations ranging from 2,000 feet in the western foothills to more than 13,000 feet in the high Sierra.

FIGURE NUMBERS

35 Yosemite Valley
36 Wawona Road
37 Tioga Road
38 Hetch Hetchy Valley
   Yosemite Nat. Park

Yosemite
National Park

The crown jewel of the Sierra Nevada lies in the center of the 400-mile mountain range with the most distinctive and spectacular glacial valley in California—or anywhere else, by many accounts. Yosemite Valley, 7 miles long and about 1 mile wide, is essentially a stage where people can merely stand and turn their heads to see internationally known landmarks, such as El Capitan, Yosemite Falls, Half Dome, and Bridalveil Fall. The view from Wawona Tunnel entering the valley from Highway 41 causes most people to immediately pull into the nearest parking lot, take out a camera, and begin snapping photographs.

The view is both the blessing and curse of Yosemite. Of the estimated 4 million people who visit Yosemite annually, 3 million of them come to the valley, which has not been considered a wilderness area in many decades. The only time visitors can get an experience uncluttered by streams of other people is in the winter when the

[*Above:* Yosemite Falls, America's tallest waterfall, has a vertical descent of 2,425 feet]

Yosemite National Park Area

Yosemite National Park includes more than 750,000 acres with much of it in the high Sierra above 8,000 feet.

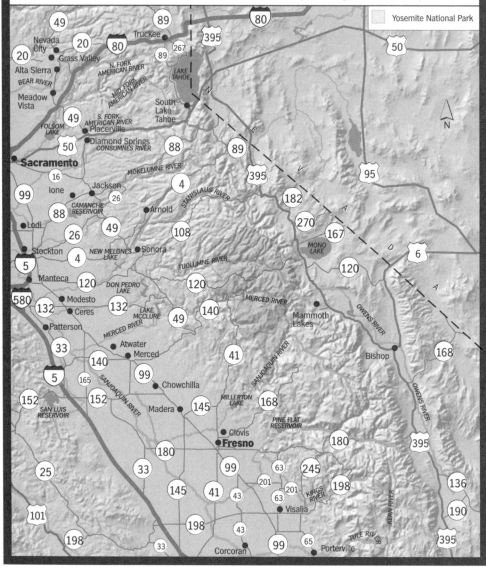

cold weather and snow keep the crowds down.

Yosemite National Park is more than 750,000 acres, much of it in the high Sierra above 8,000 feet. It spans elevations ranging from about 2,000 feet in the western foothills to more than 13,000 feet at the crest. The different elevations create micro-climates that have a wide diversity of plant and animal life.

But the geology and diminutive Yosemite Valley are the starting points for most visitors. Once people tear their attention from the cliffs and waterfalls in the valley, there is much they can learn here that will help explain the rest of the park, particularly in the geology.

The granite plutons that form the valley's bedrock are between 80 and 120 million years old. They are part of the vast Merced River drainage, which begins in Yosemite's high country about 12 miles to the east at the Sierra crest and races through a deep, rugged canyon. The river's course emerged about 80 million years ago when widespread volcanic activity came to a halt.

At one point about 33 million years ago, the Sierra weather was largely tropical with a lot of rainfall in summer. Some geologists believe the Sierra batholith uplifted more than 30 million years ago and erosion from the rainfall of millions of years cut the V-shaped gorges that were later widened into U-shaped valleys by glaciers.

Other geologists believe the granite of Yosemite Valley uplifted during a period between 25 million and 15 million years ago. They believe that as the uplift occurred, the Merced and Tuolumne rivers cut deep channels in the bedrock. In the past 2 million years, extensive glaciation and erosion opened the deep channels into wide valleys.

Either way, Yosemite was left with two distinctive valleys. Yosemite Valley is the southern feature on the Merced River, and the Hetch Hetchy Valley is to the north on the Tuolumne River. Yosemite Valley became known far and wide as explorers discovered what the glaciers had left behind. They found waterfalls suspended thousands of feet in the air, sheer granite faces mounting 3,000 feet and higher above the valley floor, and a sediment-filled lake in the valley that supported native grasses, flowers, shrubs, and trees.

Half Dome, Yosemite's emblematic feature on the east end of the valley, is a massive dome with granite that probably first formed about 80 million years ago. An Ice Age glacier knocked out the footing below the dome. Other glaciers quarried away fractured slabs of granite until a flattened rock face was fashioned. It is really more of an 80-percent dome, since about 20 percent of the dome was lost.

Yosemite's landscape dates back to about 400 million years ago when it was still beneath the Pacific Ocean. Like the rest of the Sierra, the rocks below the ocean were subject to compressing forces during the movement of the earth's tectonic plates. Over about 175 million years the Sierra slowly pushed up. The rocks metamorphosed or changed slowly from limestone, shale, and sandstone to hornfels and schists, geologists' terms for metamorphic rocks.

Granitic plutons began invading the Sierra rock about 160 million years ago, coming in at least three distinct phases lasting more than 15 million years apiece. It took about 130 million years for the pulses to finish their intrusion. Dramatic volcanics and the Sierra's uplift took place over another 25 million years. The Ice Age glaciers appeared in the last 2 million years, finally subsiding about 10,000 years ago.

But glaciers—or actually glacierets—still exist in the Yosemite high country. They are not remnants of the Ice Age that passed 10,000 years ago. They rest in the large cirques or bowl-shaped depressions cut into mountains during the Ice Age, but these glaciers are a product of the Little Ice Age, a worldwide cooling period from 1700 to 1750. They have melted down to modest ice patches in comparison to the size of Ice Age glaciers. Scientists are not certain, but many believe the ice patches seen today are not remnants of the Ice Age.

In the Yosemite high country, many glaciers can be seen at Mount Lyell, Kuna Crest, Sawtooth Ridge, Mount Conness, and Mount Dana. Most are well above 10,000 feet. The highest is at Mount Lyell at 12,800 feet.

Evidence of glaciers is everywhere in Yosemite. The most common sight is an erratic, a large rock that is definitely out of place in a meadow or perched on a ledge. Erratics were carried on glaciers and dropped in distant places when the ice melted. They can be found in such places as Glacier Point, overlooking Yosemite Valley.

Such glacial evidence is also apparent at Hetch Hetchy Valley, but it might be best viewed by wearing a wet suit and a snorkel. It is underwater beneath Hetch Hetchy Reservoir, which provides water for San Francisco.

The pure mountain water in a national park allows San Francisco the distinction of being one of the largest cities in the country without the need of surface water treatment. Early in the twentieth century, the building of O'Shaughnessy Dam, which stops the Tuolumne River, was a heart-breaking experience for John Muir, the revered naturalist-author who fought a losing battle to stop the dam.

O'Shaughnessy was built less than a century after the first European laid eyes on Yosemite. The first sighting supposedly came in the 1830s by explorer Joseph Walker. He didn't actually camp in Yosemite Valley. Historians believe his party moved through Hetch Hetchy Valley and the Tuolumne River canyon. He probably followed the old Mono Indian Trail, generally along present-day Highway 120 or Tioga Road. The trail took him from the Eastern Sierra to the western slope.

But thousands of years before Walker, the peaceful Miwok Indians lived in Yosemite Valley. They were called the Ahwaneechee (Ah-wah-nee-chee). At one point, the tribe suffered a fatal sickness that led to the evacuation of the valley. Scientists do not know what the illness was.

Many years later in the early 1800s, Tenaya, who claimed to be descended from an Ahwaneechee chief, left the Monos on the Eastern Sierra. He returned to the valley and claimed it as the birth right of his people.

During the gold rush of the late 1840s and 1850s, fighting began between Indian tribes and the Europeans who were searching for gold. Major James D. Savage was sent to quell the Mariposa Indian War. Savage found the mysterious valley—Yosemite Valley—where the tribe lived. Savage's forces were the first Europeans to actually camp in the valley. The date was March 27, 1851.

The tribe was captured and moved to a reservation near Fresno. A homesick Chief Tenaya was allowed to move back into the valley with his immediate family. He died soon after when his group was attacked by eastern Monos. In 1855, all the Indians on the reservation were allowed to return to their original homes.

Yosemite has been the object of study and passion from the 1860s through the present day. People such as Muir wrote about its wonders, setting the stage for a crush of public visitation that only grew with each passing decade in the twentieth century.

The Stoneman House, an elaborate 3.5-story structure, was built for $40,000 in 1886 near the site of the current Curry Village garage. It was one of the early hotels built in Yosemite Valley, and, like many others that followed, it burned down in 1896.

Congress set aside land for Yosemite National Park in October 1890. Muir and his powerful associates had a hand in establishing the park.

The park originally contained 1,512 square miles, excluding Yosemite Valley and the Mariposa Big Trees, which remained under state control as part of the original Yosemite Land Grant created by President Lincoln. The valley would later be turned over to federal jurisdiction. The park size was trimmed back to its present size, a little less than 1,200 square miles, in the next few decades.

Cavalry units were detailed to patrol and take charge of Yosemite. Between 1891 and 1914, military officers and various cavalry units guarded Yosemite's forests.

Camp Curry, operated by the Curry family beginning in 1898, became a center for visitor gatherings. David and Jennie Curry made the hospitality industry a priority in Yosemite.

Those were the days when people simply enjoyed the natural setting without completely understanding how the ecosystem worked. For instance, feeding the bears became a tradition. The black bear (*Ursus americanus*) became an object of delight. Chairs would be set up for people to toss food into the garbage hills where the bears would feed.

Inevitably, some bears would become bolder and begin approaching people for food. Some bears would learn they could "bluff charge" visitors and the visitors would drop their food and flee. These bears had to be killed.

Today, bears have become a major headache for wildlife managers. Though an aggressive publicity campaign about protecting food has brought down the number of human-bear encounters, black bears cause up to $500,000 of damage annually to visitors' cars and belongings. The bears can be relocated if they become chronic pests, but they must be destroyed when they become aggressive in pursuit of food.

In Little Yosemite Valley, which is along the hike to Half Dome, the bears visit the

Yosemite Valley

Yosemite Valley is 7 miles long and about 1 mile wide, and is visited by 3 million people annually.

Ref: Yosemite National Park NPS Map

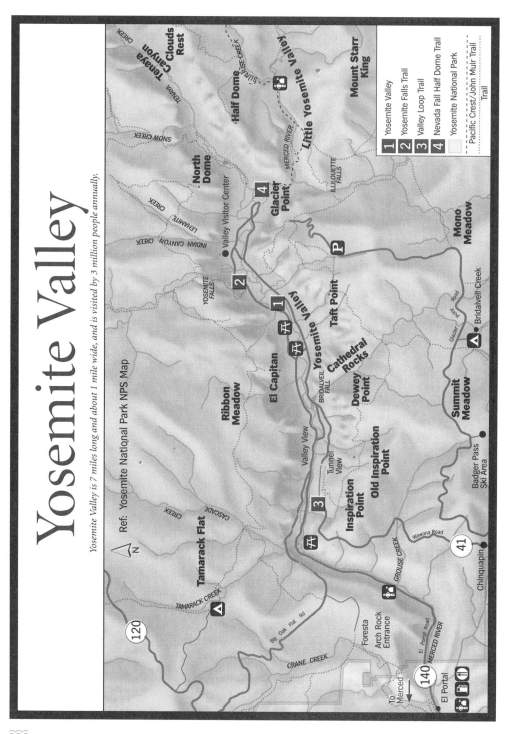

1	Yosemite Valley
2	Yosemite Falls Trail
3	Valley Loop Trail
4	Nevada Fall Half Dome Trail
	Yosemite National Park
......	Pacific Crest/John Muir Trail
	Trail

backpacker campground nightly, raiding campsites. Squirrels, raccoons, and coyotes are also known to wait outside motel doors in the Yosemite Valley for people to feed them.

The natural sources of food are abundant in Yosemite, since it has been a protected environment for more than a century. The vegetation, particularly the trees, offers protection and nourishment for animals of all kinds.

Of the 27 varieties of trees in the park, four are easiest to identify, due to their impressive size and distinctive characteristics. They include the California black oak (*Quercus kelloggii*), which is abundant in Yosemite Valley. These large deciduous trees, with yellow-green leaves and dark trunks, produce acorns, which many forest creatures, such as squirrels, eat. The other three easily identifiable trees include the ponderosa pine (*Pinus ponderosa*), with its bark made up of irregularly shaped plates; the incense cedar (*Calocedrus decurrens*), with a feathery reddish bark; and the giant sequoia (*Sequoiadendron giganteum*), the largest tree on earth.

Three groves of giant sequoias are in the park. They include the Mariposa Grove near the southern entrance at Highway 41; the Tuolumne Grove, near Crane Flat on the Tioga Road or Highway 120; and the Merced Grove, off the Big Oak Flat Road (another section of Highway 120), between Crane Flat and the Big Oak Flat Entrance.

Yosemite is home to some rare species in the Sierra, such as the peregrine falcon (*Falco peregrinus*), which has been nesting in such places as the Hetch Hetchy Valley. Other rare species include the red-legged frog (*Rana aurora, draytonii*) and the mountain yellow-legged frog (*Rana muscosa*).

Along the many streams in Yosemite Valley and at some higher elevations, visitors will find some rare lichen species as well. They include *Dermatocarpon moulinsii*, *Dimelaena oreina*, *Hydrothyria venosa*, and *Umbilicaria torrefacta*. Scientists use the lichen in air monitoring because the lichens are so sensitive to air pollution, which already has wiped out some species of lichen in other California mountain ranges, particularly in Southern California.

For travelers who wish to orient themselves quickly in Yosemite, the major roads generally lead to Yosemite Valley. Organizing visits to the areas of interests, such as Tuolumne Meadows in the high country or Glacier Point above the valley, should always provide time for stopping in the valley, which can be crowded in warmer months and even the so-called shoulder seasons in April and October.

Yosemite Valley

[Fig. 35(1)] The best way to see the magnificent cliffs, waterfalls, granite spires, domes, and meadows of Yosemite Valley is probably on a bicycle. A slow, easy ride around the 7-mile-long by 1-mile-wide valley would take no more than half a day. There are probably two dozen places where you could sit down for a picnic lunch and

In this view of the Yosemite Valley, El Capitan is to the left,
Half Dome is in the distance, and Bridalveil Fall can be seen on the right.

enjoy the view of your life. Bring the camera.

But the valley comes with a warning: Crowds and competing interests are everywhere. In this small valley, world-famous rock climbers congregate at Sunnyside
Campground near Yosemite Lodge before they ascend El Capitan. Backpackers begin
the 223-mile John Muir Trail at Happy Isles on the east end of the valley. Day hikers
crowd trails that climb to the valley rim. People rent and ride horses not far from
Mirror Lake. Open-air trams, tour buses, and cars jam the roads.

On any given weekend, researchers have found the traffic is comparable to downtown Houston rush hour. Restaurants, motels, retail outlets, a U.S. post office, and a
federal magistrate with his own courthouse and jailhouse can be found in this
outdoor paradise.

The National Park Service has been working on a restoration plan to move
campgrounds, buildings, and other developments away from the floodplain of the
Merced River. The river's 1997 flood was the biggest on record this century in the
valley. It closed the park for more than two months.

Federal officials received almost $200 million to rebuild damaged buildings, roads, and sewage systems. But the work is mired in lawsuits and delays, which have characterized planning efforts since 1980 in Yosemite Valley. Each summer, the crowds return.

In the midst of this traffic and work, nature continues. Raccoons *(Procyon lotor)* are sometimes found under soda machines waiting for people to drop food. Mountain coyotes *(Canis latrans)* are seen trotting along lines of cars stopped in front of El Capitan. Usually, somebody will throw the critters something to eat.

Mountain lions *(Felis concolor)* are rarely seen around Yosemite Valley, though scientists say there are more of them around the valley now. They do not normally attack people, but park officials warn people not to allow their children to stray without an adult nearby. Mountain lions, which are marvelous stealth hunters, prefer to strike prey that is smaller and represents an easier kill.

The lions prefer to feast on mule deer *(Odocoileus hemionus)*, which are also seen walking through meadows and crossing trails in the valley. Campers sometimes wake up in the morning with a doe browsing through nearby vegetation.

The Miwok tribes also ate from the natural food around the valley, including mushrooms, berries, bulbs, insects, and some 40 different plants. Some of the bulbs they ate were soap roots *(Camassia pomeridianum)* and corn lily *(Veratrum californiacum)*. Berries included greenleaf manzanita *(Arctostaphylos patula)* berries, whiteleaf manzanita *(Arctostphylos viscida)* berries, gooseberries *(Ribes amarum)*, currants *(Ribes roezelli)*, wild strawberries *(Fragaria vesca)*, and elderberries *(Sambucus caerulea)*.

Exotic species of plants and grasses are found throughout the valley, so don't be surprised to see the apple orchard on the east end where bears often go to feed. Park officials have begun meadow-burning projects to clear the land of invasive exotic species and allow natural grasslands to return in many places.

If there seems to be smoke in the valley, look for signs noting "management burns" of meadows or upland areas that have become too densely crowded with vegetation. Such burns either allow native plants more room to grow or they eliminate excess brush that would only fuel a much larger fire and endanger large trees.

In general, avoid Yosemite Valley on Memorial Day, the Fourth of July, and Labor Day weekends. If possible, schedule the vacation in April when the waterfalls are usually thundering during the spring thaw. But if you visit in April, remember the high country trails are most likely still under snow.

If you're driving around the valley and you've seen all the waterfalls, stop at El Capitan Meadow on the valley loop road, pull out the binoculars, and watch the rock climbers scaling El Capitan. It is considered one of the best climbing spots in the world.

Directions: Yosemite can be entered from Highway 41 from the south and Highway 140 from the west. Highway 120 or Tioga Road intersects with Highway 140, bringing in visitors from the east and northwest. From the south, drive 94 miles from Fresno on Highway 41. Follow signs about 30 miles to the valley. From the west, drive 81 miles from Merced on Highway 140 through the Arch Rock Entrance Station, and follow the signs about 12 miles to the valley.

Activities: Hiking, backpacking, camping, nature photography, horseback riding, ice skating, snowshoeing, bicycling, sight-seeing, and fishing.

Dates: Open year-round.

Fees: There is an entry fee.

Facilities: Ahwahnee Hotel, Yosemite Lodge, Curry Village tent cabins, picnic areas, restaurants, grocery store, post office, fire station, campgrounds, retailers, rentals, ice rink, and stables.

Closest town: El Portal, 14 miles.

For more information: Yosemite National Park, PO Box 577, Yosemite, CA 95389. Phone (209) 372-0529. For recorded information on traffic, weather conditions, and camping or motel reservations, phone (209) 372-0200.

YOSEMITE FALLS TRAIL

[Fig. 35(2)] People hike this trail in a day, but it's a long day. Hikers are essentially walking up to the rim of the valley. Bring lots of water—64 ounces or more. When the warm weather arrives, the streams dry up everywhere around this trail.

A lot of people hike to the top of Yosemite Falls, which combines three separate falls into a vertical descent of 2,425 feet. America's tallest waterfall was created when glaciers turned V-shaped Yosemite Valley into a U-shaped valley, scraping away the gentler slope that Yosemite Creek traversed several million years ago. The creek became "suspended," bouncing off great ledges in the granite.

The ledges were carved because of flaws in sections of granite. The upper section drops a breathtaking 1,430 feet, and its flume becomes an ice cone against the rock in winter. The middle fall plunges 675 feet, and the lower fall dives 320 feet.

The trail to the top is dusty in summer, but it has rewarding views of Half Dome and Quarter Domes to the east. The first 0.5 mile of the hike is filled with steep switchbacks through talus fields and wondrous stands of black oak (*Quercus kelloggii*), which produce leaves in the spring from reddish leaf buds.

Look closely and perhaps see a great horned owl (*Bubo virginanus*) nesting in some rotted-out crevice of an oak. The deep hooting of this owl can be heard at dawn, so get an early start. The pygmy owl (*Glaucidium gnoma*) may be a little easier to see because it is active all day long.

After climbing for about 3.5 miles on this trail, hikers turn east to meet Eagle Peak Trail. Stay to the right and follow the trail down to Yosemite Creek. The water is snowmelt, so it is cold. Stay back away from the slick boulders and stay behind the railing at the fall.

Continue on the trail over a bridge and climb for another 0.8 mile to Yosemite

Point. The view includes snow-covered Clark Range to the southeast. This panoramic view has its price: You have to turn around go and back down the way you came.

Directions: From the Wawona Tunnel on Highway 41, drive 8.3 miles to Yosemite Valley. Highway 41 becomes a loop road around the valley. Follow the signs to the west end of the valley and drive about 0.6 mile to Sunnyside walk-in campground. Park near Yosemite Lodge, across the street from Sunnyside. Walk through the Sunnyside parking lot to the marked trailhead.

Trail: 7.2 miles round-trip.

Elevation: About 2,600-foot gain, 6,600-foot peak.

Degree of difficulty: Strenuous.

Surface: Well marked, but steep with switchbacks up a talus slope.

▨ VALLEY LOOP TRAIL

[Fig. 35(3)] Views of El Capitan are stunning and close on this trail, though views of El Capitan are pretty remarkable from almost any angle. The trail is for people who don't want to gain a lot of elevation but who still want to see the high-elevation sights on foot.

Bridalveil Fall and the spires of Cathedral Rocks are also easy to see up close on the trail. East valley sights include Half Dome.

Most people need binoculars to see climbers on the big wall at El Capitan. It is about 3,500 feet to the valley rim, and climbers take many different many routes. El Capitan is a challenge known around the world.

As hikers pass, they will notice a low ridge of rock in the nearby forest. The ridge is called the El Capitan Moraine, which was left when the last glacier departed Yosemite. The moraine helped to dam the old Lake Yosemite, which filled the valley thousands of years ago.

Bridalveil Fall, which usually runs year-round, drops 620 feet with a wide spray that usually douses visitors who stand too close. Bridalveil is a classic example of what geologists call a hanging valley. It was a canyon intersecting with Yosemite Valley at one point 2 million years ago, but glaciers sliced away the place where the canyon and the valley met. So the canyon was left hanging above the valley and Bridalveil Creek became a waterfall instead of a stream flowing into the valley.

The Ahwaneechee called Bridalveil *Pohono*, meaning puffing wind. Many in the tribe had a superstition about the place being evil, though no one knows precisely why.

The Valley Loop Trail crosses the Merced River at Pohono Bridge. Hikers will notice the National Park Service is keeping people out of Bridalveil Meadow because it is restoring vegetation in the area. Follow the signs and stay on the trail.

Directions: From the Wawona Tunnel on Highway 41, drive 8.3 miles to Yosemite Valley, and drive the Highway 41 loop about 2 miles past Yosemite Lodge. You pass Leidig Meadow and come to Devil's Elbow Picnic Area. The marked trail starts just west of the picnic area.

Trail: 4 miles.
Elevation: 150-foot gain, 4,125-foot peak.
Degree of difficulty: Easy.
Surface: Open footpath, well marked.

NEVADA FALL/HALF DOME

[Fig. 35(4)] Hikers can reach at least two magnificent waterfalls on this trail. If they are ambitious—meaning, fit and ready to walk for 12 hours or so—they can also reach Yosemite's ubiquitous icon, Half Dome, by simply extending their hike from this trail. The views of the Merced River canyon and Tenaya Canyon are worth the extra wear on the legs.

The trail at Happy Isles is also the starting point of the famed John Muir Trail, which goes about 220 miles south across the Sierra to Mount Whitney and down the east side of the Sierra. Do not entertain any thoughts of being alone in the wilderness here. This is easily the busiest trailhead in Yosemite. It is sometimes called a "freeway" by experienced backpackers.

The first few miles of this walk are called the Mist Trail because of Vernal Fall, the 317-foot fall that hikers first encounter. In spring, when snowmelt swells the Merced River, the mist soaks everything, making the granite steps slippery. Take it slowly. Stay out of the seemingly placid pools above the fall. Many people have cooled off in the water and plunged to their deaths.

Hikers will see flourishing black oak (*Quercus kelloggii*) and incense cedar (*Libocedrus decurrens*) along the way. The cedar may show signs of incense cedar dry-rot fungus (*Polyporus amarus*), which opens cavities in the wood. Woodpeckers will search for the larvae and leave little depressions in "shot-hole" patterns.

Some hikers stop and turn around after 1.5 miles at the top of Vernal Fall. The hike has been enough for some people because of a strenuous 0.7-mile section with more than 500 steps carved in the granite alongside Vernal.

Those continuing will go about 2.7 miles into the hike before reaching the bottom of Nevada Fall, the 619-foot fall that thunders above Vernal. Hike another 0.6 mile up to reach some nice picnic areas. Whether you're continuing to Half Dome or taking the right fork in the trail to hike down a section of the Muir Trail back to Happy Isles, fill up on water from the river. And use your water filter to purify it.

Some people opt to hike another mile to Little Yosemite Valley and camp the night before assaulting Half Dome in the morning. You will need a wilderness permit from the National Park Service to camp. The free permits are available at the Wilderness Center in Yosemite Village.

When camping at Little Yosemite Valley, remember some of the most active bears in Yosemite live right there. Nightly food raids have been going on for a long time, so use the bear boxes to store food, toothpaste, or even chewing gum. Anything that has a scent will attract them.

Also, consider leaving all the pouches unzipped on your backpack. If squirrels get a whiff of any strong scent, they will chew a hole in your pack. With the pouches unzipped, they will simply search and leave.

To ascend Half Dome, a set of parallel cables is drilled into the granite on the backside of the dome. Hikers must walk at various angles approaching 45 degrees or worse while holding onto the cables and pulling themselves up. If you are carrying lunch in a daypack, do not leave it anywhere. The yellow-bellied marmots *(Marmota flaviventris)* are fearless and inventive food thieves. They too will chew a hole in your pack to get at your food.

One other Half Dome warning: If storm clouds are anywhere on the horizon, do not attempt climbing the cables. Thunderstorms appear very quickly above 8,000 feet in the Sierra, and lightning strikes are common on Half Dome.

Once on top of Half Dome, hikers are often surprised to find it is quite large. The views include Glacier Point to the west, the massive Merced River canyon to the southeast, and the Tenaya Canyon high country to the north. Enjoy the view, but remember you still have more than 8 miles of hiking to get back down to your car.

Directions: From the Wawona Tunnel on Highway 41, drive 8.3 miles to Yosemite Valley. Follow signs on Highway 41 to Curry Village on the east end of the valley. Park in the day-use parking lot. The trailhead is about a 1-mile walk southeast of the parking lot. Follow the signs.

Trail: 6.6 miles round-trip to Nevada Fall, 17 miles round-trip to Half Dome.

Elevation: 1,900-foot gain to Nevada Fall, 4,900-foot gain to Half Dome; 5,880-foot peak for Nevada Fall, 8,842-foot peak for Half Dome.

Degree of difficulty: Strenuous for Nevada Fall, very strenuous for Half Dome.

Surface: Granite stairway cut by federal work crews decades ago in the first few miles, some steep switchbacks on the way up to Half Dome.

CALIFORNIA BLACK OAK

(Quercus kelloggii) The ellipsoidal, 1-inchlong acorn of the California black oak was once a staple food of California Indians.

Wawona Road

Wawona Road, or Highway 41, was first officially constructed in the 1870s and rebuilt in the 1930s.

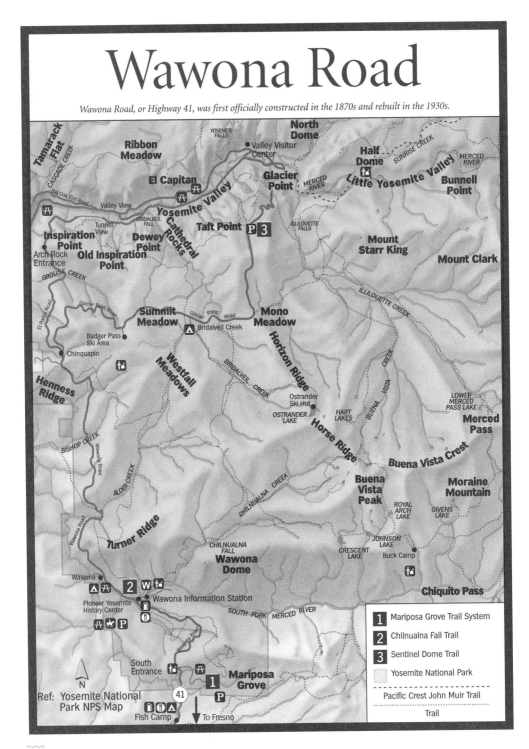

Tamarack Flat

Ribbon Meadow

YOSEMITE FALLS

North Dome

Half Dome

SUNRISE CREEK

MERCED RIVER

El Capitan

CASCADE CREEK

Big Oak Flat Road

Valley View

Glacier Point

Valley Visitor Center

MERCED RIVER

Little Yosemite Valley

Bunnell Point

Yosemite Valley

BRIDALVEIL FALL

Tunnel View

Taft Point

ILLILOUETTE FALLS

Inspiration Point

Dewey Point

Cathedral Rocks

Mount Starr King

Mount Clark

Arch Rock Entrance

Old Inspiration Point

GROUSE CREEK

ILLILOUETTE CREEK

El Portal Road

Glacier Point Road

Summit Meadow

Glacier Point Road

Bridalveil Creek

Mono Meadow

Horizon Ridge

Badger Pass Ski Area

Chinquapin

Westfall Meadows

BRIDALVEIL CREEK

Ostrander Ski Hut

OSTRANDER LAKE

HART LAKES

BUENA VISTA CREEK

LOWER MERCED PASS LAKE

Merced Pass

Henness Ridge

BISHOP CREEK

Wawona Road

ALDER CREEK

CHILNUALNA CREEK

Horse Ridge

Buena Vista Crest

Buena Vista Peak

Moraine Mountain

ROYAL ARCH LAKE

GIVENS LAKE

Turner Ridge

CHILNUALNA FALL

Wawona Dome

JOHNSON LAKE

CRESCENT LAKE

Buck Camp

Wawona

Pioneer Yosemite History Center

Wawona Information Station

SOUTH FORK MERCED RIVER

Chiquito Pass

South Entrance

Wawona Road

Mariposa Grove

N

Ref: Yosemite National Park NPS Map

41

Fish Camp

To Fresno

1	Mariposa Grove Trail System
2	Chilnualna Fall Trail
3	Sentinel Dome Trail
	Yosemite National Park
	Pacific Crest John Muir Trail
	Trail

Wawona Road

[Fig. 36] People drive up Highway 41 through Fresno and Madera counties to enter through the South Entrance, which is the logical way to go if they want to see the Mariposa Grove, the Wawona area, and Glacier Point on the way to Yosemite Valley. Highway 41 becomes the Wawona Road when it enters Yosemite.

At the gate, visitors can turn right to see the Mariposa Grove or left for Wawona, the Glacier Point, the valley, and other parts of the park. Historians believe the Wawona Road is the approximate route taken by the Mariposa Battalion in 1851 when they were hunting for Miwok encampments in Yosemite Valley. The first official Wawona Road was constructed in the 1870s and rebuilt in the 1930s.

For those who want to see the view made famous on countless postcards, the Wawona Road through the South Entrance is the place to enter Yosemite. It is called Tunnel View, 1.6 miles from the valley floor. Motorists emerge from the Wawona Tunnel and see the grand vista of Yosemite Valley, El Capitan, Half Dome, and Bridalveil Fall. Most people simply pull into the huge parking areas, climb out of the car or bus, and start snapping photographs.

The tunnel is almost 1 mile long, blasted and drilled through solid granite at a cost of almost $1 million in the 1930s. It took almost two years to complete. The idea was to provide a dramatic view without destroying the mountainside.

The small community of Wawona is the first landmark along the Wawona Road. Visitors first camped there during the Civil War. Today, Wawona is known for its golf course, hotel, and frequent visiting mule deer (*Odocoileus hemionus*). People have fed them for so many years that they boldly approach the area, searching for tidbits. Some of these deer weigh more than 200 pounds and have sharp antlers that can accidentally harm or kill people who get too close. Don't feed them, the National Park Service advises.

The drive along Wawona Road will introduce visitors to so-called "old-growth" forests in California. Old growth refers to a forested area with trees that are more than 40 inches in circumference. These trees are often hundreds of years old, but size, not age, is more important in the old-growth classification. An old-growth tree is often quite important to the ecosystem even after it dies. Many will remain a source of shelter and nutrition to animals and insects for centuries.

The road also passes a vast fire-scarred area several miles beyond Wawona. A lightning strike in dry summer of 1990—which was the third consecutive dry summer during a six-year California drought—started the fire. It burned more than 8,000 acres. Yosemite West, a private in-holding community along the Wawona Road many miles north of Wawona, survived the fire.

Beyond Yosemite West, the road passes the small rest area called Chinquapin, which is at the base of the Glacier Point Road. Badger Pass Ski Area is along the Glacier Point Road, which winds up to an overlook to view the valley, Vernal and

Nevada falls, and the high Sierra for dozens of miles in all directions. A gift shop and food service building have been added, and an amphitheater has been carved into a place near the 7,214-foot-high overlook.

In winter, the Glacier Point Road makes an excellent cross-country skiing adventure. The snow-capped view across the high Sierra is breathtaking and usually quite peaceful compared to summer months.

MARIPOSA GROVE

[Fig. 36] There are more than 500 mature giant sequoia *(Sequoiadendron gigantum)* in the Mariposa Grove, making it one of the larger groupings of the big trees among the 75 groves in the Sierra. People can stroll for hours admiring the 2,000-year-old specimens still standing and the ones that have toppled on the 250 acres.

A short, well-marked hike from Wawona Road and the parking area brings most visitors to trees that give them a good idea what the rest of the area looks like. Usually, the area near the road and parking area is crowded. For those who want to get away a bit, a longer hike will take them deeper into this moist, forested area of giants. And for those who don't want to walk at all, there are tram tours available.

It's important to understand that giant sequoias are generally part of the white fir *(Abies concolor)* forest, which occurs between 4,000 and 7,000 feet in the Sierra. The white fir forest is the richest in variety among the different elevations on the Sierra's western slope. Its growing season can be a month longer than the forest above 7,500 feet. And with 40 to 60 inches of precipitation annually, it is considerably wetter than the foothill belt below it.

The shrub layer, just above the ground cover, is golden chinquapin *(Chrysolepis sempervirens)*, scouler's willow *(Salix scoulariana)*, and ground rose *(Rosa spithamia)*. The canopy, aside from giant sequoia, includes Douglas fir *(Pseudotsuga menziesii)* and ponderosa pine *(Pinus ponderosa)*, as well as sugar pine *(Pinus lambertiana)* in Yosemite.

When the white fir forest is dominated by the giant sequoia, as it is at Mariposa Grove, it is not as densely forested as the name "grove" would imply. Instead, it can be quite open. The big trees and the other trees around them can create so much shade that the ground cover vegetation is almost nonexistent in some places. Where the sunshine is sufficient to support life, look for the hooker's fairy bell *(Disporum hookeri)*, bracken fern *(Pteridium aquilinum)*, and bedstraw *(Galium sparsifolium)*.

One of the more famous trees in the grove was the Wawona Tunnel Tree, a 234-foot-tall giant that fell in 1969. It was the tree with a tunnel about 8 feet wide, 9 feet high, and 26 feet long. The Yosemite Stage and Turnpike Company paid about $75 in the early 1880s to have the tunnel cut into a fire scar. Though it had a hole big enough to drive wagons and, later, cars through it, the Wawona Tunnel Tree was actually still alive and growing when heavy snow in its upper branches toppled it. The National Park Service does not allow similar cuts to be made now.

Another distinctive tree in the grove is the Clothespin Tree. Repeated fires in the area over the last millennium have burned out the center support of the tree. The hole is about 15 feet across at the bottom of the tree and rises to about 40 feet high.

The giants' thick bark and ability to grow despite losing part of their base allow them to survive fires. In fact, seedlings actually need the minerals created in the soil when fires burn vegetation around them. The National Park Service now controls the growth of vegetation with "managed" or "prescribed" burns in the area. The vegetation removal reduces chances of a large, hot fire that would leap to the canopies of the big trees and destroy them.

One of the older trees is Grizzly Giant, estimated to be 2,700 years old. It looks its age, having suffered through at least six lightning strikes in a single 1940s storm. Its crown is flattened. At one point in the 1860s, photographs show it leaning as it does today.

The grove was probably first seen by European settlers during the gold rush of 1849. No record has been kept on the first sighting. The first official report of the grove is recorded in 1851. Congress decided to protect the grove in 1864. Further protection laws were introduced in 1916. About 1.5 million people visit the trees each year.

Directions: From the South Entrance, turn right on Mariposa Grove Road and drive 2 miles to the parking area.

Activities: Hiking, photography, picnicking, and sight-seeing.

Facilities: Shuttle buses run between the park community of Wawona and the Mariposa Grove. There are restrooms, potable water outlets, picnic areas, a gift shop, tram rides, and the Mariposa Grove Museum.

Dates: Open year-round.

Fees: There is no fee to see the grove. There is a fee to ride the tram.

Closest town: Fish Camp, 7 miles.

For more information: Yosemite National Park, PO Box 577, Yosemite, CA 95389. Phone (209) 372-0265.

MARIPOSA GROVE TRAIL SYSTEM

[Fig. 36(1)] In the 250-acre grove, a trail winds past the many named giants. The parking area generally is filled by the afternoons and traffic is heavy. Hiking back into the forest is a good way to get away from the crowds, because many visitors simply want to sample the views and leave.

There is interpretive information at the trailhead. Signs give directions and more information along the trails. The trails will lead to both an upper and a lower section of the grove. Trail maps are available at the trailhead.

Directions: From the parking lot, follow the trail to the northeast. It is marked.

Trail: 6.3 miles round-trip

Elevation: About 1,000-foot gain, 6,600-foot peak.

Degree of difficulty: Moderate.

Surface: Mostly open footpath in the forest with some steep climbing.

WAWONA

[Fig. 36] It can be difficult to understand Wawona. The name is believed to be Native American, meaning big trees. But nobody is quite sure of that. It is also a scenic place where wildlife and views of ridgelines can be as wonderful as anything in the park. People do come here for nature, but they also come to Wawona for the golf course, the Victorian-era architecture of the Wawona Hotel, the gas station, and the grocery store.

There is also a popular Pioneer History Center in Wawona. The National Park Service has collected and placed some historic structures at the center. The buildings include an old jail and furnished cabins. In summer, the National Park Service presents informative programs.

The golf course, which was built in 1917, is in the lower part of Wawona Meadow. Before Wawona was added to Yosemite in 1932, the area was used to grow hay. Animals such as hogs and sheep often grazed here. At one point, the meadow was used as an airport.

Wawona Hotel, built in the 1870s, is on the east side of Wawona Road, across from the golf course. John and Edward Washburn built the hotel. They intended to have visitors rest overnight at Wawona on their way to Yosemite Valley in stagecoaches.

Directions: From the South Entrance, turn left onto Wawona Road and drive 8 miles.

Activities: Hiking, photography, golfing, bicycling, fishing, horseback riding, and camping.

Facilities: Hotel, grocery store, campground with 98 campsites in summer and 30 in winter, golf course, history center, stables, gas station, rental homes, and museum.

Dates: Open year-round.

Fees: There are fees to golf, camp, and stay in the hotel.

Closest town: Fish Camp, 6 miles.

For more information: Yosemite National Park, PO Box 577, Yosemite, CA 95389. Phone (209) 372-0265.

CHILNUALNA FALL TRAIL

[Fig. 36(2)] There are not a lot of good hiking trails in the Wawona area compared to many other parts of Yosemite. But the Chilnualna Fall Trail rates as one of better, less-traveled trails that visitors will find in the Wawona area. It is popular in spring when the high country destinations are often still under a blanket of snow. The trail offers panoramics of the South Fork Merced River canyon, Chilnualna Creek drainage, Wawona Dome, and, of course, the fall.

Look for mountain misery (*Chamaebatia foliolosa*), an evergreen that grows well in the dry soils on the southern end of the park. Why was it named mountain misery? The plant oozes a kind of black, sticky gum that will get all over a hiker's clothing. Avoid the misery by walking around the plants. Or just stick to the trail.

The trail runs through an interesting cross-section of Yosemite—between 4,000 and 6,400 feet—where vegetation changes as elevation increases. Hikers will pass the black oak and incense cedar on their way to stands of ponderosa pine that grow just beyond several cascades in the Chilnualna Creek.

Hikers may see a seed-eating bird called the dark-eyed junco *(Junco oreganus)*. This bird competes with lodgepole chipmunks *(Eutamias speciosus)* for seeds from the incense cedars along the trail. The junco's summertime competition includes a seasonal visitor called the chipping sparrow *(Spizella passerina)*, which nests in April and departs the Sierra as the nights grow colder in late September.

Later in the season along this trail, the snowmelt begins to dwindle. Small, warm pools form at the bottom of slick granite slides, which provide a delightful playground where hikers can cool off. It is a welcome break in late August or early September.

Flower fanatics will find a colorful array waiting along the way and at the fall. The western azaleas *(Rhododendron occidentalis)* are particularly abundant. Also look for the Sierra shooting star *(Dodecatheon subalpinum)*, which tend to collect in shady, moist niches around the fall.

Directions: From the South Entrance, turn left and drive about 8.5 miles to Chilnualna Falls Road, just beyond the Wawona store. Turn right, drive 1.7 miles to the dirt parking lot. Trailhead starts at the parking lot.

Trail: About 8 miles round-trip.

Elevation: About 2,200-foot gain, 6,400-foot peak.

Degree of difficulty: Strenuous.

Surface: Steep and easy to follow. Many switchbacks.

GLACIER POINT

[Fig. 36] The main reason to visit Glacier Point is the view. It is perched at 7,214 feet, which is about 3,200 feet above Yosemite Valley. Situated on the south rim of the granite walls around the valley, the view includes landmarks such as El Capitan and Half Dome. Those who have a map and a basic understanding of the geography can easily find Mount Hoffmann, Mount Conness, and Mount Clark. Visitors can drive to Glacier Point, park, and walk several hundred feet to see the views.

No one needs a map to see Vernal and Nevada falls bounding down the Merced River Canyon out of Little Yosemite Valley to the east. Glaciers created the stair-step appearance during the past 2 million years. There may be no better place in Yosemite—or anywhere in the world—to easily see the effects of glaciation.

John Muir believed the Merced River glacier was actually five different glaciers that met at Yosemite Valley and welded together to widen Yosemite Valley. He called them the Yosemite Creek, Hoffmann, Tenaya, South Lyell, and Illilouette glaciers. They combined to reach several thousand feet in depth, carving and slicing the uneven granite faces at Vernal and Nevada falls where the Merced cascades into Yosemite Valley. Glacial erosion was also responsible for Yosemite Falls, another sight visible from Glacier Point.

Visitors can see 619-foot Nevada Fall from Glacier Point.

During the earliest glaciation, ice rose more than 600 feet above Glacier Point. A geologic exhibit at Glacier Point describes it.

The area also has a colorful recent history. Several decades ago, people created a spectacle every night in summer by pushing a burning mound of tree bark, usually red fir *(Abies magnifica)*, over the lip of Glacier Point. To the people in the valley, the flaming embers became known as the fire fall. The National Park Service banned the practice in 1968.

A nineteenth century hotel, the Mountain House, once occupied Glacier Point. It was replaced earlier this century with a newer version, but it burned to the ground in 1969. Now, there are no overnight accommodations at Glacier Point, though the gift and snack shop and open-air amphitheater have been rebuilt recently.

The Glacier Point Road, the only paved road to the lookout, winds through a red fir and lodgepole pine *(Pinus murrayana)* forest. Badger Pass Ski Area and many trailheads can be accessed from the road.

Directions: From the South Entrance, turn left on Wawona Road and drive about 16 miles to Glacier Point Road, which is at a rest stop called Chinquapin. Turn right and drive about 15 miles to the end of Glacier Point Road and park in the lot.

Activities: Sight-seeing, hiking, skiing, and picnicking.

Facilities: Gift and snack shop, restrooms, amphitheater, historic and science exhibits.

Dates: Open May through Oct. until the road is closed by winter snow. Cross-country skiers go up the road to Glacier Point in winter.

Fees: None.

Closest town: Fish Camp, 31 miles.

For more information: Yosemite National Park, PO Box 577, Yosemite, CA 95389. Phone (209) 372-0265.

SENTINEL DOME TRAIL

[Fig. 36(3)] If Glacier Point is the best drive-up view in Yosemite, Sentinel Dome could be the best walk-up view. The view is a lot like Glacier Point, except the crowd is a lot smaller.

Sentinel Dome is photographed almost as much as Half Dome. The dome is known for a photograph of a grotesquely bent Jeffrey pine growing in a crack along the granite. The crown of the stunted tree was actually horizontal at the top of the windblown dome. It succumbed to the harsh environment in 1970, but photographs of this sideways pine tree are still quite popular.

The trail up the back of the dome fades away in the granite, but it is pretty obvious and easy to navigate the final 100 yards or so to the top of the dome. Besides Yosemite Valley, people can see the Clark Range, Clouds Rest, Half Dome, and Tenaya Canyon.

Directions: From the junction of Wawona Road and Glacier Point Road, drive about 13 miles on Glacier Point Road and park at a parking pullout to the side of the road. The trailhead, which starts at the pullout, is easy to find. After about 50 yards on the trail, take the right fork.

Trail: About 2.2 miles round-trip.

Elevation: About 400-foot gain, 8,122-foot peak.

Degree of difficulty: Easy.

Surface: Easy-to-follow trail. About 0.5 mile of closed roadway. Trail disappears in the granite near the dome, but the route is pretty obvious by then.

TAFT POINT

[Fig. 36] If a 2,500-foot sheer vertical drop is an interesting sight to you, linger and look while you're on this trail. However, a lot of people may discover they suffer mild forms of vertigo when they hike past the areas known as The Fissures, slender openings along Profile Cliff. The valley is actually visible through the openings, which were created as freezing and thawing cracked the granite.

At Taft Point, hikers will find a railing. Yosemite Falls and the Three Brothers formation are among the views at this point. The view of El Capitan is one of the best available in Yosemite.

On the way to Taft Point, look for the deep blue blossoms of the tall larkspur (*Delphinium glaucum*). The forest includes white fir and Jeffrey pine. Lodgepole pine stands are farther along the trail toward Taft Point.

Hikers may see the red crossbill (*Loxia curvirostra*) picking at lodgepole pine cones in search of seed. They are generally high in lodgepoles, using their powerful mandibles on scales of the cones to get the seeds.

Directions: Use the same directions as the hike to Sentinel Dome and take the same trailhead. Take the left fork after 50 yards.

Trail: About 2.2 miles round-trip.

Elevation: About a 200-foot gain on the return hike, starting at 7,720-foot peak.

Degree of difficulty: Easy.

Surface: Downsloping footpath with rocky outcroppings. Some steep fissures without railings, so hike carefully.

Tioga Road

Tioga Road, or Highway 120, is the longest trans–Sierra route, running 46 miles from Crane Flat to Tioga Pass.

Ref: Yosemite National Park
NPS Map

1 Lembert Dome Trail
2 Cathedral Lakes
3 High Sierra Loop to May Lake
4 Sunrise Lakes Trail
5 Porcupine Creek Trail to North Dome

Yosemite National Park

– – – Pacific Crest/John Muir Trail
········· Trail

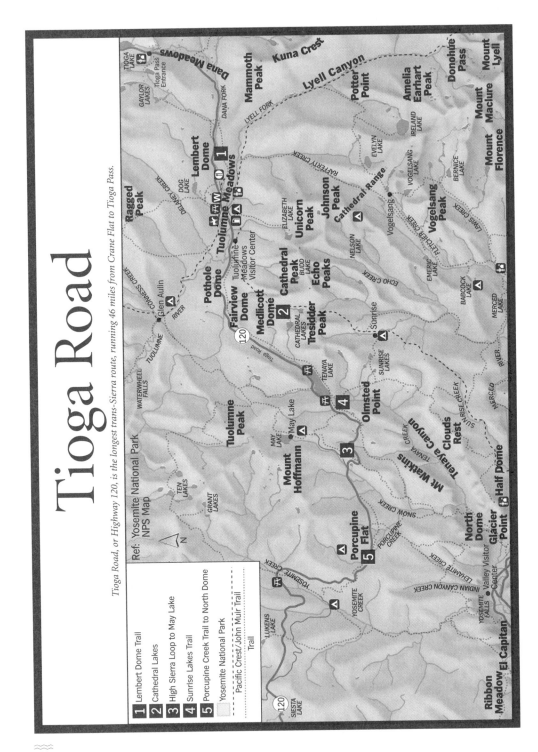

Tioga Road

[Fig. 37] Tioga Road, or Highway 120, is the longest trans-Sierra route and widely considered the most scenic. It runs 46 miles from Crane Flat, elevation 6,192 feet, to Tioga Pass, elevation 9,945 feet at the Yosemite gate.

Travelers can see an array of glacially carved mountaintops, domes, spires, and lakes, along with alpine vegetation and meadows. The tiny remnants of once mammoth glaciers can be seen in the cirques along Mount Lyell, Kuna Crest, and Mount Conness. The glaciers are mostly above 11,000 feet.

There are many places to stop, look, and explore this vast high country. Many trailheads depart from Tuolumne Meadows, a kind of Mecca for high Sierra backpacking. Other locations for camping or other recreation include White Wolf, Tenaya Lake, and May Lake.

Stop at Olmsted Point, 9 miles from the Tioga Pass gate, and look at the view. Half Dome is in the distance to the south. The Cathedral Range is just to the east. But, even more impressive, the granite landscape spreads out for miles in all directions, giving a hint of what things looked like about 55 million years ago.

At that time, the granite already had risen, but it had been eroded to the basic form that can be seen today. Many geologists believe it was several thousand feet lower then, and the erosion processes were carrying bits and pieces of it in rivers into California's 400-mile-long Central Valley.

Volcanic eruptions took place about 20 million years ago, and the faults that caused the Sierra to lift probably began about 10 million years ago. Before tons and tons of ice covered the Tioga high country about 3 million years ago, it already had risen dramatically from the faulting.

How fast could the area rise? The eastern side of the range rose more than 13 feet in a single earthquake recorded in 1872. With such events continuing every few centuries, it is conceivable that the Tioga high country could be an average of 15,000 feet high in the next few million years. That would make it higher than 14,498-foot Mount Whitney, the tallest mountain the contiguous 48 states.

But the grand scale of Tioga often becomes obscured in Yosemite because of politics and human history. The road has been mired in political infighting for decades.

Business owners on the Sierra's east side have come to rely on the road to deliver tour buses and customers to their communities, which include Bishop, Lee Vining, and Mammoth Lakes. The National Park Service must close the road each autumn with the first substantial snowfall. It does not reopen until spring when the road can be cleared of snow. But east-side business owners believe the park service is too slow to reopen the road. Park service officials defend their schedules, saying they must be sure the road is safe.

It is all part of Tioga's human history, which goes back about 2,000 years when

Granite Gilia

Many high-country hikers come across the clustered white flowers of the granite gilia (*Leptodactylon pungens*), which are found throughout the mountain range. The flowers are very noticeable near the crest in Yosemite National Park and on the Eastern Sierra. They bloom in July and August from 7,500 feet to 12,500 feet. The flowers survive in granite crags, growing like a bush and clinging to life in an inhospitable environment. Notice that the leaves are almost like needles, which allow the granite gilia to survive in the cold, arid habitat.

Native Americans from the western slope, Miwok, traveled across the Sierra to trade berries, beads, and baskets with the eastern tribes, the Mono. The Mono would trade buffalo robes, salt, and obsidian, among other things.

Miners and others completed the original dirt road in the 1880s near the current Tioga alignment. The road was rebuilt and paved in the late 1930s and 1940s. The road was completely re-aligned and rebuilt again at a cost of almost $7 million in the late 1950s and early 1960s.

Critics say the road should never have been constructed on the south side of a slick granite face at Olmsted Point. Officials built the road there because they wanted the stunning view from Olmsted. However, when snow-clearing operations take place each spring, Olmsted is notorious for being avalanche-prone. In the mid-1990s during snow plowing, a massive block of ice crushed a bulldozer, killing a park employee.

Such political battles have always been a part of Yosemite. People see the park passionately from many viewpoints—some emphasizing preservation, others pushing to open it for more people to see.

Between the politics and the geology, there is an interesting collection of vegetation at these high elevations, particularly in the meadows. Tuolumne Meadows, for instance, is a place where sod-forming sedges and grasses congregate.

Snow buries the high country meadows in late fall, winter, and spring. As it melts in June and July, swampy areas form where the sods grow. Probably the most common sight is the alpine sedge (*Carex subnigricans*), along with the Brewer's shorthair grass (*Calamagrostis breweri*). Visitors also will see such herbs as dwarf lewisia (*Lewisia pygmaea*), alpine goldenrod (*Solidago multiradiata*), and Lyall's lupine (*Lupinus lyalli*).

Shrubs are not generally abundant in this alpine environment. Near Tioga, people can find red mountain heather (*Phyllodoce breweri*) or dwarf huckleberry (*Vaccinium nivictum*), but these plants do not grow very large.

Birds, insects, and small creatures, such as chipmunks and pika (*Ochotona princeps*) are among the wildlife in the higher elevations around Tioga. Pika, though they look like rodents, are related to rabbits. They avoid human contact, living under rockslides.

The yellow-bellied marmot can grow big and fat here because people feed it. Park service officials continually warn visitors not to feed wild creatures. Often, it means the creatures will become dependent on human food and eventually die when humans leave.

The porcupine *(Erethizon dorsatum)* is known to wander through the alpine meadows. It prefers to be in a forest around trees, but hikers do see porcupine in the Tioga area. Porcupine Flat along Tioga Road is at 8,550 feet. There is no indication in historic records that porcupine lived here, but it was known as Porcupine Flat as far back as 1863.

For those entering the park from the east, through the Tioga Pass Entrance Station, the National Park Service has recently replaced the 1,000-pound gates that once hung at the entrance. The new gates are replicas made of lodgepole pine wood and granite.

TUOLUMNE MEADOWS

[Fig. 37] The trails and vistas from Tuolumne Meadows make it a worthy stop for just a half hour of picture taking or several days of backpacking. This meadow area is the largest of its kind in the Sierra, stretching for hundreds of acres as a shorthair carpet of resilient sedge and grasses at 8,600 feet and higher.

The glacial history would fill a textbook. Glaciers stretched over the expanse of the meadows because they were not limited to a streambed or canyon. They created features that are not commonly found in many parts of the Sierra.

Such features include the *roches moutonnées,* or "rock sheep" in French. They are rounded rocks that resisted the erosion of the glacier as it passed. There are small versions of them in many places around Yosemite, including Tuolumne Meadows. French geologist Horace Benedict De Saussure coined the name *roches moutonnées.*

Hikers can see Lembert Dome rising above the meadow. Climb up to see parts of the dome, which shines in the sun because of the polishing action of the ice about 145,000 years ago.

Shorthair sedge *(Carex exserta)* dominates the vegetation found in the meadows. Other sedges include beaked sedge *(Carex rostrata)* and black sedge *(Carex nigricans).* It stands up to frost

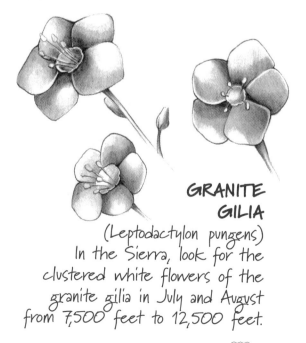

GRANITE
GILIA
(Leptodactylon pungens)
In the Sierra, look for the
clustered white flowers of the
granite gilia in July and August
from 7,500 feet to 12,500 feet.

and cold at this elevation. Look also for grasses, such as the spiked trisetum *(Trisetum spicatum)*, Hansen's bluegrass *(Poa hanseni)*, and gray wild rye *(Elymus glaucus)*. Besides surviving the cold and snow, this vegetation does well in dry soils, particularly in late summer.

The meadow will fill with snowmelt briefly in late June and July. In the swampy conditions, the snow mosquitoes *(Aedes communis)* thrive. They are often seen in clouds—usually surrounding unfortunate hikers and backpackers. Smear on repellents and sleep in tents with screens to avoid becoming a blood meal. However, it is almost impossible to avoid being bitten in late June and July.

Hikers and backpackers know Tuolumne Meadows as a kind of high country oasis. It is a place where they can get food, a shower, and even a tent with a bed. Tuolumne Meadows is one of the first major stops along the John Muir Trail for backpackers who begin at Happy Isles in Yosemite Valley.

Many hikers choose to park their cars in the valley and ride a shuttle bus to Tuolumne Meadows. From the 8,600-foot meadows, they hike back down to the 4,000-foot-elevation valley—a much easier trip than vice versa. Often, they take the Muir Trail, or they stop at another place along Tioga Road and hike back into the valley. The vistas are incredible, especially when a lot of water is flowing in late June and July.

The subalpine wildlife in this region includes the Yosemite toad *(Bufo canorus)*, which is most likely to appear during wet times in the meadows. It usually hibernates beneath the snowpack and makes its appearance in May or June. Listen for a chorus of singing around warm, shallow pools of water.

For winter sports enthusiasts, cross-country skiing along Tioga Road can bring experienced skiers all the way to Tuolumne Meadows. Always check with the rangers before embarking on such a trip, however. Blizzards can move in very quickly above 7,000 feet in Yosemite or anywhere else in the Sierra.

Directions: From Crane Flat on Highway 120 or Tioga Road, drive east about 40 miles to Tuolumne Meadows. From the Tioga Pass Entrance Station on the east side of Yosemite, drive about 6 miles west to Tuolumne Meadows.

Activities: Hiking, backpacking, camping, skiing, picnicking, and nature photography.

Facilities: Campground, gas station, restrooms, grocery store, lodge, restaurant, mountaineering school and shop, and ranger station.

Dates: For hiking and camping, May or June through early Oct. Cross-country skiing in the winter.

Fees: There is a fee for camping and services.

Closest town: Lee Vining, 15 miles.

For more information: Yosemite National Park, PO Box 577, Yosemite, CA 95389. Phone (209) 372-0265.

LEMBERT DOME TRAIL

[Fig. 37(1)] The view of the Cathedral Range directly south of Lembert Dome is spectacular. The smooth surface of the dome was created by glacial action. The dome is sometimes mistaken for a large *roche moutonnée*, but that is not what it is.

A true *roche moutonnée* has been completely overridden by ice, and Lembert Dome was merely shaped and polished by glaciers. For examples of giant *roches moutonnées*, go to Little Yosemite Valley and see the Liberty Cap.

The trail to Lembert Dome forks after 0.1 mile. Take the right fork and begin the short ascent of the dome. The trail will disappear on the granite after about 0.8 mile, but it is not difficult to see where to go.

The trail leads through lodgepole pine, which is a fairly typical tree to find in the forest surrounding a subalpine meadow such as Tuolumne Meadows. Notice the limbs of larger trees and the entire trunks of smaller ones are bent at odd angles from the heavy snowfall. Some areas experience avalanches.

Smoke In The Sierra

When driving through Yosemite National Park, visitors often notice smoke in the air. Most of the time, there's no reason to be alarmed. Park officials set fires called prescribed burns when temperatures, the wind, and humidity allow them to easily control the blaze.

The fire burns excess vegetation that could some day fuel a much larger wildfire. It also makes the forest healthier. Unfortunately, it makes the forest smokier, too. Residents in many parts of the Sierra go through the same ordeal every summer, as federal officials try to eliminate extra vegetation.

The extra vegetation has grown largely because of federal policies to extinguish every fire that was spotted in the mountains for most of the twentieth century. Now, federal officials need to burn more than 100,000 acres annually for many years to make the mountains safer.

Lembert Dome is named after a sheepherder who was tragically slain in the 1890s. Jean Baptiste Lembert also was somewhat of a naturalist who spent time in Tuolumne Meadows during the summer, living in a cabin. His body was found in a cabin near Yosemite Valley, and the case was never solved.

The hike to the dome is an easy morning walk. Some people like to stop for a picnic at the top. Don't get too close to the summit if you have difficulty with heights.

Directions: From Crane Flat on Highway 120 or Tioga Road, drive east about 40 miles to Tuolumne Meadows. Drive about 0.6 mile to the east side of Tuolumne Meadows and turn north into the Lembert Dome parking lot. The trailhead starts north from the parking lot.

Trail: 2 miles round-trip.

Elevation: 850-foot gain, 9,450-foot peak.

Degree of difficulty: Moderate.

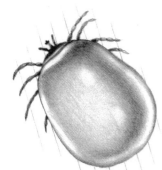

**WESTERN BLACK-
LEGGED TICK**

(Ixodes pacificus)
Tick hatchlings climb
vegetation and latch
onto a passing host.
After a meal, they
drop off, molt, and
climb onto another host,
repeating the process
until they are full-
grown.

Surface: Rocky footpath, disappearing into bare granite.

CATHEDRAL LAKE

[Fig. 37(2)] The jagged granite atop Cathedral Peak is a sight waiting for anyone who makes the ascent to the Cathedral Lakes. The glacial lake is usually reached in a day hike, though many people prefer to backpack the trail and camp around the lake.

The trail takes hikers past erratics, boulders left behind after glaciers melted. Note the smooth appearance of the granite bedrock, which was scoured by passing glaciers.

Besides lodgepole pine, fir trees are found as hikers climb higher on the trail. Both red fir and white fir occur as hikers reach elevations that reveal a view of Fairview Dome, another glacially polished feature.

Some prominent shrubs found on the hike include white mountain heather (*Cassiope mertensiana*) and bush cinquefoil (*Potentilla fruticosa*). In July and August, wildflowers found along the trail include the California valerian (*Valeriana capitata*), Bigelow's sneezeweed (*Helenium bigelovii*), and Sierra butterweed (*Senecio scorzonella*).

If a day hike is the plan, it's a good idea to start early and take it slow, especially for those coming from a sea-level area the day before. The hike begins above 8,000 feet, and even the fittest hikers experience shortness of breath unless they are acclimated to this elevation.

Directions: From Crane Flat on Highway 120 or Tioga Road, drive east about 38 miles to the Cathedral Lakes parking lot, indicated by a sign on the south side of the road. It is about 1.6 miles west of the Tuolumne Meadows campground.

Trail: 7.2 miles round-trip.

Elevation: About 1,000-foot gain, 9,580-foot peak.

Degree of difficulty: Moderate.

Surface: Well-marked and rocky, steep in places.

TENAYA LAKE/OLMSTED POINT

[Fig. 37] The Tenaya Lake/Olmsted Point area is considered the main stop in Yosemite for anyone who has very little time to spend. From Olmsted, visitors can look down Tenaya Canyon to the south, toward Half Dome and Little Yosemite Valley, near Yosemite Valley. At Tenaya, visitors can fish, hike, and see a glacially carved lake up close. The surrounding granite is one of the best examples of glacial polish in the park.

The lake was created when a glacier dug down in the Tuolumne Canyon to make a depression in the granite bedrock about 15,000 years ago. The receding ice left one of the larger and more scenic lakes in Yosemite National Park. Tenaya Lake, at an elevation of 8,149 feet, is about 1 mile in length and 0.5 mile in width.

The lake spreads in full view south of the road, attracting flocks of visitors to picnic and see the granite peaks and domes surrounding it. It can be seen from Olmsted Point, which is about 2 miles to the west on Tioga.

Tenaya Lake is where Chief Tenaya of the Ahwahnachee tribe was captured in 1851. The Mariposa Battalion caught Tenaya and escorted him down to Yosemite Valley. The lake is named for the chief. Tenaya Lake was known as "Lake of the Shining Rocks" to the tribe, because of the smooth, polished look that remained after the glacier created the lake basin.

Olmsted Point is named after Frederick Olmsted, the well-known landscape designer who directed the construction of New York's Central Park. Olmsted was the chairman of Yosemite's first Board of Commissioners in the nineteenth century.

The spectacular southeast-facing granite near Olmsted has been the source of much debate and danger over the past 30 years. Thick blocks of ice freeze at an angle on the rock during winter. In spring, as the ice melts, small sections beneath the ice liquefy and begin sending water out from beneath the ice block. During cold spring nights in May, it often refreezes, only to begin thawing again the next day.

The several tons of ice can slide without warning onto Tioga Road. A road-clearing worker was killed in a bulldozer in such an avalanche during the mid-1990s. Park officials have since hired an avalanche consultant who uses dynamite to blast unstable sections down from the dome.

On the eastern side of the Sierra, merchants and business owners wait for the road to open and bring them the tour buses that will keep their economies alive. So, each year, park officials must balance the goals of safety and access. The controversy ignites because east-side interests believe the park is being too cautious and too slow about opening the road.

Once visitors are allowed on the road, usually in late May or June, they will see Mount Conness at 12,600 feet to the east of Olmsted and Fairview Dome to the south. Among the subalpine vegetation is the mountain hemlock *(Tsuga mertensiana)*, a tough tree that thrives in areas where snow piles deep. There are not many places in Yosemite where visitors can drive past mountain hemlock. Usually, it is best seen on a hike in the high country.

Directions: Drive about 34 miles east from Crane Flat on Highway 120 or Tioga Road to Olmsted Point. Tenaya Lake is about 2 miles farther east.

Activities: Picnicking, hiking, fishing, and sight-seeing.

Facilities: Campground, picnic area, restrooms, and potable water.

Dates: Tioga Road is open June through Oct.

Fees: There is a fee for a fishing license.

Closest town: Lee Vining, 12 miles

For more information: Yosemite National Park, PO Box 577, Yosemite, CA 9538. Phone (209) 372-0265.

HIGH SIERRA LOOP TO MAY LAKE

[Fig. 37(3)] The area is popular because of its easy access: Visitors can drive most of the way to May Lake. The 1.1-mile hike to the lake from the parking lot is scenic and not too challenging. It is also a historic trail. The route is the part of the old Great Sierra Wagon Road, which preceded Tioga Road. Travelers used the route extensively in the 1880s going from east to west through Yosemite.

The lake is just below the approximate geographical center of Yosemite—Mount Hoffmann, the 10,850-foot peak that scientists believe jutted out above the last glacier about 12,000 years ago. The mountain was named after Charles Hoffmann, a topographer who passed through the area in the 1860s with the geological survey led by geologist William Brewer. May Lake is a stopping point along a 50-mile high-elevation route that circles Tuolumne Meadows. It is one of five High Sierra camps along the route. Each of the High Sierra camps is about 10 miles or a one-day hike from each other. Hikers can rent tent cabins, buy food, and rest amid the lodgepole pine and the red mountain heather.

Take time to stop along the way; turn around and see Clouds Rest to the south. The 9,925-foot summit is often surrounded with clouds in spring and fall.

Directions: Drive about 32 miles east of Crane Flat on Highway 120 or Tioga Road. Turn left on May Lake Road, and drive about 1.8 miles to parking area.

Trail: 2.2 miles round-trip.

Elevation: About 500-foot gain, 9,329-foot peak.

Degree of difficulty: Moderate.

Surface: Established trail; some rocky and sandy flats.

SUNRISE LAKES TRAIL

[Fig. 37(4)] The trail is busy but rewarding for those who want a picnic alongside one of the three Sunrise Lakes. They include lower, middle, and upper lakes. All have views of the glacially shaped landmarks and erosion process—exfoliation—that continues to change their faces.

This route is filled with mosquitoes in June and part of July. Usually, the mosquitoes are out for their blood meals in the morning and early evening hours. Put on the repellent along with the sunscreen and hike this during the warmer parts of the morning and afternoon.

The wildflowers at this elevation can bloom in July and August. Look for bud saxifrage (*Saxifraga bryophora*), Nuttall's gayophytum (*Gayophytum nuttallii*), and western blue flag (*Iris missouriensis*). The displays can be wonderful for those who like to photograph wildflowers.

This hike also will give amateur botanists the chance to see white mountain heather (*Cassiope mertensiana*), a late-summer delight to see at high elevations. The

The New Year's Day Flood

An unusual winter tropical storm began dumping rain on California in late December 1996, and the rain kept coming until the third day of January. More than 10 inches of rain fell at elevations above 8,000 feet, melting a thick snowpack in Yosemite National Park. By the time the rain stopped, the Merced River had risen 10 feet above its banks, inundating Yosemite Valley and ripping out roads, sewer lines, and campgrounds.

It was the largest flood in more than 80 years, causing more than $175 million damage to lodge units, roads, and other developments. The park was closed for more than three months. People were stranded in the valley for days, and many worried about the park's tourist season for 1997.

But the flood helped the ecosystem, spreading rich sediment for vegetation and moving boulders downstream, where they were pulverized into gravel for fish habitat.

wiry stem systems intertwine and create dense mats that are highlighted with bell-like flowers. They grow around rock ledges, and they are not generally visible from roads in Yosemite.

Directions: Drive about 36 miles east on Highway 120 or Tioga Road to the Sunrise Lakes trailhead parking area on the west side of Tenaya Lake.

Trail: 5.5 miles round-trip.

Elevation: About a 1,000-foot gain, 9,165-foot peak.

Degree of difficulty: Strenuous.

Surface: Steep in places with switchbacks on established trail.

PORCUPINE CREEK TRAIL TO NORTH DOME

[Fig. 37(5)] The view of Half Dome from North Dome makes this day hike worth the effort. Half Dome looms southeast of North Dome, separated perhaps by only 2.5 miles with Yosemite Valley yawning below and the glacially scarred Tenaya Canyon to the northeast. It almost looks as if you can reach out and touch Half Dome.

The lodgepole pine in the area is a favorite food for the American porcupine. The porcupine feed on the inner bark of the lodgepoles. They feed at night, making a soft grunt or groaning "nuh" as they move about. From North Dome, most of the geologic features at the rim of Yosemite Valley are visible, including Illilouette Fall, Clouds Rest, Glacier Point, Sentinel Rock, Three Brothers, and El Capitan. In the valley, the Ahwahnee Hotel is a recognizable landmark. The views of wildflowers in meadows near Porcupine Creek are another attraction on the hike. Look for creeping sidalcea (*Sidalcea reptans*), blue-eyed mary (*Collinsia torreyi*), and alpine lily (*Lilium parvum*). Sedges in the area include black sedge and beaked sedge.

The hike is not considered difficult, but some people are susceptible to elevation sickness. The symptoms include a pressure behind the eyes, headache, and dizziness. Severe forms of it can force people to simply stop hiking, rest, and turn around. North

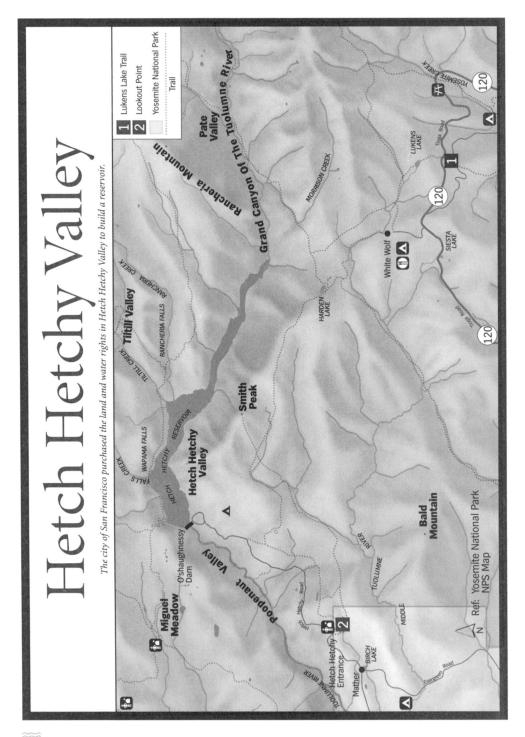

Hetch Hetchy Valley

The city of San Francisco purchased the land and water rights in Hetch Hetchy Valley to build a reservoir.

Legend:
- 1 — Lukens Lake Trail
- 2 — Lookout Point
- Yosemite National Park
- Trail

Ref: Yosemite National Park NPS Map

Dome, at 8,522 feet, probably would not cause elevation sickness for most people.

Directions: Drive about 25 miles east on Highway 120 or Tioga Road from Crane Flat. Park on the right side of the road near the sign for Porcupine Creek. The trailhead begins at the sign.

Trail: 9.8 miles round-trip.

Elevation: 400-foot gain, 8,522-foot peak.

Degree of difficulty: Moderate.

Surface: Old road, open footpath in the forest, and rocky at the dome.

Hetch Hetchy Valley

[Fig. 38] This glacial valley is an 8-mile-long reservoir for the city of San Francisco, which purchased the land and all the rights to it and the Tuolumne River in 1908 for $600,000. Even though the floor is flooded with Tuolumne River water behind O'Shaughnessy Dam, it is still an attraction for many hikers and campers because of its waterfalls and many similarities to Yosemite Valley.

Hetch Hetchy's Wapama Falls spills 1,200 feet over a granite precipice. The falls are spawned by Falls Creek, a tributary of the Tuolumne River. John Muir compared the falls to Yosemite Falls, although Wapama is only 1,700 feet compared to more than 2,400 for Yosemite Falls. Kolana in Hetch Hetchy occupies roughly the same location in this valley as El Capitan does in Yosemite Valley. Tueeulala Falls is similar to several falls in Yosemite Valley.

Muir considered Hetch Hetchy Valley to be as rare and beautiful as Yosemite Valley. He made the statement often in the course of the battle over the Tuolumne River with San Francisco. The federal government resisted several attempts by San Francisco to secure the valley, but succumbed to political pressure in 1907.

During those battles, Muir wrote: "Sad to say, this most precious and sublime feature of the Yosemite National Park, one of the greatest of all our natural resources for the uplifting joy and peace and health of the people, is in danger of being dammed and made into a reservoir to help supply San Francisco with water and light, thus flooding it from wall to wall and burying its gardens and groves 100 or 200 feet deep. This grossly destructive commercial scheme has long been planned and urged (though water as pure and abundant can be got from outside of the people's park, in a dozen different places), because of the comparative cheapness of the dam."

These days, the Sierra Club continues to advocate for restoration of Hetch Hetchy Valley. Others point out that in the last decade San Francisco has undergone brief scares over cryptosporidium, a mysterious spore found in surface water. In Hetch Hetchy, no one has proven there is cryptosporidium, which causes a variety of flulike symptoms and can be fatal to immune-deficient people. But many believe it is another reason to tear down O'Shaughnessy.

Anyone who drinks water from the reservoir or any other surface water in the Sierra should filter it or use iodine pills to purify it. Even rivers in Yosemite are considered to be too dangerous to drink unfiltered.

But many things about Hetch Hetchy have not changed since Muir fought for the valley. Muir noted Douglas fir *(Pseudotsuga menziesii)*, yellow pine *(Pinus ponderosa)*, sugar pine *(Pinus lambertiana)*, digger pine *(Pinus sabiniana)*, and incense cedar *(Libocedrus decurrens)*. He also found tangles and clumps of western azalea *(Rhododendron occidentalis)*, mountain spiraea *(Spiraea densiflora)*, woolly sunflower *(Eriophyllum congdonii)*, and spice bush *(Calycanthus occidentalis)*. With few exceptions, the vegetation is still visible in the area.

Like Yosemite Valley to the south, Hetch Hetchy Valley was a narrow or V-shaped river gorge before the Ice Age of 2 million years ago. It was covered with timber in a coniferous forest, much the same as it is today. When vast rivers of ice began moving down the Tuolumne River gorge, they filled Hetch Hetchy Valley and relentlessly ground the granite away. The valley is now U-shaped. It has a hanging valley above it where Tueeulala Falls comes down in surges with a wispy mist. Smaller glaciers came down the valley where Tueeulala now flows. The larger glaciers in Hetch Hetchy met the smaller glaciers and carved off the end of the smaller valley.

Directions: Drive 45 miles east on Highway 120 from Oakdale on the northwest side of Yosemite. About 1 mile west of Yosemite's Big Oak Flat entrance station, turn north on the Hetch Hetchy turnoff, which is Evergreen Road. Evergreen Road becomes Hetch Hetchy Road after 7.5 miles. The Hetch Hetchy entrance station is about 2 miles beyond the junction of Evergreen and Hetch Hetchy roads. Drive another 6.5 miles beyond the entrance station on Hetch Hetchy Road to the parking lot above O'Shaughnessy Dam.

Activities: Backpacking, hiking, camping, photography, and picnicking.

Facilities: Backpacker campground, vault toilets.

Dates: The road is open until the first snow storm in Nov. It reopens after the snowmelt in May.

Fees: A fee is charged for camping.

Closest town: Groveland, 18 miles.

For more information: Yosemite National Park, PO Box 577 Yosemite, CA 95389. Phone (209) 372-0265.

LUKENS LAKE TRAIL

[Fig. 38(1)] The hike to Lukens Lake is less than 1mile, but the benefits of the short walk are considerable. The lake is full of trout—mainly rainbow trout and Eastern brook trout. The ecosystem at this high country lake is also an attraction with many kinds of animals that represent the subalpine belt—6,000 to 8,000 feet—in the Sierra.

Predator animals at these elevations are generally smaller than they are below

6,000 feet. Look for the mountain coyote *(Canis latrans)*, great horned owl *(Bubo virginianus)*, and the marten *(Martes americana)*.

For wildlife photographers, the marten would be a particularly difficult and coveted subject to find. The marten, which efficiently hunts rodents, is very secretive. The marten's cousins, the long-tailed weasel *(Mustela frenata)* or the least weasel *(Mustela erminea)*, are more likely to be seen.

Directions: Drive about 16 miles east of Crane Flat on Tioga Road. Park on the south side of the road near the Lukens Lake sign. The trailhead is across on the north side of Tioga Road.

Trail: 1.6 miles round-trip.

Elevation: 200-foot gain, 8,340-foot peak.

Degree of difficulty: Easy.

Surface: Established, open footpath.

LOOKOUT POINT

[Fig. 38(2)] The trail is an easy way to find great views of Hetch Hetchy's waterfalls. Photographers like to take this short walk in spring for a photo of Tueeulala Falls and Wapama Falls to the east. This is North Mountain, where a fire lookout was established many years ago. The lookout is no longer used.

The trail is also nice walk for its natural features. Look closely at the granite on Lookout Point and see the scratches and grooves left by a glacier more than 12,000 years ago.

Trees do not grow in abundance on the granite surface. The tenacious Jeffrey pine can survive, but few other conifers grow here. In the lower and more sheltered elevations along this trail, the white fir and incense cedar grow in small stands.

The natural grasses in the lower elevations include Hansen's bluegrass *(Poa hanseni)* and western needlegrass *(Stipa occidentalis)*. But many exotic grasses have been introduced to the Sierra and California in the last 100 years.

Directions: Drive 45 miles east on Highway 120 from Oakdale to the Evergreen Road, about 1 mile west of the Big Oak Flat entrance station. Turn north on Evergreen at the Hetch Hetchy turnoff sign and drive about 7.5 miles to Hetch Hetchy Road and turn right. Drive about 1 more mile to the Mather Ranger Station and park. The trailhead is marked near the ranger station.

Trail: 3.2 miles round-trip.

Elevation: 450-foot gain, 5,265-foot peak.

Degree of difficulty: Easy.

Surface: Well-established, rocky slope.

MARTEN
(Martes americana)

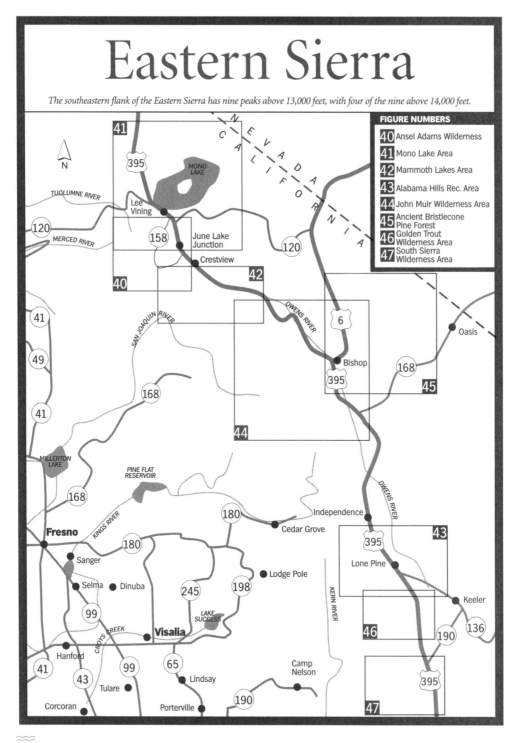

Eastern Sierra

The southeastern flank of the Eastern Sierra has nine peaks above 13,000 feet, with four of the nine above 14,000 feet.

FIGURE NUMBERS

- 40 Ansel Adams Wilderness
- 41 Mono Lake Area
- 42 Mammoth Lakes Area
- 43 Alabama Hills Rec. Area
- 44 John Muir Wilderness Area
- 45 Ancient Bristlecone Pine Forest
- 46 Golden Trout Wilderness Area
- 47 South Sierra Wilderness Area

Eastern Sierra

The stark, high desert of the Eastern Sierra contains perhaps as many natural wonders as any other region in California. The steep, sometimes barren eastern slope is almost completely within the Inyo National Forest, a 1.9 million-acre expanse where visitors can find the highest peak in the continental United States and the oldest living things on earth.

The forest covers a 165-mile area beginning in the north at Mono Lake, an almost barren Ice Age relic distinguished by its eerie tufa formations—chemical sedimentary rocks composed of calcium carbonate or silica deposited from the water draining into the lake. Around Mono Lake are cinder cones from volcanoes that have been active in the past 5,000 years.

On the ground around Mono Lake and in other places, visitors can find pumice, a spongy or porous form of volcanic glass. The extensive volcanic past is still alive and

[*Above:* A hiker among quaking aspens *(Populus tremuloides)* near Reds Meadow]

well today as magmatic activity produces clusters of small earthquakes on the Eastern Sierra.

In the Owens Valley, which is between the Sierra and the White Mountains, visitors can see parts of a volcanic caldera, or massive crater, more than 19 miles long and 10 miles wide. The caldera is so large that it cannot be viewed from ground level, but people can look at a map and guide themselves to part of the circular ridge. An enormous volcanic blast created the caldera—known as Long Valley Caldera—about 730,000 years ago. Ash from the blast has been discovered as far away as Nebraska.

To the west of the Owens Valley, the Sierra rises with Mount Whitney soaring to 14,497 feet, making it the tallest mountain in the lower 48 states. Whitney's popularity and size are so enormous that both the U.S. Forest Service and the National Park Service have a part of the mountain in their administrative territories. The majority of the mountain's management is done from the Inyo forest, but Whitney is also a part of Sequoia National Park. And the mountain can be approached from trails that begin or pass through Kings Canyon National Park. Like the Pacific Crest Trail and the Tahoe-Yosemite Trail, Whitney is considered a feature that transcends boundaries in the Sierra.

The spectacular Devils Postpile National Monument is also in the western Inyo National Forest area, though it is managed by the combined Sequoia-Kings Canyon National Parks administration on the west side of the Sierra. The linear basalt formation was created more than 100,000 years ago. Nearby, Mammoth Lakes is where millions of skiers hit the slopes at one of the highest-elevation ski resorts anywhere.

In the eastern Inyo National Forest is a separate range called the White Mountains where the bristlecone pine *(Pinus longaeva)* is found. Though it is not part of the Sierra, the range is well worth a side trip. The bristlecone pine is considered the oldest living tree, with a life-span stretching beyond 4,000 years. Scientists believe 17 of these trees have lived for more than 4,000 years.

The southern part of the Inyo National Forest contains 12,123-foot Olancha Peak. Olancha is the most southern of the Sierra's great peaks—mountains that are taller than 10,000 feet. The southeastern flank of the Sierra has nine peaks above 13,000 feet. Four of those nine are above 14,000 feet.

Why are the Sierra's tallest mountains on the southeast side? Dramatic faulting along the Sierra crest about 5 million years ago caused the mountain range to lift on the Eastern Sierra. Three distinct pulses lifted the area thousands of feet and created sheer canyons and high ridgelines that run from the crest to the Owens Valley in 10 or 12 miles. The west side is tilted in a long, gentle slope for about 50 miles from the crest.

The differences in the east and west inclines helps to explain why the climates vary so much on either side of the crest. The west slope is much wetter in winter, because Pacific storm clouds drop their moisture as they slowly rise above the mountain range. Near the crest on the Eastern Sierra, heavy snowfall can occur in places such as Mammoth Lakes, where it isn't unusual to receive 75 feet of snow in a winter. But, once the storms clear the crest, they can simply drop down the sheer eastern slope without losing any more moisture. The Eastern Sierra is left quite arid with smaller streams and sparse underbrush compared to the west slope.

The Inyo forest has 519 glacial lakes, and the southernmost of these lakes border the Golden Trout and John Muir wildernesses. They include popular Cottonwood Lakes, Consultation Lake, Meysan Lake, Lake Helen of Troy, and those within the dramatic Palisades Basin out of Big Pine. The Muir Wilderness alone has more than 27 major trailheads, and it is a favorite among backpackers and hikers because of the vast, steep canyons and the soaring granite spires. According to many backpackers and hikers, the striking views are comparable to those in Yosemite National Park, but the trailheads are nearly as crowded.

The only way that many people can see the wonders of the high Sierra is by riding on the back of a pack animal. The Eastern Sierra has many professional packers who guide trips into the high Sierra on the Inyo National Forest and also in Yosemite National Park. Appendix A lists commercial packers who rent animals and provide guides for trips into the wilderness.

The steep Eastern Sierra slope also gives hikers an extraordinary variety of vegetation and animal life to view. Abrupt changes from alpine vegetation to desert sagebrush occur within a few miles. A black-tailed jackrabbit *(Lepus californicus)* lives in the desert just a few miles from the white-tailed rabbit *(Lepus townsendi)*, which is known to roam higher elevations all the way up to 12,000 feet.

The Jeffrey pine *(Pinus jeffreyi)* forest along with the lodgepole pine *(Pinus murrayana)* and red fir *(Abies magnifica)* forest on the Eastern Sierra support many kinds of mammals, including the least chipmunk *(Eutamias minimus)*, Belding ground squirrel *(Spermophiles beldingi)*, Shasta beaver *(Castor canadensis shasta)*, and mule deer *(Odocoileus hemionus)*.

The bighorn or mountain sheep *(Ovis canadensis)* has attracted the most concern of any mammal on the Eastern Sierra because its numbers are dwindling quickly. The sheep has been added to the federal Endangered Species Act list and is considered near extinction because of predation from mountain lions *(Felis concolor)* and disease.

More than 1,000 flowering plants have been collected on the Eastern Sierra. Visitors can find thistle poppy *(Argemone munita* ssp. *rotundata)*, cow parsnip *(Heracleum lanatum)*, evening primrose *(Oenothera hookeri)*, and scarlet penstemon *(Penstemon bridegesii)*. Like those in the rest of the Sierra, the wildflowers in this area blossom first in the lower elevations and later in summer at higher elevations.

Native Americans made use of many plants. The Paiute, who inhabited the Eastern Sierra for at least the last 1,000 years, figured a way to irrigate taboose *(Cyperus esculentus)*, a plant that has an edible tuber. They also were known to eat

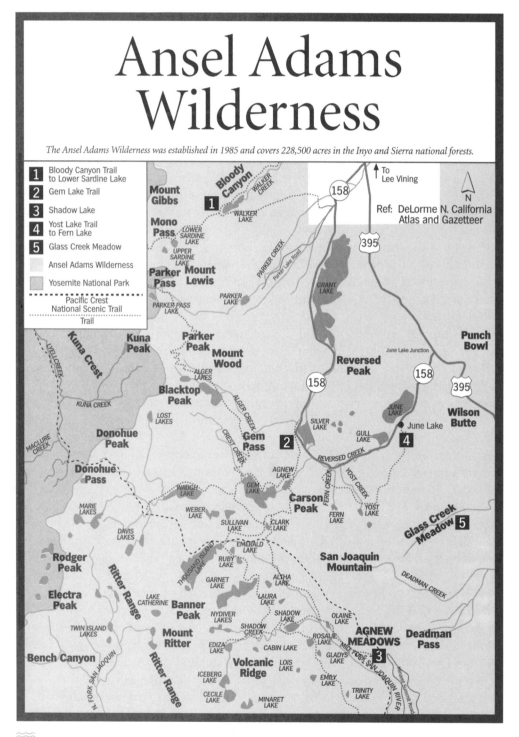

Ansel Adams Wilderness

The Ansel Adams Wilderness was established in 1985 and covers 228,500 acres in the Inyo and Sierra national forests.

1 Bloody Canyon Trail to Lower Sardine Lake

2 Gem Lake Trail

3 Shadow Lake

4 Yost Lake Trail to Fern Lake

5 Glass Creek Meadow

Ansel Adams Wilderness

Yosemite National Park

Pacific Crest National Scenic Trail

Trail

To Lee Vining

Ref: DeLorme N. California Atlas and Gazetteer

N

pinion pine *(Pinus monophylla)* nuts through the long winter.

But the Paiute and the Shoshone engaged in wars to stop European settlers from taking the land in the early 1860s. But military action stopped the Native American uprisings in the 1870s, and the Eastern Sierra economy began to grow from mining, grazing, and farming.

Mining took place in the White Mountains and in the Sierra—both sides of the Owens Valley. Miners flooded into such places as Cerro Gordo, Bodie, Mammoth City, and Lundy. By the early twentieth century, with resources dwindling and finances waning, most mining had ended in the Eastern Sierra. Many towns were left deserted. Bodie, in the White Mountains northeast of Mono Lake, is one of the more popular ghost towns for visitors.

Down in the Owens Valley, a notorious water war took place in the early twentieth century. The city of Los Angeles used political influence to bring Owens River water 200 miles south to burgeoning Southern California communities. Owens Valley farmers fought and lost the battle to keep the river. Soon Owens Lake was dried up. The film *China Town* was based on the Owens Valley dispute with Los Angeles.

After decades of bickering and rancorous debate, Inyo County filed a lawsuit in the 1980s. The county and the city of Los Angeles came to an out-of-court settlement in 1991, stopping Southern California from taking any more water. Streams throughout the Eastern Sierra are regenerating ecosystems that were lost when they were drained.

Mono Lake, which had dropped 45 vertical feet by the mid-1980s and suffered from high salinity, is rising. The tributaries in the Mono Basin had been the target of a second big push for water acquisition by Los Angeles in the 1960s. Environmentalists and scientists later played a role in raising public awareness of the problems. In 1987, the National Academy of Sciences predicted the ecosystem would collapse if water diversions had not stopped.

Ansel Adams Wilderness

[Fig. 40] The Ansel Adams Wilderness is named for the landscape photographer whose wilderness portraits of Yosemite National Park and the Sierra Nevada have been acclaimed internationally. The wilderness, established in 1985, covers 228,500 acres in the Inyo and the Sierra national forests.

It is considered an important ecological area because it contains the headwaters of the 350-mile San Joaquin River, the state's second longest river. The San Joaquin starts at Thousand Island Lake, above 10,000 feet in elevation, and runs to the Central Valley. Its 1.7 million acre-foot annual runoff passes through more than 25 powerhouses, which produce hydroelectric power for Southern California Edison.

Along the river are stands of red fir *(Abies magnifica)* and Jeffrey pine *(Pinus jeffreyi).*

STRIPED SKUNK
(Mephitis mephitis)

Visitors also will see mountain hemlock *(Tsuga mertensia)* and quaking aspen *(Populus tremuloides)*. The wildlife include the panamint kangaroo rat *(Dipodomys panamantinus)*, striped skunk *(Mephitis mephitis)*, and porcupine *(Erethizon dorsatum)*.

But land at the high elevations—ranging between 7,600 feet and 13,000 feet—is barren granite. The granite formed about 80 million years ago. Erosion of volcanic and metamorphic rock over the next 20 million years exposed the Sierra Granite, which existed as lowland compared to today's soaring mountains.

The tilting and uplifting of the Sierra began 20 million to 30 million years ago. The San Joaquin's headwaters may have been as far east as Nevada. But the Sierra rose high enough to block the ancient channel from the east, and the river's headwaters became suspended near the crest at Thousand Island Lake.

After three pulses of uplift over more than 20 million years, Ice Age glaciers 2 million years ago began to widen river and creek canyons with tons of slow-moving ice. They created cirques and scarred gorges when they departed. Some small glaciers remain on the north- and north-east facing peaks, especially in the Ritter Range near the Devils Postpile National Monument.

The retreating glaciers left many lakes, which are considered to be fishing paradises. The wilderness has excellent stream and lake fishing for rainbow *(Oncorhynchus mykiss)*, golden *(Salmo aguabonita)*, and Eastern brook trout *(Salvelinus fontinalis)*. The lakes include Gem Lake, Parker Lake, Waugh Lake, and Minaret Lake, but there are dozens of others.

Hikers, backpackers, fishing enthusiasts, and snow skiers should be aware of the dramatic weather in the Sierra, especially above 9,000 feet in this part of the range. A few puffy clouds on the horizon can become a drenching thunderstorm in less than an hour. During storms, avoid open areas such as meadows, ridges, and mountain-tops, and stay away from water and isolated trees.

Blizzards also develop rapidly any time of year, but especially in late fall, winter, and spring. Carry extra food, parkas, and dry clothing when taking a trip of more than one day. The best time to hike the Ansel Adams Wilderness is from June through September. Some access roads close after the first snowfall in autumn and do not reopen until late May or June.

Directions: From Lee Vining at Mono Lake, drive south on Highway 395 to one of three roads. The first is Road 158, also known as the North June Lake Junction, about 7 miles south of Lee Vining. The second is the South June Lake Junction, about 12 miles south of Lee Vining. The third is Highway 203, about 25 miles south of Lee Vining. From June Lake and Mammoth Lakes, there are trails into the wilderness.

Activities: Hiking, backpacking, camping, fishing, and nature photography.

Facilities: Commercial packers operate from June Lake, Agnew Meadow, and Red's Meadow. Grocery stores, hotels, and restaurants are available at Mammoth Lakes, just east of the wilderness. Also, several campgrounds are available along the eastern border of the wilderness, but no facilities, roads, or campgrounds are in the wilderness.

Dates: Open year-round.

Closest town: Mammoth Lakes, 2 miles.

For more information: Inyo National Forest Mammoth Ranger District, Highway 203, PO Box 148 Mammoth Lakes, CA 93546. Phone (760) 924-5500. Inyo National Forest supervisor's office, 873 North Main Street, Bishop, CA 93514. Phone (760) 873-2400.

▓ BLOODY CANYON TRAIL TO LOWER SARDINE LAKE

[Fig. 40(1)] Anyone who makes the tough hike to this alpine lake should be wearing insect repellant. The mosquitoes in late June, July, and early August are everywhere. The views of Walker Creek and Walker Lake along the hike make the walk interesting. Lower Sardine Lake is a small, deep glacial tarn filled with cold water and trout.

On the way to Lower Sardine, hikers will see Indian paintbrush *(Castilleja campestris)*, quaking aspen *(Populus tremuloides)*, white fir *(Abies concolor)*, and lupine *(Lupinas lepidus)*. The route is called Bloody Canyon Trail, which refers to the first time explorers with horses tried to traverse it. The sharp rocks cut their horses so badly that the trail was sprinkled with blood.

At Lower Sardine, alpine wildflowers look dazzling on the shoreline. Look for the alpine paintbrush *(Castilleja nana)*, alpine goldenrod *(Solidago multiradiata)*, and Drummond's cinquefoil *(Potentilla drummondii)*.

The view from the lake includes the Owens Valley and Mono Lake. At this elevation, visitors can expect to also see the gray-crowned rosy finch *(Leucosticte tephrocotis)*. This bird is commonly seen in flocks feeding on seeds and insects next to alpine lakes and even near snowbanks on ridgecrests.

Aside from fishing and hiking, photography is one of the big lures of Lower Sardine Lake. The glacially sculpted cliffs and waterfalls in the area make an excellent backdrop for photographers who want to capture views of the Sierra crest.

Cow Parsnip

Cow parsnip (*Heracleum lanatum*) can be found in moist areas below 8,000 feet. Hikers normally see it sticking up above the ground on long stems with bunches of white flowers. The leaves can sometimes be more than a foot wide. The root is considered edible if cooked. The stems are also edible if they are peeled. They can be eaten raw, but they are supposed to be a bit more palatable cooked.

Directions: Drive about 7 miles south from Lee Vining on Highway 395 to the North June Lake Junction at Route 158. Turn right and drive 1.5 miles to the "Parker Lake-Walker Lake" sign. Turn right onto the unpaved road for the lakes, and then veer left at the junction about 0.1 mile away. Drive 0.4 mile, then turn right toward Walker Lake. Drive about 3.4 miles to a small parking lot where the trailhead is marked.

Trail: 7 miles round-trip.

Elevation: 2,700-foot gain, 9890-foot peak.

Degree of difficulty: Strenuous.

Surface: Rocky, sometimes steep trail. Some sections have loose, sandy soil and footing can be treacherous.

GEM LAKE TRAIL

[Fig. 40(2)] The lake, named by Theodore Agnew during the mining days of the late nineteenth century, is nestled on a granite bench with soaring peaks around it. Hikers can see Carson Peak (10,909 feet) to the east and Mount Lyell (13,114 feet) to the west. Blacktop Peak (12,710 feet) and Mount Wood (12,637 feet) rise in the distance to the north.

Gem Lake is a hydroelectric reservoir owned by Southern California Edison. But miners recognized it immediately for its beauty and photogenic location among the peaks in what would become the Ansel Adams Wilderness. It was quickly known as "Gem o' the mountains."

The flora is also striking at Gem Lake. Look for the edible fruit of the dwarf huckleberry (*Vaccinium nivictum*). Small rodents in the area feed on this plant, which is fairly common in moist soils above 7,000 feet in the Sierra.

Hikers have to walk uphill a long way to see these sights. There is a 1,300-foot gain in elevation in the first 2.5 miles, so be prepared take a little time, especially this high in the Sierra.

Directions: From Lee Vining, drive south on Highway 395 about 7 miles to the North June Lake Junction. Turn right and drive about 3.6 miles to Silver Lake parking lot, about 0.1 mile south of the packing station. Trailhead is marked at the parking lot.

Trail: 7 miles round-trip.

Elevation: About 1,800-foot gain, 9,052-foot peak.

Degree of difficulty: Strenuous.

Surface: Steep, well established with many switchbacks.

SHADOW LAKE

[Fig. 40(3)] Two 13,000-foot peaks, Mount Ritter and Banner Peak in the Ansel Adams Wilderness, dominate the view around Shadow Lake. The stunning views are the main reasons to climb the trail into this lake, which is surrounded by Jeffrey pine *(Pinus jeffreyi)*, lodgepole pine *(Pinus murrayana)*, and red fir *(Abies magnifica)*. Along the streams in the area, look for the black cottonwood *(populus trichorcarpa)* and the Fremont cottonwood *(Populus fremontii)*.

The understory plants in the coniferous forest include herbaceous vegetation in the Eastern Sierra. The plants are not abundant but they are apparent. In this area, look for the white-veined wintergreen *(Pyrola picta)*, western prince's pine *(Chimaphila umbellata)*, and spotted coralroot *(Corallorhiza maculata)*.

This hike is not a long day hike, but it requires a fair amount of climbing. Take it slowly and bring plenty of water or a water pump to purify the water you find in streams or the lake. No surface water in the Sierra is considered safe from contaminants.

Directions: Drive south about 25 miles from Lee Vining on Highway 395 to the Mammoth Lakes turnoff State Route 203. Turn right on 203, drive 3.7 miles—which will take you through the town of Mammoth Lakes—to a junction with Minaret Summit Road, which forks to the right toward the Devils Postpile National Monument. Take the right fork and drive about 5.6 miles to the monument entrance. From the entrance, follow the paved road for another 2.7 miles and turn off at the sign for Agnew Meadows Campground.

Trail: About 7 miles round-trip.

Elevation: About 1,000-foot gain, 8,748-foot peak.

Degree of difficulty: Moderate.

Surface: Well established, easy to follow.

COW PARSNIP
(Heracleum lanatum)
The leaves of cow parsnip can be more than 1 foot wide.

June Lake

[Fig. 40] The view of Carson Peak at 10,909 feet soaring above June Lake is enough to make any photography buff stop for a few hours to investigate this area. But June Lake, which is at 7,680 feet in the Sierra, has a lot more activities to offer visitors. The activities include hiking, fishing, boating, snow skiing, camping, and horseback riding.

The town of June Lake has a population of 600, and it is located on the southern end of the scenic 15-mile loop of Route 158, which can be reached from Highway 395. Besides June Lake, there are three other lakes where trout fishing is done around this area—Gull, Silver, and Grant lakes. Fishing enthusiasts will find the lakes stocked with brown trout *(Salmo trutta)* and rainbow trout *(Oncorhynchus mykiss)*.

June Lake has one of the more interesting geologic histories in the Sierra. The lake is fed by Reverse Creek, which runs west toward the Sierra batholith instead of away from it. For that reason, the creek is unique in this mountain range.

The backward flow was created about 10,000 years ago when the rugged granite of Reverse Canyon resisted the erosion of a glacier. The glacier was forced uphill for a few miles as it passed through the canyon, then it spilled down toward the Owens Valley to the east.

Today, visitors on Highway 395 east of June Lake may notice evidence of the glacier; the road climbs over the rocky lateral moraine of the Reverse Canyon glacier. If travelers on Highway 395 turn west onto Route 158 into the June Lake area, they will see Reverse Creek's water flowing from June Lake back toward the Sierra into Rush Creek. The creek goes north to Grant Lake.

Visitors also will notice the heavily wooded forests, composed mostly of Jeffrey pine *(Pinus jeffreyi)*, lodgepole pine *(Pinus murrayana)*, and pinion pine *(Pinus monophylla)*. In other areas around June Lake, the wild rose *(Rosa woodsii var. ultramontana)*, Sierra chinquapin *(Castanopsis sempervirens)*, and wax currant *(Ribes cereum)* are prominent shrubs. June Lake sports some of the finest fall color along the Eastern Sierra.

For bird-watchers, mountain quail *(Oreortyx picta)* can be seen in summers when they migrate to the higher elevations. This plump blue-gray bird often nests in dense sagebrush *(Artemesia tridentata)*, the kind of vegetation found all over the Eastern Sierra. The mountain quail scurries almost everywhere on foot. It usually does not fly unless it is being pursued or some danger is nearby.

Other birds include the Steller's jay *(Cyanocitta stelleri)*, the water ouzel *(Cinclus mexicanus)*, and the mountain bluebird *(Sialia currucoides)*. The water ouzel is one of the more unusual birds on the Eastern Sierra. The bird spends its life along streams where it hunts aquatic insects and larvae. It dives into the water and occasionally walks beneath waterfalls in pursuit of food.

In winter, all levels of snow skiing are offered at June Mountain, a 10,130-foot peak, just south of the June Lake. The June Mountain Resort, based in the town of June Lake, provides courses for downhill skiers and snowboarders. For more information, the resort can be contacted at PO Box 146, June Lake, CA 93529. Phone (760) 648-7733.

Directions: From Lee Vining, drive south on Highway 395 about 7 miles to the North June Lake Junction. Turn right onto Route 158. Drive about 13 miles to June Lake.

Activities: Hiking, fishing, boating, snow skiing, camping, scenic driving, bird-watching, nature photography, and horseback riding.

Facilities: Motels, cabins, campgrounds, retail stores, and restaurants.

Dates: Open year-round. Hiking and camping are best between May and Oct. Skiing season runs from Nov. to Apr., or later in big snowfall years.

Fees: There is a charge for camping, skiing, and horseback riding.

Closest town: June Lake.

For more information: June Lake Chamber of Commerce, PO Box 2, June Lake, CA 93529. Phone (760) 648-7584.

▓ YOST LAKE TRAIL TO FERN LAKE

[Fig. 40(4)] The cold, clear water in Fern Lake is wonderful on tired feet. Plenty of people have used this small, glacially created lake to cool off before having a picnic and taking photographs of wildflowers. The scent of sagebrush and the view of the snow-capped high Sierra make this a very rewarding hike.

But it is not a hike to take lightly. Even though it is less than 2 miles to the lake, hikers must ascend more than 0.25 mile vertically. Take breaks because the upward direction of this trail—called Yost Lake Trail—is unrelenting. The trail continues past Fern Lake to Yost Lake, but Yost is not as picturesque as Fern Lake.

The familiar Jeffrey pine *(Pinus jeffreyi)* may interest photographers, but the Sierra juniper *(Juniperus occidentalis)* is probably more favored on the trail and near Fern Creek. The juniper often grows on rocky or granite ridges, such as the ones around Fern Lake. Many are bent and deformed from lightning strikes or from

BIGHORN SHEEP
(*Ovis canadensis*)

the high winds that blast through the Eastern Sierra at 9,000 feet.

For wildflower lovers, watch for mule ears *(Wyethia mollis)* and rose everlasting *(Antennaria rosea)* in late July or August. The blooms are generally more spectacular in early to mid-August.

Directions: From Lee Vining, drive about 12 miles south on Highway 395 to the South June Lake Junction or Route 158. Turn right and drive west for about 5.4 miles to an unpaved road marked only by the sign "Yost Creek Trail." Turn left and drive 0.1 mile to trailhead parking.

Trail: 3.5 miles round-trip.

Elevation: 1,700-foot gain, 9,030-foot peak.

Degree of difficulty: Moderate.

Surface: Narrow, rocky, and well established.

GLASS CREEK MEADOW

[Fig. 40(5)] Glass Creek got its name from the volcanic activity that took place about 20,000 years ago in the area. The volcanic eruptions left behind pumice, a spongy or porous form of glass. It sparkles in the sand along the creek and in many places around Glass Creek Meadow, where small streams create a swampy mountain haven for wildflowers.

Look for Brewer's lupine *(Lupinus breweri)*, monkey-flower *(Mimulus sp.)*, and marsh marigold *(Caltha howellii)*. The color groupings can be dazzling among the glittering pumice and the obsidian in the area. The trees around the outside of the meadow are lodgepole pine *(Pinus murrayana)* and whitebark pine *(Pinus albicaulis)*.

On the return trip, hikers will notice many different offshoots of the main trail just beyond the meadow. These spur trails lead in directions away from the creek. Keep the creek within earshot as you go back down and you should be able to find the right spur that leads back to the parking lot.

Directions: From Lee Vining, drive 15.7 miles south on Highway 395 to Glass Flow Road, an unpaved route. Turn right and drive 2.7 miles to a place where the road divides into three routes. Stay to the right for 0.1 mile and do not cross Glass Creek. Park at trailhead parking lot.

Trail: 4.1 miles round-trip.

Elevation: 700-foot gain, 8,850-foot peak.

Degree of difficulty: Moderate.

Surface: Rocky, sometimes difficult to distinguish as it crosses granite. Continue following the creek's upward course to the lake.

BODIE STATE HISTORIC PARK

[Fig. 41(1)] The park features the West's largest ghost town that has not been restored. Visitors can take a short self-guided tour of the town, which includes cemeteries and the wooden buildings of the past. The Miners' Union Hall is where visitors can find the museum. Books and brochures are also available at the hall.

Bodie was a mining boomtown in the late nineteenth century. It boasted many hundreds of mining claims and 10,000 residents in 1885. More than a century later, a few of the original buildings survived after a major fire in 1892 and another in 1932.

The town was named after prospector William S. Bodey, who found gold in the Bodie Hills in 1859. The incorrect spelling of his name is rumored to have been a painter's error. Many well-funded efforts followed Bodey's discovery, but it took 15 years before two Swedish miners found a vein of gold-bearing ore. Many claims followed.

Bodie expanded so quickly that there was a shortage of wood. The townsfolk were clearing out the pinion pine and irritating the Native Americans, the Paiute. In the late 1870s, logging near Mono Lake began bringing in wood from vast Jeffrey pine forests.

MONARCH BUTTERFLY

(Danaus plexippus)
This brown to orange-brown butterfly has wings with white-spotted black borders and dark veins.

The town had a reputation for being wild. Gunfights, robberies, stagecoach holdups, and gambling occurred regularly. But the mining was Bodie's biggest claim to fame. By 1888, the area had produced about $30 million in gold and silver. But the supply was mostly exhausted.

The town continued as a shadow of its former self for several decades as small veins were found. When the town's school closed down in 1940, the few remaining people just left.

The state took over the town in 1962 to preserve its mining past. The state added it to the historic park system in 1964. Several government agencies combined in 1997 to buy 600 acres of land east of town. They are now included in the park.

Directions: Drive 15 miles north of Lee Vining on Highway 395 to Bodie Road and turn right. Drive 13 miles east to Bodie. The last 3 miles are unpaved.

Activities: Self-guided walking tour, photography.

Facilities: Museum, restrooms, and interpretive center.

Dates: The museum is open Memorial Day through mid-Sept. The park is open year-round, but the road is subject to winter closures because of snow.

Fees: There is an entry fee to the park.

Closest town: Bridgeport, 18 miles.

For more information: Bodie State Historic Park, PO Box 515, Bridgeport, CA 93517. Phone (760) 647-6445.

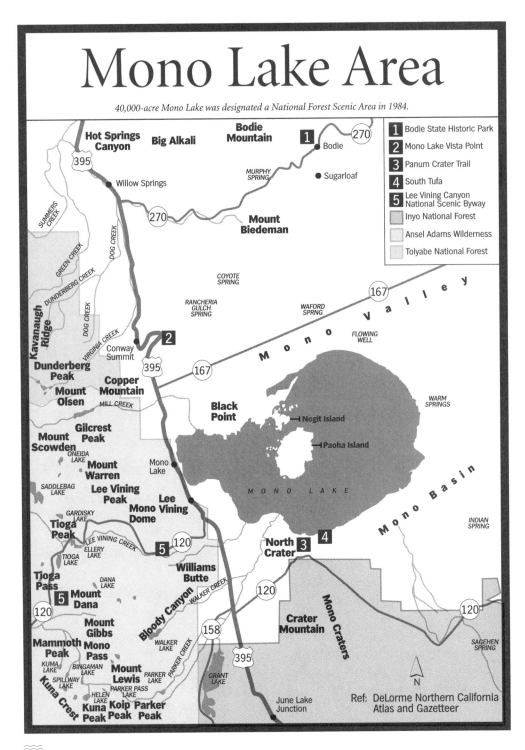

Mono Lake Area

40,000-acre Mono Lake was designated a National Forest Scenic Area in 1984.

1 Bodie State Historic Park
2 Mono Lake Vista Point
3 Panum Crater Trail
4 South Tufa
5 Lee Vining Canyon National Scenic Byway
Inyo National Forest
Ansel Adams Wilderness
Toiyabe National Forest

Hot Springs Canyon
Big Alkali
Bodie Mountain
1
270
Bodie
395
Willow Springs
MURPHY SPRING
Sugarloaf
SUMMERS CREEK
270
Mount Biedeman
DOG CREEK
GREEN CREEK
DUNDERBERG CREEK
COYOTE SPRING
RANCHERIA GULCH SPRING
WAFORD SPRNG
167
Mono Valley
Kavanaugh Ridge
DOG CREEK
VIRGINIA CREEK
Conway Summit
2
395
167
FLOWING WELL
Dunderberg Peak
Copper Mountain
MILL CREEK
Black Point
Negit Island
WARM SPRINGS
Mount Olsen
Gilcrest Peak
ONEIDA LAKE
Mount Scowden
Mount Warren
Mono Lake
Paoha Island
SADDLEBAG LAKE
Lee Vining Peak
MONO   LAKE
Mono Basin
GARDISKY LAKE
Lee Vining
Mono Dome
Tioga Peak
LEE VINING CREEK
ELLERY LAKE
5
120
North Crater
3
4
INDIAN SPRING
TIOGA LAKE
Williams Butte
WALKER CREEK
120
Tioga Pass
DANA LAKE
120
5 Mount Dana
Bloody Canyon
158
Crater Mountain
Mono Craters
120
Mount Gibbs
WALKER LAKE
PARKER CREEK
SAGEHEN SPRING
Mammoth Peak
Mono Pass
KUMA LAKE
BINGAMAN LAKE
PARKER LAKE
GRANT LAKE
395
N
KUNA LAKE
Mount Lewis
PARKER PASS
SPILLWAY LAKE
HELEN LAKE
PARKER PASS CREEK
Ref: DeLorme Northern California Atlas and Gazetteer
Kuna Crest
Kuna Peak
Koip Peak
Parker Peak
June Lake Junction

Mono Lake

[Fig. 41] Visitors can see one of the oldest lakes in North America just east of Yosemite National Park. Mono Lake, an alkaline body of water with curious mineral formations called tufa, offers bird-watching, swimming in briny water, walks along volcanoes that are still rumbling deep in the earth, canoeing, boating, and dramatic views of the high Sierra.

In 1984, Congress protected 40,000-acre Mono Lake and its ecosystems by designating it the Mono Basin National Forest Scenic Area. California, three years earlier, granted protections for the tufa mineral columns around the lake. The state designated the area as the Mono Lake Tufa State Reserve.

Mono Lake is a terminal lake, a depression in the earth where streams enter but do not leave. It is at the foot of Lee Vining Canyon, which descends from the Yosemite park line east of Lee Vining. The lake is the destination for several streams that have carried water and sediment into the lake bed since the Ice Age.

The origins of the lake bed can be traced back about 10 million years to when Mono Basin's floor began slipping downward as the Eastern Sierra lifted and tilted west along faults beneath the earth's surface. The lake probably began holding water about 1 million years ago.

To check the age of Mono Lake in the early part of the twentieth century, a well was drilled 1,400 feet deep on Paoha Island, one of Mono Lake's two volcanic islands. It struck light pink rock known as Bishop Tuft, which came from a massive volcanic blast more than 700,000 years ago. There were no saline layers in between, indicating the lake had not dried up for at least 700,000 years.

When the massive faulting began along the Eastern Sierra about 10 million years ago, a vast redwood forest covered the area. As the Sierra rose in the west, it began to block storms coming from the Pacific Ocean.

A "rain shadow" developed, meaning the west side of the Sierra absorbed most of the moisture from the storms and the east side became arid. The redwood forest changed to vegetation more tolerant of dry conditions, such as Indian manzanita (*Arctostaphylos mewukka*), pinion pine (*Pinus monophylla*), and, eventually, sagebrush (*Artemesia tridentata*).

The dry conditions created this sparse, desert vegetation, which enhances the stark, almost moonscape appearance around Mono Lake. John Muir described it as "a country of wonderful contrasts." These contrasts between the desert and the high Sierra in the background have captured photographers' imaginations for many decades.

The two volcanic islands are particularly interesting for photographers and boaters, who like to paddle out and explore them. They are Negit Island and Paoha Island. Paoha is the more eerie of the two. Erupting into existence about three centuries ago, Paoha has little vegetation. On its north and south ends, cinder cones

Gulls At Mono Lake

The California gull (*Larus californicus*) colony at Mono Lake is considered one of the biggest in the world. The breeding population is estimated between 30,000 and 40,000 birds. They come to Mono Lake—most to Negit Island—in March and April to nest. Their chicks typically hatch in June.

Mono Lake provides gulls with brine shrimp and flies in great abundance. Negit Island is far enough from the edge of land that it provides isolation and protection against such predators as coyotes (*Canis latrans*).

That protection was lost in 1979 when the Mono Lake water level dropped low enough to create a land bridge to Negit Island. Coyotes raided the nests and drove off the gulls, which did not return for the next six years. A wet year in 1985 allowed the lake to again turn Negit into an island. Gulls have since returned and continued to nest in great numbers on Negit Island.

mark the place where the island began with lava flows. Negit is about 1,700 years old. It is darker and much smaller than Paoha.

The lake contains some of the saltiest water in California or anywhere else. It comes from natural salinity left by the ocean many millions of years ago. As streams carry it into Mono Lake, the salt content becomes more concentrated. It is almost three times as salty as the Pacific Ocean and 1,000 times saltier than Lake Tahoe. Mono Lake contains about 280 million tons of dissolved salts.

As a result of the salts, it is virtually impossible to sink in Mono Lake. The south shore at Navy Beach attracts a lot of swimmers. A word of caution: Don't open your eyes in this water. It will sting.

Chemically, the lake's water contains a lot of chlorides, carbonates, and sulfates, which are carried in from the mountain streams around the lake. There are few places on earth where this combination exists, and it helps to create tufa, the strange, jagged columns sticking out of the water and scattered about the periphery of the lake.

Tufa towers have been described as fossilized underwater springs. They form from fresh underwater springs that contain calcium carbonate, a mineral in limestone. The tufa form in a chemical process occurring when the calcium in the spring water encounters the brine in Mono Lake. They combine and create a solid, composed of calcite or aragonite.

The process goes on in the surrounding beach areas as well as the lake bottom. Ground water seeps into the sandy areas to combine with the briny water, and tufa towers begin to grow a few millimeters annually.

Within such briny, mineral-laden water, one might suspect there would be little life. Indeed, there are no fish or vascular plants. About eight invertebrate species are visible to the eye in Mono Lake, and there are about 25 microscopic species.

Because there are no fish to feed on them, the hardy creatures that survive in this water have few predators. The alkali fly (*Ephydra hians*) and the Mono brine shrimp

(*Artemia monica*) are the most noticeable forms of life. They are everywhere in great numbers. They are considered "osmoregulators," meaning they have evolved the ability to pump unwanted substances out of their bodies.

The Mono brine shrimp cannot live anywhere else on earth. They are not even like other brine shrimp. They produce cysts, not eggs, and the cysts hatch in warmer water. Biologists have found 50,000 of them in a single cubic yard of Mono Lake water.

The alkali flies are also abundant at Mono Lake, and they are eaten in great numbers by shorebirds in the area. Thousands of the flies, which usually have no interest in even landing on humans, can be found in each square foot along the shore.

The Wilson phalarope (*Steganopus tricolor*), the eared grebe (*Podiceps caspicus*), and the California gull (*Larus californicus*), along with many other kinds of birds, will fly hundreds, even thousands of miles to dine for a season at Mono Lake. In the fall, for instance, more than 700,000 grebes fly to Mono Lake from breeding grounds as far away as western Canada. They feast on the insect life, and they prefer the Mono Lake winter climate to Canada's.

These huge gatherings of birds were impacted in the mid-twentieth century when Los Angeles began tapping into the Mono Lake creek system for water. By 1970, Los Angeles was diverting water from Lee Vining, Walker, Parker, and Rush creeks around Mono Lake. By 1981, Mono Lake had dropped 45 vertical feet and salinity had doubled. Negit Island had become a peninsula, and predators were decimating the bird population.

After an environmental lawsuit was filed in the late 1980s, the issue of Mono Lake's decline came before the California Water Resources Control Board, which determined in 1994 that the lake and ecosystem had been damaged by water diversions. An advocacy group, the Mono Lake Committee, and Los Angeles forged a settlement calling for the restoration of the ecosystem. The water diversions are no longer taking place.

Scientists believe it will take several decades for the lake to recover. But the lake already has risen more than 12 feet, and scientists have been encouraged by the rebounding ecosystem.

Directions: From Tioga Gate at the east side of Yosemite National Park, drive about 7 miles east on Highway 120 to Highway 395. Turn left and drive 1 mile to Lee Vining where the lake can be viewed. For self-guided walking tours, drive another 12 miles north to Mono Lake Vista Point.

Activities: Hiking, swimming, camping, photography, canoeing, and scenic driving.

Facilities: Motels, restaurants, and retail outlets can be found in Lee Vining. Campsites are available in various places.

Dates: Open year-round.

Fees: There is a fee for camping.

Closest town: Lee Vining.

For more information: Inyo National Forest, Mono Basin Scenic Area Manager,

PO Box 429, Lee Vining, CA 93541. Phone (760) 647-3040. Lee Vining Chamber of Commerce, PO Box 29, Lee Vining, CA 93541. Phone (760) 647-6595.

🟦 MONO LAKE VISTA POINT

[Fig. 41(2)] People bring their large lenses, cameras, and binoculars to this vista point to enjoy the sweeping view. This is the western edge of the geological domain called the Great Basin, which stretches hundreds of miles to Nevada and Utah. From this point, Mono Lake to the southeast is 1,000 feet below. It is an awesome depression with streams draining into it. Keep looking southeast on a clear day to see the White Mountains beyond Mono Lake. White Mountain Peak juts out at 14,246 feet. Just west of the White Mountains, you will see Glass Mountain, an 11,123-foot volcano. It erupted almost 1 million years ago.

Farther west, the Mono Craters are visible. And, the Sierra Nevada stands high in the west with jagged granite peaks etched into the skyline. Mono Lake is one of the Great Basin's many terminal lakes, which do not allow water to drain into the ocean. The Great Salt Lake is another well-known terminal lake.

Directions: Drive about 12 miles north of Lee Vining on Highway 395. Pull into a wide turnout to the right just before reaching the Conway Summit sign.

Activities: Scenic viewing and photography.

Facilities: None.

Dates: Open year-round.

Fees: None.

Closest town: Lee Vining, 12 miles.

🟦 PANUM CRATER TRAIL

[Fig. 41(3)] The view from Panum Crater, near the southern shore of Mono Lake, takes in the Mono Craters, Koip Peak, Mount Gibbs, Mount Lewis, and Mount Dana. Looking east, between Gibbs and Lewis, visitors can see two lateral moraines near the mouth of Bloody Canyon.

Panum Crater is a rounded pumice feature, one of the latest of the Mono Craters. It formed as magma moved up from the earth and worked its way through the underground aquifer. The hot magma created pressure in the aquifer and caused it to open up with a violent explosion. The explosion made the crater. For bird watchers, it is interesting to note several species in the area, including green-winged teal (*Anas crecca*), Canada goose (*Branta canadensis*), American avocet (*Recurvirostra americana*), and western sandpiper (*Calidris mauri*).

Directions: From Lee Vining, drive south on Highway 395 about 1 mile and turn left on Highway 120 at the Mono Lake South Tufa sign. Drive about 3.5 miles east on Highway 120 and turn left on a dirt road that is marked with a Panum Crater sign. Drive about 1 mile to the parking area. The short trail to the crater begins at the parking lot.

Trail: About 0.5 mile round-trip.

Elevation: About 200-foot gain, 6,400 feet.
Degree of difficulty: Easy.
Surface: Open footpath.

▨ SOUTH TUFA

[Fig. 41(4)] Walk through the tufa towers along the south shore of Mono Lake and see how eerie they are up close. But don't climb on them or take any part of them as a souvenir. State law protects the tufa.

The towers are created by the combination of the salty lake water and freshwater springs from beneath the lake and beach. The main ingredients are calcium from the fresh water and carbonates from the tufa. The chemical result is the same as limestone. As you walk along the water's edge, stick your toes in and experience how slick it is. If you taste Mono Lake water, it is briny and bitter.

The beach is filled with alkali flies *(Ephydra hians)*—swarms of them. But they are not interested in humans. They will flee as people approach. They may seem a bit disgusting, but Native Americans have long considered them a delicacy.

Directions: From Lee Vining, drive south on Highway 395 about 1 mile and turn left on Highway 120 at the Mono Lake South Tufa sign. Drive about 6 miles east and turn left toward Mono's shore at the South Tufa sign. Drive 1 mile to the South Tufa parking lot.

Activities: Sight-seeing, bird-watching.
Facilities: Restrooms, interpretive signs.
Dates: Open year-round.
Fees: None.
Closest town: Lee Vining, 7 miles.

The Lee Vining Canyon Scenic Byway

[Fig. 41(5)] Visitors can travel 12 miles from alpine meadows and tarns to sagebrush and pumice along the Lee Vining Canyon Scenic Byway. If someone is driving through Yosemite National Park on Tioga Road or Highway 120 to the east side of the park, it is not a long detour to see this glacial canyon. The drive is a breathtaking descent from the 9,945 feet at Tioga Pass to the 6,000-foot-elevation Mono Lake in the Great Basin.

The last glacier passed through Lee Vining Canyon about 13,000 years ago. Glacial scientists estimate its depth was 2,500 feet of ice. Lee Vining Creek, Mono Lake's largest tributary, cuts through this canyon, but it is clear from the evidence that the glacier had more to do with the current shape of the canyon than the creek. The canyon is U-shaped, much like Yosemite Valley. If the creek was the only influence, the canyon would be V-shaped.

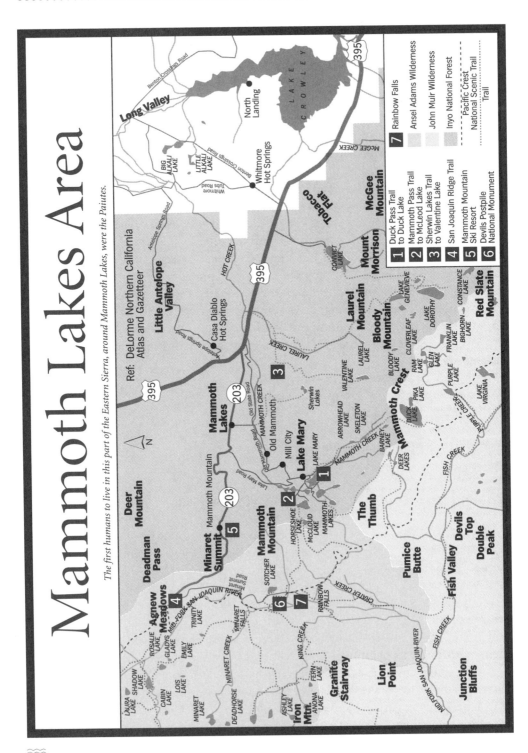

Mammoth Lakes Area

The first humans to live in this part of the Eastern Sierra, around Mammoth Lakes, were the Paiutes.

Ref: DeLorme Northern California Atlas and Gazetteer

7 Rainbow Falls

Ansel Adams Wilderness

John Muir Wilderness

Inyo National Forest

Pacific Crest National Scenic Trail
Trail

1 Duck Pass Trail to Duck Lake

2 Mammoth Pass Trail to McLeod Lake

3 Sherwin Lakes Trail to Valentine Lake

4 San Joaquin Ridge Trail

5 Mammoth Mountain Ski Resort

6 Devils Postpile National Monument

On the drive down the canyon, visitors will get a clear view of Mono Lake and the line of Mono Craters. If the day is clear, people will be able see the White Mountains, a range to the east of the desert floor. The rocks in the White Mountains are thought to date back to the Mesozoic Era, ranging from 135 million to 200 million years old.

About 3 miles before Highway 120 reaches the bottom of the canyon, visitors can turn right on Power House Road and drive about 0.2 mile to Lee Vining Diversion Dam. Water was diverted at one time from the creek into the Los Angeles Aqueduct. The water is no longer exported to Los Angeles because of an agreement to restore Mono Lake.

Higher up the canyon, the glacier carved a cliff and suspended Lee Vining Creek, cutting the canyon into upper and lower halves. The water drops almost 1,700 feet through a penstock into a powerhouse that generates hydroelectricity.

When visitors reach Owens Valley below, they will most likely see low sagebrush (*Artemisia arbuscula*), common rabbitbrush (*Chrysothamnus viscidiflorus*), and antelope bitterbrush (*Purshia tridentata*). All are quite common in this part of eastern California. Less common shrubs include cottonthorn (*Tetradymia axilleris*), hopsage (*Grayia spinosa*), and littleleaf horsebrush (*Tetradymia glabrata*).

The canyon and the small town on the edge of Mono Lake are named after LeRoy Vining and some companions who scouted the area after gold was discovered here in 1852. Vining built a sawmill on the creek in the 1860s. He sold lumber in Nevada. Vining died several years later in Nevada when his own pistol accidentally went off in his pocket, and he bled to death.

Directions: From Crane Flat in Yosemite National Park, drive 46 miles east on Highway 120 or Tioga Road to Tioga Pass. Continue about 12 miles to the junction of Highway 120 and Highway 395.

Activities: Scenic driving and photography.

Facilities: There are none on Highway 120. But visitors can turn north on Highway 395 and drive about 2 miles to Lee Vining where restaurants, motels, and retail shops are available.

Dates: The road is not plowed in winter.

Fees: None.

For more information: Inyo National Forest, Mono Basin Scenic Area Manager, PO Box 429, Lee Vining, CA 93541. Phone (760) 647-3040.

Mammoth Lakes

[Fig. 42] In many ways, Mammoth Lakes epitomizes the Eastern Sierra—in climate, recreation opportunities, geologic features, and vegetation. Visitors can see a place where scientists found a 500 million-year-old rock. They can swim or boat in glacial tarns tucked below the Sierra crest on the Eastern Sierra. They can ski or snowshoe in winter. They can find the full range of Eastern Sierra vegetation on the different elevations.

And visitors can feel the earth move under their feet. Swarms of earthquakes—literally thousands—hit Mammoth Lakes. Federal officials have an alert system that is triggered anytime the Mammoth Lakes area has an earthquake registering 6.0 or higher on the Richter scale.

There is active magma below the Sierra in this region. Mammoth Mountain, though it has not been active in thousands of years, could still erupt some day, according to the U.S. Geological Survey. Located just 3 miles west of the town of Mammoth Lakes, it is venting huge plumes of carbon dioxide. The gas has been so concentrated that it has killed more than 20 acres of conifers near Horseshoe Lake.

Scientists say there is no danger at the moment because the carbon dioxide is cool. Mount St. Helens in the Pacific Northwest belched hot carbon dioxide before it blew 20 years ago. But people get nervous about Mammoth Mountain anyway. The mountain is one of a series of volcanoes on the shoulder of a massive and ancient blast that left a valley 19 miles long and 10 miles wide. The blast that created Long Valley Caldera, as it is now called, occurred 730,000 years ago.

Mammoth Mountain began building on the edge of the caldera about 180,000 years ago as lava filled with feldspar and mica poured out of it. Mammoth is the oldest in the series of volcanoes that stretch about 30 miles north to Mono Craters. The younger volcanoes began building about 40,000 years ago, and many have been active in the last 500 years.

The cold climate above ground plays a big role in the lives of people, wildlife, and plant life around Mammoth Lakes. Snowfall at Mammoth Mountain averages about 30 feet a year. Winter is long and cold around the scenic lakes, including Twin, Horseshoe, McLeod, and TJ lakes as well as Lake Mary, Lake George, and Lake Mamie. The tree communities include hardy conifers such as the lodgepole pine (*Pinus murrayana*), red fir (*Abies magnifica*), whitebark pine (*Pinus albicaulis*), and mountain hemlock (*Tsuga mertensiana*).

Only 15 miles or so to the east, the plant communities are dramatically different. Plants here adapt to the lack of moisture; only 10 inches of rain falls in the desert east of the Sierra. Inyo bush lupine (*Lupinus excubitus*), bee plant (*Cleome lutea*), and hopsage (*Grayia spinosa*) are flowering varieties of the plants visitors can expect to see.

For fishing enthusiasts, there are five kinds of trout in the lakes and streams around Mammoth Lakes. The rainbow trout is planted throughout the area and is widely fished. Other fish include the golden trout (*Oncorhynchus aguabonita*), Lahontan cutthroat trout (*Oncorhynchus clarki henshawi*), Eastern brook trout (*Salvelinus fontinalis*), and brown trout (*Salmo trutta*).

Visitors to the higher elevations will no doubt hear the shrill call of the chickaree (*Tamiasciurus douglasii*). The small squirrel usually remains high in trees, watching for intruders and searching for food. Its biggest enemy is the pine marten (*Martes americana*).

The first humans to live in this part of the Eastern Sierra were the Paiutes. They traded with the nearby Kuzedika, who lived around Mono Lake. The Kuzedika were known as fly eaters, because they collected the fly larvae of the alkali fly around Mono Lake, dried it, and ate it. They also traded it to Paiutes.

These Native American groups generally lived in peace. They survived the extreme temperatures on the Eastern Sierra by fashioning shelters from bent poles and covering them with grass and sagebrush bark. They ground pine nuts from the Jeffrey pine into a kind of meal. The pine nuts gathered in warmer months had to last through the long winters.

Directions: Drive about 28 miles south of Lee Vining on Highway 395 to Route 203. Turn right on Route 203 and drive about 2.8 miles to the town of Mammoth Lakes.

Activities: Hiking, backpacking, camping, skiing, photography, fishing, and scenic driving.

Facilities: Motels, restaurants, and retail shops are available in Mammoth Lakes.

Dates: Open year-round.

Fees: Motel rates change seasonally.

Closest town: Mammoth Lakes.

For more information: Mammoth Lakes Visitors Bureau, PO Box 48, Mammoth Lakes, CA 93546. Phone (760) 934-2712. Mammoth Lakes Ranger District, PO Box 148, Mammoth Lakes, CA 93546. Phone (760) 924-5500.

CONVICT LAKE

[Fig. 42] Some people come here because it's an easy walk for the family. Others like the view of 12,275-foot Mount Morrison. Fishing enthusiasts find a lot of rainbow trout (*Oncorhynchus mykiss*). But if you like looking at the geology around a lake, this is a special place.

Tiny fossils found at the base of Mount Morrison have been determined to be 500 million years old. Fifteen thousand-year-old glacial moraines are apparent at the mouth of Convict Canyon. And the metamorphic rock layers and formations in the hillsides next to the lake are among the oldest in the Sierra, dating back some 350 million to 400 million years.

The white boulders scattered along the hillside near the lake are 135 million-year-old granodiorite that rode out of the backcountry on glaciers. Look for sandstone, marble, phyllite, and chert.

Convict Lake has a fair amount of human history, some of which is not pleasant. The lake's name came from an 1870s incident involving a prison break by 29 inmates at the Nevada State Penitentiary in Carson City. Six of the 29 went south toward Mammoth Lakes and apparently killed a mail rider who looked like one of the prison guards.

A posse tracked the six outlaws to Convict Canyon where a shootout occurred. Robert Morrison, posse leader, died in the gun battle. Mount Morrison is named after him. The six inmates escaped the area but were recaptured near Bishop a few days later.

Another more recent tragedy involved the deaths of seven people at Convict Lake in 1990. Three teenagers began playing on the lake's ice on a February day. The ice broke and the three teens died. Four adults also died trying to save them from the icy water.

Directions: Drive 32.5 miles south of Lee Vining on Highway 395 to Convict Lake Road and turn right. Drive 2.4 miles to the parking lot.

Trail: 2.8 miles round-trip.

Elevation: 30-foot gain, 7,670-foot peak.

Degree of difficulty: Easy.

Surface: Rocky in places, but well established and basically flat.

MAMMOTH PASS TRAIL TO MCLEOD LAKE

[Fig. 42(2)] The lake is in a beautiful setting just beneath the Mammoth Crest. It is about as far west as you can go to find a glacial lake in this area. People catch and release fish, but swimming is not allowed in this lake because federal officials want to preserve its cold, pristine water and ecosystem. Picnics on the sandy beaches are popular here.

Depending on the time of year, visitors may have a lot of company on the short, steep trail to the lake. Try hiking this trail on a weekday.

The rugged mountains around the lake are dotted with red fir *(Abies magnifica)* and whitebark pines *(Pinus albicaulis)* with an occasional mountain hemlock *(Tsuga mertensiana)*. On the trail up to the lake, note the water birch *(Betula occidentalis)*, considered common along streams on the Eastern Sierra but rare on the western slope.

The wildlife at the lake includes the mountain yellow-legged frog *(Rana muscosa)*, which is found between 7,000 feet and 11,500 feet in the Sierra around lakes. The tadpoles of these frogs spend the winter in ice-covered lakes and emerge as frogs the following year.

Directions: Drive about 28 miles south of Lee Vining on Highway 395 to Route 203. Turn right on Route 203 and drive about 3.5 miles to the junction with Lake Mary Road, which continues straight while Route 203 forks to the right. Drive straight on Lake Mary Road for about 5 miles to the end of the road and the parking lot beside Horseshoe Lake.

Trail: 1.4 miles round-trip.

Elevation: About a 300-foot gain, 9,320-foot peak.

Degree of difficulty: Easy.

Surface: Rocky, well established.

SHERWIN LAKES TRAIL TO VALENTINE LAKE

[Fig. 42(3)] The trail to Valentine Lake is almost the length of a 10-kilometer race, but very few people race up this course. You will spend most of your morning walking this trail. And the views at Valentine Lake will not disappoint you after all the effort.

This lake at almost 10,000 feet is filled with outdoor delights. To the east, hikers will see 11,800-foot Laurel Mountain. To the west, the Mammoth Crest juts out at more than 10,000 feet.

In meadows nearby the lake, see wildflowers in August. Look for Sierra primrose (*Primula suffrutescens*), alpine saxifrage (*Saxifraga tolmei*), and shaggy hawkweed (*Hieracium horridum*).

Directions: Drive about 28.5 miles south of Lee Vining on Highway 395 to Sherwin Creek Road and turn right. Drive about 3.5 miles west on Sherwin Creek Road to the sign for Sherwin Lakes trailhead and turn right. Park at the lot about 0.4 mile from the turn.

Trail: 12.2 miles round-trip.

Elevation: About 1,900-foot gain, 9,710-foot peak.

Degree of difficulty: Strenuous.

Surface: Steep with many switchbacks in some areas.

SAN JOAQUIN RIDGE TRAIL

[Fig. 42(4)] The hike starts at 9,265 feet, so visitors should be ready for high-elevation walking. They should also be ready for some of the best views on the Eastern Sierra. That's the reason people come up to walk on this Sierra rooftop. Bring the camera and film as well as plenty of water and a windbreaker for the windy mountaintops.

The trail traces the Sierra divide, meaning the precipitation that falls to your left goes out streams to the Pacific Ocean and the precipitation on the right goes down to the lakes on the Owens Valley floor. The color of the soil in many places is white with pumice fragments launched by volcanic eruptions about 20,000 years ago.

Directions: Drive south about 25 miles from Lee Vining on Highway 395 to the Mammoth Lakes turnoff or State Route 203. Turn right on 203, drive 3.7 miles—which will take you through the town of Mammoth Lakes—to a junction with Minaret Summit Road, which forks to the right toward the Devils Postpile National Monument. Take the right fork and drive 5.5 miles to Minaret Vista access road, just before the Postpile entrance. Drive 0.3 mile to the Minaret Vista parking lot. The trailhead is at the parking lot.

Trail: 4.8 miles round-trip.

Elevation: About 1,000-foot gain, 10,255-foot peak.

Degree of difficulty: Moderate.

Surface: Part of the trail is a rutted, four-wheel-drive road. The rest of the trail is a rocky footpath.

MAMMOTH MOUNTAIN SKI RESORT

[Fig. 42(5)] Mammoth Mountain is considered one of the most exciting downhill runs in California. The longest run is about 3 miles with a vertical drop of 3,100 feet. But skiers of all experience levels can experience Mammoth Mountain.

About 30 percent of the resort's slopes are devoted to novices, and another 40 percent are for intermediate skiers. The remaining 30 percent are for advanced skiers.

Mammoth provides more than 3,500 acres of skiing that include wide-open bowls, steep chutes, and tree-lined runs. There are 150 trails with names like Hangman's Hollow and Sesame Street. Twenty-eight lifts move people between the lodges at the resort, called Main Lodge, Canyon Lodge, and Juniper Springs, and the tops of the ski runs.

Though the season runs from November to June, people have skied on Mammoth on the Fourth of July. This area near the Sierra crest sometimes gets more than 50 feet of snow in a winter. But, in the California drought from 1987 to 1992, the area suffered just like the rest of the state, and skiing could sometimes end before Memorial Day.

Directions: Drive south about 25 miles from Lee Vining on Highway 395 to the Mammoth Lakes turnoff or State Route 203. Turn right on 203, and drive 3.7 miles to Mammoth Lakes. Stay on Route 203 by bearing right at the junction of Route 203 and Lake Mary Road. Drive 4 more miles on Route 203 to Mammoth Mountain Ski Resort.

Activities: Downhill skiing and snowboarding.

Facilities: Rentals, restaurants, cafeterias, ski school, warming hut, and child care.

Dates: Open mid-Nov. to June.

Fees: There is a fee for daily ski lift passes and rentals.

Closest town: Mammoth Lakes, 4 miles.

For more information: Mammoth Lakes Ski Resort, PO Box 24, Mammoth Lakes, CA 93546. Phone (888) 462-6668.

Devils Postpile National Monument

[Fig. 42(6)] The Devils Postpile offers visitors an outdoor classroom in volcanic history of the Sierra Nevada. The Postpile basalt has been studied and analyzed for many years by many people because it is such a spectacular sight. Hundreds of individual, vertical basalt columns came together as a single formation. They look as though someone purposely tried to create a bizarre backdrop for a horror movie.

Around the Postpile, visitors can find waterfalls, dense forest, and many other volcanic formations. The 100,000 people who come to this area each year are usually headed for the Postpile to see one of the famous columns.

The columns have an average diameter of about 24 inches and some are as long as 60 feet. They are the remains of a lava flow that probably occurred about 100,000 years ago. For many years, the Postpile was mistakenly dated at 600,000 years old. More recent methods of dating the rock indicate it is much younger.

Though the Postpile began as a molten mass, it shrank as it cooled, and it began to crack. Temperatures inside the lava bed were consistent enough to allow the cooling basalt to form six-sided columns. The Postpile's regularity of shape is probably its most remarkable feature. Temperatures are rarely consistent enough to form the columns seen at the Postpile.

The Postpile is a remnant of a much larger flow. It was perhaps 400 feet deep, emanating from the glaciated valley of the San Joaquin River's Middle Fork. The basalt lava probably filled the valley for about 3 miles, though no one knows for sure. Later glaciers pulverized most of the lava formations and stream erosion carried away other parts of it. There are indications that the smallest of the ice flows was 1,000 feet thick.

In the 10,000 to 12,000 years that have passed since the last glacier, columns have fallen from the formation, creating a heap of broken rock at the base of the Postpile. On top of the formation, visitors will see how the glaciers polished the rock. The top of the Postpile is probably the most spectacular angle for visitors to see.

This striking feature was hardly mentioned in the literature of the late nineteenth century. Little is known about the Postpile before the turn of the century. Miners were active in the area. Red-bearded "Red" Sotcher settled into nearby Reds Meadow in the late 1870s, but history does not connect him with the Postpile.

The feature was known locally in the 1890s as the Devils Woodpile. It was first recognized as the Devils Postpile in 1901 on various maps. The Postpile was part of Yosemite National Park in the late 1800s when Congress designated its boundaries. It was removed from the park in 1905 when Congress removed 500 square miles from the park under pressure from mining and lumber lobbying interests.

By 1910, a proposal was made to dynamite the Postpile and use it dam the San Joaquin River. Members of the Sierra Club and University of California professor Joseph LeConte, who was also a mountaineer, successfully campaigned against the project. On July 6, 1911, President William Howard Taft proclaimed the area a national monument and extended full protection of the federal government.

The typical Eastern Sierra forest greets hikers as they make their way to the Postpile—red fir (*Abies magnifica*), Jeffrey pine (*Pinus jeffreyi*), and lodgepole pine (*Pinus murrayana*). The slender cinquefoil (*Potentilla gracilis* ssp. *nuttalii*) is particularly noticeable in this area, along with alpine shooting star (*Dodecatheon alpinum*) in August. For bird watchers, look for the dark-eyed junco (*Junco oreganus*) and the white-crowned sparrow (*Zonotrichia leucophrys*) in the summer months.

Management of the monument can be a bit confusing. It is almost completely surrounded by the Inyo National Forest, yet Inyo officials have nothing to do with the management. Inyo officials can answer any of your questions, but Sequoia National Park on the western slope of the Sierra manages the monument.

To approach the Postpile, visitors need to enter from Inyo National Forest to the east. In the short hike, visitors pass from the arid Eastern Sierra to the lusher western slope. Besides the imposing and irregular outcroppings of granite along the way, the geology includes pumice and some basalt.

Directions: Drive south about 25 miles from Lee Vining on Highway 395 to the Mammoth Lakes turnoff or State Route 203. Turn right on 203, drive 3.7 miles—which will take you through the town of Mammoth Lakes—to a junction with

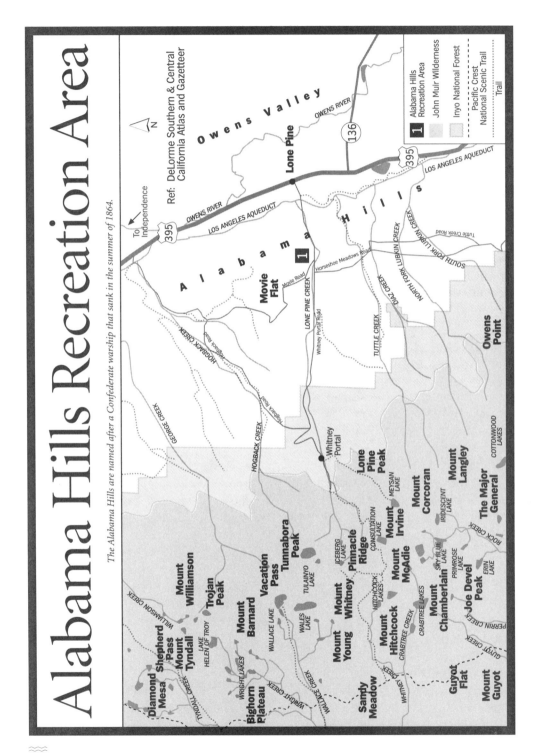

Alabama Hills Recreation Area

The Alabama Hills are named after a Confederate warship that sank in the summer of 1864.

Ref: DeLorme Southern & Central California Atlas and Gazetteer

Minaret Summit Road, which forks to the right toward the Devils Postpile National Monument. Take the right fork and drive about 5.6 miles to the monument entrance. Walk along trail from the parking lot for about 0.4 mile to the Postpile.

Activities: Hiking, bird-watching, and sight-seeing.

Facilities: Picnic areas, restrooms, interpretive signs, and brochures.

Dates: Open from about May to Oct. The road closes at the first snowfall.

Fees: There is an entrance fee.

Closest town: Mammoth Lakes, 9 miles.

For more information: Mammoth Lakes Ranger District, PO Box 148, Mammoth Lakes, CA 93546. Phone (760) 924-5500.

▒ RAINBOW FALLS

[Fig. 42(7)] People stand at Rainbow Falls in summer around the noon hour and just watch the rainbows forming in the constant mist. The San Joaquin River plunges 101 feet down Rainbow Falls in a thundering crescendo all through the summer. There is no shortage of water and, most days, there is no shortage of people. Don't expect to get away from the crowds here.

The hike to the falls from the Devils Postpile takes visitors through the shade of white fir *(Abies concolor)*. Depending on the time of year, the wildflowers can be dazzling in the moist meadows. Look for the broad-seeded rockcress *(Arabis platysperma)* in the rock crannies. The cutleaf daisy *(Erigeron compositus)* and the shaggy hawkweed *(Hieracium horridum)* are also seen in this area.

There's a bonus when you hike into the falls: You'll be going downhill. However, remind the children that they will be gaining about 300 feet in elevation on the way back. Bring the camera and a sandwich, but don't get too close to the falls or the slippery rocks around them.

Directions: From the Devils Postpile National Monument, hike downstream along the San Joaquin River. The signs at the Postpile will direct you to the trail for Rainbow Falls.

Trail: About 4 miles round-trip.

Elevation: About 300-foot gain, 7,660-foot peak.

Degree of difficulty: Easy.

Surface: Rocky in places, easy to follow.

Alabama Hills Recreation Area

[Fig. 43(1)] These hills at the foot of the stunning eastern escarpment provide views, history, and interesting geology for visitors. To the west of this 30,000-acre area, managed by the U.S. Bureau of Land Management, Mount Whitney and a few other wind-whipped 14,000-foot peaks stand high above the Alabamas, creating

Throughout the summer, the San Joaquin River plunges 101 feet down Rainbow Falls, where rainbows form in the constant mist.

striking photographic opportunities for visitors.

The Alabama Hills have been an attraction for prospectors in the nineteenth century, Native Americans, and filmmakers. The first two groups are not too unusual for the Eastern Sierra, but Hollywood filmmakers are not generally interested in this part of California unless they're shooting a western.

Since the early 1920s, the Alabamas have been the backdrop for such western characters as Tom Mix, Hopalong Cassidy, Gene Autry and the Lone Ranger. Film classics such as *Gunga Din*, *Springfield Rifle*, and *How the West Was Won* were filmed at sites now known as "Movie Flats" and Movie Flat Road in the Alabama Hills. Some of Mel Gibson's scenes in the movie *Maverick* also were shot here.

Television advertisements shot in the Alabama Hills have had such sponsors as Reebok, Nissan, Eveready Battery Company, Saab, Mazda, and Jeep-Eagle. Filmmakers like the wide-open look of the Eastern Sierra and dramatic background provided by the Sierra.

But the Alabama Hills also offer a very distinctive appearance. The rounded, weathered Alabamas look as though they were transported from another place, in contrast with sculptured ridges of the Sierra. But the same cataclysmic uplifting in the Sierra batholith 100 million years ago shaped both features.

Over the millennia, wind-blown sand has blasted across the Alabamas and helped create the cracked, weathered granite. Geologists believe the weathering occurred during a time when the Eastern Sierra climate was moister than it is now. The rock was covered with soil, and moisture worked its way into the granite. The moisture and the soil chemically combined to erode the granite, geologists think. As the climate dried out, the wind slowly stripped away the soil from around the granite.

The name, Alabama Hills, comes from a Confederate warship responsible for wreaking havoc on union shipping during the Civil War. Prospectors who were sympathetic to the Confederate cause named their mining claims after the *Alabama* and eventually the name stuck to these hills.

The warship *Alabama* was both brilliant and short lived. Yankee warships cornered the *Alabama* and sank it in a running gun battle. The Northern steam-sail ship,

U.S.S. *Kearsarge* sank the *Alabama* in the Atlantic Ocean during the summer of 1864. Miners who sympathized with the North in the Civil War indulged in "one-up-manship," by naming a whole mining district, a mountain pass, a peak, and a town "Kearsarge." Those names are still part of the Eastern Sierra as well.

In the arid hills, wildflowers bloom earlier in the season—May and June—than in the higher Sierra elevations. For anyone driving along Highway 395 on the long stretch between Los Angeles and Lake Tahoe, a short stop in spring will be rewarding. The more common and attractive wildflowers include prairie smoke *(Geum ciliatum)*, low evening primrose *(Oenothera caespitosa)*, lowly penstemon *(Penstemon humilis)*, and desert paintbrush *(Castilleja chromosa)*.

The pinion pine *(Pinus monophylla)* dominates the woodland areas in this part of the Eastern Sierra. Understory vegetation includes basin wild rye *(Elymus cinereus)* and Idaho fescue *(Festuca idahoensis)*. Also, look for shrubs, such as western chokecherry *(Prunus demissa)* and spiny hopsage *(Grayia spinosa)*.

To survive in this arid climate, shrubs must send down large taproots or large systems of spreading roots to take advantage of any moisture available. Visitors may notice the hairiness on some of the shrubs, such as winter fat *(Ceratoides lanata)*. It is another adaptation to this area. The hairs reflect sunlight and lower the temperature of the plant in desert conditions. The reflected light gives many of these plants the pastel or light colors associated with the area. The hairs also offer protection and insulation from the heat and the wind.

The animals of this area are also interesting. They include the Merriam's shrew *(Sorex merriami)*, Great Basin kangaroo rat *(Dipodomys microps)*, and southern grasshopper mouse *(Onychomys torridus)*.

Visitors might encounter the speckled rattlesnake *(Crotalus mitchelli)*, though the snake avoids human contact at all costs and bites only in self-defense. The heat-sensing pits on this snake's snout help it find warm-blooded prey. It can be found below boulders in this area. Watch your step.

Another interesting creature is the sage grouse *(Centrocercus urophasianus)*, a bird with a distinctive ritual to determine which male will be the "master cock" during mating. The birds will gather in an open area during spring to strut and reveal their plumage, often having mock battles. A hierarchy develops and a single male emerges with a few others serving as guards against the unsuccessful males attempting to mate with the female population.

The Alabama Hills are laced with trails and dirt access roads for people to hike and climb to see the sights. But there are mine shafts and tunnels in the area, and they could be dangerous. False bottoms might give way or tunnels collapse because of deterioration of the timbers that support the tunnels.

Directions: Drive 16 miles south of Independence on Highway 395 to Lone Pine and turn right at Whitney Portal Road. Drive 2.8 miles west on Whitney Portal Road to Movie Road and turn right. Continue about 1 mile to see Movie Flat, a graded dirt

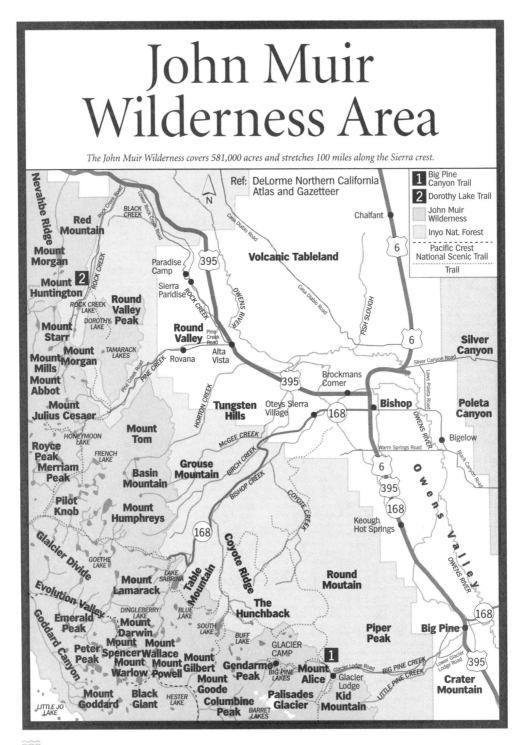

John Muir Wilderness Area

The John Muir Wilderness covers 581,000 acres and stretches 100 miles along the Sierra crest.

Ref: DeLorme Northern California Atlas and Gazetteer

1	Big Pine Canyon Trail
2	Dorothy Lake Trail
	John Muir Wilderness
	Inyo Nat. Forest
---	Pacific Crest National Scenic Trail
....	Trail

Chalfant

Nevahbe Ridge

BLACK CREEK
Rock Creek Road
Lower Rock Creek Road

Red Mountain

Mount Morgan

Paradise Camp

Volcanic Tableland

Casa Diablo Road

Casa Diablo Road

FISH SLOUGH

6

6

Mount Huntington **2**

ROCK CREEK

Sierra Paridise

Round Valley Peak

ROCK CREEK LAKE
DOROTHY LAKE

395

OWENS RIVER

Silver Canyon

Mount Starr

Round Valley

Pine Creek Road

Rovana

TAMARACK LAKES

Alta Vista

Silver Canyon Road

Mount Mills
Mount Morgan

Pine Creek Road

PINE CREEK

Mount Abbot

HORTON CREEK

395

Brockmans Corner

Laws Poleta Road

Poleta Canyon

Mount Julius Cesaer

HONEYMOON LAKE

Mount Tom

Tungsten Hills

Oteys Sierra Village

168

Bishop

OWENS RIVER

Royce Peak

FRENCH LAKE

McGee Creek

Bigelow

Warm Springs Road

Merriam Peak

Basin Mountain

Grouse Mountain

BIRCH CREEK

6

Black Canyon Road

Pilot Knob

Mount Humphreys

BISHOP CREEK

COYOTE CREEK

395

168

Owens Valley

Glacier Divide

GOETHE LAKE

168

Keough Hot Springs

OWENS RIVER

Evolution Valley

Mount Lamarack

LAKE SABRINA

Table Mountain

Coyote Ridge

Round Moutain

DINGLEBERRY LAKE

BLUE LAKE

The Hunchback

168

Goddard Canyon

Emerald Peak

Mount Darwin

SOUTH LAKE

BUFF LAKE

Piper Peak

Big Pine

Peter Peak

Mount Spencer

Mount Wallace

GLACIER CAMP

Lower Glacier Lodge Road

395

Mount Gilbert

Gendarme Peak

1

Mount Alice

Glacier Lodge Road

BIG PINE CREEK

Mount Warlow

Mount Powell

BIG PINE LAKES

LITTLE PINE CREEK

Crater Mountain

LITTLE JO LAKE

Mount Goddard

Black Giant

HESTER LAKE

Mount Goode

Columbine Peak

Palisades Glacier

Glacier Lodge

Kid Mountain

BARRET LAKES

N

road where many films have been shot. For the Tuttle Creek Campground, drive 3.2 miles west of Lone Pine on Whitney Portal Road and turn left at the sign for Horseshoe Meadow and the Tuttle Creek Campground. Drive 1.6 miles and stay to the right for the campground, which is about 1 mile farther.

Activities: Hiking, photography, camping, backpacking, rock climbing, and bird-watching.

Facilities: There are restaurants and motels in Lone Pine. Tuttle Creek Campground has 85 sites, picnic tables, and restrooms. But there is no drinking water. Bring your own water pump and get water from Tuttle Creek.

Dates: Open year-round. Campground is open Apr. through Oct.

Fees: None.

Closest town: Lone Pine, 3 miles.

For more information: Alabama Hills Recreation Area, Bureau of Land Management, 785 N. Main, Suite E, Bishop, CA 93514. Phone (619) 872-4881.

John Muir Wilderness

[Fig. 42, Fig. 43, Fig. 44] The John Muir Wilderness offers visitors a lot of room for hiking, backpacking, fishing, camping, horseback riding, and bird-watching. At 581,000 acres, it is about two-thirds the size of Yosemite National Park. And the Muir wilderness has no traffic-filled hub like Yosemite Valley, although there are parts of this Eastern Sierra area that are filled with people.

The wilderness stretches almost 100 miles along the Sierra crest in Central California, ranging from the upper foothills at 5,000 feet to the alpine areas above 14,000 feet. The majority of the wilderness is on the Eastern Sierra where the Inyo National Forest manages it. But there are substantial sections of the wilderness on the western slope, which the Sierra National Forest manages.

The John Muir Wilderness contains many streams, lakes, and glacially carved canyons. Dozens of glacial tarns include Duck Lake, Lake Virginia, Big Bear Lake, Desolation Lake, Merriam Lake, and Consultation Lake. Most high-elevation lakes are filled with snowmelt and teeming with rainbow trout (*Oncorhynchus mykiss*) and Eastern brook trout (*Salvelinus fontinalis*). The southernmost glacier in the United States is located in the Muir wilderness, and a major part of Mount Whitney is in the wilderness. At 14,497 feet, it is the tallest mountain in the contiguous United States.

Also within the wilderness is the Bighorn Sheep Zoological Area where the California bighorn (*Ovis canadensis*) is protected. This 200-pound mammal is nearing extinction. The sheep have died in great numbers after having brief contact with domestic sheep. The domestic sheep pass a common virus that is fatal to bighorn. But the bigger danger, by far, is the mountain lion (*Felis concolor*), a tenacious predator that has been specially protected in California since the early 1990s.

As the mountain lion populations have grown in the 1990s, the bighorn have been forced to feed at higher elevations, even in colder weather, to avoid contact with the big cat. The result has been a higher mortality rate for young sheep and many deaths by avalanche.

These mountain sheep have dwindled to a total of about 100 animals, one-third the number that existed about eight years ago. They have received emergency protection under the U.S. Endangered Species Act. Federal officials hope they can fend off the mountain lion long enough to bring back the populations in the Muir wilderness, which has most of the remaining bighorn in the Sierra.

The wilderness was named after John Muir, America's most famous and influential naturalist and conservationist. Muir was known for solo journeys into the Sierra Nevada, among Alaska's glaciers, and across the world. Muir, the first president of the Sierra Club, traveled these parts as well.

He might recognize the geologic features, the flora, and the fauna these days, but things have changed a lot since Muir hiked these mountains. Some trails have become so crowded that quota systems have been established to protect the wilderness and the solitude of hikers and backpackers. Overnight trips require an entry permit in this wilderness, but day trips do not require a permit.

Those who venture very far into the Muir wilderness will see the highest part of the Sierra. This is where uplift of the Sierra batholith has been the most dramatic over the past 5 million years. Whitney is not the only 14,000-foot peak. Mount Russell, north of Whitney, is 14,086 feet; Mount Muir to the south is 14,015 feet.

Geologists say these mountains continue to rise. The jagged peaks form a saw-tooth against the horizon because of vertical joints that developed in the batholith many millions of years ago. Though the granite in the Muir wilderness looks pretty worn and old in some places, it is among the youngest rock in this part of the range—forming perhaps 80 million years ago, as opposed to some that formed more than 150 million years ago.

The glacial erosion is not difficult to see in many places in the wilderness area. For instance, at 14,200-foot North Palisade, there is an obvious knife-edged ridge or *arete*, as geologists call it. It is a sharp rock ridge with cirques on either side of it. The cirques look like deep canals flowing on either side of the ridge, a high spot in the granite that resisted the glacial flow.

To see these features, visitors have to hike or ride stock animals into the wilderness. No motorized or mechanized transportation, including bicycles, is allowed in the wilderness. Wheelchairs are permitted. The wilderness can be entered from the west through Sequoia-Kings Canyon National Parks and from several major trails on the eastern side.

Directions: Drive about 28 miles south of Lee Vining on Highway 395 to Route 203 and turn right. Drive about 3.5 miles to the junction with Lake Mary Road, which continues straight while Route 203 forks to the right. Drive straight on Lake

Mary Road for about 4 miles and turn left onto Road 4S09 for the Lake Mary campground and drive 3.6 miles. Turn left toward Coldwater Campground and drive 0.8 mile to the Emerald Lake parking lot. The Emerald Lake Trail will lead into the wilderness from the parking lot. Wilderness entry points can be found south of Mammoth Lakes by driving south on Highway 395. At Big Pine, Independence, and Lone Pine, there are access roads that take visitors to campgrounds, packing stations, and trailheads just outside the wilderness.

Long Valley Caldera

In the Owens Valley, against the steep escarpment of the Sierra, the Long Valley Caldera is a huge depression caused by a massive volcanic blast more than 700,000 years ago. The blast sent out 140 to 150 cubic miles of lava, buried everything for more than 300 square miles, and left the 19-mile-long and 10-mile-wide depression that is still visible today.

Why was this blast so big? Chemistry played a big part, scientists say. The rhyolite found in the Bishop Tuff is almost three-fourths silica, which is dense and does not flow easily. This thick magma has the capacity to capture more gases. The gases build in the magma. In the case of Long Valley Caldera, their release was an epic explosion.

Activities: Hiking, backpacking, fishing, camping, horseback riding, bird-watching and photography.

Facilities: None in the wilderness. Campgrounds and pack stations can be found just outside the wilderness off of access roads from Highway 395. The towns of Mammoth Lakes, Big Pine, Independence, and Lone Pine have retail outlets, restaurants, and motels.

Dates: Open year-round. The best hiking and camping time is May through Oct.

Fees: There are fees at many campgrounds. Overnight trips require a free permit that can be picked up at the ranger station in Mammoth Lakes.

Closest town: Mammoth Lakes, 4 miles on the north. Big Pine, Independence, and Lone Pine are also about the same distance from the wilderness.

For more information: Mammoth Ranger District, PO Box 148, Mammoth Lakes, CA 93546. Phone (760) 924-5500. White Mountain Ranger District, 798 North Main Street, Bishop, CA 93514. Phone (760) 873-2500. Mount Whitney Ranger District, PO Box 8, Lone Pine, CA 93545. Phone (760) 876-6200.

DUCK PASS TRAIL TO DUCK LAKE

[Fig. 42(1)] This is a hike for people determined to see the John Muir Wilderness. As with many hikes into the Muir wilderness, it is not easy, but it is worth the view of Duck Lake and Pika Lake from Duck Pass at 10, 800 feet. Don't bring the children on this hike, but make sure you have the camera and give yourself some time. There is a lot to see along the way.

The high Sierra on this trail is striking. The lodgepole pine *(Pinus murrayana)* and the mountain hemlock *(Tsuga mertensiana)* are a graceful backdrop, particularly in the spring when snow lingers. Notice that the tips of saplings may not be completely straight after a long winter and a lot of snow. Watch for small groupings of silver pine *(Pinus monticola)*, a beautiful pine tree that is not abundant but can survive above 9,000 feet in this part of the Sierra.

Up on the wind-blown pass above 10,000 feet, wildflowers cling to life in the rock crannies. Look for mountain sorrel *(Oxyria digyna)* and rock fringe *(Epilobium obcordatum)*. Down by the lake, where people relax in the afternoon, the alpine buttercup *(Ranunculus eschscholtzii)* blooms a bright yellow flower in wet meadows nearby. They are most noticeable just days after the snowmelt.

Directions: See directions for Emerald Lake Trail from John Muir Wilderness.

Trail: 8.6 miles round-trip.

Elevation: 1,900-foot gain, 10,800-foot peak.

Degree of difficulty: Strenuous.

Surface: Steep, rocky, well defined, many switchbacks.

BIG PINE CANYON TRAIL-PALISADES GLACIER

[Fig. 44(1)] For those who want to see Big Pine Canyon, Big Pine Lakes, and part of the Palisades Glacier from a distance, this walk is for you. It can be done in one day, though it is a tough hike. The hike rewards visitors with wonderful views of the high Sierra.

Many of the glacial features studied so extensively in Yosemite National Park are present here. The "chatter" or scars and gouges left in the granite are visible in the canyon along the creek. About 6 miles into the hike among the Big Pine Lakes, visitors will see a

MOUNTAIN
HEMLOCK
(Tsuga mertensiana)

small portion of the Palisade Glacier. The glacier's bergschrund, a geologist's term for a crack in the head wall of the glacier, is not visible from the trail, but the newly formed moraine—long hills of sand and gravel at the end of a glacier—can be partially seen.

There are other, smaller glaciers higher in the surrounding Sierra. Most are between 11,000 and 13,000 feet in places such as Mount Goddard, Mount Humphreys, and Glacier Divide. Nestled in cirques and north-facing mountainsides, they are puny compared to their Ice Age ancestors. They are not even mentioned in the same breath with today's large glaciers in Antarctica or on Mount Everest where they can have a head wall more than a mile high.

But the tarns left in the Eastern Sierra are impressive. Big Pine Lakes area consists of five lakes, plus Summit Lake and Black Lake. These bodies of water are featured in this hike. The lakes are various shades of blue and turquoise, depending on the season and the time of day. In warm weather, look for the mountain bluebird *(Sialia currucoides)* and the Clark's nutcracker *(Nucrifraga columbiana)*. But when the weather starts turning in early September, these birds leave for lower elevations.

Directions: Drive about 14 miles south of Bishop on Highway 395 to Big Pine and turn right on Glacier Lodge Road at the sign for Big Pine Creek. Drive west on Glacier Lodge Road for 10.5 miles to a parking area at the end of the road. The trailhead is marked Big Pine Trail.

Trail: 13-mile loop.

Elevation: 3,000-foot gain, 10,800-foot peak.

Degree of difficulty: Strenuous.

Surface: Steep, rocky, narrow with many switchbacks.

DOROTHY LAKE TRAIL

[Fig. 44(2)] People walk to Dorothy Lake to get away from crowds for some fishing or picnicking, or both. It will not take up much of the morning to hike in and find a nice spot to fish for rainbow trout or Eastern brook trout.

In the moist meadows along this hike, look for Suksdorf's monkeyflower *(Mimulus suksdorfi)* and glaucous larkspur *(Delphinium glaucum)*. Also notice the meadow penstemon *(Penstemon rydbergii)*.

Directions: Drive about 15 miles south of the South Mammoth Lakes Junction on Highway 395 to Rock Creek Road and turn right. Drive southwest for about 8.9 miles, then bear left toward Rock Creek Lake and drive another 0.5 mile to the parking lot where the trailhead begins.

Trail: 6 miles round-trip.

Elevation: About an 800-foot gain, 10,560-foot peak.

Degree of difficulty: Easy.

Surface: Short climbs, some marshy areas.

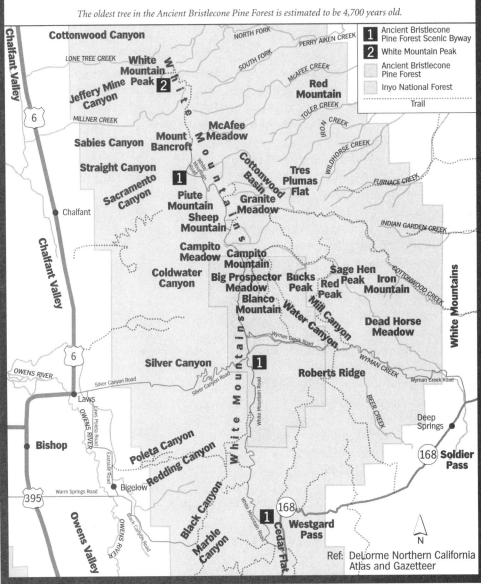

Ancient Bristlecone Pine Forest

The oldest tree in the Ancient Bristlecone Pine Forest is estimated to be 4,700 years old.

Legend:
- **1** Ancient Bristlecone Pine Forest Scenic Byway
- **2** White Mountain Peak
- Ancient Bristlecone Pine Forest
- Inyo National Forest
- Trail

Cottonwood Canyon

NORTH FORK

PERRY AIKEN CREEK

LONE TREE CREEK

SOUTH FORK

McAFEE CREEK

Chalfant Valley

White Mountain Peak **2**

Jeffery Mine Canyon

Red Mountain

MILLNER CREEK

TOLER CREEK

IRON CREEK

McAfee Meadow

Sabies Canyon

Mount Bancroft

WILDHORSE CREEK

Straight Canyon

Cottonwood Basin

Tres Plumas Flat

FURNACE CREEK

Sacramento Canyon

1

Piute Mountain

Granite Meadow

White Mountain Road

Chalfant

Sheep Mountain

INDIAN GARDEN CREEK

Campito Meadow

Campito Mountain

Coldwater Canyon

Big Prospector Meadow

Bucks Peak

Sage Hen Peak

Iron Mountain

COTTONWOOD CREEK

Red Peak

White Mountains

Blanco Mountain

Chalfant Valley

Water Canyon

Mill Canyon

Dead Horse Meadow

Wyman Creek Road

6

OWENS RIVER

Silver Canyon

1

Roberts Ridge

WYMAN CREEK

Wyman Creek Road

Silver Canyon Road

Silver Canyon Road

White Mountain Road

BEER CREEK

Deep Springs

Laws

Laws Poleta Road

OWENS RIVER

Eastside Road

168 Soldier Pass

Bishop

Poleta Canyon

Redding Canyon

White Mountains

395

Warm Springs Road

Bigelow

Black Canyon Road

OWENS RIVER

Black Canyon

White Mountain Road

1

168

Westgard Pass

Marble Canyon

Cedar Flat

Owens Valley

N

Ref: DeLorme Northern California Atlas and Gazetteer

Ancient Bristlecone Pine Forest And Scenic Byway

[Fig. 45(1)] The White Mountains east of the Owens Valley are not in the Sierra Nevada, nor are they particularly easy to reach on Highway 168 and the White Mountain Road, a scenic byway that becomes a dirt road at one point. But there's a real good reason to take a full day out of the Sierra and journey across the desert to this arid, desolate-looking range: the bristlecone pine *(Pinus longaeva)*, the oldest organism known.

Visitors should be aware that in this distant and forbidding mountain range, there are no gas stations or restaurants. You can find restrooms, picnic areas, a visitor's center, and trailhead camping at 14,246-foot White Mountain Peak, but there are no services here. Bring water and food for the trip to see these old trees.

The oldest tree, named after Methuselah, an Old Testament symbol of longevity in the Bible, is estimated to be 4,700 years old. If the estimates are true, this tree was alive 2,700 years before Christ was born.

Bristlecones grow in Utah and Nevada, and a related species, *Pinus aristata*, grows in Arizona. But there are more of these squat, twisted conifers growing in the White Mountains—the 58,000-acre Ancient Bristlecone Pine Forest—than anywhere else.

Science has been studying the trees since the 1950s when researcher Edmund Schulman first discovered the trees' age. The University of California White Mountains Research Station, north of the Schulman Grove, has pieced together a climate record dating back almost 9,000 years by examining and counting the tree rings on dead bristlecone pines.

The bristlecone's dead wood can linger in the ecosystem for thousands of years because of the dense cell structure. Parts of a bristlecone pine can continue living even after most of the tree has died.

Research also indicates bristlecones have evolved for the harsh conditions of the White Mountains, preferring the soils where there is less competition for the nutrients. The dry alkaline soils in the White Mountains accommodate those needs well. The soils do not support a lot of vegetation. The bristlecones send out a wide, shallow root system to gather all the nutrients available for their slow growth—about 1 inch in diameter per century on exposed, steep hills. Sheltered

BRISTLECONE PINE
(Pinus aristata)
Bristlecone pines, with cones covered in scales with sharp prickles, live for thousands of years on dry, rocky slopes and ridges.

bristlecones in comparatively good soil do not live half as long as those that get far less moisture or nutrients.

The trees contort in the high winds, which have blown sand and ice around these trees for centuries. They grow no higher than 25 or 30 feet. Their wood becomes almost golden with age. Photographers love what they see—the stark mountains and these golden, ancient trees.

The bristlecone is not the only tree in the forest. The closest tree species, limber pine *(Pinus flexilis)* resembles the bristlecone, but it does not have bristles on its cones. The limber pine's needles are slightly longer than the bristlecone's 2-inch needles. And, generally, neither species is grouped very closely with the other.

The drive to the forest is interesting but slow. The winding road goes about 25 miles from Owens Valley. It passes from the high desert scrub to pinion-juniper woodland to higher or montane vegetation before reaching the bristlecone pine forest above 9,500 feet. Do not expect to drive up White Mountain Road in the winter. Snowfall closes the road periodically from November to May.

The slower driving speeds will allow visitors to see some of the same wildlife that can be found in the different life zones or elevations of the Eastern Sierra. As the road moves up the slope, look for one-awned spineflower *(Chorizanthe uniaristata)* in sandy or gravelly areas. Higher up, visitors will see mountain sorrel *(Oxyria digyna)* and mountain clover *(Trifolium wormskioldii)*, especially in July and August.

For bird watchers, the sights become interesting as the road approaches ridgelines where golden eagles *(Aquila chrysaetos)* and white-throated swifts *(Aeronautes saxatillis)* seem to float high above their prey. Also look for mountain bluebirds *(Sialia currucoides)* and mountain chickadee *(Parus gambeli)*.

The first recommended stop on the drive is Sierra View Overlook at 9,000 feet. The display at the overlook helps people identify the 100 miles of the Sierra visible from this location. Mount Whitney can be seen from this spot.

Ten miles down the road, there is a visitor's center at the Schulman Grove where people can get information or have a picnic. The grove has two self-guided trails—the Discovery Trail and the Methuselah Trail. On the 1-mile Discovery Trail, people will pass the Pine Alpha tree, the first tree Schulman determined to be more than 4,000 years old. On the 4.5-mile Methuselah Trail, visitors will walk by the oldest tree, Methuselah. Only the scientists know exactly where the trees are in the grove. For their protection, they are not marked.

The Patriarch Grove is 11 miles down the road, which becomes a dirt road. It is closer to the ridgeline, so sparse sagebrush vegetation below the trees gives way to sparse alpine species. The Patriarch Tree at 11,000 feet is considered the largest of the bristlecone pines. It measures more than 35 feet in circumference.

Directions: From Big Pine, drive east on Highway 168 for 13 miles to White Mountain Road and turn left. Drive about 8 miles to Sierra View Overlook. From the overlook, continue on White Mountain Road another 10 miles to Schulman Grove and a visitor's center. To reach Patriarch Grove, continue another 11 miles on White Mountain Road, which becomes a dirt road at Schulman Grove.

Activities: Hiking, photography, bird-watching, and scenic driving.

Facilities: Restrooms and picnic areas at Schulman Grove. There are no overnight accommodations at Sierra View Outlook, Schulman Grove, or Patriarch Grove. There is a campground at Cedar Flat off of Highway 168 just before the turn for White Mountain Road or at the trailhead for White Mountain Peak, which is 4.6 miles beyond Patriarch Grove.

Dates: Open from May through Nov.

Fees: None.

Closest town: Big Pine, 18 miles from Sierra View Overlook.

For more information: White Mountain Ranger Station, 798 North Main Street, Bishop, CA 93514. Phone (760) 873-2500.

WHITE MOUNTAIN PEAK

[Fig. 45(2)] The physical challenge and the views bring people to this long, steep day hike. At 14,246 feet, White Mountain Peak offers a grand view of the Owens Valley and the Sierra Nevada. The climb is a shorter walk with less gain in elevation than the hike up Mount Whitney, which can be seen from White Mountain Peak. But it is only the third tallest mountain in California; Whitney at 14,497 is the tallest.

For people who wish to get there the night before and sleep above 11,000 feet, camping is allowed near the trailhead as long as a permit is secured for use of a camping stove. No fires are allowed. Bring a lot of water because you won't find much water here. Also, take it slowly. The elevation takes some adjustment if you have come from anyplace close to sea level.

Directions: Take the route to the Patriarch Grove as explained in the previous site. Continue another 4.6 miles on the dirt road past the Patriarch Grove to the trailhead.

Trail: 15 miles round-trip.

Elevation: 2,600-foot gain, 14,246-foot peak.

Degree of difficulty: Strenuous.

Surface: Steep with a lot of switchbacks and rocky outcroppings.

Golden Trout Wilderness

[Fig. 46] The 303,287-acre Golden Trout Wilderness, on the southeastern flank of the Sierra Nevada, attracts backpackers, hikers, fishing enthusiasts, and horseback riders. Almost two-thirds of the wilderness is in the Inyo, and the rest is in Sequoia National Forest on the western slope. The Golden Trout is considered an ideal choice for novice backpackers and stock users because its gentle hills and lower elevations are easily accessible in spring when

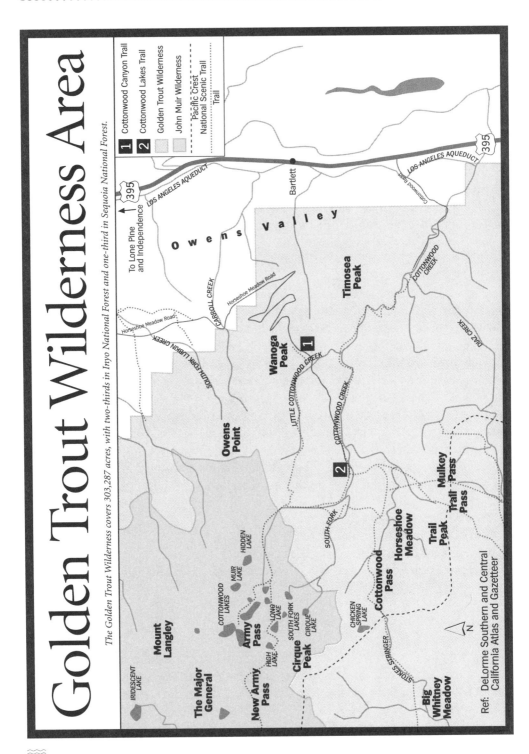

Golden Trout Wilderness Area

The Golden Trout Wilderness covers 303,287 acres, with two-thirds in Inyo National Forest and one-third in Sequoia National Forest.

Legend:

1	Cottonwood Canyon Trail
2	Cottonwood Lakes Trail
	Golden Trout Wilderness
	John Muir Wilderness
- - -	Pacific Crest National Scenic Trail
······	Trail

To Lone Pine and Independence

395 · LOS ANGELES AQUEDUCT · Bartlett · 395 · LOS ANGELES AQUEDUCT

Owens Valley

CARROLL CREEK · Horseshoe Meadow Road · COTTONWOOD CREEK · DIAZ CREEK

Timosea Peak

SOUTH FORK LUBKIN CREEK

Wanoga Peak

LITTLE COTTONWOOD CREEK

Owens Point

COTTONWOOD CREEK

Mulkey Pass · Trail Pass

Horseshoe Meadow

Trail Peak

SOUTH FORK

Mount Langley

IRIDESCENT LAKE

The Major General

COTTONWOOD LAKES · MUIR LAKE · HIDDEN LAKE

Army Pass

New Army Pass

HIGH LAKE · LONG LAKE · SOUTH FORK LAKES · CIRQUE LAKE

Cirque Peak

Cottonwood Pass

CHICKEN SPRING LAKE

STOKES STRINGER

Big Whitney Meadow

N

Ref: DeLorme Southern and Central California Atlas and Gazetteer the high country is still under snow. There are many trails on the eastern portion of the wilderness, which is on the Kern Plateau, a broad, high plateau above the Kern River Canyon. The plateau covers about 600,000 acres in the Southern and Eastern Sierra.

The golden trout *(Salmo aguabonita)*, California's state fish, is native to the streams in this area, existing for perhaps thousands of years in the drainages of the upper Kern River. It developed as a distinct species from the rainbow trout, and it has been transplanted into many streams throughout the Central Sierra. Two subspecies of golden trout are also found in the wilderness. They are called Volcano Creek golden trout *(Oncorhynchus aguabonita)* and Little Kern River golden trout *(Salmo aguabonita whitei)*, considered a threatened species. The golden trout fisheries have been threatened by the introduction of the brown trout *(Salmo trutta)*, a European native fish. The brown trout prey on golden trout. Another problem for the golden trout is interbreeding with the rainbow trout. Of the 117 miles of streams in the Little Kern River drainage, fewer than 10 miles now contains pure populations of golden trout. A golden trout restoration program has been ongoing for many years.

The Kern River Canyon, where the golden trout occurs, is considered an anomaly of sorts in the Sierra Nevada. All the major canyons of the Sierra are roughly parallel to each other and cut at right angles to the crest of the mountain range. The Kern, however, runs due south, winding up at a terminal lake in the southern San Joaquin Valley. It is different simply because faults in the Sierra developed in a north-south direction in this part of the range.

The elevations in the Golden Trout Wilderness run from about 5,000 feet at the Forks of the Kern River to 12,900-foot Cirque Peak at the edge of the John Muir Wilderness. The Golden Trout's lower elevations, below 6,500 feet, are dominated by the ponderosa pine *(Pinus ponderosa)* and Jeffrey pine *(Pinus jeffreyi)*. Between 6,000 feet and 10,000 feet, there are three distinct forest communities. They include the white fir *(Abies concolor)* forest and sugar pine *(Pinus lambertiana)* forest, the red fir *(Abies magnifica)* forest, and the Sierra juniper *(Juniperus occidentalis)* forest. The foxtail pine *(Pinus balfouriana)* is a hardy tree found high in the Kern Plateau. Another high Sierra conifer found here is the limber pine *(Pinus flexilis)*, which grows in isolated places and is rarely seen by hikers. To see this pine, you'll have to get off trails and perhaps scramble over boulders to find the dry, rocky, secluded places where it grows. Unless you have a compass, a map, and good path-finding skills, it is not a good idea to leave any trail in the Sierra.

The wildlife of the Golden Trout Wilderness include the marten *(Martes americana)*, beaver *(Castor canadensis)*, mountain lion *(Felis concolor)*, mountain coyote *(Canis latrans)*, black bear *(Ursus americanus)*, wildcat *(Lynx rufus)*, and mule deer *(Odocoileus hemionus)*. About 6,000 acres of the Tule River deer herd range are within the wilderness. The Kern River deer herd and the Monache deer herd also are found here.

The peregrine falcon *(Falco peregrinus anatum)*, the bald eagle *(Haliaetus leucocephalus)*, and the California bighorn sheep *(Ovis canadensis californiana)* are endangered species found in the wilderness. The wolverine *(Gulo luscus)*, the Kern Canyon slender salamander *(Batrachoseps simatus)*, and the fisher *(Martes pennanti)* are considered rare species here. Cattle and sheep grazing took place in this area more than a century ago. Sheep were excluded from the Kern Plateau in 1893 because the meadows were becoming too degraded. Cattle grazing continued in major meadows, which were converted into "cow camps" where the ranchers set up their summertime headquarters. Although the cow camps have decreased in number since the 1950s, they continue today. The ranchers and the timber industry established many of the current trails.

Though mining is not a big activity in the Golden Trout, geologists know the area has tungsten, molybdenum, titanium, lead, and gold. Tungsten is mined at the Pine Tree Mine, the only active mine in the area. But thousands of years before grazing or mining, the Golden Trout Wilderness and the rest of the Kern Plateau served as a summer destination for Native Americans who hunted and gathered food here. The tribes are still around this area today. They are the Paiute and the Shoshone on the eastern side of the plateau.

Travel in the Golden Trout Wilderness requires a wilderness permit for overnight camping. Hikers and equestrians both use the area. Campfires are allowed with a proper campfire permit where no resource damage will be done. Permits can be obtained from the ranger station at Lone Pine. Use of backpacker stoves instead of campfires is encouraged.

Directions: From Lone Pine, drive west on Whitney Portal Road about 4 miles to Horseshoe Meadows Road and turn left. Drive about 22 miles southwest on Horseshoe Meadows Road to parking areas. At several points before reaching the parking area, there are other places to park for trailheads into the wilderness. They include Little Cottonwood Creek and Cottonwood Canyon Trail.

Activities: Hiking, backpacking, picnicking, fishing, horseback riding, and photography.

Facilities: None in the wilderness. On the edge of the wilderness at several trailheads, there are campgrounds, picnic areas, potable water, and restrooms.

Dates: Open year-round. The hiking season is roughly May through Oct. Campgrounds are also closed Nov. to May 1.

Fees: There are campground fees.

Closest town: Lone Pine, 22 miles. Permits are required for overnight camping and campfires. The permits can be obtained at the ranger station in Lone Pine.

For more information: Mount Whitney Ranger Station, PO Box 8, Lone Pine, CA 93545. Phone (760) 876-6200.

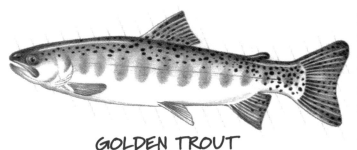

GOLDEN TROUT
(Oncorhynchus aguabonita)
This trout has been introduced to more than 300 mountain lakes and streams in the Sierra Nevada.

COTTONWOOD CANYON TRAIL

[Fig. 46(1)] The trip down Cottonwood Creek Canyon is laced with history, an Eastern Sierra stream ecosystem, and views in the Golden Trout Wilderness. Start the trip early because it is all downhill on the way, but hikers have to turn around and go back uphill for the return trip.

The human history here includes the Stevens Sawmill, which supplied timber to the mining town of Cerro Gordo in the Inyo Mountains. The mill was abandoned in the late 1800s, and fire destroyed it. An old log cabin, once used by loggers, remains farther along the trail. A little more than 1 mile into this hike, you must cross Cottonwood Creek at about 7,800 feet. Most of the time, it is not a big concern, but it is dangerous in times of heavy snowmelt. In late May and June, it is wise to avoid this crossing and this trail. Like most Sierra streams, the flow can be deceiving—low in the morning and quite high in the afternoon as the snowmelt picks up. The vegetation in the area is typical at this elevation. Red fir *(Abies magnifica)* and lodgepole pine *(Pinus murrayana)* dominate. Also look for the blue elderberry *(Sambucus caerulea)* and red elderberry *(Sambucus racemosa)*, especially in the moist, open areas along the trail.

Directions: From Lone Pine, drive west on Whitney Portal Road about 4 miles to Horseshoe Meadows Road and turn left. Drive about 21 miles to trailhead parking on the right side of the road marked for Little Cottonwood Creek. Trail begins across the street on the south side of the road.

Trail: 11.4 miles round-trip.

Elevation: 3,400-foot gain, 9,300-foot peak.

Degree of difficulty: Strenuous.

Surface: Partly on a dirt road. Mostly on a rocky, sometimes steep footpath.

COTTONWOOD LAKES TRAIL

[Fig. 46(2)] The views and the fishing are the attractions on this trail. Most of it is in the Golden Trout Wilderness, but the Cottonwood Lakes are actually in the John Muir Wilderness. Nevertheless, if golden trout fishing is your passion, this is a prime fishing area for you. From this trail, hikers get the full view of pinion pine *(Pinus monophylla)* and Sierra juniper *(Juniperus occidentalis)* in the surrounding meadows. In fall, the leaves of the quaking aspen *(Populus tremuloides)* turn golden yellow and quiver in any breeze. Beavers *(Castor canadensis)* rely on the bark of the quaking aspen for food.

Closer to the streams, hikers will see the water birch *(Betula occidentalis)*, a tree that is found only sporadically through the Sierra. Understory vegetation in many areas includes Idaho fescue *(Festuca idahoensis)* and basin wild rye *(Elymus cinereus)*. At the end of the trail, hikers come to the striking Cottonwood Lakes. Among these glacial lakes are Long Lake, High Lake, Muir Lake, and Hidden Lake.

Directions: From Lone Pine, drive west on Whitney Portal Road about 4 miles to Horseshoe Meadows Road and turn left. Drive about 24 miles to the sign for Cottonwood Lakes Recreation Area about 0.2 mile before reaching the end of the paved road and turn

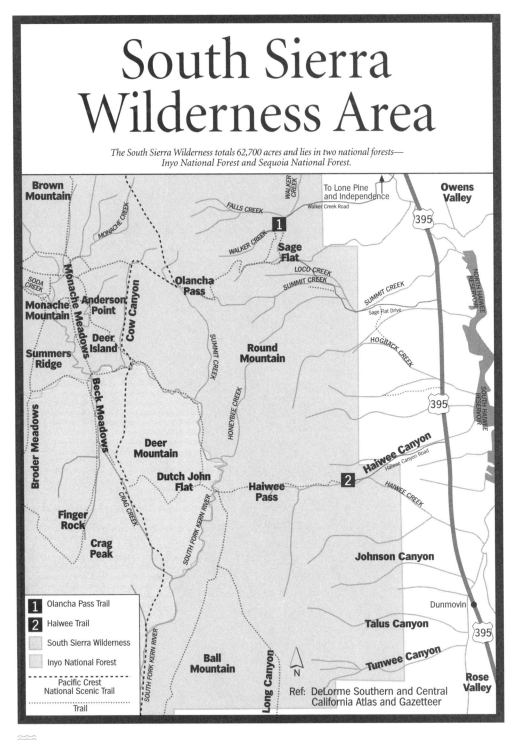

South Sierra Wilderness Area

*The South Sierra Wilderness totals 62,700 acres and lies in two national forests—
Inyo National Forest and Sequoia National Forest.*

Brown
Mountain

WALKER CREEK

FALLS CREEK

To Lone Pine
and Independence

Walker Creek Road

Owens
Valley

395

MONACHE CREEK

WALKER CREEK

Sage
Flat

LOCO CREEK

SUMMIT CREEK

SUMMIT CREEK

Olancha
Pass

SODA CREEK

Monache
Mountain

Anderson
Point

Cow Canyon

Deer
Island

Sage Flat Drive

NORTH HAIWEE RESERVOIR

Summers
Ridge

Beck Meadows

SUMMIT CREEK

Round
Mountain

HOGBACK CREEK

395

SOUTH HAIWEE RESERVOIR

Broder Meadows

Deer
Mountain

HONEYBEE CREEK

Haiwee Canyon

Haiwee Canyon Road

Dutch John
Flat

CRAG CREEK

SOUTH FORK KERN RIVER

Haiwee
Pass

2

HAIWEE CREEK

Finger
Rock

Crag
Peak

Johnson Canyon

1   Olancha Pass Trail

2   Haiwee Trail

Dunmovin

South Sierra Wilderness

Talus Canyon

395

Inyo National Forest

Pacific Crest
National Scenic Trail

SOUTH FORK KERN RIVER

Ball
Mountain

Long Canyon

N

Tunwee Canyon

Rose
Valley

Trail

Ref: DeLorme Southern and Central
California Atlas and Gazetteer

right. Continue on the access road for 0.4 mile and park at the trailhead parking lot.

Trail: 9.8 miles round-trip.

Elevation: 1,200-foot gain, 10,900-foot peak.

Degree of difficulty: Moderate.

Surface: Some switchbacks, narrow, but well established.

South Sierra Wilderness

[Fig. 47] The South Sierra Wilderness is 62,700 acres straddling the southern crest of the Sierra. Much of its acreage is in the Inyo National Forest on the rugged Eastern Sierra. The west slope acreage in this wilderness—amounting to about 24,000 acres— is in the comparatively gentle terrain of the Sequoia National Forest.

It is a vast, arid expanse of the Sierra, compared to the Central and Northern areas of this mountain range. Elevations range from 6,100 feet near Kennedy Meadows at the southern tip of the wilderness to 12,123 feet at Olancha Peak on the eastern flank. The South Fork of the Kern River, federally protected as a Wild and Scenic River, runs through the heart of the wilderness. Like the Golden Trout Wilderness just to the north, the South Sierra has open meadows that were once grazed extensively in the late 1800s. And like the Golden Trout, the historic grazing patterns continue today with fewer animals under federal permit programs.

But compared to many other areas around the Sierra, including the Golden Trout, this wilderness gets a lot less attention from hikers and backpackers. There are no visitor permits required to enter the wilderness, and the federal government has imposed no quotas on hikers and backpackers. If solitude is what you seek, the South Sierra may be a good destination for you. Bring water, food, warm clothing, and a tent if you intend to stay overnight. There are no facilities in this wilderness.

Don't get the idea that this place is untouched by humans, though. People have been in the South Sierra for at least 6,000 years, according to archaeologists. Though the wilderness has not been completely surveyed, scientists have found bedrock mortars and obsidian objects that Native Americans used. It is believed that Owens Valley Paiute and the Panamint Shoshone once lived in these parts.

Farther back in time, the granite of the South Sierra formed between 100 million and 150 million years ago. Volcanic eruptions took place about 1 million years ago near the South Fork of the Kern. Basalt lava flows can be seen in rock formations near the river.

The high Sierra in this wilderness is above the timberline, which is roughly 9,000 feet. Besides 12,200-foot Olancha Peak, Deer Mountain is 9,418 feet, and Round Mountain is 9,884 feet. The coniferous forests around the ridges contain several kinds of trees, including the foxtail pine, ponderosa pine, lodgepole pine, and red fir.

But the combination of a dryer climate and high elevation produces chaparral-type vegetation in the center of the wilderness, called montane chaparral. It is a bit different from other places in the Sierra because chaparral appears most often in dry foothill locations. In such higher elevations, chaparral communities commonly contain snow bush *(Ceanothus cordulatus)*, mountain snowberry *(Symphoricarpos vaccinioides)*, golden chinquapin *(Chrysolepis sempervirens)*, and Corville's ceanothus *(Ceanothus pinetorum)*. These shrubs adjust to the colder temperatures and deeper snowfalls in the higher elevations, yet they thrive when the temperatures warm up and the precipitation virtually disappears. Most of these high-elevation chaparral species are not found below 5,000 feet.

The South Sierra also has three endemic species that federal officials watch closely. They are the Nine Mile Canyon phacelia *(Phacelia novenmillensis)*, the Kern River daisy *(Erigeron multiceps)*, and the Tulare horkelia *(Horkelia tularensis)*. Though no endangered species are known to live in this wilderness, there are several species that are considered "sensitive" or possibly in danger of dwindling in number. Of those species, the Sierra Nevada red fox *(Vulpes vuples necator)* is the creature studied the most in this area. The marten and the pine fisher *(Martes pennanti)* are also considered sensitive species. Another species, the wolverine *(Gulo luscus)*, was last seen in the South Sierra Wilderness during the 1950s.

Directions: From Lone Pine, drive about 28 miles south on Highway 395 to Sage Flat Road and turn right. Drive about 5 miles west on Sage Flat Road to the trailhead for Olancha Pass. Trailhead parking is available. Another access road to the wilderness can be found by driving 4 miles south of the Sage Flat Road turnoff on Highway 395 to Haiwee Canyon Road and turning right. Drive about 2.8 miles to trailhead parking and hike into the wilderness.

Activities: Hiking, backpacking, picnicking, photography, and fishing.

Facilities: None.

Dates: Open year-round, but the best hiking season is May through Oct.

Closest town: Olancha, 5 miles.

For more information: Mount Whitney Ranger Station, PO Box 8, Lone Pine, CA 93545. Phone (760) 876 6200.

OLANCHA PASS TRAIL

[Fig. 47(1)] The views on this hike are interesting coming and going. When hikers reach Olancha Pass at more than 9,200 feet, they will be rewarded with views of Summit Creek. About three miles north, Olancha Peak juts out at 12,123 feet. On the way back, the Owens Valley, Sage Flat Creek, and Haiwee Reservoir are the sights.

For hikers interested in seeing a high-elevation meadow, continue about 0.5 mile past Olancha Pass and see Summit Meadow near Summit Creek. Notice the lichen on the granite near the meadow. It is tenacious map lichen *(Rhizocarpon geographicum)*. The lichen spreads its thread-like appendages all over the rocks to absorb the minerals needed to survive. It can survive cold and sunlight, a tough combination to contend with in the South Sierra Wilderness.

The white-crowned sparrow *(Zonotrichia leucophrys)* and the western meadow-lark *(Sturnella neglecta)* are common residents in the meadow during the summer months. They leave for the lower elevations in September when the evenings begin to cool off. Hikers, too, should probably stay away in the colder months; because cold and blustery storms appear quickly at this elevation.

Directions: From Lone Pine, drive about 27 miles south on Highway 395 to Sage Flat Road and turn right. Drive 4.5 miles west on Sage Flat Road to the end of the road where parking places and the trailhead can be found.

Trail: 6 miles round-trip.

Elevation: About 1,500-foot gain, 9,220-foot peak.

Degree of difficulty: Moderate.

Surface: Rocky footpath and open meadow.

HAIWEE TRAIL

[Fig. 47(2)] The biggest reason to hike this trail is to get a good look at the Wild and Scenic South Fork of the Kern River. Depending on the time of year, hikers can see a swollen, raging river or a fairly quiet mountain creek. If you want to see it full and running, hike in late May and June. And, don't bother trying to ford it. Just admire it from a distance, enjoy the picnic lunch, and hike back out. If your hike takes place in late August, however, the cold water might feel good on your feet.

The view from 8,180-foot Haiwee Pass includes 9,455-foot Crag Peak to the west and 9,418-foot Deer Mountain to the northwest. Both are on the west side of the South Fork Kern. Hikers can see meadow shrubs, such as the bush cinquefoil *(Potentilla fruticosa)*, Sierra bilberry *(Vaccinium nivictum)*, and western blueberry *(Vaccinium occidentale)*, in areas near the Kern. Also, look for wildflowers in June and July. Common wildflowers of the area include California valerian *(Valeriana capitata)* and wandering daisy *(Erigeron peregrinus)*.

Probably the most frequently seen large animal in the area is the mule deer *(Odocoileus hemionus)*. The deer are most noticeable in the summer months after the birth of fawns. Mortality for deer in the Sierra is high because of starvation, hunting, and predation. The deer's biggest enemy is the mountain lion *(Felis concolor)*, which hikers probably will not see because it is so secretive.

Directions: From Lone Pine, drive about 31 miles south on Highway 395 to Haiwee Canyon Road and turn right. Drive west on Haiwee Canyon Road for about 2.2 miles to parking and the trailhead.

Trail: 7.5 miles round-trip.

Elevation: About 900-foot gain, 8,180-foot peak.

Degree of difficulty: Moderate.

Surface: Some switchbacks, rocky.

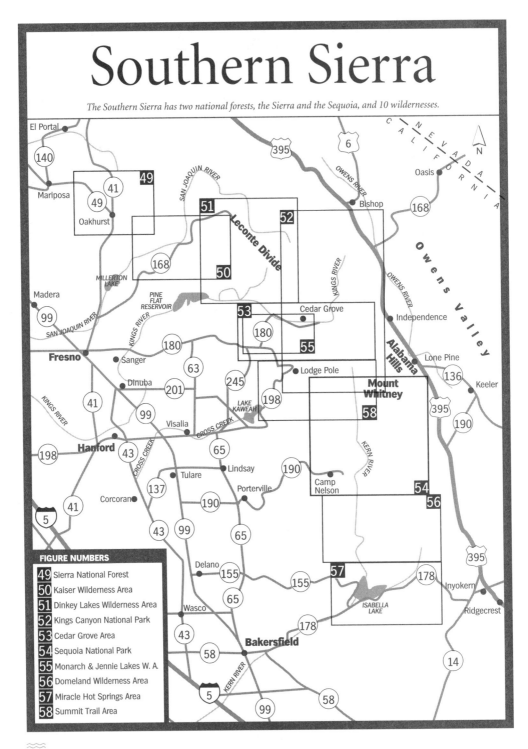

Southern Sierra

The Southern Sierra has two national forests, the Sierra and the Sequoia, and 10 wildernesses.

FIGURE NUMBERS

49 Sierra National Forest
50 Kaiser Wilderness Area
51 Dinkey Lakes Wilderness Area
52 Kings Canyon National Park
53 Cedar Grove Area
54 Sequoia National Park
55 Monarch & Jennie Lakes W. A.
56 Domeland Wilderness Area
57 Miracle Hot Springs Area
58 Summit Trail Area

Southern Sierra

South of Yosemite National Park and west of the Sierra Nevada crest, nearly 3.5 million acres of trails, lakes, canyons, and high country vistas offer almost every recreational opportunity possible in this mountain range. The wildernesses in the Southern Sierra are among the most popular hiking destinations in the world, rivaling even Yosemite. But visitors have lots of options: scenic driving, whitewater rafting, bird-watching, photography, camping, backpacking, fishing, swimming, skiing, snowshoeing, and picnicking are available in some of the most beautiful places in the range. The elevations go from about 900 feet in the western foothills to more than 14,000 feet at the crest, so there is a lot of diversity in the southern ecosystems.

The Southern Sierra begins with the 1.3-million-acre Sierra National Forest, just south of Yosemite. Sequoia and Kings Canyon national parks cover a combined

[*Above:* A group of giant sequoias (*Sequoiadendron giganteum*) in Sequoia National Park]

856,000 acres southeast of the Sierra forest. The 1.2-million-acre Sequoia National Forest is at the southern end of the range. In case there is confusion, the Sierra forest is a part of the Sierra Nevada range—Sierra within the Sierra. The Sequoia forest is separate from Sequoia National Park.

The two public agencies—the National Park Service and the U.S. Forest Service—manage land quite differently from each other. The Forest Service, which is part of the Department of Agriculture, has historically allowed grazing, mining, logging, hunting, and off-road vehicle recreation in addition to hiking, camping, and other recreation. Land managed by the Park Service, which is part of the Department of Interior, is considered a wildlife sanctuary where commercial enterprises such as grazing, mining, and logging do not generally take place.

The Sequoia park and forest contain most of the giant sequoia (*Sequoiadendron giganteum*) left in the world. Sequoia National Park has the largest tree in the world in the ancient grove at Giant Forest. The General Sherman tree, estimated to be more than 2,000 years old, has a circumference of about 103 feet at ground level. At 275 feet tall, it is not the tallest tree—the coastal redwood (*Sequoia sempervirens*) has been measured at more than 380 feet tall near the California coast. But the weight of the Sherman tree is estimated to be almost 1,400 tons, easily making it the largest living tree on earth.

Kings Canyon National Park, which the National Park Service manages under one administration with Sequoia National Park, has an interesting natural distinction as well. The Kings River canyon is the deepest river canyon in the United States. It is about 8,000 feet deep—deeper than the Grand Canyon in Arizona.

The two forests of the Southern Sierra, the Sierra and the Sequoia, have a combined 10 wildernesses. Both share wildernesses with the Inyo National Forest to the east. The Sierra, for instance, shares the John Muir and the Ansel Adams wildernesses, while Sequoia shares the Golden Trout and South Sierra wildernesses with Inyo. Both the Sierra and the Sequoia contain pieces of the Monarch Wilderness.

In the Sierra forest, a chain of hydroelectric lakes northeast of

GIANT SEQUOIA

(Sequoiadendron giganteum)
While bristlecone pines grow older and redwoods grow taller, no trees are more massive than giant sequoias, which can measure more than 100 feet around their base.

Fresno provides power and recreation. The hydro construction began around the turn of the century as Southern California Edison searched for ways to supply growing Los Angeles with power. The hydro chain is one of the oldest in California.

But most people do not think of electricity when they see these human-made lakes. They think of fishing and boating. Huntington and Shaver lakes are stocked with rainbow trout *(Oncorhynchus mykiss)* and brook trout *(Salvelinus fontinalis)*. A sailing regatta is held every summer at Huntington.

Just south of the hydro chain, the Kings River provides kayaking and whitewater rafting opportunities for visitors. The middle and south forks of the Kings are designated for federal protection under the Wild and Scenic Rivers Act. Combined with the Merced River, which flows out of Yosemite to the north, the Sierra has 224 miles of Wild and Scenic rivers.

Archaeologists say western Piute, Mono, and Chuckchansi tribes came to the Sierra forest to spend summers about 5,000 years ago. Loggers began working in the area during the late nineteenth century. The warmer seasons are longer here compared to the Central and Northern Sierra, so human activities could begin earlier and end later in the year than in most other places in the mountain range.

The farther south visitors travel, the milder the climate becomes in the lower elevations of the Sierra. The peaks and high country still get pasted with big storms and a lot of snow, but the Southern Sierra below 5,000 feet has short winters and long, dry summers. Consequently, spring can come as early as March in some foothill areas, even though the wildflowers do not start blooming until July in many high country meadows.

Plants that would normally occur at 3,000 feet farther north in the mountain range begin appearing at 5,000 feet and up in the Southern Sierra because they can adapt to the drier conditions at these elevations here. The foothill vegetation of chaparral, such as bush poppy *(Dendromecon rigida)* or poison oak *(Toxicodendron diversilobum)*, will occur at greater elevations on the western slope in the Southern Sierra than it does in the Central Sierra. Many of the animal communities also range higher in this part of the Sierra.

Among the more important parts of the animal community in this part of the range is the bat, which can be found in many parts of the Southern Sierra. With few natural enemies—owls and some hawks sometimes hunt for them—they are voracious consumers of insects. A bat can eat its own weight in insects during one night feeding. There are more than a dozen species in this area of the Sierra, including the little brown bat *(Myotis lucifugus)* around Kings Canyon National Park and the big-eared bat *(Plecotus townsendii)* in Sequoia National Forest.

Farther south, the Kern River presents an intimidating flow of water each spring, particularly in the dangerous upper reaches where rapids are often too turbulent even for experienced whitewater boaters. Between the upper reaches and Isabella Lake, just above Bakersfield, the river annually drowns about eight people. The river drops 28 feet

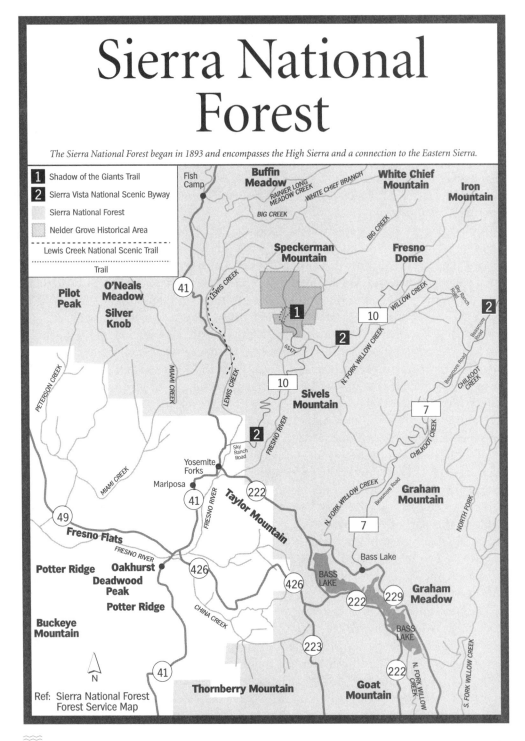

Sierra National Forest

The Sierra National Forest began in 1893 and encompasses the High Sierra and a connection to the Eastern Sierra.

1 Shadow of the Giants Trail
2 Sierra Vista National Scenic Byway
   Sierra National Forest
   Nelder Grove Historical Area
-------- Lewis Creek National Scenic Trail
.... Trail

Fish Camp

Buffin Meadow

RAINIER LONG MEADOW CREEK
WHITE CHIEF BRANCH

White Chief Mountain

Iron Mountain

BIG CREEK

BIG CREEK

Speckerman Mountain

Fresno Dome

Pilot Peak

O'Neals Meadow

Silver Knob

41

LEWIS CREEK

WILLOW CREEK

Sky Ranch Road

2

1

10

2

PETERSON CREEK

MIAMI CREEK

6S41Y

10

Sivels Mountain

N. FORK WILLOW CREEK

Beasmore Road

CHILKOOT CREEK

7

LEWIS CREEK

FRESNO RIVER

CHILKOOT CREEK

2

Sky Ranch Road

Yosemite Forks

Mariposa

MIAMI CREEK

222

41

Taylor Mountain

FRESNO RIVER

N. FORK WILLOW CREEK

Beasmore Road

Graham Mountain

NORTH FORK

7

Bass Lake

49

Fresno Flats

FRESNO RIVER

Potter Ridge

Oakhurst

Deadwood Peak

Potter Ridge

Buckeye Mountain

426

CHINA CREEK

426

BASS LAKE

222

229

Graham Meadow

BASS LAKE

223

N

41

Thornberry Mountain

Goat Mountain

222

N. FORK WILLOW CREEK

S. FORK WILLOW CREEK

Ref: Sierra National Forest
     Forest Service Map

per mile, a steep run compared to the Mississippi River, which averages about 2 feet per mile. In the hands of professionals, whitewater kayaking and rafting can be more exciting here than any other place in the Sierra. But this is no place for novices.

The cultural history of this region includes mining in the nineteenth century. Mining is what opened up one of the more stunning locations in the Southern Sierra, Mineral King in Sequoia National Park (*see* page 282). James Crabtree claimed the White Chief mine in 1873 and started a rush of miners who searched for silver. They did not find much silver, but they were successful in building a road that would eventually be extended to picturesque Mineral King, which is a glacial canyon up against the western divide of the Sierra. The road is 24 miles of winding, gut-turning switchbacks. The payoff at the end of this unsettling journey is well worth the trouble, but motorists should drive this road carefully and slowly.

Sierra National Forest

[Fig. 49, Fig. 50, Fig. 51, Fig. 52] The Sierra National Forest can mean many different things to many visitors. For those who come here from Los Angeles or the San Francisco Bay area each year, the forest means camping or renting a cabin at Huntington Lake and sailing every day. For fishing enthusiasts, it means fishing in a backcountry reservoir such as Lake Thomas Edison or Florence Lake. And, for backpackers, the Sierra forest means hiking near the crest at 13,986-foot Mount Humphreys. Four million people visit this forest every year.

From a practical standpoint, the Sierra forest represents a marriage of commercial interests—hydroelectric companies, cattle grazers, and others—and nature. Hydro companies have left the most noticeable imprint on the mountain ecosystems here.

There are 29 powerhouses on the San Joaquin River watershed, and Southern California Edison's chain of hydro lakes includes 11 major reservoirs. The reservoirs' combined storage is more than 500,000 acre-feet of water—roughly enough water to supply a California city of about 2 million people for an entire year. Two massive reservoirs, Courtright and Wishon, are part of the Pacific Gas & Electric Company hydroelectric network on the Kings River. In one place in the Sierra forest, Pacific Gas & Electric blasted a cavern several thousand feet deep inside a granite mountain to bury a massive powerhouse.

Yet, a few dozen miles away from the hydro projects, the Ritter Range within the Sierra Nevada displays small glaciers, jagged 12,000-foot peaks, and deep canyons. It is as primitive as any part of the Sierra crest. And, all through the high country, there are more than 350 natural lakes left by the receding glaciers more than 10,000 years ago.

Forest managers have been given a tool for keeping this forest wild—wildernesses. The eastern side of the Sierra forest is lined with wildernesses, including the Ansel

Douglas Fir Tussock Moth

More than 20,000 acres of fir trees in the Southern Sierra were defoliated in the late 1990s by the Douglas fir tussock moth *(Orgyia pseudotsuga)*. The larvae of this moth feed on many types of fir trees, including the white fir *(Abies concolor)*. But that's not the biggest problem for outdoor enthusiasts; in its caterpillar stage, the tussock's hairs cause itching and rashes for many people. Outbreaks of tussocks can last up to three years, dying off in a viral outbreak that is harmless to people.

Adams, John Muir, Dinkey Lakes, Kaiser, and Monarch wildernesses. The best Monarch Wilderness access is in Sequoia National Forest, so the Monarch will be detailed in the Sequoia forest section of this chapter (*see* page 295).

Together, the Sierra forest wildernesses provide a kind of natural corridor between Yosemite National Park on the north and Kings Canyon National Park on the south. Only the Kaiser Wilderness, just north of Huntington Lake, is an island away from the contiguous string of wildernesses.

The Sierra forest began in 1893 under the name of Sierra Forest Reserve, encompassing more than 4 million acres and most of the Southern Sierra. Over the next several decades, it shrank as other forests and national parks were established. But the Sierra forest has always contained the high Sierra and a connection to the Eastern Sierra.

There is no way to get from the western slope to the Eastern Sierra by passenger car. This area is part of the longest block of wild lands in the Sierra where no paved pass exists to cross the mountain range. Visitors interested in crossing the range have to drive north to Yosemite and cross on Tioga Pass, or drive more than 100 miles south to Highway 178 in Kern County.

In 1879, there was earnest discussion of building a road from Fresno to Mono County through the present-day Sierra forest, but the attempt was doomed because Mammoth Mining Company closed the next year. With no financial support, the idea

DOUGLAS FIR TUSSOCK MOTH
(Orgyia pseudotsuga)
The larvae of this moth feed on and defoliate many types of fir trees, including the white fir. In its caterpillar stage, the moth's hairs cause itching and rashes for many people.

fizzled. Other proposals have been entertained over the last century, but none has panned out.

Now Beashore Road to Clover Meadow in the northern Sierra National Forest is as far as developed roads go. The road and its access roads stop about 18 miles short of crossing the crest and reaching Mammoth Lakes. The only way to cross the Sierra in this area is to walk, ride a stock animal, or fly by plane—although there is no commercial landing strip in the forest. And a lot of people want this part of the mountain range to remain a haven for plants, animals, and recreation rather than cars.

Unlike the steep escarpment of the Eastern Sierra, the western slope rises gradually over a long distance—40 miles or so in the Sierra forest. So foothills are a big part of the ecosystem. A large variety of animals reside in the foothills year-round because of the milder climate. The animals include Gilbert's skink *(Eumeces gilberti)*, the screech owl *(Otus asio)*, Bewick's wren *(Thyromanes bewickii)*, and spotted skunk *(Spilogale gracilis)*.

Several kinds of woodland oaks provide habitat for many kinds of animals. The oaks range from the San Joaquin Valley floor to 6,000 feet in the Sierra. Species include the valley oak *(Quercus lobata)*, black oak *(Quercus kelloggii)*, blue oak *(Quercus douglasii)*, and Oregon oak *(Quercus garryanai)*.

The foothill woodlands also are known for adjacent grasslands. Nineteenth century California had millions of grassland acres that have since become farmland. But some grasslands still exist, and they are easy to see from the roads as visitors drive into the forest. In spring, look for wildflower displays that include baby blue-eyes *(Nemophila menziesii)*, long-spurred plectritis *(Plectritis ciliosa)*, evening snow *(Linanthus dichotomus)*, and American vetch *(Vicia americana)*.

Native Americans, the Western Paiutes, lived in the grasslands and foothill areas of the Sierra forest hundreds of years before other humans arrived. Other tribes also came into the Sierra on a seasonal basis. The Mono tribe came from the Eastern Sierra to Mono Hot Springs, just south of Lake Thomas Edison, to participate in spiritual cleansing rites during the summer. Some tribes left behind holes in the granite bedrock near the San Joaquin River where they ground acorns for food. There is also evidence of Native Americans around the Kings River.

Today, the Kings River, on the forest's extreme southern boundary, is considered a fine whitewater rafting stream. When the snow melts in spring and summer, about 1.7 million acre-feet of water roll down the river over several months. That amount of water varies wildly because California's capricious weather can spin off five or six consecutive drought years, followed by three or four near-record rainfall years.

▨ SIERRA VISTA NATIONAL SCENIC BYWAY

[Fig. 49(2)] The Sierra Vista National Scenic Byway is the best way to see the Sierra National Forest from your car. Indeed, it may be the quickest and easiest way to see a huge cross-section of life in the Sierra Nevada. It runs from the foothills at about 2,800 feet in elevation around North Fork to more than 7,000 feet at Globe

Rock, Cold Springs Summit, and Fresno Dome.

Make sure your gas tank is full and your tires are properly inflated. This route is about 100 miles, and 20 of them are not paved. In other words, this trip will probably take most of the day. Allow at least four or five hours.

Visitors can fill up with gas and find food in the small community of North Fork. They can also visit the Mono Indian Cultural Museum. The scenic byway begins about 3 miles south of North Fork at Minarets Road, which can be reached from Road 223 in North Fork. Before they start the drive, visitors may want to take a 6-mile detour down Italian Bar Road to see the geographic center of California. The much-debated subject of the state's geographic center was settled with Global Information System instruments several years ago. The area is marked along Italian Bar Road. Return to Road 223 and continue driving southeast until you reach Minarets Road.

Along the Sierra Vista National Scenic Byway, Redinger Overlook at 3,700 feet provides a good view of the foothills and vegetation. Redinger Lake, which can be seen from the overlook, is part of the hydroelectric system built by Southern California Edison Company. In the chaparral plant communities of this area, common shrubs are birchleaf mountain mahogany (*Cercocarpus betuloides*), coyote bush (*Baccaris piluaris*), and California coffeeberry (*Rhamnus californica*).

About 6 miles farther along, as the road slowly begins to wind north, there is Ross Cabin at 4,000 feet in elevation. Jessie Blakey Ross built the cabin in the 1860s. Jessie had moved west with his parents for the Gold Rush. His log cabin is among the oldest still standing in this area.

The next stop is Mile High Vista at 5,300 feet. The Kaiser Wilderness and Mammoth Pool Reservoir, another hydroelectric lake belonging to Southern California Edison Company, stretch before visitors. The U.S. Forest Service closes the Mammoth Pool area between May 1 and June 15 to allow migrating deer to pass through safely. Apparently, before the pool was constructed, the area was a meadow along a corridor where mule deer (*Odocoileus hemionus*) migrated annually from the foothills to the higher elevations. The deer apparently have not changed their route over the last century. Campgrounds in the Mammoth Pool area include Placer and Sweetwater.

Arch Rock at 6,200 feet is the next stop, about 14 miles from Mile High Vista. It can be seen from a marked turnout, but visitors may want to take the short hike to see how erosion formed the granite into an arch. About 5 miles beyond Arch Rock is the Clover Meadow Forest Service Station and the Granite Creek Campground. Turn right on the marked access road and drive 2 miles. The Ansel Adams Wilderness is a few miles beyond the campground next to the access road.

Minarets Road becomes Beashore Road at the Clover Meadow turnoff. The pavement ends here, and it will not begin again for about 20 miles. The Minarets Pack Station is about a 0.5-mile hike south of Beashore Road. About 11 miles down Beashore Road, visitors will see Globe Rock at 7,152 feet. It features a large granite rock perched and balanced on a smaller rock, a phenomenon caused by freezing and erosion at the base of the formation. Campgrounds along Beashore include Chilkoot, Graggs Camp, and Upper Chiquito.

Lodgepole pine *(Pinus murrayana)* and red fir *(Abies magnifica)* are common in the forest here. The vegetation below the trees must be able to grow without a lot of sun. Look for the alpine prickly currant *(Ribes montigenum)*, tobacco bush *(Ceanothus velutinus)*, and Labrador tea *(Ledum glandulosum)*.

About 8 miles beyond Globe Rock, visitors have the choice of turning right from Beashore onto Sky Ranch Road or continuing straight on Beashore to Bass Lake. Either way, visitors will wind up on Highway 41 where the byway concludes just north of Oakhurst. Along Sky Ranch, visitors can see the giant sequoia. Bass Lake, known as a fine fishing hole, is another picturesque mountain lake formed by a Pacific Gas and Electric Company hydroelectric project.

Directions: From Fresno, drive 22 miles northeast on Highway 41 and turn right on Road 200. A scenic byway sign is posted. Drive about 16 miles northeast on Road 200 to North Fork and turn right on Road 223. Drive another 0.4 mile and turn right on Road 225. Drive south about 3 miles on Road 225 and bear left at the fork. Drive 0.3 mile to where the route becomes Minaret Road and the byway begins.

Activities: Scenic driving, hiking, camping, photography, fishing, and backpacking.

Facilities: Clover Meadow Forest Service Station for permits and information, Minarets Pack Station, Jones Store at Beashore Meadow, campgrounds, motels and gas stations in Bass Lake, and Mono Cultural Indian Museum in North Fork.

Dates: The byway is open May through Oct.

Fees: There is no fee to drive the byway, but campgrounds do have fees.

Closest town: North Fork, 3 miles.

For more information: Sierra National Forest, PO Box 10, North Fork, CA 93643. Phone (559) 877-2218. Mono Indian Cultural Museum. Phone (559) 877-2218.

SHADOW OF THE GIANTS TRAIL

[Fig. 49(1)] Nelder Grove has more than 100 giant sequoias in its 1,500 acres, and the Shadow of the Giants Trail offers visitors an up-close look at many of them. At the end of the trail is the Bull Buck Tree, once considered the largest sequoia in the country. The General Sherman Tree in Sequoia National Park holds that distinction now.

Along the trail, visitors may notice incense cedar *(Libocedrus decurrens)* and white fir *(Abies concolor)* in the grove. Some of the incense cedars appear to have cavities running parallel to the grain of the bark. These are the work of a dry-rot fungus *(Polyporus amarus)*.

Another interesting part of Nelder Grove is the Graveyard of the Giants, not far from the Shadow of the Giants Trail. Visitors will find nearby Nelder Grove Campground, which has no piped water. However, there is no fee to stay in this campground.

Directions: Drive the scenic byway about 80 miles, veer right on Sky Ranch Road, and drive about 6 miles to Forest Road 6S47Y and turn right. Drive 0.2 mile and bear left at the fork. Drive 0.2 mile to the trailhead. From Oakhurst, drive about 3 miles north of Oakhurst on Highway 41 and turn right on Sky Ranch Road. Drive about 4.5 miles northeast on Sky Ranch Road to Forest Road 6S47Y and turn left. Drive 0.2 mile and bear left at the fork. Drive 0.2 mile to the trailhead.

Trail: 2 miles.

Elevation: About 50-foot gain, 6,100-foot peak.

Degree of difficulty: Easy.

Surface: Open footpath.

ANSEL ADAMS WILDERNESS/JOHN MUIR WILDERNESS

The Ansel Adams [Fig. 40, Fig. 41, Fig. 42] and John Muir [Fig. 42, Fig. 43, Fig. 44, Fig. 46] wildernesses straddle the crest of the Sierra Nevada, falling into both the Sierra and Inyo national forests. Together, the wildernesses spread over 800,000 acres of the high Sierra. Many of their most famous features—such as part of Mount Whitney, the Devils Postpile National Monument (*see* page 226), and Thousand Island Lake—are reached from the Eastern Sierra. For a fuller description of each wilderness, see the Ansel Adams Wildernes, (page 205) and the John Muir Wilderness (page 233) in the chapter on the Eastern Sierra. In the Southern Sierra, the Sierra National Forest has its share of wilderness features, too. Fishing, camping, horseback riding, backpacking, and hiking are the main activities.

Though there are dozens of picturesque glacial lakes carved into the granite on the western side of these two wildernesses, the four lakes known best in these parts are hydroelectric lakes. They are Lake Thomas A. Edison, Florence Lake, Courtright Reservoir, and Wishon Reservoir. All are massive compared to the natural lakes in this area.

Edison and Florence, part of Southern California Edison Company's hydroelectric chain of lakes, help harness the 1.7-million-acre-foot runoff each year coming down the granite canyons of the San Joaquin River watershed. Courtright and Wishon are in the Kings River watershed to the south, and they are part of the Pacific Gas and Electric Company hydroelectric complex. None of the four lakes is technically inside a wilderness, but the wilderness surrounds Edison and Florence. And wilderness borders Courtright and Wishon. Campgrounds and other attractions can be found near the lakes. About 3 miles from Edison, visitors will find Mono Hot Springs, which provides people a chance to experience an exhilarating dip in mineral waters.

Fishing enthusiasts like the lakes because they can find plenty of rainbow trout, brown trout, and Eastern brook trout. Hikers and backpackers enjoy the high Sierra vistas, dominated by granite that began forming 80 million to 100 million years ago.

The backcountry trails in these wildernesses are heavily used, and they traverse some of the most rugged country anywhere in this mountain range. Like the trails in the Central Sierra, these trails require physical fitness because they are many miles from civilization.

In the 6,000- to 8,000-foot forest belt dominated by lodgepole pine, ponderosa pine, and red fir, the California spotted owl *(Strix occidentalis)* can be found within 0.25 mile of streams. The owl prefers living in mixed conifer parts of the forest dominated by red fir and white fir where old-growth trees of more than 30 inches in diameter can be found. The owl is considered a "Forest Service sensitive species," meaning its numbers have dwindled and its habitat is disappearing.

The rare plants in this part of the forest include golden annual lupine *(Lupinus citrinus)* and unexpected larkspur *(Delphinium inopinum)*. The lupine is endemic to the Sierra forest. Other endemics found here are the two-lobed clarkia *(Clarkia biloba* ssp. *australis)*, Kings River buckwheat *(Eriogonum nudum* var. *regirivum)*, many-flowered lily *(Erythronium pluriforum)*, and Rawson's flaming trumpet *(Collomia rawsonia)*.

Directions: Drive 65 miles northeast of the Fresno-Clovis area on Highway 168 to Huntington Lake. Continue on Highway 168 over Kaiser Pass. The road becomes Kaiser Pass Road. Drive another 11 miles and turn left where the route forks. It is marked with a road sign. Drive another 5 miles to Lake Thomas A. Edison. Both the Adams and Muir wildernesses can be entered from Edison. If visitors bear right at the fork, they can drive another 12 miles to Florence Lake. The road narrows to one lane for several miles.

Activities: Fishing, hiking, backpacking, camping, bird-watching, and photography.

Facilities: Just outside the wildernesses, Vermillion and Mono campgrounds, ferry to cross Thomas A. Edison Lake, and restrooms.

Dates: Open June through Oct. The road is not plowed past Kaiser Pass in winter.

Fees: There is a fee for camping and for the ferry ride.

Closest town: Huntington Lake, 16 miles.

For more information: Sierra National Forest, 1600 Tollhouse Road, Clovis, CA 93611-0532. Phone (559) 297-0706.

MAXSON TRAIL

[Fig. 51(1)] People hiking the Maxson Trail to Post Corral Meadows consider this trek to be a light weekend of walking. They camp around the meadows and return the next day. So, if you're interested in a short backpack into the John Muir Wilderness, this is a good sampler filled with views of the high Sierra. You will need a wilderness permit for an overnight stay. For the wilderness permit, write the forest at 1600 Tollhouse Road, Clovis, CA 93611-0532, or stop on your way to the wilderness.

There is one area of interest around Courtright Reservoir where the trail begins. It is called the Courtright Intrusion Zone Geologic Contact Area. Geologists say visitors can see the edge of two massive plutons meeting at this place, which is just east of the parking area. The edge of metamorphic rock, once part of an ancient seabed about 180 million years ago, is visible as reddish hornfels along the intrusion zone of the two plutons. Another interesting geologic feature is the outline of an old, inactive fault between the two plutons.

Directions: Drive 45 miles northeast of Fresno-Clovis on Highway 168 to Shaver Lake and turn right on Dinkey Creek Road. Drive 12 miles to the McKinley Grove

Kaiser Wilderness Area

The 22,700-acre Kaiser Wilderness, formed in 1975, has elevations ranging from 8,000 feet to 10,320 feet.

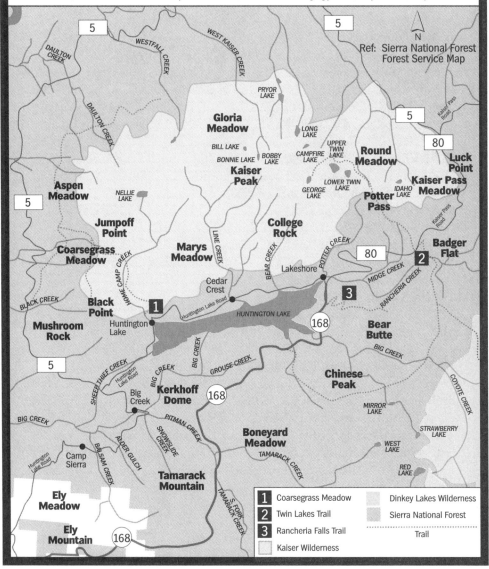

Ref: Sierra National Forest
Forest Service Map

1 Coarsegrass Meadow
2 Twin Lakes Trail
3 Rancheria Falls Trail
◻ Kaiser Wilderness
◻ Dinkey Lakes Wilderness
◻ Sierra National Forest
······· Trail

Botanical Area on Dinkey Creek Road, which becomes McKinley Grove Road at the botanical area. Continue another 7 miles on the McKinley Grove Road and turn left at the Courtright-Wishon reservoirs sign on Forest Road 40. Drive 1 mile to the junction with Courtright Road and turn left. Drive another 8 miles to Courtright Reservoir. At the reservoir, take the right fork and drive 0.2 mile to the Maxson trailhead parking.

Trail: 15 miles round-trip.

Elevation: About 700-foot gain, 8,800-foot peak.

Degree of difficulty: Moderate.

Surface: Mostly granite, but some old dirt road.

WOODCHUCK TRAIL

[Fig. 51(2)] It's hard work, but most people appreciate the views after climbing several hundred feet of granite at the start of this trail. Wishon Reservoir stretches below. To the southeast, visitors will see Mount Hoffman at 9,622 feet. The glacial advances over the last 1.5 million years buried this area under ice several times. The last of the retreating glaciers, about 11,000 years ago, finished the job of carving the spectacular spires and domes visible to the north.

Some people like to walk up the first 2 to 3 miles of Woodchuck just to see the views and turn around. Visitors do not need a wilderness permit for a day hike. In September, the quaking aspen (*Populus tremuloides*) is dazzling as it lights up meadows with yellow leaves. Lost Peak at 8,476 feet is to the north, and Loper Peak at 10,059 feet can be seen in the distance as the trail enters the John Muir Wilderness.

Farther into the John Muir Wilderness, the Woodchuck Trail comes to bridges made from local timber. Soon hikers reach Moore Boys Camp, the end of the line for this hike. For bird watchers, there is plenty to observe in summer. The willow flycatcher (*Empidonas tralii*), considered a sensitive species in danger of becoming rare, can be seen in this area. Also, look for the poor-will (*Phalaenoptilus nuttalli*) and mountain quail (*Oreortyx pictus*).

Directions: Follow the directions for the Maxson Trail (*see* page 261) to the junction of McKinley Grove Road and Courtright Road. Continue on McKinley Grove Road for about 2 more miles to the Woodchuck Trail parking lot at the south end of Wishon Lake. The trail begins at the southern end of the parking area.

Trail: 12 miles round-trip.

Elevation: About 1,700-foot gain, 8,700-foot peak.

Degree of difficulty: Strenuous.

Surface: Granite, rocky, sometimes narrow, crossing Woodchuck Creek.

KAISER WILDERNESS/HUNTINGTON LAKE

[Fig. 50] The 22,700-acre Kaiser Wilderness, formed in 1975, gives visitors opportunities to hike, backpack, take photographs, cross-country ski, and fish at elevations between 8,000 and 10,320 feet. But the real attraction of Kaiser is just outside the wilderness boundary—Huntington Lake to the south. Visitors rent summer cabins and spend vacations sailing, hiking, and seeing nature. In winter, downhill skiing enthusiasts flock to nearby Sierra Summit Ski Area. The Kaiser Wilderness gives folks a chance to get away from the development around the lake.

The mule deer *(Odocoileus hemionus)* is probably the easiest large mammal to find in this area, but there are also marten *(Martes americana),* fisher *(Martes pennanti),* striped skunk *(Mephitis mephitis),* and black bear. Black bears are not considered dangerous, although they occasionally have been known to break into cabins in search of food.

With the development of homes and summer cabins around Huntington, natural fires become more of a concern because there are people and property to protect. A fire in the mid-1990s charred thousands of forest acres near the lake and the community of Big Creek several miles away. Homes and wilderness acreage were threatened, but there was no damage to either.

The human history of the area starts with the Native Americans, particularly the Mono tribe. They hunted and gathered here for centuries, and obsidian used in their tools and weapons has been found in archeological digs in the wilderness.

Huntington Lake, named after utility entrepreneur Henry Huntington, is not natural. Pacific Power and Light Company, now known as Southern California Edison Company, began constructing Huntington dams in 1911, and the lake began holding water in 1913.

Directions: Drive 60 miles northeast of the Fresno-Clovis area on Highway 168 to Huntington Lake. Trails into the wilderness depart from the Huntington Lake area.

Activities: Sailing, swimming, skiing, hiking, camping, backpacking, cross-country skiing, fishing, photography, bird-watching, and picnicking.

Facilities: Cabins, summer cottages, resorts, gas stations, restaurants, campgrounds, boat launches, visitor center, and Sierra Summit Ski Area.

Dates: The lake and wilderness are open year-round, but camping takes place from May to Oct.

Fees: There are fees for rentals, campgrounds, resorts, snow skiing, and other commercial outlets.

Closest town: Huntington Lake.

For more information: Sierra National Forest, 1600 Tollhouse

FISHER
(Martes pennanti)

Road, Clovis, CA 93611-0532. Phone (559) 297-0706.

COARSEGRASS MEADOW TRAIL

[Fig. 50(1)] Hikers enter the Kaiser Wilderness after walking 0.25 mile on the trail to Coarsegrass Meadow. The views are filled with red fir, Jeffrey pine, and seasonal wildflowers.

Look for the yarrow (*Achillea landulosa*) and the meadow fritillary (*Fritillary brandegei*). On many wet years, the hike passes by pussy paws (*Calyptridium umbellatum*) and wild strawberry (*Fragaria californica*).

Directions: Follow directions to Huntington Lake (*see* page 261) and continue to the northeast side of the lake. Turn left on Huntington Lake Road and drive 5.2 miles west to Huntington Lake Resort. Park on the roadside near the resort entrance. Walk about 0.1 mile to the trailhead on the east side of Home Camp Creek, which is just west of the resort entrance. Look for the Coarsegrass Meadow-Aspen Meadow sign.

Trail: 5.5 miles round-trip.

Elevation: 700-foot gain, 7,900-foot peak.

Degree of difficulty: Easy.

Surface: Granite with several creek crossings.

TWIN LAKES

[Fig. 50(2)] Visitors can see some small natural lakes on the Twin Lakes hike. There are quiet fishing holes in the lakes, but they will require a bit of searching to find. Rainbow trout are found in the lakes.

The views from Potter Pass include Banner and Ritter peaks, which are both higher than 12,000 feet. The peaks jut

Valley Tassels

A beautiful member of the snapdragon family, the valley tassel (*Castilleja attenuata*) looks like a big-nosed character from an animated Disney movie. Its flowers usually contain several blossoms with dark spots on either side of a long, cream-colored extension. The flowers can be found in the grasslands along the foothills on the western slope of the Sierra. They bloom in May.

VALLEY TASSELS (*Castilleja attenuata*) The flowers of the valley tassel, which blooms in May, can be found in the grasslands along the foothills on the western slope of the Sierra.

Dinkey Lakes Wilderness Area

The Dinkey Lakes Wilderness is a 30,000-acre area southeast of Huntington Lake and northwest of Courtright Reservoir.

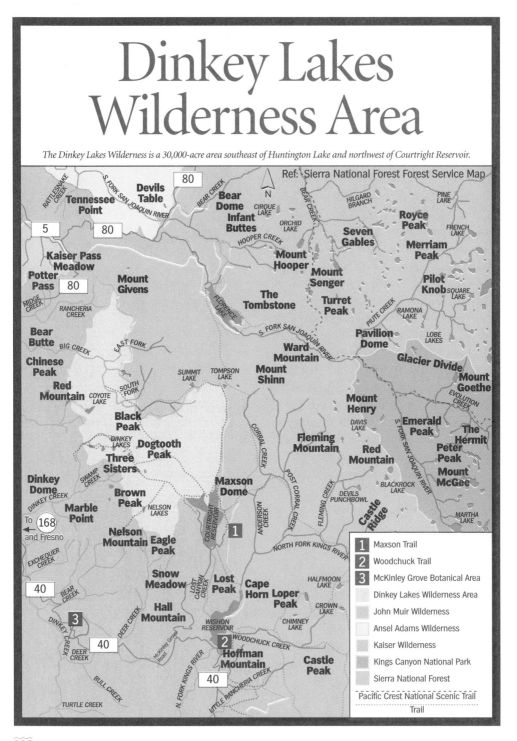

Ref: Sierra National Forest Forest Service Map

1	Maxson Trail
2	Woodchuck Trail
3	McKinley Grove Botanical Area
	Dinkey Lakes Wilderness Area
	John Muir Wilderness
	Ansel Adams Wilderness
	Kaiser Wilderness
	Kings Canyon National Park
	Sierra National Forest
	Pacific Crest National Scenic Trail
	Trail

into the skyline at the Sierra crest many miles north of Potter Pass.

Directions: Drive 65 miles northeast of the Fresno-Clovis area on Highway 168 and continue past Huntington Lake. The road becomes Kaiser Pass Road. Drive about 5 miles on Kaiser Pass Road to Badger Flat and park on the south side of the road near the D & F Pack Station sign. The trailhead is marked.

Trail: 6.9 miles round-trip.

Elevation: 500-foot gain, 9,000-foot peak.

Degree of difficulty: Moderate.

Surface: Rocky, granite with some open meadow.

RANCHERIA FALLS TRAIL

[Fig. 50(3)] Hikers like the shaded walk to Rancheria Falls in spring, summer, or fall. It passes along understory vegetation such as buckbrush *(Ceanothus cuneatus)*, white-stemmed gooseberry *(Ribes inerme)*, and chinquapin *(Castanopsis chrysophylla)*.

The falls are about 150 feet high and 50 feet wide. Unlike many falls that dry up by August, the water keeps flowing consistently through the year at Rancheria. The falls continue because the area is in the high Sierra and close to places where a healthy snowpack slowly melts into the streams feeding Rancheria Creek.

Directions: Follow directions to Huntington Lake (*see* page 264) and turn right on Forest Road 8S31. Drive 1.3 miles and bear right at the fork. Drive another 2 miles to the trailhead.

Trail: 2 miles round-trip.

Elevation: 300-foot gain, 8,120-foot peak.

Degree of difficulty: Easy.

Surface: Granite, rocky.

🏵 DINKEY LAKES WILDERNESS

[Fig. 51] The Dinkey Lakes Wilderness is a 30,000-acre area southeast of Huntington Lake and northwest of Courtright Reservoir. Hikers and visitors on pack animals traverse miles of trails for the fishing, views, and camping between the two massive watersheds of the San Joaquin River to the north and the Kings River to the south.

The wilderness is a bit of an oddity because its eastern boundary is an unpaved route, called the Ershim/Dusy Off-Highway Vehicle Route. It forms the boundary between the Dinkey Lakes and John Muir wildernesses and allows off-road vehicles to travel about 31 miles through the heart of wilderness areas. Vehicles can take a back road from Huntington Lake to Courtright Lake.

The highest point, Three Sisters Peak, stands 10,619 feet just to the south of First Dinkey Lake and southwest of Second Dinkey Lake, which are natural bodies of water. Red Mountain at 9,874 feet is just outside the northwest shoulder of the wilderness, but it is a striking volcanic feature in an area dominated by granite. Red Mountain was created more than 3 million years ago by an andesite flow. People do climb the peaks, but there are not maintained trails on them.

The trout fishing in the Dinkey Lakes Wilderness is considered excellent. Rainbow trout and Eastern brook trout are caught in the Dinkey Lakes, Swede Lake, and many others. The tough part is getting to the lakes. The closest paved roads are at Courtright and near Huntington. A gravel road will bring visitors within about 0.7 mile of the wilderness. The rest is done on foot. A free wilderness permit is required for overnight visits. To get the permit, write or go to the Sierra National Forest headquarters, 1600 Tollhouse Road, Clovis, CA 93611-0532. Phone (559) 297-0706.

Directions: Regular passenger cars can drive about 45 miles northeast of Fresno-Clovis on Highway 168 to Shaver Lake and turn right on Dinkey Creek Road. Drive about 10 miles to Rock Creek Road and turn left. Drive about 12 miles to the end of the road and park. You can hike to Mystery Lake, which is about 0.7 mile away. For four-wheel-drive vehicles, drive northeast from Huntington Lake on Kaiser Pass Road about 8 miles to an unnamed gravel access road and turn right. Drive 0.2 mile to the Ershim/Dusy Off-Highway Vehicle Route and continue between the Dinkey and Muir wildernesses. Lakecamp Lake is the first of many stops visitors can make along this 31-mile route to Courtright Lake.

Activities: Fishing, hiking, camping, and swimming.

Facilities: None.

Dates: Open May through Oct. Roads close for the winter.

Fees: None.

Closest town: Dinkey Creek, 12 miles.

For more information: Kings River Ranger District, 34849 Maxson Road, Sanger, CA 93567. Phone (559) 855-8321.

🔲 MCKINLEY GROVE BOTANICAL AREA

[Fig. 51(3)] The McKinley Grove features about 165 giant sequoia, some of which can be seen from McKinley Grove Road as it passes through the area. Visitors can stroll through much of the 100 acres, which include massive sugar pine and Jeffrey pine, as well as white fir.

The General Washington Tree is the largest of the grove. It is 65 feet in circumference and a small brook actually flows below the root system. Around the trees, visitors will find carpet clover (*Trifolium monanthum*) and thimbleberry (*Rubus parviflorus*). Also look for the Sierra gooseberry (*Ribes roezlii*).

The grove remained a bit of an enigma to local residents for decades after it was discovered in the 1860s. The reason: There was little publicity about the grove, and it was not easy to find. Cattle owners grazed their animals near it, and a hydraulic miner worked a claim on Laurel Creek near the grove. But there was no easy way to the grove until 1930. Many historians and environmentalists believe the isolation may have helped the grove survive.

Directions: Drive 45 miles northeast of Fresno-Clovis on Highway 168 to Shaver Lake and turn right on Dinkey Creek Road. Drive 12 miles from Shaver Lake to the

McKinley Grove Botanical Area on Dinkey Creek Road, which becomes McKinley Grove Road at the botanical area.

Activities: Hiking, photography, picnicking, scenic driving.

Facilities: Picnic grounds with vault toilets, but no potable water.

Dates: Open May through Oct.

Fees: None.

Closest town: Shaver Lake, 12 miles.

For more information: Sierra National Forest, 1600 Tollhouse Road, Clovis, CA 93611-0532. Phone (559) 297-0706.

🏞 WHITEWATER RAFTING ON THE KINGS RIVER

The Kings River has turbulent rapids, huge whirlpools, and smooth open water. It has been attracting boaters for many years. Three companies are known for their professionally guided tours during the whitewater season. They include Kings River Expeditions, Spirit Whitewater, and Zephyr Expeditions.

The companies generally take people of many skill levels. Teens are allowed to go, but it is best to check with the companies on children 12 years old and younger. In May and even June, the water can be quite cold, so wet suits are often recommended. The companies rent wet suits, life jackets, and often provide meals and overnight camping. The season stops when the snowmelt slows down—usually in late July or August.

For more information: Kings River Expeditions, 211 North Van Ness Avenue, Fresno, CA 93701. Phone (559) 233-4881 or (800) 846-3674. Spirit Whitewater, 1849 Crane Lane, Squaw Valley, CA 93675. Phone (559) 332-2227 or (800) 400-7138. Zephyr Expeditions, PO Box 510, Columbia, CA 95310. Phone (559) 532-6249 or (800) 431-3636.

Kings Canyon National Park

[Fig. 52] Kings Canyon National Park offers some of the wildest and untouched natural views in the Southern Sierra. The park consists of more than 400,000 acres of land surrounding the deepest river canyon in North America. The Kings River canyon drops 8,200 feet from high in the Sierra to the San Joaquin Valley. It is deeper than Hell's Canyon on the Snake River in Idaho and the Grand Canyon in Arizona. With a canyon that drops more than 1.5 miles, it may not be surprising to learn that visitors come to Kings Canyon for the views.

The canyon developed its depth over the past 5 million years as the Sierra batholith uplifted and the Kings River eroded down into the granite. The combination of lifting up and eroding down resulted in the steep canyon. Wind, water, and geologic rumblings continue causing erosion. It also occurs through avalanches that

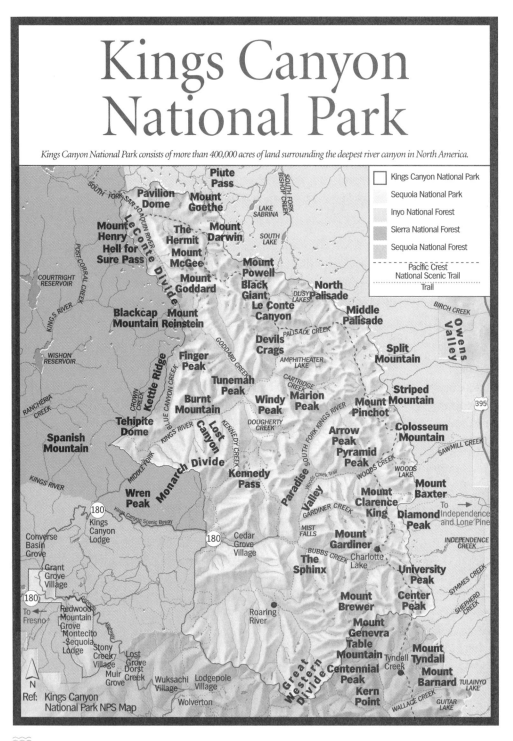

Kings Canyon National Park

Kings Canyon National Park consists of more than 400,000 acres of land surrounding the deepest river canyon in North America.

Kings Canyon National Park
Sequoia National Park
Inyo National Forest
Sierra National Forest
Sequoia National Forest
Pacific Crest
National Scenic Trail
Trail

Ref: Kings Canyon
National Park NPS Map

promote large rock falls. Chutes or slides have developed over many centuries in the highest places on the eastern side of the park.

People have known about the inspiring sights of Kings Canyon for the last century. The park was established in 1940, decades after John Muir and the Sierra Club began a campaign to move it into National Park Service protection. Muir reacted to the widespread logging that took place in the 1890s in the giant sequoia groves of the area.

Visitors can see these logged areas by following trails in the area. Perhaps the most interesting view is of the meadow left by clear-cutting in Converse Basin. The basin extends more than 4,500 acres, and huge stumps of downed sequoias are found throughout the area. Unfortunately, there are a lot of places around Kings Canyon National Park where visitors can find stumps left behind by logging in the late nineteenth and early twentieth centuries.

But there are still many magnificent specimens remaining. The General Grant Tree, for instance, is the Nation's Christmas Tree. At about 6,500 feet in elevation, it is found at Grant Grove, just beyond the Big Stump Entrance Station on Highway 180 at the western tip of the park. This 2,000-year-old tree stands 267 feet high, and in December it towers above the snow as the annual celebration of the Nation's Christmas Tree takes place at its base. The tree was discovered in 1862 and named for Ulysses S. Grant. Grant Grove was its own national park in 1890. It was a little more than 2,000 acres, and it was added to Kings Canyon in 1940.

Prior to the arrival of European settlers, the Wobonuch tribe of Native Americans lived just west of Grant Grove. The Wobonuch, like the Waksachi, were part of the Monache tribe that crossed the Sierra crest from the Eastern Sierra about five centuries ago. Grant Grove was a summer gathering place for the Wobonuch.

The Redwood Mountain Grove, not far from Grant Grove, is one of the few places left on earth where visitors can find more than 2,000 giant sequoias in one place. Visitors can also see the red or creek dogwood (Cornus sericea) along Redwood Creek.

Cedar Grove is where Kings Canyon views can be found. Highway 180 or Kings Canyon Highway winds down the canyon into Cedar Grove, which has campgrounds along the river. Cedar Grove is the starting point for many hikes, including backcountry treks. From this area, backpackers can walk to some of the most pristine areas found anywhere in the Sierra. Many backpackers depart from Cedar Grove to hook up with John Muir Trail at the crest and walk all the way to Mount Whitney.

But Cedar Grove is a well-known haunt for black bears, which grow to 300 or 400 pounds eating the fatty scraps and leftovers they find in the garbage. Like black bears in Yosemite National Park, these creatures learn quickly and persistently pursue food. Bears have been known to rip car doors off to get at a piece of candy. Some bears must be destroyed if they become too aggressive.

Bears in the backcountry have not learned as much about human food as those in partially developed areas such as Cedar Grove. But backpackers must still place their

Grant Grove & Cedar Grove Area

The third largest tree in the world—the 267-foot tall General Grant—can be found at Grant Grove.

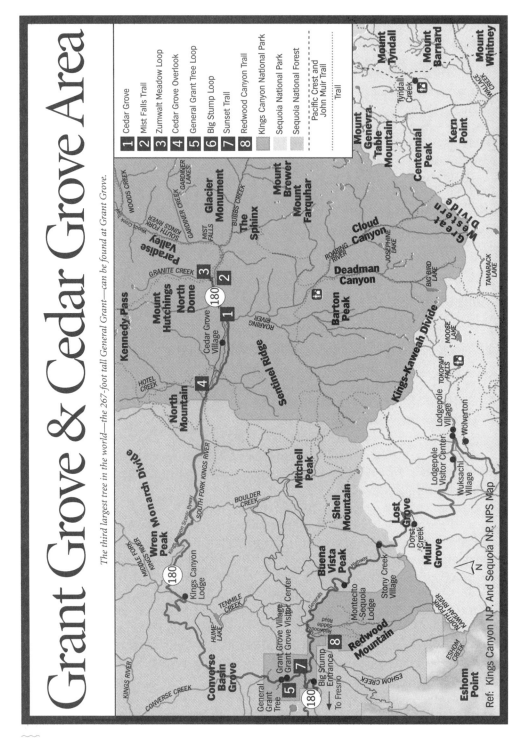

Legend:
1. Cedar Grove
2. Mist Falls Trail
3. Zumwalt Meadow Loop
4. Cedar Grove Overlook
5. General Grant Tree Loop
6. Big Stump Loop
7. Sunset Trail
8. Redwood Canyon Trail

Kings Canyon National Park
Sequoia National Park
Sequoia National Forest

Pacific Crest and John Muir Trail
Trail

Ref: Kings Canyon N.P. And Sequoia N.P. NPS Map

food in bags and carefully hang the bags from tree limbs to keep the food away from bears or other animals. If the food is hung high above the ground and far enough away from the trunk of the tree, many animals cannot reach it. The lodgepole chipmunk *(Eutamias specious)* and the yellow-bellied marmot *(Marmota flaviventris)* are also known to take food whenever possible.

Marmots can be seen on some of the high Sierra trails in the backcountry of Kings Canyon. In the granite rising above beautiful Rae Lakes on the eastern side of Kings Canyon, marmots munch Sierra saxifrage *(Saxifraga aprica)* and alpine goldenrod *(Solidago multiradiata)* until their bellies are full. Then they bask in the afternoon sunshine.

The eastern part of Kings Canyon remains primitive and relatively untouched compared to the western part. The eastern side has no paved entrance. From the east, the only way to enter is on a trail through passes, such as Kearsarge Pass at 11,823 feet. But the eastern part of the park contains the John Muir Trail, one of the busiest high Sierra walking routes and one of the best-known high-elevation trails in the world. While it may look pretty remote on the map, there are many people walking this trail.

CEDAR GROVE

[Fig. 53(1)] Backpackers and campers can find the wild Kings River and some of the most beautiful hiking trails in the Southern Sierra at Cedar Grove. Trails radiate in many directions to the backcountry, and from the campgrounds visitors can hear the river thundering in May and June as the snowmelt swells the Kings.

For hikers, it is usually best to start early in the day anywhere in the Sierra, but early is definitely much better at Cedar Grove. At about 4,600 feet in elevation—a mere 600 feet higher than Yosemite Valley—it gets warm in the afternoon at Cedar Grove. But the elevation also provides better weather earlier in the year for hiking. Some of the hikes can be steep and treacherous, so take care.

This is an area once considered for a highway through to the Eastern Sierra. But the plan was dropped in 1965, and the high Sierra beyond Cedar Grove remains free of paved roads, unlike the Northern and Central Sierra.

Cedar Grove also was considered as a place to dam the Kings River and create a reservoir, much as the city of San Francisco did at Hetch Hetchy Valley in Yosemite National Park. Los Angeles made the pitch early in the twentieth century, but Central Californians fought and delayed the effort long enough for supporters to run out of momentum.

In the meadows at the higher elevations around Cedar Grove, look for several kinds of grasses, including tufted hairgrass *(Deschampsia cespitosa)* and spiked trisetum *(Trisetum spicatum)*. Visitors also will find black sedge *(Carex nigricans)* and beaked sedge *(Carex rostrata)*, which are common in this part of the Sierra.

Directions: From the Big Stump Entrance Station on Highway 180, drive northeast for about 22 miles to the Cedar Grove Village.

Activities: Hiking, backpacking, camping, bird-watching, photography, and fishing.

Facilities: Four campgrounds with a total of 350 sites. The campgrounds include Canyon View, Sentinel, Sheep Creek, and Moraine. Ranger station, lodge, and pack station.

Dates: Highway 180 or Kings Canyon Highway is open in the warmer months only, generally mid-Apr. through Oct.

Fees: There is a fee to enter Kings Canyon National Park. There are also fees for camping.

Closest town: Squaw Valley, 22 miles.

For more information: Sequoia and Kings Canyon National Park, 47050 Generals Highway, Three Rivers, CA 93271. Phone (559) 565-3341.

MIST FALLS TRAIL

[Fig. 53(2)] Hikers who want to get a good look at Kings Canyon without pushing themselves too hard should consider the Mist Falls Trail. Many trails around this area gain elevation so quickly that it's just too much work to enjoy the view. This trail gains about 600 feet in elevation in full view of the South Fork Kings River as it tumbles and blasts through the rocks along this gorge.

In various places along this trail, hikers will see interesting combinations of chaparral in the driest areas and some sparse Jeffrey pine and lodgepole pine. In the chaparral community, look for the flower ash *(Fraxinus dipetala)*, birchleaf mountain mahogany *(Cercocarpus betuloides)*, and chaparral honeysuckle *(Lonicera interrupta)*. They are a few of the many species living close together in these plant communities.

Glacially carved features are easy to spot along the trail. A granite spire called The Sphinx can be seen to the east of the trail. Glaciers polished the granite in many places, leaving it smooth and sometimes slippery when wet. Do not climb around the rocks near the river because they are slippery and you could fall into the river.

The nicest thing about the Mist Falls Trail is that hikers can stop in many places for a picnic lunch and simply turn around if they are tired. The views are grand throughout the hike.

Directions: From the Big Stump Entrance Station on Highway 180, drive northeast for about 27 miles to Roads End at Cedar Grove and park in the first lot where wilderness information is available. The trailhead is on the east side of the parking lot.

Trail: 8 miles round-trip.

Elevation: 600-foot gain, 5,650-foot peak.

Degree of difficulty: Moderate.

Surface: Smooth granite, east to follow.

ZUMWALT MEADOW LOOP

[Fig. 53(3)] Stop here with the children for a quiet, easy stroll through nature. Visitors can see where Native Americans lived and created mortar holes into the granite as they ground acorns into a meal. The area is between the parking lot and the river where visitors might see mule deer *(Odocoileus hemionus)* browsing.

The acorns in this area come from the black oak *(Quercus kelloggii)*, a common tree here. Hikers also can find California hazelnut *(Corylus californica)* and thimbleberry *(Rubus parviflorus)*. The views include North Dome at 8,700 feet to the north.

The meadow is named after Daniel Zumwalt, a Tulare County lawyer who was instrumental in getting Congress to designate Sequoia and Kings Canyon as national parks. Zumwalt once owned the meadow.

Directions: From the Big Stump Entrance Station on Highway 180, drive 22 miles northeast to the Cedar Grove Village and ranger station. Continue on the same road for another 4.5 miles to the Zumwalt Meadow parking area, marked by a sign.

Trail: 1.5 miles.

Elevation: 50-foot gain, 5,000-foot peak.

Degree of difficulty: Easy.

Surface: Flat, open footpath. There is a short, wooden causeway near the end of the hike.

HOTEL CREEK TRAIL TO THE CEDAR GROVE OVERLOOK

[Fig. 53(4)] The Cedar Grove Overlook is where hikers go to see for miles all the way to the Great Western Divide to the east. From the overlook, people can look down the U shape of Kings Canyon.

But there's a price for this breath-taking view. You have to climb 1,400 feet to the top of the canyon. Carry a lot of water and start hiking early in the day.

The route to the overlook is called the Hotel Creek Trail. It was named for a camp that was established in the 1890s. Native Americans also used this area and the trail. They ate acorns from the black oak and the interior live oak *(Quercus wislizenii)*.

The live oak is easily distinguished from black oak because it is evergreen. Various year-round bird residents favor this tree for the insects that it attracts. Look for the Hutton's vireo *(Vireo huttoni)*, which nests in these trees.

Directions: From the Big Stump Entrance Station on Highway 180, drive 22 miles northeast to the Cedar Grove Village and turn left at the first access road. Drive 0.3 mile to the parking area near the pack station. The trail begins at the parking area.

Trail: 5 miles round-trip.

Elevation: 1,400-foot gain, 6,000-foot peak.

Degree of difficulty: Strenuous.

Surface: Granite with many short switchbacks.

GRANT GROVE

[Fig. 53] The third largest tree in the world—the 267-foot-tall General Grant—can be found at Grant Grove, where short loop trails allow visitors to tour both living and felled giant sequoia. For people in a hurry, Grant Grove is the easiest place to see in a short amount of time.

Congress first set this area aside in 1890 as the General Grant National Park. In all, Congress preserved about 2,400 acres along a historic migration route for Native

Americans in the area. Fifty years after Congress established it, the little park was absorbed into Kings Canyon National Park.

On the map, it still looks like an addition or appendage to the Sequoia-Kings Canyon National Parks. Grant Grove is at the western end of Sequoia-Kings Canyon along Highway 180, near the Big Stump Entrance Station where visitors choose either the Kings Canyon Highway to the left for Kings Canyon or the Generals Highway to the right for Sequoia National Park.

The height of the General Grant tree is impressive, but it is not among the tallest trees in the world. Its circumference is 107 feet, its volume of wood is estimated to be more than 47,000 cubic feet, and it probably weighs more than 2 million pounds. At more than 1,800 years old, the General Grant was growing a full millennium before Christ was born.

Along with the giant sequoia, the wild or western azalea *(Rhododendron occidentalis)* is particularly abundant and attractive at Grant Grove. It is found mostly in moist places below 7,500 feet. Grant Grove is at about 6,600 feet.

Within Grant Grove is a private community called Wilsonia. Such private communities inside national parks are not rare. Near Yosemite National Park, Yosemite West is a similar private community in the midst of public lands where development is restricted.

Directions: From Fresno, drive 52 miles east on Highway 180 to the Big Stump Entrance Station. Beyond entrance station, turn left on Kings Canyon Highway and drive about 1 mile to Grant Grove Visitor Center.

Activities: Hiking, photography, picnicking, camping, bicycling, snowplay, and bird-watching.

Facilities: Campgrounds include Azalea, Crystal Springs, and Sunset. There are more than 200 campsites available. Gas station, lodge, ranger station, restaurant, gift shop, and picnic areas.

Dates: Open year-round, but there are some temporary snow-related road closures in the winter. The best time to hike and camp is from May to Nov.

Fees: There is a fee for camping.

Closest town: Squaw Valley, 5 miles.

For more information: Sequoia-Kings Canyon National Parks, 47050 Generals Highway, Three Rivers, CA 93271. Phone (559) 565-3341.

GENERAL GRANT TREE LOOP

[Fig. 53(5)] A lot of people take this short loop trail because there is so much to see, and it is an easy jaunt for children. Often, children have fun playing around the Fallen Monarch, a giant sequoia that fell more than a century ago and has been hollowed out by fire. The fallen giant provided shelter for horses during storms when the park was first established in the 1890s.

The General Grant Tree is not much farther along the path. The tree, discovered in 1862 by Joseph Thomas, became the Nation's Christmas Tree in 1926. An annual event takes place on the second Sunday in December around the base of the tree to mark the holiday.

Other features along the trail include the massive Centennial Stump and Gamlin Cabin, which was one of the first ranger stations in General Grant National Park. Homesteader Israel Gamlin built the cabin in the 1870s. The Centennial Stump was part of a sequoia that was taken down in the 1870s.

Directions: From the Big Stump Entrance Station, turn left onto Kings Canyon Highway from Highway 180 and drive about 1.3 miles to the General Grant Tree Road, turn left. Drive 0.8 mile to the General Grant Tree parking area. The trail starts on the north side of the parking lot.

Trail: 0.5 mile.

Elevation: 75-foot gain, 6,400-foot peak.

Degree of difficulty: Easy.

Surface: Flat, paved footpath.

BIG STUMP LOOP

[Fig. 53(6)] The sights at Big Stump illustrate the history of logging among the giant sequoia in this part of the Sierra. Early in the 1880s, almost an entire grove of the giants had disappeared. The names of some trees and stumps speak for themselves: Shattered Tree, Burnt Monarch, Sawed Tree, and the Mark Twain Stump.

The Twain Stump is interesting because it was cut down after General Grant National Park was formed in 1890. Apparently the Twain tree was just outside the old boundary, which was updated 75 years later to include the stump in the protection of the park. A slice or cross-section of the tree was shipped to New York for display in the American Museum of Natural History.

One living specimen teaches an interesting lesson about the giant sequoia. A lightning strike took off the top 20 or 25 feet of the Resurrection Tree many years ago. The resilient tree appears to be growing a new top.

Directions: From Fresno, drive 52 miles east to Big Stump Entrance Station. Follow the signs to the parking area. The trail begins at the southern end of the parking lot, near the restrooms.

Trail: 1 mile.

Elevation: About 150-foot gain, 6,400-foot peak.

Degree of difficulty: Easy.

Surface: Open footpath, easy to follow.

SUNSET TRAIL

[Fig. 53(7)] Along this trail, hikers are likely to encounter herbaceous species such as Hartweg's ginger *(Asarum hartwegii)*, bride's bonnet *(Clintonia uniflora)*, and rattlesnake orchid *(Goodyera oblogifolia)*. The flora—including mountain dogwood *(Cornus nuttalli)*—is not found above about 7,000 feet in the Sierra. So, aside from the giant sequoia, the other vegetation makes this trail an attraction for many people.

Hikers will see a waterfall along Sequoia Creek, called Ella Falls. The banks and meadows around the creek contain white alder *(Alnus rhombifolia)* and arroyo willow *(Salix lasiolepis)*.

The hike also allows visitors to see Sequoia Lake from a distance. The lake was created in the late 1880s when Sequoia Creek was dammed. Lumber companies used the lake as part of their flume operations, which sent logs down to the San Joaquin Valley.

Directions: From the Big Stump Entrance Station on Highway 180, drive 1 mile to the junction of Highway 180, Kings Canyon Highway, and Generals Highway. Turn left on Kings Canyon Highway and drive about 1 mile to the Grant Grove Visitor Center and park. Trail signs will direct you across the highway—in the crosswalk—to the Sunset Campground where the trail begins.

Trail: 6 miles.

Elevation: 1,200-foot gain, 6,600-foot peak.

Degree of difficulty: Moderate.

Surface: An old fire road, granite and dirt trail with a bridge crossing over a creek.

REDWOOD MOUNTAIN

[Fig. 53] Visitors can find the sixth largest grove of giant sequoia in the world at Redwood Mountain. It was logged briefly in the late nineteenth century, but more than 2,000 giants remain at Redwood Mountain and several trails offer hikers spectacular views of the trees. Among the giants are sugar pines *(Pinus lambertiana)*, which can grow to 200 feet tall and 5 or 6 feet in diameter at the base, but visitors will have little trouble distinguishing between these two types of trees.

The giants thrive in white fir forests, which receive 40 to 60 inches of precipitation per year. But the giants must have moist soil even during the summer months, and the ones that receive adequate moisture throughout the year will grow the largest.

One of the more curious sights in Redwood Canyon is Redwood Log Cabin. It truly is a "log" cabin—a cabin made from one very large, hollow sequoia log. Park officials believe it was built by a tungsten miner in the late 1800s. The miner apparently placed boards over holes in the floor and built stone fireplaces at each end. The cabin can be seen along Redwood Canyon Trail.

The federal government bought the Redwood Mountain area in 1940 after mining and logging had ended. It was included in Kings Canyon National Park by presidential order. Today the Redwood Mountain area is probably the least noticed among visitors, but it has much natural history to offer.

Directions: From the Grant Grove Visitor Center *(see* page 276), drive about 5.2 miles southeast on Highway 180, which becomes the Generals Highway. From the Generals Highway, turn right on narrow, unpaved Redwood Saddle Road, and drive another 2 miles to the parking area, which will be on your left.

Activities: Hiking, backpacking, picnicking, photography, and bird-watching.

Facilities: None.

Dates: Open May through Nov. The area is closed in the colder months.
Fees: None.
Closest town: Grant Grove Village, 4 miles, or Squaw Valley, 5 miles.
For more information: Sequoia-Kings Canyon National Parks, 47050 Generals Highway, Three Rivers, CA 93271. Phone (559) 565-3341.

REDWOOD CANYON TRAIL

[Fig. 53(8)] Aside from the Redwood Log Cabin about 5 miles from the trailhead, the giant sequoia and the gorgeous views are the main reasons to hike this trail. Redwood Mountain, a 7,001-foot granite peak to the west, is framed perfectly for photographing between the giants along the first 2 miles of the hike. To the east, hikers will see 7,605-foot Buena Vista Peak.

Many hikers with children choose to just walk about 2.5 miles to the Redwood Creek crossing and turn around. The trail runs along the creek for almost 2 miles, showing off greenish-yellow blossoms on the California dogwood (*Cornus nuttallii*). In May, the blossoms are particularly beautiful. By early autumn, the trees' pink and reddish leaves light up the forest.

The migratory birds in this and other areas along the Redwood Canyon Trail are richly diverse. Look for the yellow warbler (*Dendroica petechia*), the MacGillivray's warbler (*Oporornis tolmiei*), and the Swainson's thrush (*Catharus ustulatus*).

The giants include the Hart Tree and Fallen Goliath. The Hart tree was named for William Hart, who owned a sawmill and almost 100 acres in this area during the 1880s. But there are hundreds of unnamed sequoias, many with diameters larger than 10 feet. In the surrounding forest, there are incense cedars and white firs.

At one point near the end of the trail, which concludes at Big Springs, hikers will see a sign warning them to stay away from a research area where scientists want to study the ecosystem without human disturbance. The area is one of several places where researchers studied the effects of fire on sequoia ecosystems in the 1960s and 1970s.

Like most trees in the Sierra, the sequoia periodically needs a fairly hot fire to burn out the underbrush and give the trees room to grow and reproduce. For many decades in the twentieth century, federal officials snuffed fires at the first sign of smoke. The result was a lot of brush growth and the potential for very large fires that would reach the canopies of large trees and destroy groves of older trees. Federal officials now incorporate fire into forest management, allowing some blazes to burn.

Directions: The Redwood Canyon Trail begins on the east side of the parking lot at Redwood Saddle (*see* directions to Redwood Mountain, page 278).
Trail: 13 miles round-trip.
Elevation: 1,600-foot gain, 6,400-foot peak.
Degree of difficulty: Moderate to strenuous.
Surface: Well-established granite and dirt trail. One section includes an old four-wheel-drive roadbed.

Sequoia National Park

The 275-foot-tall General Sherman, the largest living tree in the world, is estimated to weigh almost 1,400 tons and is located in Giant Forest.

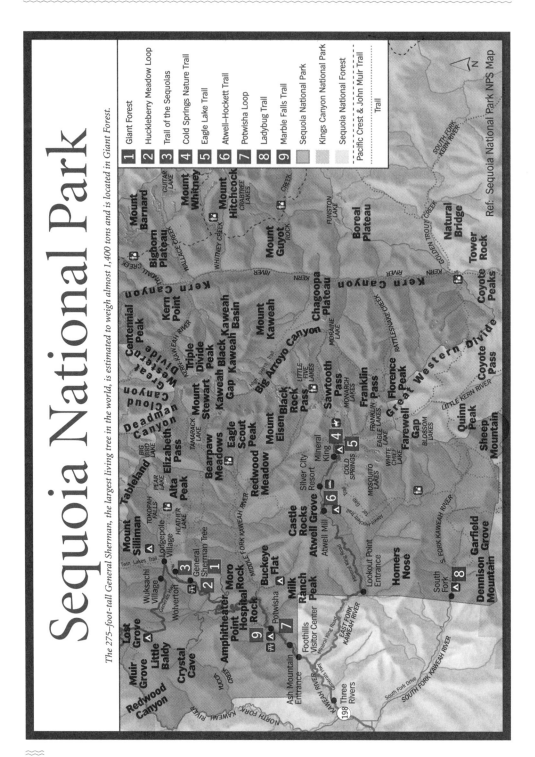

1 Giant Forest
2 Huckleberry Meadow Loop
3 Trail of the Sequoias
4 Cold Springs Nature Trail
5 Eagle Lake Trail
6 Atwell–Hockett Trail
7 Potwisha Loop
8 Ladybug Trail
9 Marble Falls Trail

Sequoia National Park
Kings Canyon National Park
Sequoia National Forest
Pacific Crest & John Muir Trail
Trail

Ref: Sequoia National Park NPS Map

Sequoia National Park

[Fig. 54] About 100 miles north of Sequoia National Park, millions of people crowd into the outdoor cathedral of Yosemite National Park to see the wonders of the Sierra Nevada. But the visitors in Sequoia are counted in tens of thousands, not the millions, and they see a less crowded version of Sierra paradise.

Established in 1890, the 400,000-acre Sequoia National Park has 12,000-foot peaks to the east, extensive foothill trails to the west, and several of the most stunning giant sequoia groves in the world, including Giant Forest. The 275-foot-tall General Sherman, the largest living tree in the world, is estimated to weigh almost 1,400 tons and is in Giant Forest.

In honor of the big trees in Giant Forest, George Stewart, editor of a Visalia newspaper and a long-time advocate for giant sequoias in the area, suggested the name, Sequoia National Park, when the park was established in September 1890. Austrian scholar Stephen Endlicher gave the tree its scientific name in 1947. No documentation exists to establish why he named it "sequoia," but most experts agree the new genus name was to honor Sequoyah, the Cherokee Indian.

There are 73 sequoia groves or grove systems in the Sierra, according to the latest federal surveys. Mapping of the groves shows there is one in Tahoe National Forest, two in the Calaveras Big Trees State Park in the Central Sierra, three in Yosemite National Park, and two in the Sierra National Forest. The rest are in Sequoia National Forest and Sequoia-Kings Canyon National Parks. And, the largest of the trees are in Sequoia National Park.

But there is more to Sequoia National Park than trees. The North, Middle, and South forks of the Kaweah River drain the western section of the park, while the Kern River runs south through the eastern side of the park. On the farthest east flank of the park, 14,498-foot Mount Whitney is partially within the boundary.

Hiking, backpacking, and cross-country skiing are the biggest activities in Sequoia National Park, but people also like the scenic driving along the Generals Highway. The highway enters from the northwest, bringing vehicles from Highway 180 in Kings Canyon. The Generals Highway also enters the park from the southwest at Ash Mountain where the name changes from Highway 198 to the Generals Highway. The Mount Whitney Power Company originally built part of the road early in the twentieth century to provide access for flume construction in the area. The federal government finished the road in the 1920s.

Along the Generals Highway, about 3 miles from the General Sherman Tree, is the Lodgepole Campground where visitors will find the Walter Fry Nature Center. The center has hands-on exhibits and displays of natural processes in Sequoia park. It bears Fry's name because he was so deeply involved with a nature tour program for the public that started in 1922.

Fry came to Sequoia in the late 1880s as a logger, but it didn't take him long to join the movement to preserve Sequoia. He later worked as a ranger at Sequoia. Eventually, he became a U.S. Commissioner, or a judge, in the federal parks system. After he retired in 1930, he devoted himself to informing the public about Sequoia and the natural processes throughout the park.

Visitors take the Mineral King Road on a slow, windy trip to a settlement in one of the most beautiful alpine settings in the Sierra—Mineral King. Remnants of the logging industry are still along this road, particularly at the Atwell Mill. Though Mineral King began in the 1870s with mining claims, it became known for logging and recreation.

Mineral King supporters fought to protect trees from logging many decades ago. Then, in the 1970s, they waged a successful fight against the Disney Corporation to prevent a commercial ski resort from being built. These days, the fight is between families who had long-term use permits on cabins and the National Park Service, which contends the land belongs to the public.

Mineral King Valley's floor is 7,500 feet, so vegetation is different from the foothills in Sequoia. In the moist meadows of the valley, the Sierra bilberry *(Vaccinium nivictum)*, marsh marigold *(Caltha howellii)*, and wandering daisy *(Erigeron peregrinus)* may be found.

Sequoia National Park's natural charms are not immune from the ecological pressures of a burgeoning population in the nearby San Joaquin Valley. Ground-level ozone, or smog, from the valley drifts up to the park in the summer, causing needle damage to many Jeffrey pines.

The ozone, created mostly by automobile emissions during warm, sunny days, does not seem to bother the mature giant sequoias, but it does appear to affect their seedlings. Experts say there is no way to determine if the valley's air—which ranks among the dirtiest in the nation—will eventually begin to damage the giants.

But the smog story gets even worse for the Sierra. Smog levels curiously appear to remain higher for longer periods of time in the Sierra because there is not as much evening traffic here as there is in the valley. The additional emissions from traffic in the valley appear to scavenge ozone and reduce it. Because the Sierra traffic is almost nonexistent at night, there is no scavenging or reduction on calm, windless evenings.

Directions: From Visalia, drive 35 miles east on Highway 198 to the Ash Mountain Entrance. The Sequoia-Kings Canyon National Park headquarters is located at the entrance.

Activities: Hiking, camping, swimming, picnicking, photography, backpacking, fishing, and bird-watching.

Facilities: Bathrooms and picnic tables.

Dates: Open year-round.

Fees: There is an entrance fee.

Closest town: Three Rivers, 4 miles.

For more information: Sequoia-Kings Canyon National Parks, 47050 Generals

Highway, Three Rivers, CA 93271-9651. Phone (559) 565-3341.

🏛 GIANT FOREST

[Fig. 54(1)] People come to Giant Forest to visit the largest living things on earth—the giant sequoia. Trails cross in many directions, giving people the chance to walk at the feet of trees that are estimated to be between 1,800 and 3,200 years old. There are hundreds of giants of that age in Giant Forest.

The 1,800-acre Giant Forest has about 8,400 trees with a diameter of at least 18 inches. The Redwood Mountain grove,

Golden Trout

The golden trout (*Oncorhynchus aguabonita*) is native to the upper Kern River basin, where it was isolated and evolved separately from other trout. It is believed to be a hybrid of rainbow trout (*Oncorhynchus mykiss*) and cutthroat trout (*Oncorhynchus clarki*). The golden trout are found in cold, high mountain lakes above 8,000 feet. Usually fishing enthusiasts have to hike into the wilderness to catch one of these fish.

with more than 15,000 sequoias, has more trees, but Giant Forest is extraordinary because it has so many of the largest giants. Three of the five biggest sequoias in the world are in Giant Forest. They include the General Sherman, the Lincoln, and the Washington trees.

The largest sequoia is the General Sherman, which is about 272 feet tall and almost 37 feet in diameter. A closer look at the Sherman tree reveals why Giant Forest grows so many large trees. It stands in moist soil at about 6,700 feet in elevation, and it grows like no tree anywhere on earth. In the last five decades, it has grown enough wood to build an average-sized home in Central California. Its lowest branch, more than 7 feet in diameter, would crush a car if it fell off. The Sherman tree is estimated to be more than 2,000 years old, but nobody has invented a coring instrument yet that can extract a sample deep enough in the tree to confirm the age.

The Sherman tree, and likewise hundreds of others in this area, has shallow roots that spread hundreds of feet in all directions. Giant Forest has plenty of moisture in the soil, even during summer, and plenty of room for the roots to spread. The trees' ideal growing conditions exist on the western slope of the Sierra in a belt between 5,000 and 7,000 feet. It is uncommon to find giant sequoia outside of this belt in the Sierra.

In the last century, people have built roads, buildings, and trails around these trees. The National Park Service has even had a primitive sewage treatment plant in this grove to process the wastes from motel cabins, a restaurant, and restrooms. Scientists are not certain how the trees have been affected, but the federal government is not waiting for one of the giants' shallow root systems to be compromised and a tree to fall over.

Throughout the 1990s, the federal government has slowly closed down the motel and restaurant operations at Giant Forest Village. Now, nobody spends the night at the feet of the giants. The motel rooms, cabins, and a hodge-podge of buildings have been torn down and removed. People visit during the day, and they can still find a natural history museum to visit as well as restrooms. But the trees and the wildlife are left alone at night.

About 5 miles north of Giant Village, the federal government and the park concessionaire have designed and constructed Wuksachi Village, which has a hotel, restaurant, gift shop, and other amenities. Wuksachi is out of the giant sequoia belt. It is built on granite, not the soil that supports the giant sequoias' shallow root systems.

Hiking is the main activity around Giant Forest, but there is also cross-country skiing in the winter. The trails are clearly marked with yellow triangles for skiers. A favorite cross-country skiing area at Giant Forest is Wolverton, which is northeast of the Sherman tree.

Directions: From the Ash Mountain Entrance Station where Highway 198 turns into the Generals Highway, drive 12 miles north to Giant Forest. From the Big Stump Entrance Station on Highway 180 in Kings Canyon National Park, drive about 1 mile to the junction of Highway 180 and the Generals Highway. Turn right on the Generals Highway and drive about 26 miles to Giant Forest.

Activities: Hiking, photography, bird-watching, skiing, and picnicking.

Facilities: Restrooms, bookstore, and museum.

Dates: Open year-round, but subject to closures during winter snowfall.

Fees: There is a fee to enter Sequoia National Park. There is no day-use fee at Giant Forest.

Closest town: Three Rivers, 16 miles.

For more information: Sequoia and Kings Canyon National Park, 47050 Generals Highway, Three Rivers, CA 93271. Phone (559) 565-3341.

HUCKLEBERRY MEADOW LOOP

[Fig. 54(2)] The meadows, Squatter's Cabin, and Native American grinding stones or mortars make the Huckleberry Meadow Loop an interesting hike. The trail begins at Hazelwood Nature Trail, which goes about 0.4 mile to a junction with the trail that goes to Bear Hill. Decades ago at Bear Hill, the park landfill for many years, visitors would gather to watch the black bears sort through the garbage. The dump was closed in 1940 after bears became more aggressive in their search for handouts.

Jeffrey pines surround the meadows in high rocky places around the area. In the meadows and below the trees, visitors may see white-veined wintergreen (*Pyrola picta*), spotted coralroot (*Corallorhiza maculata*), and pinedrops (*Pterospora andromedea*).

An unnamed settler built Squatter's Cabin next to Huckleberry Meadow in the 1880s as an attempt to claim the land. However, rancher Hale Tharp, who owned the property, had already homesteaded the land.

The Native Americans around Giant Forest were probably a Mono-related tribe, such as the Tubatulabal. The bedrock mortars they left behind can be found beyond Huckleberry Meadow as the trail loops back toward Generals Highway.

Directions: From the Ash Mountain Entrance Station, drive about 12.5 miles on the Generals Highway to the Hazelwood Nature Trail parking area just east of Giant Village. The Huckleberry Meadow Loop coincides with the Hazelwood Nature trail for about 0.4 mile.

Trail: 4 miles.

Elevation: 500-foot gain, 6,900-foot peak.

Degree of difficulty: Moderate.

Surface: Granite and dirt with a few short, steep climbs.

TRAIL OF THE SEQUOIAS

[Fig. 54(3)] The Trail of the Sequoias is the trail of choice for those who want to experience the giant sequoia forest. It begins and ends at the General Sherman Tree, which was discovered by James Wolverton in the late 1870s. The tree's name was briefly changed to the Karl Marx Tree in the 1880s when a group of socialists tried to settle in the area. They soon departed, and the name reverted to General Sherman.

Hikers may notice the cones hanging from the giant sequoia. There are sometimes 30,000 or 40,000 of them on a single mature giant. Seeds drop from the cones in a variety of ways. The cones also react to fire. The heat opens them and the lightweight seeds spill in all directions onto the ash below.

Yet, the tens of thousands of seeds rarely take hold and produce a giant sequoia. Seedling studies show that almost 99 percent of young sequoias die in the first two summers. Very few make it to maturity.

Hikers may be able to see a permanent resident of the sequoia—the white-headed woodpecker *(Dendrocopus albolarvatus)*. It is often in plain view high in the giant trees. Other birds in the forest include the dark-eyed junco *(Junco oreganus)*, black-headed grosbeak *(Pheucticus melanocephalus)*, and golden-crowned kinglet *(Regulus satrapa)*.

Directions: From the Ash Mountain Entrance Station, drive about 13 miles north on the Generals Highway to the parking lot at the General Sherman Tree. The trail-head is on the northeast end of the parking lot.

Trail: 6-mile loop.

Elevation: About 500-foot gain, 7,300-foot peak.

Degree of difficulty: Moderate.

Surface: Well-established dirt path.

▓ MINERAL KING

[Fig. 54] In spring, just after the snowmelt, Mineral King Valley is one of those places that seems unaffected by the passing of time. The twisting little two-lane road, the lack of big crowds, and the stunning, granite ridgelines help hikers experience the unvarnished wonder of nature. Unfortunately, the valley is not always serene and free of conflict. In midsummer, it can be just as crowded as any other destination in the Sierra. And Mineral King has never had a shortage of controversy.

Visitors have been coming to Mineral King for hiking, swimming, backpacking, camping, and fishing for most of the twentieth century. It is still an outdoor recreational haven, but its land is now managed by the National Park Service, not the U.S. Forest Service. The difference is not subtle.

As part of the Forest Service, which is an arm of Department of Agriculture, the valley was open for many commercial ventures—mining, generating hydroelectric power, grazing, and developing downhill ski resorts. As part of the Park Service, an arm of the Department of Interior, Mineral King became a sanctuary for wildlife and virtually untouchable for commercial development.

The move came in 1978 in Mineral King after a protracted battle between commercial interests and environmentalists. Both sides were among the many people who have coveted this glacial valley at 7,500 feet. In the late 1800s, miners struck gold and silver, but their luck didn't hold very long. In the early twentieth century, hydroelectric companies built dams at the outlets of several Mineral King Lakes and generated electrical power. Logging of giant sequoia also took place early in the century.

By the 1970s, the Walt Disney Corporation wanted to widen Mineral King Road into a highway and build a massive commercial ski resort to attract thousands of Southern Californians in the winter. To dozens of families who have leased cabins at Mineral King for decades, the Disney plan was unthinkable. Joining environmentalists, they successfully fought to move Mineral King out of Sequoia National Forest and into Sequoia National Park.

These days, there's no controversy over development, but that doesn't mean there is no controversy. Now, the National Park Service is interested in allowing public access to the park land where the cabins are located. That one has not yet been resolved.

The latest argument has little impact for hikers and backpackers traveling the steep trails around Mineral King. They will see meadow vegetation such as marsh marigold *(Caltha leptosepala* var. *biflora)*, squirreltail *(Elymus elymoides)*, and beaked sedge *(Carex utriculata).* The jagged granite of the Sierra is visible toward 11,680-foot Franklin Pass to the south. Nearby, Florence Peak is 12,432 feet. Some people say the scene reminds them a lot of the Alps.

The birds at Mineral King are quite an attraction as well. In summer, hikers can see seasonal residents such as the white-throated swift *(Aeromautes saxatalis)*, hermit warbler *(Dendroica occidentalis)*, solitary vireo *(Vireso solitarius)*, and olive-sided flycatcher *(Nuttalornis borealis).*

Directions: From Three Rivers, drive about 2 miles northeast on Highway 198 and turn right on Mineral King Road. Drive about 25 miles east to Mineral King.

Activities: Hiking, backpacking, camping, fishing, bird-watching, and photography.

Facilities: Ranger station, two campgrounds west of the ranger station (Cold

Springs Campground with 37 sites and Atwell Mill campgrounds with 21 sites), pack station, and restrooms.

Dates: Open from May to Oct. The Mineral King Road closes each winter.

Fees: There is a fee to camp and a fee to enter Sequoia National Park on the Mineral King Road.

Closest town: Silver City, 7 miles.

For more information: Sequoia and Kings Canyon National Park, 47050 Generals Highway, Three Rivers, CA 93271. Phone (559) 565-3341.

COLD SPRINGS NATURE TRAIL

[Fig. 54(4)] The Cold Springs Nature Trail is considered a good starting point for anyone visiting Mineral Springs Valley for the first time. If you have just driven the 25-mile Mineral King Road, you may be a bit dizzy from the windy route. Mineral King Valley is also 7,500 feet in elevation, which is high enough to cause shortness of breath for some people. The Cold Springs Nature Trail is an easy walk that allows visitors to start adjusting to the thinner air.

In June the flowers are colorful and plentiful. They are red, blue, white, pink, and many other shades. The splash of color set against the snow-capped ridges to the east is almost startling. Look for American wintercress *(Barbarea orthoceras)*, alpine veronica *(Veronica americana)*, and mouse-ear chickweed *(Cerastium glomeratum)*. Signs along the self-guided nature trail describe many other plants of Mineral King.

The cabins seen on the first part of the hike were part of an 1870s settlement that resulted from the gold and silver mining in the area. The settlement lasted about 30 years before the mining craze died down and an avalanche struck the cabins, wiping many of them out.

Directions: From Three Rivers, drive about 2 miles northeast on Highway 198 and turn right on Mineral King Road. Drive about 26 miles, bear right at the fork in the road, and park at the Eagle-Mosquito parking area. It is the end of Mineral King Road. The trailhead is at the northwest end of the parking lot.

Trail: 2 miles round-trip.

Elevation: About 350-foot gain on the way back, 7,850-foot peak.

Degree of difficulty: Easy.

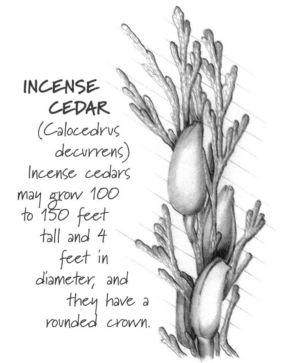

INCENSE CEDAR
(Calocedrus decurrens)
Incense cedars may grow 100 to 150 feet tall and 4 feet in diameter, and they have a rounded crown.

Surface: Open granite and dirt walkway.

EAGLE LAKE TRAIL

[Fig. 54(5)] For many fishing enthusiasts, a day of fun at Mineral King means a short but tough hike up to Eagle Lake and a relaxing time hauling in trout. Hikers like this trail because it passes by a sink hole where Eagle Creek disappears and the views of the surrounding high Southern Sierra are breathtaking.

Wildflower lovers will enjoy this trip as well. In the first mile or so near Eagle Creek, hikers may see streamside bluebells *(Mertensia ciliata)*, corn lily *(Veratrum californicum)*, and California hesperochiron *(Hesperochiron californicus)*. Farther along the trail, look for the blue and white of the Torrey's blue-eyed Mary *(Collinsia torreyi)*. Higher in the open areas, there is timberline phacelia *(Phacelia hastata* ssp. *compacta)*, a white flower that can be found at elevations to 10,000 feet in June and July.

The sinkhole is at about 9,000 feet. Around the sink hole, notice the white-and-gray marble mixed in with the granite. Farther along the trail as you pass red fir trees, the vegetation becomes sparser toward 10,000 feet.

Eagle Lake was affected by efforts to generate hydroelectric power in the early twentieth century. There is a dam on the north end of the lake. The lake was used decades ago as a regulating reservoir for a hydroelectric generating project near Three Rivers.

Directions: Follow the directions given for Cold Springs Nature Trail, page 287. The trailhead is at the south end of the Eagle-Mosquito parking area.

Trail: 7 miles round-trip.

Elevation: 2,400-foot gain, 10,000-foot peak.

Degree of difficulty: Moderate.

Surface: Granite with steep switchbacks.

ATWELL-HOCKETT TRAIL

[Fig. 54(6)] People can compare the giant sequoia with the massive sugar pine and see the difference along this trail. And there is a significant difference. Some sugar pines can grow as tall as 200 feet with a diameter of 7 feet. But some of the smaller, mature sequoias are 13 feet in diameter. Their thick, fibrous bark is cinnamon colored, quite different from the grainy bark of the sugar pine. The sugar pine, however, does have a larger cone.

The stumps along the first part of the trail are worth seeing as well. Around the old Atwell Mill, there are stumps left by loggers who cut down giant sequoias in the 1870s and 1880s. The stumps are pretty impressive. In the old logging mill, hikers can see machinery dating back to the nineteenth century.

Toward the Kaweah River on this trail, wildflower enthusiasts may see the scarlet monkeyflower *(Mimiulus cardinalis)*, whisker brush *(Linanthus ciliatus)*, and perhaps explorer's gentian *(Gentiana calycosa)*. Also, if hikers arrive in late May or early June, they may catch a glimpse of mitten-leaf nemophila *(Nemophila spatulata)*, which appears briefly as meadows slowly begin drying out for the summer.

Directions: From the junction of Highway 198 and Mineral King Road just north of Three Rivers, drive about 20 miles east on Mineral King Road and turn right into the Atwell Mill Campground parking lot. The trailhead is on the west end of the parking lot.

Trail: 4 miles round-trip.

Elevation: 800-foot gain, 6,600-foot peak.

Degree of difficulty: Easy to moderate.

Surface: Granite.

🌾 FOOTHILLS

To those who do not understand the diverse and compelling ecosystem in the foothills, it may appear they are something to be endured along the drive to the high country. It is understandable why the foothills in the Southern Sierra are not popular compared to the coniferous forests at higher elevations. In the summer, it is hot. Who wants to take a sweaty hike around a bunch of boulders, plain-looking brush, and dried grasslands?

But a quick look around the foothill areas of Sequoia National Park will give hikers a good reason to spend time in the foothills—in fall, winter, or spring. Go to a soothing stream near the Kaweah River and see trees that cannot be found in higher elevations. Fremont cottonwood *(Populus fremontii)*, sandbar willow *(Salix exigua)*, white alder *(Alnus rhombifolia)*, and western sycamore *(Platanus racemosa)* are just a few.

Periodic drought plagues the Southern Sierra foothills, just as it does the Central Valley of California. At 2,000 feet and below, Sequoia National Park headquarters routinely receives less than 15 inches of rainfall a year, compared to more than 35 inches at 7,000 feet. By midsummer, only the most drought-tolerant plants can survive. The blue oak *(Quercus douglasii)* is one of the more resilient trees found living in dry conditions around the foothills.

But, if hikers arrive in early April, the wildflowers will be waiting. The more common ones include popcorn flower *(Plagiobothrys nothofulvis)*, purple owl's clover *(Castilleja exserta)*, wind poppy *(Stylomecon heterophylla)*, California milkmaids *(Cardamine californica)*, and tower mustard *(Arabis glabra)*.

The grasslands are lush and green with such introduced species as foxtail fescue *(Vulpia myuros)* and soft chess *(Bromus hordeaceous)*. The bunchgrasses that once dominated the California foothills are now largely gone. They have been replaced by European species that arrived with settlers in the nineteenth century. With a keen eye, visitors might be able to spot native grasses such as purple needlegrass *(Nassella pulchra)*.

The animal communities swell with migrants every fall and winter. Birds particularly like to look for food in the foothills. Common birds include the red-winged blackbird *(Agelaius phoeniceus)*, American kestrel *(Falco sparverius)*, golden eagle *(Aquila chrysaetos)*, and western bluebird *(Sialia mexicana)*. And there are many more species—far more than in the higher elevations.

The mammals are interesting as well. The foothills provide habitat for the ornate shrew *(Sorex ornatus)*, San Joaquin Valley pocket mouse *(Perognathus inoratus)*, and broad-handed mole *(Scapanus latimanus)*. The reptile and amphibian populations are considerably larger and more diverse here as well.

The western rattlesnake *(Crotalus viridis)* is the most lethal reptile in the foothills. It hides in wait for its prey, strikes, and injects poisonous venom. It does not hunt humans, nor is it easy to see. Most of the time when people are bitten, it is because they have not watched the trail carefully. Western rattlesnake bites are dangerous, but few people actually run into the snakes on the trails.

Directions: From Visalia, drive about 32 miles northeast on Highway 198 to the Ash Mountain Entrance. Many foothill hikes are within about 8 miles of the entrance along on the Generals Highway. But other trails can be found near the town of Three Rivers, about 5 miles south of the entrance on Highway 198.

Activities: Hiking, camping, swimming, bird-watching, and photography.

Facilities: Potwisha Campground offers 44 sites, flush toilets, amphitheater, and sanitary disposal station for recreational vehicles. Buckeye Flat Campground offers 21 sites and flush toilets but no recreational vehicle sites or facilities. There is a picnic area at Hospital Rock.

Dates: Open year-round, but subject to periodic closures in winter due to weather.

Fees: There is a fee to enter the park and to use the campgrounds.

Closest town: Three Rivers, 4 miles.

For more information: Sequoia-Kings Canyon National Park, 47050 Generals Highway, Three Rivers, CA 93271. Phone (559) 565-3341.

POTWISHA LOOP

[Fig. 54(7)] The Native American bedrock mortar or grinding holes and the pictographs are the main reasons to stop at Potwisha Loop, but the white-leaf manzanita *(Arctostaphylos viscida)* is beautiful in bloom. The bell-shaped white and rose-colored flowers can be seen as early as March around Potwisha. Other vegetation in this lower-level part of the Southern Sierra includes chaparral honeysuckle *(Lonicera interrupta)*, holly-leaf redberry *(Rhamus ilicifolia)*, and California coffeeberry *(Rhamus californica)*.

Archaeologists say a Monache tribe once lived around here. The pictographs, which are supposed to refer to tribal women, can be found on rocks near the grinding holes. The Middle Fork of the Kaweah River provides a few places where visitors can swim. Anyone who has spent a 90-degree day in the foothills during summer when water levels are low knows it is quite an advantage to have a place to cool off.

Directions: From the Ash Mountain Entrance Station, drive about 4 miles east on the Generals Highway to Potwisha Campground on the left. Instead of turning into the campground, turn right on a paved access road and drive about 0.2 mile to the end of the road. The trailhead and a restroom can be found at the end of the road.

Trail: 0.6 mile.

Elevation: 100-foot gain, 2,100-foot peak.

Degree of difficulty: Easy.

Surface: Well-worn granite and dirt path.

LADYBUG TRAIL

[Fig. 54(8)] The fishing along the South Fork of the Kaweah River is one of the big attractions on the Ladybug Trail. Rainbow trout, brown trout, and golden trout are caught on this stretch of river.

A lot of the other wildlife in the area is not usually found in the higher elevations. Along the Kaweah, visitors may see the tiger salamander *(Ambystoma tigrinum)*, ensatina *(Ensatina eschscholtzi)*, and California newt *(Taricha torosa)*. Mammals often found in this area are the ornate shrew *(Sorex ornatus)*, ringtail *(Bassariscus astutus)*, and gray fox *(Urocyon cinereoargenteus)*.

A little more than 1 mile beyond the trailhead, hikers will find a grove of giant sequoia. The sequoias here are considered to be among the lowest elevation giants in the world.

Directions: From Three Rivers on Highway 198, turn right on South Fork Drive and continue about 14 miles to the park line at South Fork Campground. The trailhead is at the end of the dirt road in the campground. It is marked with a sign.

Trail: 6 miles round-trip.

Elevation: 1,380-foot gain, 4,990-foot peak.

Degree of difficulty: Moderate.

Surface: Granite and dirt path, one bridge.

MARBLE FALLS TRAIL

[Fig. 54(9)] Hikers can see evidence of marble deposits in the Sierra granite along the Marble Fork Trail. The marble is visible in white and gray streaks of rocky outcroppings near Marble Falls.

The foothills of Sequoia National Park and Sequoia National Forest have many of these areas where marble, or crystalline limestone, occur. This is rock dating back more than 150 million years—perhaps as far back as 250 million years. It changed over time into marble because it was calcareous and crystalline.

The Marble Fork of the Kaweah River along the Marble Falls Trail is also known as a great stretch of fishing, though fishing enthusiasts must take care in the steep areas. The water is not laced with dissolved minerals, but it does

TIGER SALAMANDER (*Ambystoma tigrinum*)

contain plenty of dissolved oxygen, which trout need to survive.

For those who know nothing of poison oak *(Toxicodendron diversilobum)*, this hike would be a good place for a crash course. The plant is a widespread shrub in the foothills of Sequoia park. In autumn its red foliage is beautiful and most impressive along the Marble Falls Trail. Unfortunately, it can cause severe skin irritation and rashes on many people. Don't touch it. In fact, even contact with clothing that has touched it will often produce the skin irritation, especially in this part of the Sierra where poison oak grows large and healthy.

Directions: From the Ash Mountain Entrance Station, drive about 4 miles east on the Generals Highway and turn left into Potwisha Campground. At the north end of the campground, park in a small lot and find the trailhead nearby.

Trail: 6 miles round-trip.

Elevation: 2,500-foot gain, 4,550-foot peak.

Degree of difficulty: Strenuous.

Surface: Gravel road, granite, and dirt. It is steep with switchbacks in a few areas.

Sequoia National Forest

[Fig. 52, Fig. 53, Fig. 54] The majority of the giant sequoia groves in the Sierra can be found in the Sequoia National Forest, but this forest is much more than a place to see the big trees. The 1.2 million-acre Sequoia forest, established in 1908, contains about 25 percent of the flora species found in California. More than 100 species of plants have been found at Bald Mountain, including the Bald Mountain potentilla *(Horkelia tularensis)*, which cannot be found anywhere else in the world.

People come to the Sequoia primarily for the hiking, backpacking, horseback riding, river rafting, and fishing. At the southern end of the Sierra Nevada, spring comes earlier in the year, so the snowmelt starts earlier than in northern parts of the range. Hikers find they can get into the backcountry in the Southern Sierra weeks ahead of hikers in the Central and Northern Sierra.

The reason the Southern Sierra is relatively dry is that Pacific Ocean storms typically approach from the northwest. The storms usually lose much of their precipitation in the Northern and Central Sierra before they reach the Southern Sierra. However, storm patterns can shift and come from the southwest, packing a lot of precipitation. As always in the Sierra, it is best to be prepared for storms at any time in Sequoia National Forest.

The most primitive and pristine sights in the Sequoia can be found in vast wildernesses along the range's crest, including the Monarch, Dome Land, Jennie Lakes, and parts of the South Sierra and Golden Trout wildernesses. The South Sierra and Golden Trout wildernesses are shared with the Inyo National Forest in the Eastern Sierra.

The glacial canyons are deep and the rivers are wild in this part of the Southern

Sierra. Photographers love the landscape here. Throughout Sequoia forest, visitors will see remnants of previous times when logging, grazing, and mining were more widespread than they are today. Indeed, the Sequoia has slowly become more of a recreational forest as logging and grazing have been scaled back.

Logging will be drastically reduced by 2003 when the full restrictions of the Giant Sequoia National Monument apply. The monument, designated in 2000 by President William Clinton under the 1906 Antiquities Act, covers 328,000 acres of the forest, providing huge protection buffer zones for 19,000 acres of giant sequoias. Some logging will be allowed until 2003 so that surrounding timber mills have a short transition period.

The Sequoia is divided into four sections, with the Hume Lake Ranger District 15 miles north of the main forest and two other sections southeast of the main forest. The Hume Lake district, which has more than a dozen giant sequoia groves, is next to Sequoia-Kings Canyon National Parks. The district includes the Boole Tree, the largest tree in any national forest in the United States. It is 269 feet tall and 112 feet in circumference.

The two other forest sections—each less than 100,000 acres—are south and east of Isabella Lake, an artificial lake created when the Kern River was dammed. The section farthest east contains the 88,000-acre Kiavah Wilderness, which encompasses the Scodie Mountains within the Sierra range. The Kiavah, established in 1994, is an interesting transition zone from the Mojave Desert on the east to the Sierra. Visitors will see many desert community plants, such as burro bush (*Hymenoclea monogyra*), creosote bush (*Larrea tridentata*), and Joshua tree (*Yucca brevifolia*). The Sierra vegetation in this area includes the canyon oak (*Quercus wislizenii*), pinion pine (*Pinus monophylla*), and Sierra juniper (*Juniperus occidentalis*).

In the main body of the forest, people will find the dangerous Kern River, which regularly claims the lives of unsuspecting swimmers. Because of the warmer, drier weather in this part of California—Bakersfield annually receives less than 6 inches of rain—people are lulled into thinking the placid-looking pools on the Kern are shallow and calm. But powerful subsurface currents can drag even the best swimmers down into cold, turbulent water. The message from the Forest Service is clear: Don't swim here.

There can be dangers in other large streams of the Sequoia as well. Experienced boaters and professional guides are probably the safest bet on the Kings River and the South Fork Kings River, both of which are designated for federal protection as Wild and Scenic Rivers.

But there are streams and bodies of water that are not dangerous in the Sequoia. There are some very pleasant hot springs on the Greenhorn Ranger District, which extends far south in the Sequoia. Isabella Lake provides trout fishing for the area. One quirky note for those using a map to find Isabella Lake: The name of the town next to the body of water is Lake Isabella.

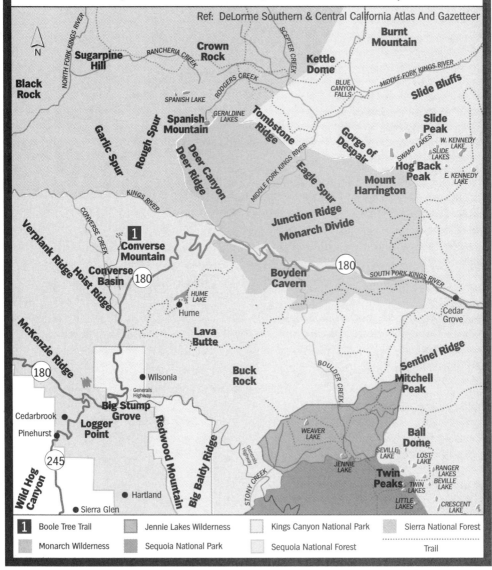

Monarch & Jennie Lakes Wilderness Areas

Monarch and Jennie Lakes wilderness areas have 56,000 acres and more than 26 miles of trails.

Ref: DeLorme Southern & Central California Atlas And Gazetteer

NORTH FORK KINGS RIVER

Sugarpine Hill

RANCHERIA CREEK

Crown Rock

SCEPTER CREEK

Kettle Dome

Burnt Mountain

Black Rock

RODGERS CREEK

SPANISH LAKE

BLUE CANYON FALLS

MIDDLE FORK KINGS RIVER

Slide Bluffs

Garlic Spur

Rough Spur

Spanish Mountain

GERALDINE LAKES

Tombstone Ridge

Deer Canyon

Deer Ridge

MIDDLE FORK KINGS RIVER

Gorge of Despair

SWAMP LAKES

Slide Peak

W. KENNEDY LAKE

SLIDE LAKES

E. KENNEDY LAKE

Eagle Spur

Hog Back Peak

Mount Harrington

KINGS RIVER

CONVERSE CREEK

Junction Ridge

Monarch Divide

Verplank Ridge

Hoist Ridge

1 Converse Mountain

Converse Basin

180

HUME LAKE

Hume

Boyden Cavern

180

SOUTH FORK KINGS RIVER

Cedar Grove

McKenzie Ridge

Lava Butte

180

Wilsonia

Generals Highway

Buck Rock

BOULDER CREEK

Sentinel Ridge

Mitchell Peak

Cedarbrook

Pinehurst

Big Stump Grove

Logger Point

Redwood Mountain

Big Baldy Ridge

STONY CREEK

WEAVER LAKE

Generals Highway

JENNIE LAKE

SEVILLE LAKE

LOST LAKE

Ball Dome

RANGER LAKES

BEVILLE LAKE

245

Wild Hog Canyon

Hartland

Sierra Glen

Twin Peaks

TWIN LAKES

LITTLE LAKES

CRESCENT LAKE

1 Boole Tree Trail	Jennie Lakes Wilderness	Kings Canyon National Park	Sierra National Forest
Monarch Wilderness	Sequoia National Park	Sequoia National Forest	Trail

▓ MONARCH WILDERNESS/JENNIE LAKES WILDERNESS

[Fig. 55] Though the 45,000 acres of the Monarch Wilderness are almost evenly divided between the Sierra National Forest and Sequoia National Forest, visitors probably will be more interested in the Sequoia side. The Sequoia side is the easiest to get into because the Kings Canyon Highway—outside of Kings Canyon National Park—runs right through the southern part of the wilderness. The highway has been designated as a scenic byway.

To the south, if visitors entering from the west turn right on the Generals Highway, they can easily reach the Jennie Lakes Wilderness, which is almost 11,000 acres of meadows, forests, lakes, and streams. The wilderness has 26 miles of trails, including walking access to both Sequoia and Kings Canyon national parks. The Big Meadows area is a popular cross-country skiing spot. Jennie and Weaver lakes are big attractions for fishing.

The beautiful Monarch Wilderness starts at about the 2,000-foot elevation along the Wild and Scenic South Fork Kings River. As the wilderness rises in elevation, there are lush mountain meadows, spectacular geological formations, and interesting groupings of vegetation that include the whitebark pine *(Pinus albicaulis)*. The Monarch is the only place in Sequoia where the whitebark can be found.

As with many wildernesses, there are no facilities, but visitors can find a picnic ground off of Kings Canyon Highway at Grizzly Falls, which is only a short distance from the highway on a well-marked route. Visitors often stop for a picnic lunch on their way to Cedar Grove in Kings Canyon National Park.

Just a few miles after entering the wilderness area on the highway, visitors may notice the Boyden Cave sign. The cave is just inside the wilderness beneath steep walls of marble. The whole family can tour the lighted trail through the cave between May and October.

Directions: For the Monarch Wilderness, drive 52 miles east on Highway 180 from the Big Stump Entrance Station. Beyond the entrance station, turn left on Kings Canyon Highway and drive about 12 miles and the highway enters the Monarch Wilderness. For the Jennie Lakes Wilderness, drive to the Big Stump Entrance Station and turn right on the Generals Highway. Drive about 5.5 miles to Forest Route 14S11 and turn left. Drive about 3.5 miles to Big Meadows. Other turnoffs from the Generals Highway to Jennie Lakes trailheads include Forest Route 13S14 and 14S21.

Activities: Hiking, camping, picnicking, photography, and fishing.

Facilities: Picnic grounds at Grizzly Falls along the Wild and Scenic South Fork Kings River.

Dates: Open May through Oct. The highway closes each winter.

Fees: None.

Closest town: Hume Lake, 3 miles.

For more information: Hume Lake Ranger District, 35860 East Kings Canyon Road, Dunlap, CA 93621. Phone (559) 338-2251.

CONVERSE BASIN

[Fig. 55] Converse Basin evokes a range of reactions from many people. Visitors make the long drive from the San Joaquin Valley heat and find a cool, green meadow with soaring granite mountains in the background. People love that first moment. But soon they begin looking around the meadow at the massive stumps of 2,000-year-old giant sequoia. Their hearts sink when they realize they have entered a graveyard of big trees.

Perhaps the most famous of the remains is the Chicago Stump, standing 20 feet high. It and others were left after loggers cleared the giants in the late 1800s and early 1900s. Hundreds of giants were cleared from the area before the U.S. Forest Service acquired about 20,000 acres in the vicinity of Hume Lake in 1935.

For hundreds of years before the loggers arrived in this area, Native Americans gathered here during the summer to gather food and hunt. The groups included the Choinimne, Yokuts, and Michahai. A fair amount of trading went on between tribes of the Eastern Sierra and the western slope. Both digger pine (Pinus sabiniana) and sugar pine provided pine nuts for the tribes.

These days, the acorn woodpecker (Melanerpes formicivorus) is among the creatures most interested in harvesting the local trees. For bird watchers, Converse Basin can be a delight. Look for the mountain chickadee (Parus gambeli), belted kingfisher (Megaceryle alcyon), and brown creeper (Certhia familiaris).

Directions: Drive about 8 miles northeast on Kings Canyon Highway from the Big Stump Entrance Station at Sequoia-Kings Canyon National Parks. Turn left from Kings Canyon Highway onto Forest Road 13S55 or Converse Basin Road and drive about 0.7 mile to Stump Meadow.

Activities: Hiking, photography, bird-watching, and picnicking.

Facilities: None.

Dates: Open May through Oct. The highway closes each winter.

Fees: There is a fee to enter the national parks, even though the destination is in a national forest.

Closest town: Hume Lake, 1 mile.

For more information: Hume Lake Ranger District, 35860 East Kings Canyon Road, Dunlap, CA 93621. Phone (559) 338-2251.

BOOLE TREE TRAIL

[Fig. 55(1)] The Boole Tree stands almost alone, the largest giant sequoia saved from the loggers who came through the grove in the late 1800s. It is named after Frank Boole, the manager of the Sanger Lumber Company, which logged the area. No one is sure why the tree was named after Boole, but the tree is 269 feet tall and 112 feet in circumference, making it the largest tree in any of America's national forests. The General Sherman Tree in Sequoia National Park is larger, however.

The Boole Tree Trail traverses the area where the General Noble Tree was cut down in 1895. The tree was carved into 14-foot sections and shipped to Chicago for the Columbian World Exposition.

For loggers, the wood from the giant sequoia was not particularly useful because it was so brittle. It was used mostly to make fence posts and roofing.

Directions: Drive about 8 miles northeast on Kings Canyon Highway from the Big Stump Entrance Station at Sequoia-Kings Canyon National Parks. Turn left from Kings Canyon Highway onto Forest Road 13S55 and drive about 0.5 mile to Stump Meadow. Turn right on an unpaved forest access road and drive 0.2 mile. Park at the trailhead.

Trail: 3-mile loop.

Elevation: 650-foot gain, 6,750-foot peak.

Degree of difficulty: Easy.

Surface: Open granite footpath.

BELTED KINGFISHER
(Megaceryle alcyon)

🌸 DOMELAND WILDERNESS/CANNELL MEADOW

[Fig. 56] The Domeland Wilderness is aptly named. Here, hikers, backpackers, and horseback riders can see rugged, eroding granite spires and domes between 7,000 and 9,000 feet in one of the more arid sections of the Sierra Nevada. Visitors will not see much of the wilderness area from a car. Though it can be reached from north, south, east or west, passenger cars cannot get close enough for the good views. You have to walk or ride an animal to really see the Domeland.

Sequoia forest visitors are more likely to start their explorations of this upper Kern River Canyon area in Cannell Meadow, which borders the wilderness on the east. Cannell Meadow can be approached from the southwest on Sierra Way, which connects with a small, east-west route that passes just north of the Domeland Wilderness.

The Cannell Meadow and surrounding areas provide a few campgrounds and several pastures for those who bring their own horses. For those who would like to take a professionally guided whitewater rafting trip down the Kern River, there are several outfitters. They include **Chuck Richards Whitewater**, PO Box WW, Lake Isabella, CA 93240, phone (760) 379-4444; **Kern River Tours**, PO Box 3444, Lake Isabella, CA 93240, phone (760) 379-4616; **Whitewater Voyages**, 5225 San Pablo Dam Road, El Sobrante, CA 94803-3309, phone (510) 222-5994; and **Sequoia Outdoor Center**, PO Box S, Kernville, CA 93238, phone (760) 376-3776.

Campers, hikers, fishing enthusiasts, and backpackers need to know about plants in this part of the forest that cause skin irritation. Look for stinging nettle (*Urtica dioica*) and poison oak.

Domeland Wilderness Area

The Domeland Wilderness is named for its eroding granite domes ranging between 7,000 and 9,000 feet.

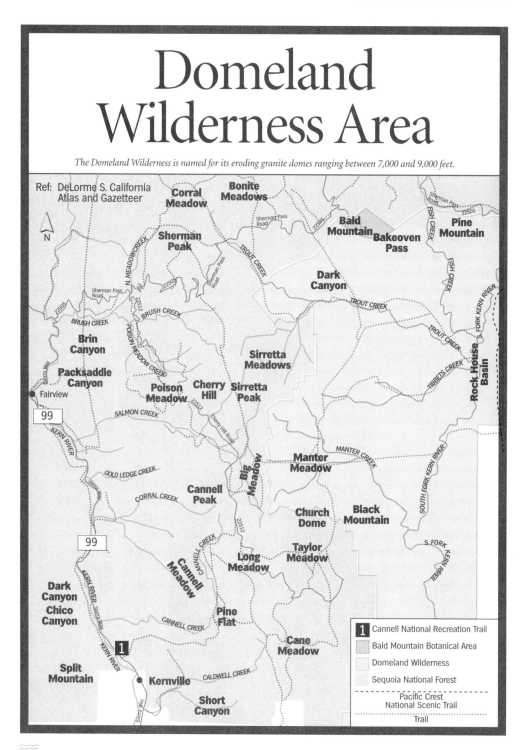

Ref: DeLorme S. California Atlas and Gazetteer

N

Corral Meadow

Bonite Meadows

Sherman Pass Road

Bald Mountain

Bakeoven Pass

Pine Mountain

Sherman Peak

TROUT CREEK

N. MEADOW CREEK

Sherman Pass Road

Dark Canyon

TROUT CREEK

FISH CREEK

Sherman Pass Road

22S05

22S12

BRUSH CREEK

POISON MEADOW CREEK

BRUSH CREEK

Brin Canyon

Sirretta Meadows

S. FORK KERN RIVER

Rock House Basin

Packsaddle Canyon

Sierra Way

Fairview

Poison Meadow

Cherry Hill

Sirretta Peak

TIBBETS CREEK

99

SALMON CREEK

22S12

Cherry Hill Road

KERN RIVER

GOLD LEDGE CREEK

Sierra Way

Big Meadow

Manter Meadow

MANTER CREEK

SOUTH FORK KERN RIVER

CORRAL CREEK

Cannell Peak

Church Dome

Black Mountain

99

22S12

CANNELL CREEK

Taylor Meadow

S. FORK KERN RIVER

Dark Canyon

KERN RIVER

Sierra Way

Cannell Meadow

Long Meadow

Chico Canyon

CANNELL CREEK

Pine Flat

Cane Meadow

Split Mountain

1

Kernville

CALDWELL CREEK

Sierra Way

Short Canyon

1 Cannell National Recreation Trail

Bald Mountain Botanical Area

Domeland Wilderness

Sequoia National Forest

Pacific Crest National Scenic Trail

Trail

Directions: From Kernville, drive 17 miles north on Mountain Route 99 or Sierra Way to Forest Service Road 22S05 or Sherman Pass Road and turn right. Drive about 5 miles to Forest Service Road 22S12 or Cherry Hill Road and turn right. Drive about 6 miles before reaching trailheads and access points for Poison Meadow, Horse Meadow, and unpaved roads to Cannell Meadow. For Domeland Wilderness access, follow the same directions to Sherman Pass Road and drive east about 14 miles before reaching trailheads that will lead into the wilderness.

Activities: Horseback riding, river rafting, camping, hiking, backpacking, bicycling, and fishing.

Facilities: Campgrounds. Services such as gasoline, food, and motel rooms are available in nearby towns along Sierra Way, such as Fairview.

Dates: Open May through Oct.

Fees: There are fees for campgrounds.

Closest town: Fairview, 12 miles.

For more information: Cannell Meadow Ranger District, PO Box 9, 105 Whitney Road, Kernville CA 93238. Phone (760) 376-3781.

CANNELL NATIONAL RECREATION TRAIL

[Fig. 56(1)] The most direct route to Cannell Meadow is a hiking trail over the rugged, roadless area from just north of Kernville. For some folks, it may actually be quicker to walk there than to drive for hours on a circuitous route that runs north along the Kern River canyon. But, for average hikers, this is a lot of walking and almost 1 mile in elevation gain. That's a lot of work, but the views of the Kern River valley are stunning.

If you try this one in the summer, make sure you bring a lot of water—maybe 64 ounces. The trail does not provide a lot of shade. In spring and summer, watch for the western rattlesnake, which has poisonous venom. The rattler generally is a shy snake that remains hidden. Just keep your eyes on the trail as you walk through rocky areas.

Directions: From Kernville, drive north on Sierra Way about 2 miles to the horse corrals just beyond Camp Owens. The trailhead begins at the corrals.

Trail: 12 miles round-trip.

Elevation: 4,700-foot gain, 7,520-foot peak.

Degree of difficulty: Strenuous.

Surface: Granite, rocky, two creek crossings.

BALD MOUNTAIN BOTANICAL AREA

[Fig. 56] This is an easy hike to see some wonderful views of the Southern Sierra and also experience Bald Mountain Botanical Area, a 440-acre site on the northern tip of the Domeland Wilderness. More than 100 species of plants have been recorded among the sedimentary rocks that date back more than 135 million years, which is a bit unusual in an area dominated by granite.

The biggest plant attraction is the Bald Mountain potentilla *(Horkelia tularensis)*, which occurs nowhere else in the world. Once you have seen this plant, however, check

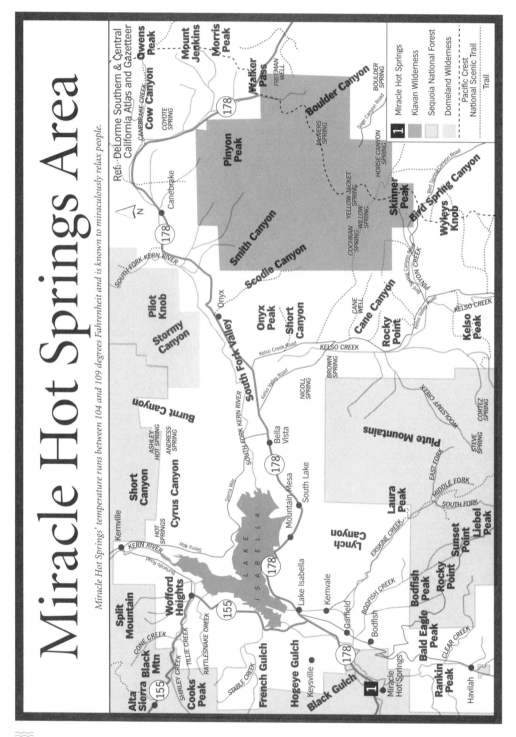

Miracle Hot Springs Area

Miracle Hot Springs' temperature runs between 104 and 109 degrees Fahrenheit and is known to miraculously relax people.

Ref: DeLorme Southern & Central California Atlas and Gazetteer

N

1	Miracle Hot Springs
	Klavan Wilderness
	Sequoia National Forest
	Domeland Wilderness
	Pacific Crest National Scenic Trail
	Trail

out the view from the 40-foot-high fire lookout on the mountain. It spans a breathtaking several hundred square miles of the Domeland and South Sierra wildernesses.

Directions: From Kernville, drive 17 miles north on Mountain Route 99 or Sierra Way to Forest Service Road 22S05 or Sherman Pass Road and turn right. Drive about 18 miles east on Sherman Pass Road to the access road into the botanical area and the Bald Mountain Lookout. Turn right, drive 0.1 mile, and park near the padlocked gate across the access road. The trail is just to the right of the gate.

Trail: 0.75-mile round-trip.

Elevation: 150-foot gain, 9,400-foot peak.

Degree of difficulty: Easy.

Surface: Smooth, open footpath alongside an access road.

MIRACLE HOT SPRINGS

[Fig. 57(1)] Miracle Hot Springs run between 104 and 109 degrees Fahrenheit. Most people find it a soothing, comfortable temperature, especially in the fall or spring when the air is cool at the 2,200-foot elevation of the hot springs. Hot springs are scattered all along the Kern River, venting water that has been heated by the earth's magmatic core. The water absorbs minerals during its underground course through the heated geological formations along the Kern. The minerals found in the hot springs around the Kern are sulfur, magnesium, iron, and borax.

A hobo camp with bathhouses developed at Miracle when the Borel Power Plant was being built in 1901. It was called Hobo Hot Springs in those days. Now, Hobo Campground is about 0.12 mile from the hot springs. The name was changed from Hobo to Miracle in the 1940s when it became known as a place to miraculously relax people.

Directions: From Lake Isabella, drive southwest on Highway 178 about 4 miles to the Borel Road turnoff. Exit southeast on Borel Road and drive about 0.25 mile to the parking lot with the Miracle Hot Springs sign. Park and walk about 0.1 mile to the hot springs.

Activities: Relaxing in a hot springs tub.

Facilities: Several rock tubs, Hobo Campground, potable water, and restrooms.

Dates: Open year-round.

Fees: There is a fee for parking.

Closest town: Lake Isabella, 4 miles.

For more information: Greenhorn Ranger District, PO Box 3810, Lake Isabella, CA 93240. Phone (760) 379-5646.

GOLDEN TROUT WILDERNESS/SOUTH SIERRA WILDERNESS

[Fig. 58] The Golden Trout and the South Sierra wildernesses combine to cover more than 365,000 acres along the Sierra crest, but almost two-thirds of those acres are on the Eastern Sierra. Individual descriptions of both wildernesses can be found in the Eastern Sierra chapter.

Visitors will find 150 miles of trails for hikers and horseback riders in the 111,146 acres

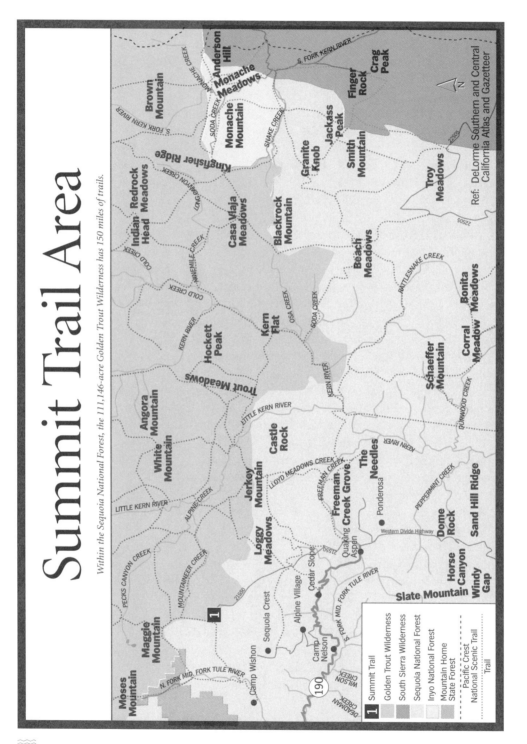

Summit Trail Area

Within the Sequoia National Forest, the 111,146-acre Golden Trout Wilderness has 150 miles of trails.

Ref: DeLorme Southern and Central California Atlas and Gazetteer

Legend:

1 Summit Trail
Golden Trout Wilderness
South Sierra Wilderness
Sequoia National Forest
Inyo National Forest
Mountain Home State Forest
Pacific Crest National Scenic Trail
Trail

of Golden Trout Wilderness in the Sequoia forest. In the smaller South Sierra wilderness, southeast of the Golden Trout, there are about 30 miles of trails in about 24,650 acres. On the Sequoia forest, the Golden Trout Wilderness ranges from about 4,800 feet in elevation to mountain peaks more than 12,000 feet high. The South Sierra Wilderness terrain is a bit less dramatic on the Sequoia forest. But peaks still reach higher than 9,000 feet.

Visitors will find campgrounds on the way to the Golden Trout Wilderness on the Sequoia forest. The South Sierra Wilderness, however, is farther east in less developed areas and has only a few neighboring campgrounds.

Directions: For the Golden Trout Wilderness, drive about 24 miles east on Highway 190 from Success Lake in Tulare County to the junction of Highway 190 and the Western Divide Highway. Turn left on Forest Road 21S50 and drive another 1.5 miles to some of the wilderness trailheads. For the South Sierra Wilderness, start at Kernville near Isabella Lake and drive 17 miles north on Mountain Route 99 or Sierra Way to Forest Service Road 22S05 or Sherman Pass Road and turn right. Drive about 22 miles northeast and turn right on another section of Sherman Pass Road. Drive southeast about 5 miles until you see trailheads for the South Sierra.

Activities: Hiking, camping, backpacking, fishing, horseback riding, and photography.

Facilities: Campgrounds can be found near the western boundaries of both wildernesses, but no facilities can be found inside the wildernesses.

Dates: Open May through Oct.

Fees: None.

Closest town: For the South Sierra, Fairview, 25 miles; for Golden Trout, Camp Nelson, 5 miles.

For more information: For Golden Trout, Tule Ranger District, 32588 Highway 190, Springville, CA 93265. Phone (559) 539-2607. For South Sierra, Cannell Meadow Ranger District, PO Box 9, 105 Whitney Road, Kernville CA 93238. Phone (760) 376-3781.

SUMMIT TRAIL

[Fig. 58(1)] The Summit Trail offers hikers many views on the way to scenic Maggie Lakes in the Golden Trout Wilderness. It starts above 8,000 feet where moist meadows often light up with greater elephant's head *(Pedicularis groenlandica)*, which has rose-colored blooms that emerge in July at this elevation.

Up higher near Maggie Lakes, the scenery includes alpine buttercup *(Ranunculus eschscholtzii)* and Anderson's alpine aster *(Alpigenus* var. *andersonii)*. In the meadows above 9,000 feet, visitors also can see dwarf huckleberry *(Vaccinium nivictum)* and red mountain heather *(Phyllodoce breweri)*. Two streams—Mountaineer Creek and Pecks Canyon Creek—should be crossed with care, particularly early in the season when small creeks often swell with snowmelt in the afternoons. Later in the summer, they are not difficult to cross.

Directions: Drive about 24 miles east on Highway 190 from Success Lake in Tulare County to the junction of Highway 190 and the Western Divide Highway. Just beyond the junction, turn left from Highway 190 onto Forest Road 21S50 and drive about 10 miles north to the trailhead at the southwestern edge of the Golden Trout Wilderness.

Trail: 11.3 miles round-trip.
Elevation: 1,500-foot gain, 9,920-foot peak.
Degree of difficulty: Moderate.
Surface: Steep in places, granite.

JACKASS PEAK

[Fig. 58] From Jackass Peak, a fairly quick hike that should not be too challenging, there are interesting views into the South Sierra Wilderness. Albanita Meadow spreads below to the southeast, flanked by 9,145-foot Finger Rock and 9,455-foot Crag Peak. To the southwest, just outside the wilderness, is 9,515-foot Smith Mountain, and 9,050-foot Granite Knob is to the northwest. Though Jackass Peak is above 9,000 feet, hikers can still see vegetation that can be found at lower and drier places in the Central Sierra foothills. That's because it is drier and warmer in this part of the mountain range. Look for the mountain whitethorn *(Ceanothus cordulatus)* and tobacco brush *(Ceanothus velutinus)*. Also, visitors may see the popcorn flower *(Plagiobothrys torreyi)*.

Directions: From Kernville near Isabella Lake, drive 17 miles north on Mountain Route 99 or Sierra Way to Forest Service Road 22S05 or Sherman Pass Road and turn right. Drive about 22 miles northeast and continue straight on Blackrock Road or Forest Route 21S03. Drive about 3 miles on Blackrock Road to Monache Jeep Road and bear right onto Monache Jeep Road. Drive about 1 mile and turn right on Forest Road 21S36. Drive 0.7 mile to the end of the road and park. The trailhead for Jackass Peak is at the end of the road.

Trail: 2 miles round-trip.
Elevation: 780-foot gain, 9,287-foot peak.
Degree of difficulty: Moderate.
Surface: Rocky, granite, and some road surface before the short ascent.

KIAVA WILDERNESS

[Fig. 57] The Kiava Wilderness is not a typical, lush mountain place, but visitors still like to take a lot of photographs around it. The Kiava is 88,290 acres of transition lands filled with characteristics of the Mojave Desert to the east and the Sierra to the northwest. People hike, camp, and take photographs of the eroding landscape and the interesting vegetation. Carry water when you hike this area, and hike it during the spring and fall. Water sources are scarce.

The Kiava, which was established in 1994, is basically the Scodie Mountains, a collection of hills and canyons on the southern extreme of the Sierra. Like the Tehachapi and Piute mountains in this part of California, it is subject to five different wind patterns—the subtropical, Pacific, polar, continental and Gulf wind patterns. It does not receive much more than 10 to 15 inches of rain annually. The climate creates "bajadas" or foot slopes of desert mountains where eroded soil and rocks have accumulated. Groupings of plants might include a digger pine and a Joshua tree. A cactus might grow within 100 yards of a canyon oak. It's not a common sight in the Sierra.

Migratory birds in Kiava are diverse as well. Visitors might see an interesting combination of a rough-legged hawk *(Buteo lagopus)*, yellow-headed blackbird *(Xanthocephalus xanthocephalus)*, gray-crowned rosy finch *(Leucosticte tephrocotis)*, and sage sparrow *(Amphispiza belli)*, depending on the time of the year.

PINION PINE
(Pinus monophylla)

The Kiava is part of the Bureau of Land Management's Jawbone-Butterbredt Area of Critical Environmental Concern. The area was designated to protect the wildlife and Native American sites.

Directions: From Isabella Lake, drive about 30 miles east on Highway 178 to find trailheads near the parking areas for Walker Pass Lodge, which is on the northeastern boundary of the wilderness. Or continue another 3.5 miles to Walker Pass where the Pacific Crest Trail crosses Highway 178. The Pacific Crest Trail enters the wilderness and intersects with trails in Kiava.

Activities: Hiking, camping, photography, and scenic driving just outside the wilderness.

Facilities: None.

Dates: Open year-round.

Fees: None.

Closest town: Ridgecrest, 15 miles.

For more information: Cannell Meadow Ranger District, PO Box 9, 105 Whitney Road, Kernville CA 93238. Phone (760) 376-3781. Bureau of Land Management Ridgecrest Field Office, 300 South Richmond Road, Ridgecrest, CA 93555. Phone (760) 384-5400.

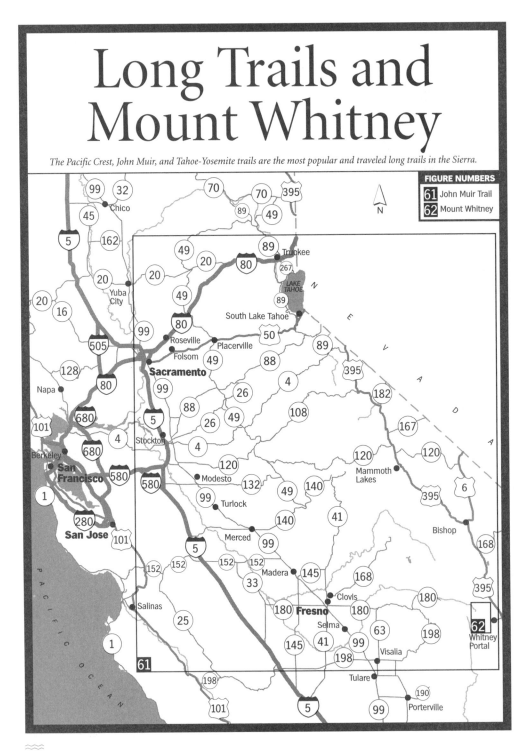

Long Trails and Mount Whitney

The Pacific Crest, John Muir, and Tahoe-Yosemite trails are the most popular and traveled long trails in the Sierra.

FIGURE NUMBERS

61 John Muir Trail
62 Mount Whitney

Long Trails and
Mount Whitney

In the Sierra Nevada, the critters and the weather greet you and help you to
quickly understand that this is not city life. Even experienced backpackers must
spend the first day of a multiday hike adjusting to Sierra conditions. At first, you
have to think about when to put on the next layer of clothes, how to protect the pack
from marauding squirrels and black bears, and where the ground is high enough to
stay out of a mud puddle if the skies open up and rain overnight.

But by the second or third day, most people stop thinking and begin feeling the
rhythm of physical exertion in pristine, wild places. It becomes almost second nature
to protect yourself and adjust to outdoor mountain living. Soon, you're completely
absorbed in the Sierra's ancient granite, the high-country meadows, and the rush of
powerful rivers that bring water to the dry lowlands of California's Central Valley.

There are many long trails in the Sierra, but there are only a few that stand above

[*Above:* A view of the Owens Valley and White Mountains from the trail to Mount Whitney]

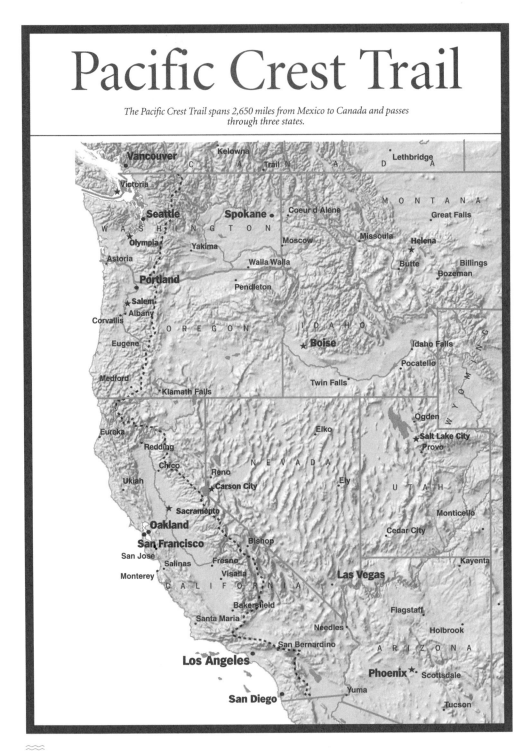

Pacific Crest Trail

The Pacific Crest Trail spans 2,650 miles from Mexico to Canada and passes through three states.

the others in popularity and acclaim. The Pacific Crest Trail, the John Muir Trail, and the Tahoe-Yosemite Trail are probably the most popular and most traveled of the long trails in the Sierra. The Tahoe Rim Trail should be mentioned in the same breath, but it is so connected to Lake Tahoe that it has been included in the Lake Tahoe chapter (*see* page 137). Another trail, the historic French Trail, is a trans-Sierra route that travels west to east and is located in the Southern Sierra, but it is obscure compared to the Pacific Crest, John Muir, and Tahoe-Yosemite routes.

It also may seem odd that Mount Whitney is included in a long trails chapter, but Whitney defies a neat, single category. It can on the shoulder of Sequoia National Park and the John Muir Wilderness in the Inyo National Forest. It can also be reached from several directions and trailheads. Like the few other trails covered in this chapter, it poses challenges that cross many physical and psychological boundaries. And, perhaps, no other trail gets as much attention each year.

Of all the trails passing through the Sierra Nevada, the Pacific Crest would have to be considered the backbone. It is mentioned in the same breath with the Continental Divide Trail and the venerable Appalachian Trail as one of America's premier long trails. In the Sierra, the Pacific Crest passes through the highest, the wildest, and the best of California's high mountains.

Pacific Crest Trail

[Fig. 60] The 2,650-mile Pacific Crest Trail covers more ground than any other route on the West Coast. The Pacific Crest stretches over 24 national forests and 33 wildernesses from the Canadian border to the Mexican border. In California alone, the trail is 1,723 miles long. It covers more than 500 miles in the Sierra Nevada.

There are people who walk for four to six months and complete an end-to-end trip. Richard Watson is reportedly the first person ever to hike the whole trail. He did it in 1972. But many folks hike the Pacific Crest in segments. In fact, some people hike segments of the segments because even smaller chunks of the Pacific Crest can be pretty long.

The longest Pacific Crest stretch in California is 177 miles of high-elevation trail that coincides with a large part of the John Muir Trail from the Southern Sierra to Yosemite National Park. That stretch takes most experienced and fit hikers three weeks to a month.

There are many strategies for walking the Pacific Crest Trail, but the common thread among them is packing and traveling light. Two decades ago, people commonly carried a 50-, 60-, or even 70-pound pack. Now, with ultralight backpacking techniques, people carry 20- to 25-pound packs and travel much farther in a single day. Other people use llamas to pack their provisions. Llamas, which are native to high-elevation areas, adapt well to carrying loads in the high Sierra.

The history of the Pacific Crest Trail can be traced to the 1920s when the first serious discussions about it began. The trail was the product of many minds. Clinton C. Clarke, a Southern California resident and chairman of the Mountain League of Los Angeles, organized the Pacific Crest Trail System Conference in 1932. But the idea had been considered since the mid-1920s among several groups on the West Coast.

It took several decades of exploration, trail work, and lobbying before the federal government included the Pacific Crest in a 1968 law called the National Trails System Act. The act established the existing Appalachian Trail and the Pacific Crest as the first two National Scenic Trails. A general trail route was federally approved for the Pacific Crest in the early 1970s.

The Pacific Crest National Scenic Trail Advisory Council was named to develop the detailed route and management plan for the trail. The council held its first meeting in 1970. There were representatives of all three states involved—Washington, Oregon, and California—as well as cattle ranchers, timber and mineral interests, youth organizations, and Native Americans.

In 1977, the Pacific Crest Trail Association was incorporated as construction of the trail progressed. The association acted as an advocacy group for the trail and assisted the government with volunteer work crews to maintain and protect the trail. Today the group continues its advocacy and trail work and provides information on everything from trail ethics to food supply points along the route.

The association worked with the U.S. Forest Service, the National Park Service, the Bureau of Land Management, and a dizzying array of local governments and private landowners to establish and maintain the trail. In 1993, after years of land acquisition, trail cutting, and work on mapping, the trail was officially dedicated as a National Scenic Trail, a quarter of a century after it had been established as a National Scenic Trail.

ROOSEVELT ELK
(Cervus canadensis roosevelti)
During the elks' fall mating season, bulls challenge each other with loud snorting and bugling, and with short, false charges. Their occasional battles produce the loud sounds of colliding antlers.

The Pacific Crest has five sections, each several hundred miles long. The Southern California section is 648 miles; Central California is 505 miles; Northern California is 567 miles; Oregon is 430 miles; and Washington is 500 miles. Much of the trail is under snow throughout the winter, especially in the Sierra Nevada. The optimum travel months in the Sierra are July, August, and September.

The trail is marked with signs, not blazes. Even so, do not attempt any lengthy section of the Pacific Crest without a good topographic map, compass, and path-finding skills. Plan the trip many months in advance to make sure you get the proper permits, which can be obtained from U.S. Forest Service in each of the forests through which the trail passes. In many parts of the Sierra, exit routes may mean a halfday or more of hiking. The Pacific Crest has a remarkable amount of foot traffic, so you probably will not be alone. But be prepared to handle problems on your own.

For more information: Pacific Crest Trail Association, 5325 Elkhorn Boulevard, Suite 256, Sacramento, CA 95842-2526. Phone (916) 349-2109.

John Muir Trail

[Fig. 61] Hikers and backpackers come from around the globe to hike the John Muir Trail. There are some days on the Muir Trail when hikers hear only foreign languages and the sounds of nature. In fact, the Muir Trail's pristine granite scenes— at an average elevation of 9,000 feet and miles from any civilization—are sometimes crowded.

The trail runs about 220 miles from Happy Isles in the north to the Whitney Portal in the south. The official southern terminus of the trail is considered to be the top of Whitney at 14,497 feet, which makes the trail closer to 212 miles. But to leave the mountains, hikers must walk down to Whitney Portal on the Eastern Sierra. About 177 miles of the Muir Trail coincides with the Pacific Crest Trail.

On the trail, hikers walk along the Sierra spine through three national parks and two national forests. Besides Yosemite, the trail cuts through a large portion of Kings Canyon National Park and a smaller part of Sequoia National Park. It runs through Sierra and Inyo national forests.

Many people plan and hike the entire length in three weeks to a month. With new ultralight backpacking methods, some prefer to walk it in 17 or 18 days. Others like to hike parts of it over a number of summers. No matter which approach people choose, the Muir Trail is considered a true collector's item among people who bag long-distance hikes.

Photography is one of the biggest passions of hikers along the Muir Trail. For those who surf the Internet, type "John Muir Trail" into your search engine and see the eye-popping Muir Trail photographs loaded onto many personal pages.

There are literally thousands of placid glacial lakes displaying mirror images of

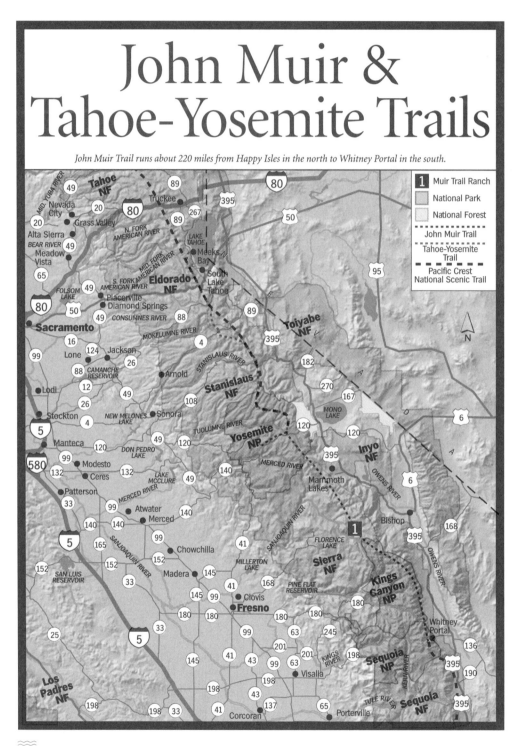

John Muir & Tahoe-Yosemite Trails

John Muir Trail runs about 220 miles from Happy Isles in the north to Whitney Portal in the south.

jagged granite peaks and snow-rimmed cirques. Hikers spend a lot of time above timberline, where vegetation is sparse and the views are sweeping and wide. And at the rooftop of California, the skies are much deeper blue and much clearer than anywhere else in the state.

State and federal officials recognized the significance of the trail in the nineteenth century. It was explored and mapped by several men. Joseph LeConte, Theodore Solomons, and Bolton Brown are credited with doing much of the early exploration. Solomons is considered the person who provided the inspiration for the trail. The National Park Service and the U.S. Forest Service began cutting the trail in 1908 and finished it eight years later.

These days, the trail is pretty easy to follow, though a good topographic map and a compass are always recommended in the backcountry. Many backpackers prefer to walk from Yosemite south to Whitney because the climb up Whitney at the start of the trek is grueling. Starting from Whitney, you gain more than 5,000 feet—about 1 mile—in elevation over about 8 miles. In Yosemite, you climb almost 6,000 feet, but it is spread over 16 miles.

Either way, this is one hike that requires physical conditioning. But, as Muir himself said in his wilderness essays: "How glorious a greeting the sun gives the mountains! To behold this alone is worth the pains of any excursion a thousand times over."

Some people prefer starting from Whitney anyway, because it allows them the safety of approaching steep passes from the south. The southern faces normally have less snow and ice early in the season. The travel season for the Muir Trail is July through October, but the snow does not fully melt until August in places higher than 12,000 feet. Be ready for thunderstorms and even snow in July or August.

Wilderness permits are required for any overnight stay, so contact ranger stations in advance. For people hiking all the way through the Muir Trail, restocking food supplies is a major concern because there is no easy access to stores or towns along much of the trail. In some places, it will take hikers more than a day to hike out of the backcountry.

There are two small stores near the trail at Reds Meadow near the Devils Postpile National Monument and Tuolumne Meadows in Yosemite. Hikers can mail food packages to Vermillion Valley Resort at Thomas Edison Lake and Muir Trail Ranch at Florence Lake in the Sierra National Forest. Vermillion and the ranch will hold the packages for a specified time and give them to hikers. But there's about a 60-mile stretch in Kings Canyon National Park where there are no quick exits to the trail.

Here are the addresses for mailing food packages: Vermillion Valley Resort, PO Box 258, Lakeshore, CA 93634. Phone (559) 259-4000 (in spring and summer), (559) 855-6558 (office). Muir Trail Ranch, Box 176, Lakeshore, CA 93634 (in spring and summer). The ranch has no telephone. In fall and winter, write to PO Box 269, Ahwahnee, CA 93601. Phone (209) 966-3195.

For more information: Inyo National Forest, Mt. Whitney Ranger District, PO

Box 8, Lone Pine, CA 93545. Phone (760) 876-6200. Sequoia-Kings Canyon National Park, Three Rivers, CA 93271. Phone (559) 565-3341. Yosemite National Park, PO Box 577, Yosemite, CA 95389. Phone (209) 372-0310 or (209) 372-0285.

▨ MUIR TRAIL RANCH

[Fig. 61(1)] The Muir Trail Ranch is at the midpoint on the John Muir Trail; from here it's 109 miles north to Happy Isles and about 109 miles south to the Whitney Portal. Hikers can stop to buy matches or batteries at a small store at the ranch, which is only 0.25 mile from the Muir Trail.

Guests here enjoy horseback riding, short hikes, or fishing. Muir Trail Ranch, located in the John Muir Wilderness, is a place to get away from the daily grind. There are no telephones, but the ranch stays in contact with the outside world via two-way radio. The comforts of a warm bed and an indoor bathroom are available in the log cabin accommodations, but many visitors choose to camp. There are also two enclosed natural hot spring baths available. And for views, just look up to Ward Mountain at 10,862 feet across the San Joaquin River from Blayney Meadow on the ranch.

Directions: From Fresno, drive northeast on Highway 168 about 65 miles to Huntington Lake. Continue on Highway 168 over Kaiser Pass. The road becomes Kaiser Pass Road. Drive another 11 miles and bear right at the fork. Drive another 12 miles to Florence Lake. Check in at the Florence Lake Store and find out where to park and unload your car. Pack animals or trucks will haul luggage to the ranch. Visitors take the 15-minute ferry ride across Florence Lake to the trailhead to the ranch. You can either ride a pack animal for the moderate 5-mile trip or walk it.

Activities: Horseback riding, fishing, hiking, camping, and photography.

Facilities: Cabins with bathrooms, tent cabins, campsites, stables, hot springs, dining hall, small store, and barbecue terrace.

Fees: There is a fee for staying at the ranch.

Closest town: Mono Hot Springs, 14 miles.

For more information: Muir Trail Ranch, PO Box 269, Ahwahnee, CA 93601. Phone (209) 966-3195.

Tahoe-Yosemite Trail

While the John Muir Trail offers majestic high country views and one of the most primitive stretches in the Sierra, the Tahoe-Yosemite Trail adds volcanic rocks and a little more lush vegetation to the panoramic views. The 186-mile trail stretches between Meeks Bay at Lake Tahoe and Tuolumne Meadows in Yosemite National Park, and such volcanic mountains as Dardanelles Cone and Relief Peak stand out along the trail on the granite of the Sierra.

The Tahoe-Yosemite Trail does not have the same type of pedigree as the Muir

Trail, which was publicly established and constructed early in the twentieth century. The Sierra Club and the U.S. Forest Service discussed the Tahoe-Yosemite Trail around 1916 and worked on the trail around Meeks Bay and around Echo Lake, but they did not formally establish it. The Tahoe-Yosemite Trail evolved informally and unofficially in hiking and conservation circles. Outdoor author Thomas Winnett eventually brought the trail before the public in 1970 after he and others personally walked, measured, and researched the route. His guidebook contains maps, measurements, history, and advice, so backpackers and hikers can enjoy the trail.

The trail is not part of the Pacific Crest Trail, which certainly can be traversed from the Desolation Wilderness beside Tahoe to the high country of Yosemite. But the two trails do not coincide for about half of the Tahoe-Yosemite route.

The Tahoe-Yosemite Trail touches parts of Yosemite, Lake Tahoe Basin Management Unit and Tahoe, Eldorado, and Stanislaus national forests. Elevations range from about 5,200 feet to more than 10,000 feet. There are many high-elevation lakes and vistas, similar to those along the Muir Trail. But the Tahoe-Yosemite Trail does not consistently reach the high elevations of the Muir Trail. Because it is north of Yosemite, however, the Tahoe-Yosemite Trail passes through areas that average more annual precipitation, giving it more abundant vegetation than the Muir Trail.

Look for the whitebark pine *(Pinus albicaulis)*, which survives in harsh conditions at high elevations. Other typical Sierra conifers can be seen as well—the sugar pine *(Pinus lambertiana)*, lodgepole pine *(Pinus murrayana)*, and mountain hemlock *(Tsuga mertensiana)*. Other Sierra vegetation, wildflowers especially, can be seen along many parts of the Tahoe-Yosemite Trail. A good example is the colorful shooting star *(Dodecatheon jeffreyi)*.

As with any long-distance Sierra trail, it is always a good idea to plan many months in advance of a backpack on the Tahoe-Yosemite Trail. The rigors of daily hiking at high elevation require backpackers to get into good physical condition before the trip. It is also wise to carry a topographic map and a compass.

Hikers should also plan to encounter thunderstorms, which come up very quickly in July, August, and September in the Sierra. Carry a radio and be alert to weather forecasts. Keep an eye on the horizon for storm clouds.

There are several Tahoe-Yosemite trailheads on the northern end of the route near Lake Tahoe, but there are long stretches without such accommodations in the Stanislaus National Forest and Yosemite. Generally speaking, there are towns closer to the Tahoe-Yosemite than there are to the Muir Trail, so bailing out of a long trek may be easier on the Tahoe-Yosemite.

For more information: Lake Tahoe Basin Management Unit, 870 Emerald Bay Road, South Lake Tahoe, CA 96150. Phone (530) 573-2600. Eldorado National Forest, 2070 Camino Heights Drive, Camino, CA 95709. Phone (530) 644-6048. Stanislaus National Forest, 19777 Greenley Road, Sonora, CA 95370. Phone (209) 532-3671. Yosemite National Park, PO Box 577, Yosemite National Park, CA 95389. Phone (209) 372-0529.

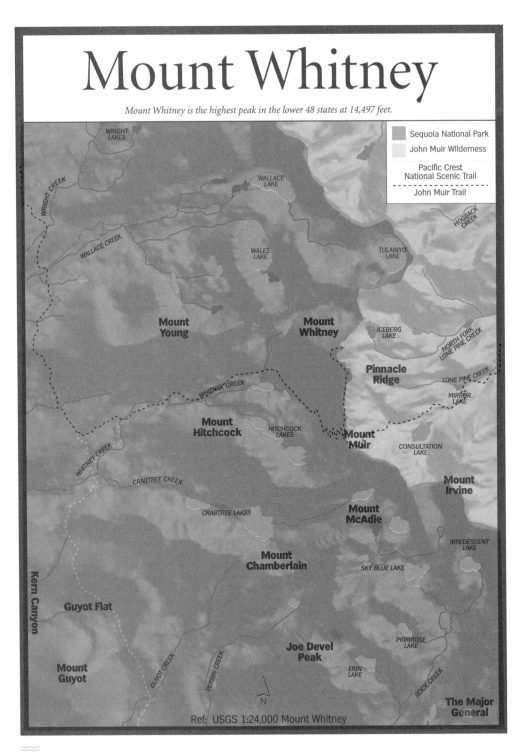

Mount Whitney

Mount Whitney is the highest peak in the lower 48 states at 14,497 feet.

Sequoia National Park

John Muir Wilderness

Pacific Crest
National Scenic Trail

John Muir Trail

WRIGHT
LAKES

WRIGHT CREEK

WALLACE
LAKE

WALLACE CREEK

HOGBACK
CREEK

WALES
LAKE

TULAINYO
LAKE

Mount
Young

Mount
Whitney

ICEBERG
LAKE

NORTH FORK
LONE PINE CREEK

Pinnacle
Ridge

LONE PINE CREEK

MIRROR
LAKE

WHITNEY CREEK

Mount
Hitchcock

HITCHCOCK
LAKES

Mount
Muir

CONSULTATION
LAKE

WHITNEY CREEK

CRABTREE CREEK

Mount
Irvine

CRABTREE LAKES

Mount
McAdie

IRREDESCENT
LAKE

Kern Canyon

Mount
Chamberlain

SKY BLUE LAKE

Guyot Flat

PRIMROSE
LAKE

GUYOT CREEK

PERRIN CREEK

Joe Devel
Peak

ERIN
LAKE

ROCK CREEK

Mount
Guyot

N

The Major
General

Ref. USGS 1:24,000 Mount Whitney

Mount Whitney

[Fig. 62] The walk up to the top of Mount Whitney could be done as a day hike, so it might seem a little out of place in a chapter about long trails. But anyone who has done Whitney in a day will attest that this is no ordinary day hike. If you're acclimated to high elevation and you're in good shape, it's a challenging 12-hour hike.

If you're not in shape, don't bother trying a one-day roundtrip on this 14,497-foot monster. Adjusting to the elevation alone is worth spending two or three days on Whitney. From Whitney Portal on the Eastern Sierra, the trail starts at 8,360 feet and climbs 2,000 feet in less than 4

A view of Mount Whitney from the east.

miles. That would be a brutal start to any hike, but it's just the warm-up. Hikers still have to climb another 4,000-plus feet over the next 7 miles. As you climb higher, the air gets thinner and your body loses efficiency.

There are other reasons why Whitney should be singled out for special consideration as a long trail in the Sierra. It is the highest peak in the lower 48 states, yet people of all ages and abilities can conquer it. So tens of thousands of people do it every year. At any given time from July to September, the 11-mile trail resembles a freeway of hikers and backpackers. Some have derisively dubbed it "Disneyland with a nosebleed." Sometimes, hikers find groups of 50 or 60 people at the summit.

Many backpackers also come from the western slope of the Sierra. Whitney's flanks easily stretch to the western slope where the mountain is partially in Sequoia National Park. Trans-Sierra backpackers come from many trails. Cedar Grove in Kings Canyon National Park is a popular takeoff point to challenge Whitney. Some prefer to walk from places in Sequoia. From almost any part of Sequoia-Kings Canyon National Parks or Sequoia National Forest, the trip will take several days, sometimes more than a week.

The crowds on the eastern side of the mountain have contaminated the high-elevation lakes, such as Consultation Lake. Hikers should purify water by boiling, chemical treatment, or water filter. The U.S. Forest Service has installed solar restrooms at 10,640-foot-elevation Outpost Camp and 12,039-foot Trail Camp, and

How Tall Is Mount Whitney?

On the U.S. Forest Service's map, Mount Whitney is 14,495 feet tall. On the U.S. Geological Survey map, it is 14,491 feet tall. And, in the National Geodetic Survey's records, Whitney is 14,497 feet tall. Who is right? It's the Geodetic Survey, according to the agency's top officials and other federal officials. The Geodetic Survey is the government's official mountain-measuring agency, so most federal officials—including the Geological Survey—agree it is probably the closest to being correct. However, federal officials say they cannot financially justify changing many thousands of maps for just a few feet.

Why the different measurements? The confusion starts with sea level, which is a moving target. The Pacific Ocean's level is more than 3 feet higher than the Atlantic's. In the late 1980s, American and Canadian researchers chose the mouth of the St. Lawrence Seaway as sea level. It was considered both a scientific and political compromise for North America.

At the top of Whitney, there are several bench marks established on boulders of varying height. The Geodetic Survey believes it has chosen the highest boulder.

hikers are encouraged to use them.

For those who camp on the way up, Outpost Camp has some high-elevation pine trees, which many consider more attractive than the barren camping places above the timberline. However, bears occasionally stray up to the area in search of food from backpacks. Trail Camp, on the other hand, is well above the timberline. You won't find much vegetation, but you probably won't encounter large mammals. The yellow-bellied marmot *(Marmota flaviventris)* can be a formidable and clever pest, however. An average adult marmot might weigh 7 pounds, but the Trail Camp marmots grow several pounds larger as they fatten up on inattentive backpackers' food.

The weather is another consideration on Whitney. Even in August, backpackers may have to cross snow fields. Visitors also will notice some lakes still have ice on them in the summer. It might be 100 degrees Fahrenheit on the floor of Owens Valley to the east, yet the temperature might be in the 50s with 30-mile-per-hour winds at the summit. On summer nights, the wind sometimes gusts up to 40 or 50 miles per hour, and temperatures drop into the 20s. Snow storms have battered the mountain well after the Fourth of July.

Probably the biggest concern for those planning a Whitney trek is a wilderness permit. The U.S. Forest Service limits the number of day hikers and overnight visitors between May and October. Visitors must request a permit in writing between March 1 and May 31. There are so many requests that the trail quota quickly fills in March. Fees are charged for overnight camping. Be advised, rangers patrol the trail and ask to see permits. The rangers will issue citations, and most people caught without a permit are fined.

Entry from the western side of the Sierra is easier. Sequoia-Kings Canyon National

Parks issue free overnight permits. Some are available on a first-come, first-served basis.

The crowding problems on Whitney are a recent phenomenon, dating back to the 1970s when 10,000 visitors ascended Whitney in one summer. Now, 20,000 or more visit the summit each year. People have been ascending the peak since it was discovered in 1864 by the California Geological Survey. William H. Brewer led the team. Clarence King and Richard Cotter, who were part of Brewer's team, attempted to climb the highest mountain in the area. When they reached the top of the 14,000-foot peak later named Mount Tyndall, they realized they did not climb Whitney. The Brewer party named the tallest mount after Josiah Dwight Whitney, who founded the California Geological Survey.

King attempted to climb Whitney again seven years later but wound up on the wrong mountain again. In August 1873, three Owens Valley men—Charley Begole, Al Johnson, and Johnny Lucas—climbed to the summit of Whitney. Many other climbs were made, but the first trail from the east side was not constructed until 1904. Residents of Lone Pine built it. A shelter was built on the summit for federal scientists who studied the weather in the early part of the twentieth century.

Today, a shelter remains atop Whitney. There is also a registry where people sign and make comments when they reach the top. The views include eight peaks that are 14,000 feet or higher. The highest grouping is to the north where visitors can see five peaks higher than 14,000 feet.

The rocks on top of Whitney are granite that formed more than 60 million years ago below the earth's surface. Throughout the Whitney area, visitors will find granite with mineral content of mica, quartz, and biotite. The steep eastern escarpment of the Sierra is basically igneous, but the formations that can be seen from the summit just west of Whitney are made up of older metamorphic rocks. Of course, the views to the west also take in the vast San Joaquin Valley, the lower portion of California's Central Valley that stretches 400 miles.

For more information: Mount Whitney Ranger Station, PO Box 8, Lone Pine, CA 93545. Phone (760) 876-6200. Sequoia-Kings Canyon National Park, 47050 Generals Highway, Three Rivers, CA 93271. Phone (559) 565-3341.

Bart Bartholomew

Orland "Bart" Bartholomew is recognized as the first person to ever ski the high Sierra between Mount Whitney and Yosemite National Park. Even with the high-technology equipment available now, the 300-mile trek is done only occasionally these days. Bartholomew did it alone in 1929 on heavy, wooden skis, and he carried a 70-pound pack.

A snow surveyor and hydrographer by profession, Bartholomew went through avalanche-prone areas and frozen granite passes, taking photographs with a folding-bellows camera. He took a photograph of himself standing at the summit of 14,497-foot Mount Whitney, after becoming the first person to scale the mountain in winter.

Appendices

A. Outfitters, Guides, and Suppliers

▓ **WESTERN SLOPE**
NORTHERN AND CENTRAL SIERRA

Crystal Springs Llamas, 2478 Rimrock Road, Placerville, CA 95667. Phone (530) 642-1120. Training people how to pack and use llamas. No rentals or guide service.

Sierra Nevada Llama Treks, 3394 Cimmarron Court, No. 2, Cameron Park, CA 95682. Phone (530) 676-7536. Renting llamas and guiding backpacking treks for all skill levels into the Central Sierra. The company emphasizes backpacking without leaving a trace.

Reid Horse and Cattle Company, headquarters, 1540 Chandler Road, Quincy, CA 95971. Gold Lake Pack Station & Stables, phone (530) 836-0940. Bucks Lake Pack Station & Stables, phone (530) 283-2532. Greagle Stables, phone (530) 836-0430. Offering trail rides, family pack trips, horse programs for children's camps, and wagon rides.

Great Basin Guides, PO Box 2841, Truckee, CA 96160. Phone (530) 587-5412. Offers guided llama treks in the Northern Sierra. Families with children are welcome.

Kennedy Meadows Resort and Pack Station, Emigrant Wilderness and Yosemite backcountry trips in warmer months. The winter address is PO Box 4010, Sonora, CA 95370. Phone (209) 532-9663. Rents horses for riding and packing. Also offers horseback riding pack trips.

YOSEMITE NATIONAL PARK

Yosemite Trails Pack Station, 8314 Santa Fe Drive, Chowchilla, CA 93601. Phone (559) 665-1123. Rides on scenic trails for families, groups, or individuals. Instruction included. Family and group rates offered.

Minarets Pack Station, Southern Yosemite National Park, PO Box 15, O'Neils, CA 93645. Phone (559) 868-3405. Offering flexible trips where the packer can drop off campers, backpackers or fishing enthusiasts in their favorite places, or guide an entire trip.

SOUTHERN SIERRA

D & F Pack Station, Badger Flat and Edison Lake, winter, 14153 Oakview Drive, Prather, CA 93651. Phone (559) 299-4451. Offering flexible pack trips for people who want to be dropped off or guided, fishing trips, and guided horseback riding.

High Sierra Pack Station, based at Edison Lake, Florence Lake in summer. The winter address is PO Box 1166, Clovis, CA 93613. Phone (559) 299-8297. High

Sierra-guided rides on horses, guided overnight trips, and walking mule trips.

Muir Trail Ranch, Blayney Meadow, PO Box 269, Ahwahnee, CA 93601. Phone (209) 966-3195. Offering horseback rides and pack trips on strong, sure-footed horses that were born and reared in the Sierra. Visitors can stay in a tent cabin by a river or in a log cabin with a bathroom.

Lost Valley Pack Station, Blayney Meadow, 2352 Magnolia Court, Hanford, CA 93230. Phone (559) 584-9132. The pack station is located at Florence Lake during warmer months, and it offers burros as pack animals. Also, packing and placing of food cache are available for long-distance backpackers.

Balch Park Pack Station, Garfield-Redwood Grove, PO Box 852, Springville, CA 93265. Phone (559) 539-3908. Offering a variety of guided trips, horse rentals, and pack animals. Special photography and fishing trips available.

Golden Trout Wilderness Pack Trains, PO Box 756, Springville, CA 93265. Phone (559) 539-2744. Guided horseback tours and pack trips offered. Food, shelter, and showers are available at the lodge, but bring your own bedroll.

Horse Corral Pack Station, Big Meadow Road, Sequoia National Forest, PO Box 701, Kings Canyon National Park, CA 93633. Phone (559) 565-3404. Offering horses to ride, pack animals to carry gear, and several types of guided trips.

▓ EASTERN SLOPE

Frontier Pack Train, Star Route 3, Box 18, June Lake, CA 93529. Phone (760) 648-7701. Offering pack trips into wilderness areas, rides on cattle drives, and trips for fly fishing.

Virginia Lakes Pack Outfit, Box 1070, Bridgeport, CA 93517. Phone (760) 937-0326. Offering four-, five-, or seven-day trips in the Inyo National Forest and Yosemite National Park for groups or families. Special group rates.

Reds Meadows Pack Station and Agnew Meadows Pack Train, PO Box 395, Mammoth Lakes, CA 93546. Phone (760) 934-2345. Overnight accommodations available at Reds Meadow Resort with a reservation. Pack trips are available to more than 100 lakes.

Mammoth Lakes Pack Outfit, PO Box 61, Mammoth Lakes, CA 93546. Phone (760) 934-2434. Offering custom mule pack trips for all skill levels. Hike or ride an animal into the high Sierra.

McGee Creek Pack Station, Route 1, Box 162, Mammoth Lakes, CA 93456. Phone (760) 935-4324. Guided rides allow visitors to see the McGee Canyon and a 12,000-foot pass opening to remote sections of the John Muir Wilderness.

Rock Creek Pack Station and Mount Whitney Pack Trains, PO Box 248, Bishop, CA 93515. Phone (760) 935-4493. Offers rides on cattle drives, guided pack tours, horseback riding, and packing schools. Trail rides are 4 to 12 days long.

B. Books and References

50 Best Short Hikes in Yosemite and Sequoia/Kings Canyon by John Krist, Wilderness Press, Berkeley, CA 1996.

A Field Guide to Western Birds by Roger Tory Peterson, Houghton Mifflin, Boston, MA 1990.

A Sierra Nevada Flora by Norman F. Weeden, Wilderness Press, Berkeley, CA 1996.

A Sierra Club Naturalist's Guide by Stephen Whitney, Sierra Club Books, San Francisco, CA 1979.

Amphibians and Reptiles of California by Robert C. Stebbins, University of California Press, Berkeley, CA 1972.

Assembling California by John McPhee, Farrar, Straus and Giroux, New York, NY 1993.

California National Forests by Andrew Horan, Falcon Press Publishing Company, Helena and Billings, MT 1989.

California Forests and Woodlands by Verna R. Johnston, University of California Press, Berkeley, CA 1994.

California Rivers and Streams by Jeffrey F. Mount, University of California Press, Berkeley, CA 1995.

Discovering Sierra Mammals by Russell K. Grater, Yosemite Association/Sequoia Natural History Association, Los Angeles, CA 1978.

Geologic History of Middle California by Arthur D. Howard, University of California Press, Berkeley, CA 1979.

Geology of the Sierra Nevada by Mary Hill, University of California Press, Berkeley, CA 1975.

Guide to the John Muir Trail by Thomas Winnett and Kathy Morey, Wilderness Press, Berkeley CA 1998.

History of the Sierra Nevada by Francis P. Farquhar, University of California Press, Berkeley, CA 1965.

Mammoth Lakes Sierra by Dean Rinehart, Elden Vestal, and Bettie E. Willard, Gennie Smith Books, Mammoth Lakes, CA 1993.

Mono Lake Guidebook by David Gaines, Kutsavi Books, Lee Vining, CA 1989.

Pacific Crest Trail, Vol. I: California by Jeffrey P. Schaffer, Ben Schifrin, Thomas Winnett, and Ruby Johnson Jenkins, Wilderness Press, Berkeley, CA 1997.

Place Names of the Sierra Nevada by Peter Browning, Wilderness Press, Berkeley, CA 1992.

Native Trees of the Sierra Nevada by Victor P. Peterson and Victor P. Peterson Jr., University of California Press, Berkeley, CA 1975.

Roadside Geology of Northern California by David D. Alt and Donald W. Hyndman, Mountain Press Publishing Company, Missoula, MT 1996.

Sierra Centennial by Gene Rose, Three Forests Interpretive Association, Auberry, CA 1994.

Sierra Nevada Ecosystem Project by the Centers for Water and Wildland Resource, University of California, Davis, Davis, CA 1996.

Sierra Nevada Natural History by Tracy I. Storer and Robert L. Usinger, University of California Press, Berkeley, CA 1963.

The Archaeology of California by Joseph L. Chartkoff and Kerry Kona Chartkoff, Stanford University Press, Palo Alto, CA 1984.

The Mountains of California by John Muir, Doubleday & Company, Garden City, NY 1961.

The Tahoe Sierra by Jeffrey P. Schaffer, Wilderness Press, Berkeley, CA 1998.

Wildflowers of the Sierra Nevada and the Central Valley by Laird R. Blackwell, Lone Pine Publishing, Edmonton, Canada 1999.

C. Calendar of Events

Before making plans to attend an event, please call to verify dates as they are subject to change.

JANUARY

Yosemite Winter Club/Snowboard Competition, Badger Pass, Yosemite National Park, early January. Phone (209) 372-8430.

Ranger-led Snowshoe Walk, near Mineral in Lassen Volcanic National Park, throughout January on weekends. Phone (530) 595-4444.

Ford Downhill Series, Mammoth Mountain, early January. Phone (760) 934-0642.

Lakes Basin 15km Freestyle Cross-Country Ski Race, Tamarack X-C Ski Center, Mammoth Mountain, mid-January. Phone (760) 934-2442.

FEBRUARY

Whiskey Flat Days, Western festival, Kernville, mid-February. Phone (760) 376-2629.

Winterfest, snowmobile events, Chester, mid-February. Phone (800) 326-2247.

Lake Davis Dog Sled Races, Portola, late February. Phone (800) 995-6057.

Snowfest, Tahoe City, late February. Phone (775) 832-7625.

MARCH

Cowboy Poetry, Vinton, mid-March. Phone (530) 993-4692.

Annual Nordic Holiday Ski Race, Badger Pass Ski Area, Yosemite National Park, early March. Phone (209) 372-8430.

Annual Mariposa Storytelling Festival, Mariposa, mid-March. Phone (209) 966-3155.

California Fire/Police Olympics, Mammoth Mountain, mid-March. Phone (760) 934-0642.

APRIL

Badger Pass Spring Festival, Yosemite National Park, early April. Phone (209) 372-8430.

Annual Passport Weekend, wine tasting, El Dorado County wine country, mid-April. Phone (916) 967-1299.

Kern River Festival, Kernville, mid-April. Phone (760) 376-2629.

Annual Slalom Kayak Race, Kernville, late April. Phone (760) 376-2629.

MAY

Annual World Championship Cribbage Tournament, Quincy, early May. Phone (530) 283-0800.

Wild Wild West Marathon, Lone Pine, early May. Phone (760) 876-4444.

Annual Mariposa County Blue Grass Festival, Mariposa, mid-May. Phone (209) 966-3155.

Calaveras County Fair & Jumping Frog Jubilee, Angels Camp, mid-May. Phone (209) 736-2561.

Annual Grand Spring Art Tour Sites, Mariposa, late May. Phone (209) 966-3155.

JUNE

Whitewater Wednesday, Kernville, mid-June. Phone (760) 376-2629.

Plumas County Old-Fashioned Picnic, Quincy, early June. Phone (530) 283-6272.

Columbia Diggins, Columbia, early June. Phone (209) 532-4301.

Annual Pioneer Wagon Train and Cowboy Poetry, Mariposa, early June. Phone (209) 742-6596.

Chocolate Festival, Susanville, mid-June. Phone (530) 257-5222.

Living History Days, Johnsville, Plumas-Eureka State Park, one day each in late June, late July, and late August. Phone (530) 836-2380.

High Sierra Music Festival, Quincy, late June. Phone (530) 283-6272.

JULY

Solar Cook-Off, Taylorsville, early July. Phone (530) 283-3402.

Daily Days at Amador Flower Farm, Plymouth, mid-July. Phone (209) 245-6660.

Golddigger Days, Greenville, mid-July. Phone (530) 284-6633.

Ghost Walking Tours, Columbia, mid-July. Phone (800) 532-1479.

Wa She Shu it Deh, Native American arts festival, South Lake Tahoe, late July. Phone (702) 265-4191.

AUGUST

Mammoth Mountain Half Marathon & 10K, Mammoth Lakes, early August. Phone (760) 934-4299.

Wine & Art Show at Sheep Ranch, Murphys, mid-August. Phone (209) 754-1774.

Mammoth Festival of Beers & Bluesapalooza, Mammoth Lakes, mid-August. (760) 934-0606.

Railroad Days, Portolla, mid-August. Phone (530) 832-5444.

Jeffrey Bear's Picnic at the Pope, South Lake Tahoe, late August. Phone (530) 541-5227.

SEPTEMBER

Restoration Days, Mono Lake, early September. Phone (760) 647-6595.

Antique Wings & Wheels, Quincy, mid-September. Phone (530) 283-0188.

Northern Sierra Indian Days, Greenville, mid-September. Phone (530) 283-3402.

Annual Great Gatsby Interpretive Days, South Lake Tahoe, mid-September. Phone (530) 544-3029.

Annual Joaquin Murrieta Days, Coulterville, mid-September. Phone (209) 878-3074.

Yosemite Bug Cross-Country Mountain Bike Race, Mariposa, mid-September. Phone (209) 966-6666.

High Sierra Fall Century Bike Ride, Mono Lake, mid-September. Phone (760) 934-2908.

OCTOBER

Gold Rush Days, Marshall Gold Discovery State Historic Park, Coloma, early October. Phone (530) 622-0390.

Mountain Harvest Festival, Quincy, early October. Phone (530) 283-3402.

Calaveras County Wine Association Grape Stomp, Murphys, early October. Phone (209) 728-0733.

Art & Wine Festival, Placerville, mid-October. Phone (530) 672-3436.

NOVEMBER

Annual Hornitos Candlelighting Ceremony, Hornitos, early November. Phone (209) 966-2522.

Tellabrations, Storytelling Festival, Mariposa, mid-November. Phone (209) 966-3155.

Festival of Lights, Placerville, late November. Phone (530) 672-3436.

DECEMBER

A Victorian Christmas Celebration, Coulterville, early December. Phone (209) 878-3085.

Lights of the Lake Boat Parade, Lake Isabella, early December. Phone (760) 376-2629.

Christmas in Coloma, early December. Phone (530) 622-0390.

The Bracebridge Dinner, the Ahwahnee Hotel, Yosemite National Park, late December. Phone (559) 252-4848.

D. Conservation Organizations

California Native Plant Society, 1722 J Street, Suite 17, Sacramento, CA 95814. Phone (916) 447-2677.

Central Sierra Environmental Resource Center, PO Box 396, Twain Harte, CA 95383. Phone (209) 586-7440.

Coalition for United Recreation in the Eastern Sierra, 300 Mendich Street, Bishop, CA 93514. Phone (760) 873-0264.

Friends of Plumas Wilderness, PO Box 225, Taylorsville, CA 95983. Phone (530) 283-6649.

Foothill Conservancy, PO Box 1255, Pine Grove, CA 95665. Phone (209) 296-5734.

Kern River Preserve, PO Box 1662, Weldon, CA 93283. Phone (760) 378-2531.

Quincy Library Group, 208 Fairground Road, Quincy, CA 95971. Phone (530) 283-6270.

League to Save Lake Tahoe, 955 Emerald Bay Road, South Lake Tahoe, CA 96150. Phone (530) 541-5388.

Mariposans for Environmentally Responsible Growth, 4512 Varain Road, Mariposa, CA 95338. Phone (209) 966-2915.

Mono Lake Committee, PO Box 29, Lee Vining, CA 93541. Phone (760) 647-6595.

The Nature Conservancy, 785 Market Street, 5th Floor, San Francisco, CA 94103. Phone (415) 777-0487.

Pacific Crest Trail Association, 5325 Elkhorn Boulevard, Suite 256, Sacramento, CA 95842-2526. Phone (800) 817-2243.

Placer Land Trust and Nature Center, 3700 Christian Valley Road, Auburn, CA 95602. Phone (530) 878-6053.

Save Our Ancient Forest Ecology, PO Box 1438, Modesto, CA 95359. Phone (209) 577-0883.

Sierra Club, field offices. Sacramento: 1414 K Street, Suite 300, Sacramento, CA 95814-3929. Phone (916) 557-1100. **San Francisco:** 85 Second Street, Second Floor, San Francisco, CA 94105. Phone (415) 977-5730. **Los Angeles:** 3435 Wilshire Boulevard, Suite 320, Los Angeles, CA 90010-1904. Phone (213) 387-6528.

Sequoia Forest Alliance, PO Box 922, Kernville, CA 93238. Phone (760) 376-4126.

South Yuba River Citizens League, 240 Commercial Street, Suite E, Nevada City, CA 95959. Phone (530) 265-5961.

Truckee Donner Land Trust, PO Box 8816, Truckee, CA 96162. Phone (530) 542-5580.

Tule River Conservancy, PO Box 723, Porterville, CA 93258. Phone (559) 542-2196.

Tule Oaks Land Trust, Route 2, Box 226, Springville, CA 93265. Phone (559) 529-2482.

Wilderness Society, California/Nevada Region, Presidio Building 1016, PO Box 29241, San Francisco, CA 94129-0241. Phone (415) 561-6641.

E. Glossary

Acre-foot—A measurement of water equal to 325,900 gallons, or 1 acre of water 1 foot deep.

Ari mutillak—Commonly known as a "stone boy," it is a pile of rocks the sheepherders made to pass the time.

Basalt—Dark igneous rock in lava flow.

Batholith—Igneous rock that has melted from pressures within the earth. The rock then moves into or intrudes other rock formations.

Caldera—A large basin or depression resulting from a volcanic blast.

Cirque—A hollowed-out area high on a mountain valley; typically a place where glacial snow accumulates.

Crag—A rugged rock formation jutting out from a cliff.

Crevasse—A deep chasm that forms within glaciers. They can be more than 100 feet deep.

Cryptosporidium—A mysterious spore found in surface water or rivers and lakes. It affects the human immune system, causing a flu-like illness.

Erratics—Boulders that are clearly out of place in meadows or on mountaintops. Receding glaciers deposited them.

Firefall—Flaming embers that were pushed off the side of Glacier Point to fall to the floor of Yosemite Valley. The practice was stopped in the 1960s.

Firn—The granular edge of snowfield that has remained frozen through the summer but is not yet considered glacial.

Garbage hills—Refuse piles where bears would feed and people would watch. The ritual was stopped decades ago.

Giardia—A protozoan found in surface water in many places. It causes a serious illness with flu-like symptoms, such as vomiting and fevers.

Glacial polish—A granite surface ground smooth and clean by a glacier.

Hanging valley—Usually a river valley or small canyon that has been cut across by a glacier, leaving it at a high elevation above a larger valley floor. Several waterfalls in Yosemite Valley flow through hanging valleys.

Hydroelectric—The creation of power through use of energy of falling water to turn an electric generator.

Hydraulic mining—A technique used in the nineteenth century in which miners would use a strong blast of water through a large hose to strip away soil, rock, and other material from an area to bare a vein of gold or silver.

Igneous—Rock that was formed in a molten state or by fire, such as volcanic rock.

Limestone—Fine-grained rock that comes from shells or reefs. The rock is basically calcium carbonate.

Metamorphic—Rocks that are changed over time by temperatures and pressures into different kinds of rocks.

Microclimates—The climate in a small area of a region, usually affected by the local geography.

Moraine—The debris and boulders left when a glacier passes through an area. Usually moraines are deposited to the sides, lateral moraine, or dropped when the glacier melts, terminal moraine.

Old growth—Refers to a forested area with trees that are more than 40 inches in circumference. These trees are often hundreds of years old, but size, not age, is more important in the old growth classification.

Ozone—Ground-level gas created by the combination of sunlight and chemicals from combustion sources, such as automobiles.

Prescribed burn—A fire intentionally set after assessing the temperature, humidity, and wind conditions. The fire is intended to burn off a buildup of vegetation.

Pumice—A type of lava that is porous and mostly glass. In solid form, it is used in powdered forms as an abrasive.

Taproot—A deep root usually belonging to a plant that must survive dry conditions.

Tarn—A lake left by a receding glacier.

Terminal lake—A body of water with no outlet to the ocean.

Timberline—The elevation where trees stop growing. It is usually between 9,000 and 10,500 feet.

Tufa—Calcareous deposits found in eerie rock forms at Mono Lake.

Tuff—Volcanic ash that has been compacted to become rock.

Index